MIRROR MIRROR

MIRROR MIRROR

REFLECTIONS ON DESIGN AT CHATSWORTH

Rizzoli Electa FRIEDMAN BENDA

THE DUKE OF DEVONSHIRE

FOREWORD

Mirror Mirror is installed. After several years of increasingly urgent discussions and planning, Dr Glenn Adamson and Dr Alexandra Hodby, the co-curators, have pulled off a tour de force. Although it has always been the case that most generations of my family have added art and design that they like to the inside and to the outside of the house (and that change is ever-present), this new exhibition is more than a generational update; it is a significant intervention into the formal spaces of a house built more than three hundred years ago. It is at the very least startling, and it shall be very interesting to see how our various audiences receive it. For me, it is exactly what I believe Chatsworth represents: a wonderful stage on which to showcase contemporary design from a wide variety of talented makers. The curators have fitted the very different objects into the available spaces, some of which are very grand. Only two of the artists were at all familiar with Chatsworth when they were invited to participate, so for most of them there must have been a good deal of thinking to be done when considering their works here. The objects are treated variously: some are entirely appropriate for the settings in a practical as well as visual sense, such as Fernando Laposse's agave armchair and cabinet in the State Bedchamber. Other works are displayed as if in a gallery, such as the works of Faye Toogood in both the Chapel and the Oak Room. Others again, notably the glass by Ettore Sottsass (1917–2007), is set up as a semi-sculptural object. It is appropriate that this is the case, as most of the rooms that house this exhibition were built for show. The Library, with the remarkable lighting installation by Michael Anastassiades, is a combination of the two.

For those of us lucky enough to be intimate with Chatsworth, this exhibition is a wonderful display in its own right. It also makes one question how these spaces *should* be displayed and certainly, in some cases, less is more. So I am sure that our attitude in planning future exhibitions will have changed by what has been created here.

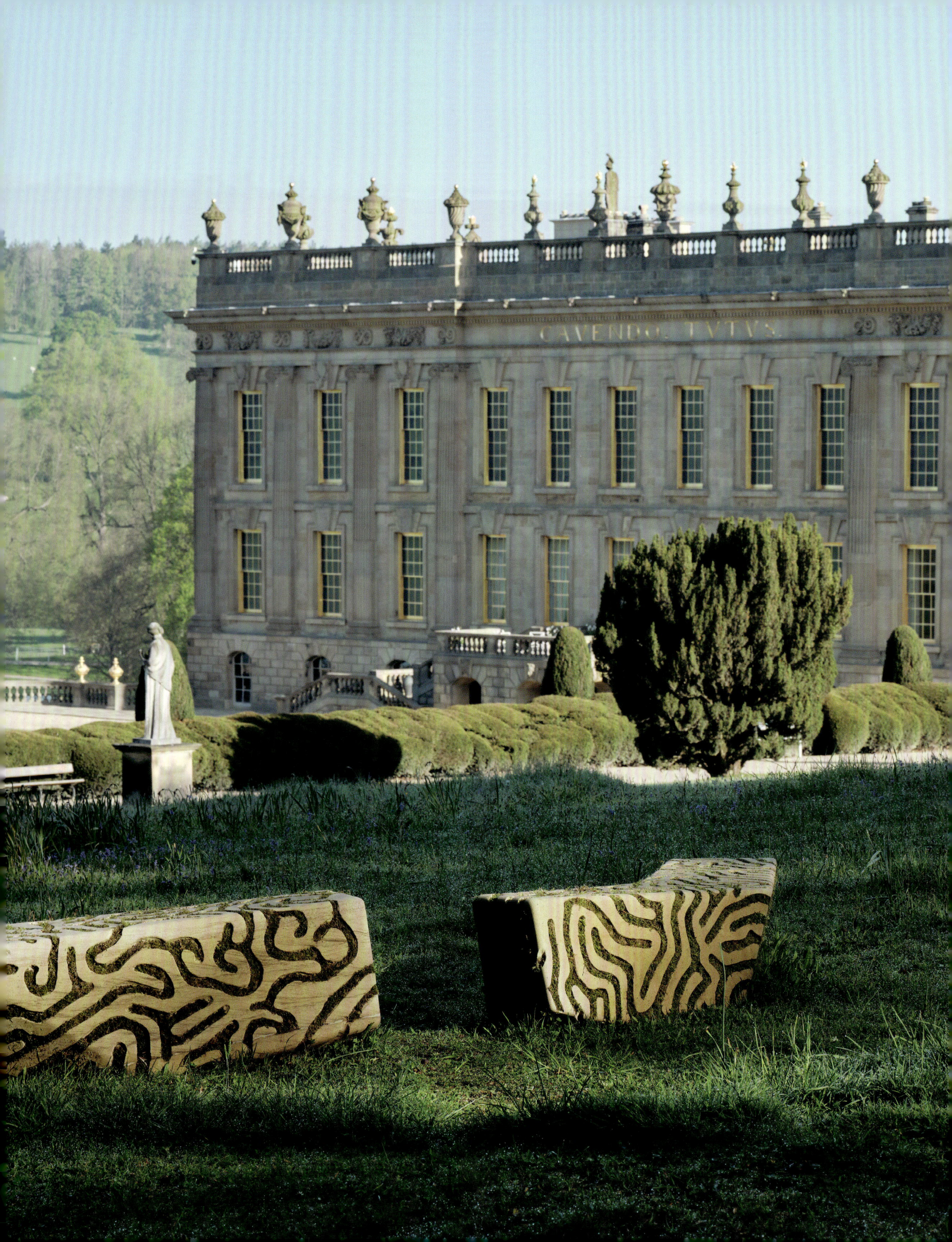
CAVENDO TVTVS

LOOKING INTO THE MIRROR

DEYAN SUDJIC

Chatsworth today is the accumulation of layer upon burnished layer of skill, taste, patronage, and cultural ambition. That history has taken in the baroque architects William Talman and Thomas Archer, Italian and French artists, and English carvers of wood and stone; it is also shaped by the inventive brilliance of Joseph Paxton, head gardener to the 6th Duke of Devonshire. It was here that Paxton designed and built the Great Conservatory, an extraordinary prefabricated greenhouse, sadly demolished. It was the prototype for his Crystal Palace which, along with the Eiffel Tower, must be counted as amongst the most remarkable works of construction of the nineteenth century.

In *Mirror Mirror*, work from sixteen design studios is installed in and around this great English country house. The success of the project depends on an intimate and detailed knowledge of the architecture, its setting, and its history in the ownership of many generations of the Devonshire family, as well as an openness to the many forms and languages adopted by contemporary practitioners of what is sometimes described as design and, in other contexts, decorative art, or craft.

We know how over-used the term 'curator' has become. We should also know that its original meaning lies in a duty of care, owed to the objects in one's charge. That responsibility has not stopped some from using the work of others to advance arguments of their own, foregrounding the curator at the expense of the artist. But as shown by Alexandra Hodby and Glenn Adamson, two curators with very different histories working together on this ambitious project, there is more to curation than the framing of an argument. It can be about helping us to see things more clearly.

The project clarifies, for example, the extent to which patronage remains a living tradition at Chatsworth. This can be seen in the Michael Craig-Martin–designed porcelain dinner service laid out in the State Dining Room and in family portraits painted by Lucian Freud, hung almost casually in a corridor. It is also a place thickly encrusted with allegory. Antonio Verrio's seventeenth-century painted ceilings reflect the politics of the period: the 1st Duke of Devonshire earned his title for his part in the replacement of James II with the Protestant monarchs William and Mary. Trompe l'oeil is part of the repertoire of the interior architecture, and walls are hung with full-height mirrors, all suggesting a degree of self-awareness.

There is so much to see in the house that, without some help, it can become an overwhelming blur of ideas, images, and art. The participants that Hodby and Adamson assembled for *Mirror Mirror* provide just that kind of articulated emphasis. They span a broad range, geographically and ideologically. One is a South Korean working in Seattle, another an American based in Switzerland. There is a designer moving between Mexico City and London, and a ceramicist from Cape Town who has spent time in Cornwall. Some of these practitioners work with their own hands; others combine mass production and limited editions. Some play with the ideas of open-source design, parametrics, and digitally-controlled manufacturing; some employ traditional materials of craft, such as silver, clay, and wood.

About half of the exhibition is composed of newly-commissioned pieces, while other studios, such as Formafantasma from Milan, are represented by existing work. These pieces too have been carefully selected for their contextual relevance. Formafantasma's exquisite series of blown glass and charcoal fragments was originally conceived for an exhibition at the Vitra Design Museum in 2012. They collaborated with Doris Wicki, one of the few practitioners of the ancient craft of charcoal burning, still working in Switzerland. Their pieces explore the tension between the misuse of the skill—charcoal's impact on forests and climate was different when it was used as an iron smelting fuel—and the material's alternate use as a means of purifying water. Charcoal burning has had both these identities in and around Chatsworth.

Wendell Castle and Ettore Sottsass are sadly no longer with us, but their contribution comes to life in *Mirror Mirror*: Castle completed the bronze castings shown here in 2014–15, while Sottsass's glass pieces date back to 1999. Castle, though trained as an industrial designer, is perhaps best described as a sculptor who was ready to work with his own hands, but also to question the nature of craftsmanship. Near the end of his life, he revisited his earliest pieces using robotic technology to expand the possibilities of his studio. Sottsass, one of the towering figures of twentieth-century design, was equally capable of giving a mainframe computer a convincing presence and transforming a ceramic vase into an abstract sculpture. His glass is beautifully placed in the Great Chamber, under Verrio's painted ceiling—titled *Return of the Golden Age*—and shown in an off-kilter arrangement that Sottsass himself might have made. On a good day, sunshine streams in from the heroically proportioned south-facing windows to animate the dangling appendages of the vases. Castle's fascination with making intuitive and innovative shapes, and Sottsass's search for memory and meaning in objects, provide a framework for the younger generations who are featured at Chatsworth.

Joseph Walsh, the Irish furniture maker, has a long-standing association with Chatsworth and contributes a bed that represents a tour de force of craftsmanship. Andile Dyalvane, the South African ceramicist, has installed a sequence of expressive stoneware and porcelain vases. Ndidi Ekubia, a silversmith from Manchester, hammered her vessels into shape for the State Closet, where they are placed beneath a seventeenth-century silver chandelier. Beirut-born Najla El Zein had solid stone shaped into a limpid, flesh-like form in the Rose Garden.

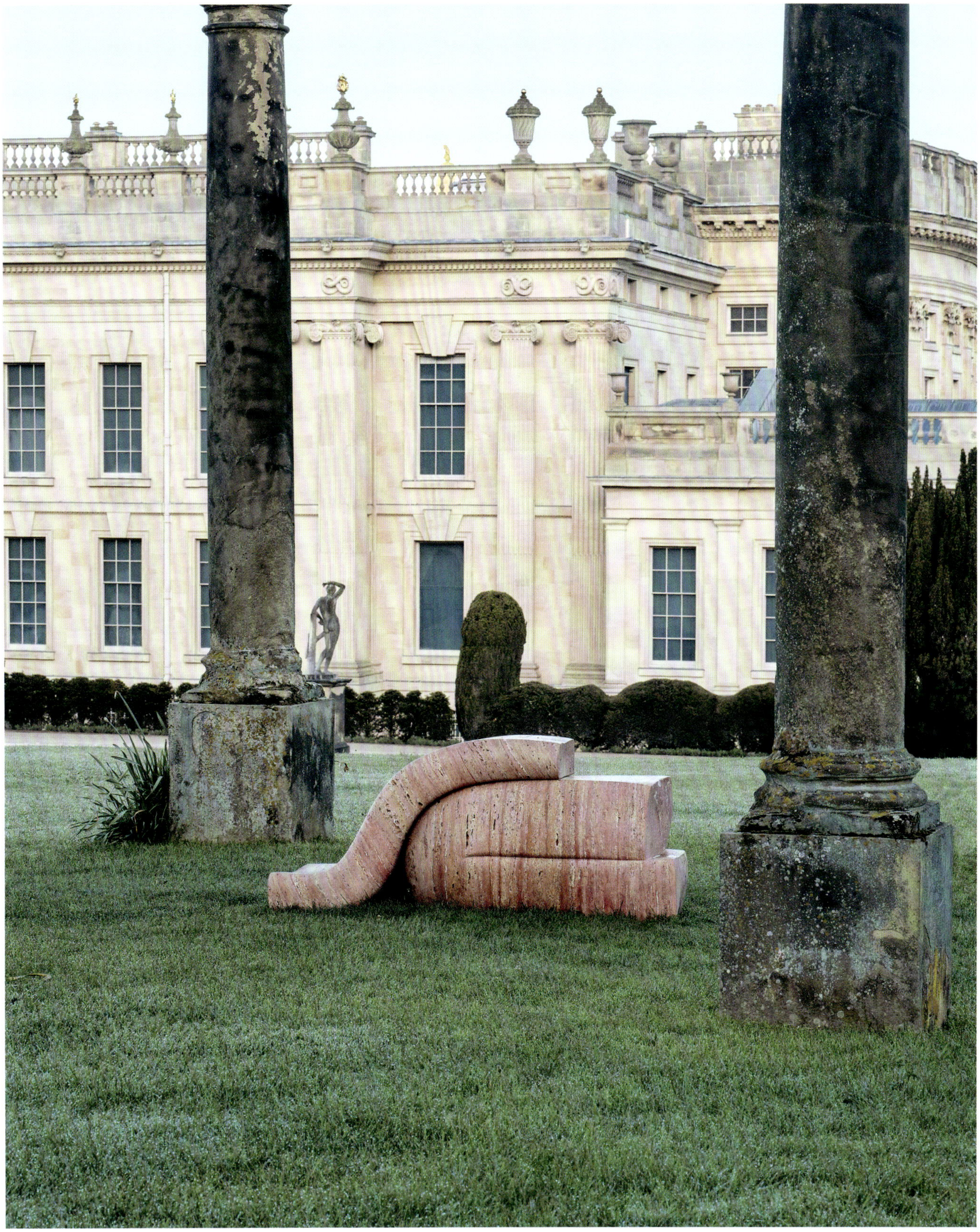

Max Lamb made a pair of chairs from a single beam of cedarwood, carefully crafting them to avoid wasting any of the precious timber. They are positioned in the State Drawing Room, making a pointed contrast with predecessors from previous centuries whose work is also in the room, Samuel Watson and Katherine Naish. The curators positioned Lamb's chairs in front of Naish's monumental coronation thrones in a manner that evokes a Velazquez court portrait—a couple of diminutive infantas guarded by their imposing, grander forebears.

Elsewhere in the exhibition, works are positioned to offer a visual rhyme with their setting. Joris Laarman's pair of *Maker* benches in the Painted Hall, with their intricate, digitally-fabricated, geometric patterns, echo the black and white marble floor. Chris Schanck's *Cryo Cabinet* in the Grotto, the space tucked underneath the elaborate staircase in the Painted Hall, is made from materials that are anything but precious: scraps of foil-wrapped timber, metal, and foam, all coated in resin. Though they are more than three centuries later than the bas-relief showing Diana, the Roman goddess of hunting and the moon, surrounded by Watson's carved ornament, there is a curious echo of form and detail.

In the Sculpture Gallery, similarly, Samuel Ross's work echoes the curves and materials of *Sleeping Endymion*, commissioned by the 6th Duke of Devonshire directly from Antonio Canova. But Ross's work—titled *Amnesia or platelet apparition?*—though it offers a visual rhyme, and is partly made of marble, too, is about other things. It is a sharp material collage of textured marble seemingly entangled with vivid orange steel, a clear reference to the clarity of modernist sculpture.

Jay Sae Jung Oh, who repurposes found objects by tightly wrapping them in leather, has created a response to Chatsworth's State Music Room. The space's most seductive feature is Jan Van Der Vaardt's trompe l'oeil violin, painted directly on a door in 1723, and moved from Devonshire House in London before a disastrous fire at the beginning of the nineteenth century. Oh has fashioned a throne from a collection of broken musical instruments—including an electric guitar, a drum, and a French horn—all given a single identity by the fine leather cord that she has painstakingly wrapped around them. The room itself is lined with gold-embossed leather, a fact of which you may only become aware by understanding the nature of the materiality, equally far from obvious, of Oh's work.

Fernando Laposse's pieces are in the State Bedchamber, occupied by the bed in which George II may, or may not, have died at Kensington Palace. They are friendly, rather hairy, slightly improbable—and somehow subvert the formal splendour of the room. Laposse uses sisal, harvested from the agave plant in Mexico where he has worked with rural communities to revive a sustainable local industry; the material and the skill with which the fibre is worked echoes the stuffing which seventeenth-century bedmakers used for the royal mattress.

Other works in *Mirror Mirror* have a different kind of specificity. Laarman's *Symbio* benches, outdoors on the Salisbury Lawn, are made of gritstone from Chatsworth's own quarry, the material from which the house itself is mostly built. Over the months of the installation, the landscape literally grows into the objects' carved channels. Michael Anastassiades worked in the Library, transformed by the 6th Duke from a picture gallery, which accounts for its impressive array of windows. Anastassiades is fascinated by the potential of bamboo, and has used the material to create clusters supporting vertical lighting tubes, tied into place with thread, all atop feet of puddled pewter.

Faye Toogood's *Standing Stones* occupy the Chapel, with its spectacular altarpiece completed in 1693—who says England did not do baroque? Her works are made from fossil-rich Dorset limestone, traditionally used to embellish churches. Toogood compares them to a neolithic stone circle, but they could also be seen as populating the chapel, a kind of congregation. They are accompanied by two equally sombre groups: a bronze pew and chairs, also in the Chapel; and a carved oak table, flanked by bog oak stools in the adjoining Oak Room.

Mirror Mirror shows how curators can offer insight into both the work and its context. In the glorious baroque interiors of Chatsworth, where dark cave-like spaces are embellished with gleaming gold highlights, the pieces that have been positioned so tactfully are like torches, offering just enough light to reveal a little more detail about their settings. How a piece is positioned is always important; in this case, placement is the way that meaning is underscored.

It is a thought that occurred to me on the rain-soaked March evening that I arrived at Chatsworth. The taxi delivering me to the gates was graced by a tiny representation of Lord Ganesha, the elephant god and remover of obstacles, placed on the dashboard of the Japanese-made automobile that took me from Chesterfield station. As I emerged from the car, I took a Zoom call from an American journalist who was working on a piece about Narendra Modi's drastic plans to leave his mark on New Delhi, and wanted to talk about the political uses of architecture. The journalist caught sight of Chatsworth behind me, making me feel as if I deliberately chose it as a backdrop.

That image is a useful counterpoint to the exhibition's title, which suggests that sense of the uncanny that comes from catching a glimpse of yourself in an ancient mirror. You are caught between past and present, much like switching on an ancient valve-driven radio and hearing Taylor Swift rather than the received pronunciation of a BBC announcer reading the news in a dinner jacket. Adamson and Hodby have said that what they were trying to do was to add a layer to Chatsworth, not to make a disruptive 'intervention'. Certainly the work that they selected is only fully realised within the context of its setting.

It's a lesson that I learned only gradually, getting to understand the exhibition step-by-step and in stages. For me it began with a list of the participants, and then some drawings of the pieces that they were preparing, followed in some cases by photographs as the works emerged from the workshops in which they were made. But the actual experience of the show is something else altogether. Chatsworth adds a dimension quite different from that of a commercial gallery, or a conventional museum setting. The house makes itself felt not just in its material qualities and its historical resonances, but also its sheer scale, something that the contemporary generation of designers rarely experiences.

Chatsworth's rooms are huge, but the skill of its architects over the years has ensured that they do not feel overwhelming or intimidating. But as Ini Archibong told me, placing his work in the context of Chatsworth meant dealing with something different from anything he had experienced before. Archibong's blown glass chandelier, which is enormous by any contemporary standard, looks no more than appropriate in the vestibule that forms the approach to Chatsworth's Sculpture Gallery. Archibong has created an installation that includes sound as well as light, filling the space with a complex soundtrack of his own composition.

Mirror Mirror is a project in which context and content illuminate each another through multiple layers of technique, meaning, and resonance. It encourages you to look hard at objects, to understand them from multiple perspectives. It's a rich survey of the field. It shows the evolution of a form of creativity that has its roots in the decorative arts as represented by Chatsworth House. That form is conventionally described as *design*—a word that has sometimes been used as a means of creating distinctions. Design, it is often said, is not art, and not craft. But as the work at Chatsworth eloquently demonstrates, design is part of a cultural continuum that includes all these and more, just as it did in the eighteenth century. The modern world that its gardener Joseph Paxton helped to build has given design an additional industrial meaning, one that Ettore Sottsass did so much to enrich. Adamson and Hodby have brought together a wide range of responses, occupying the field that Sottsass's generation did so much to open up. The context of Chatsworth is an ideal home for this extraordinarily wide range of work: a true reflection of design today.

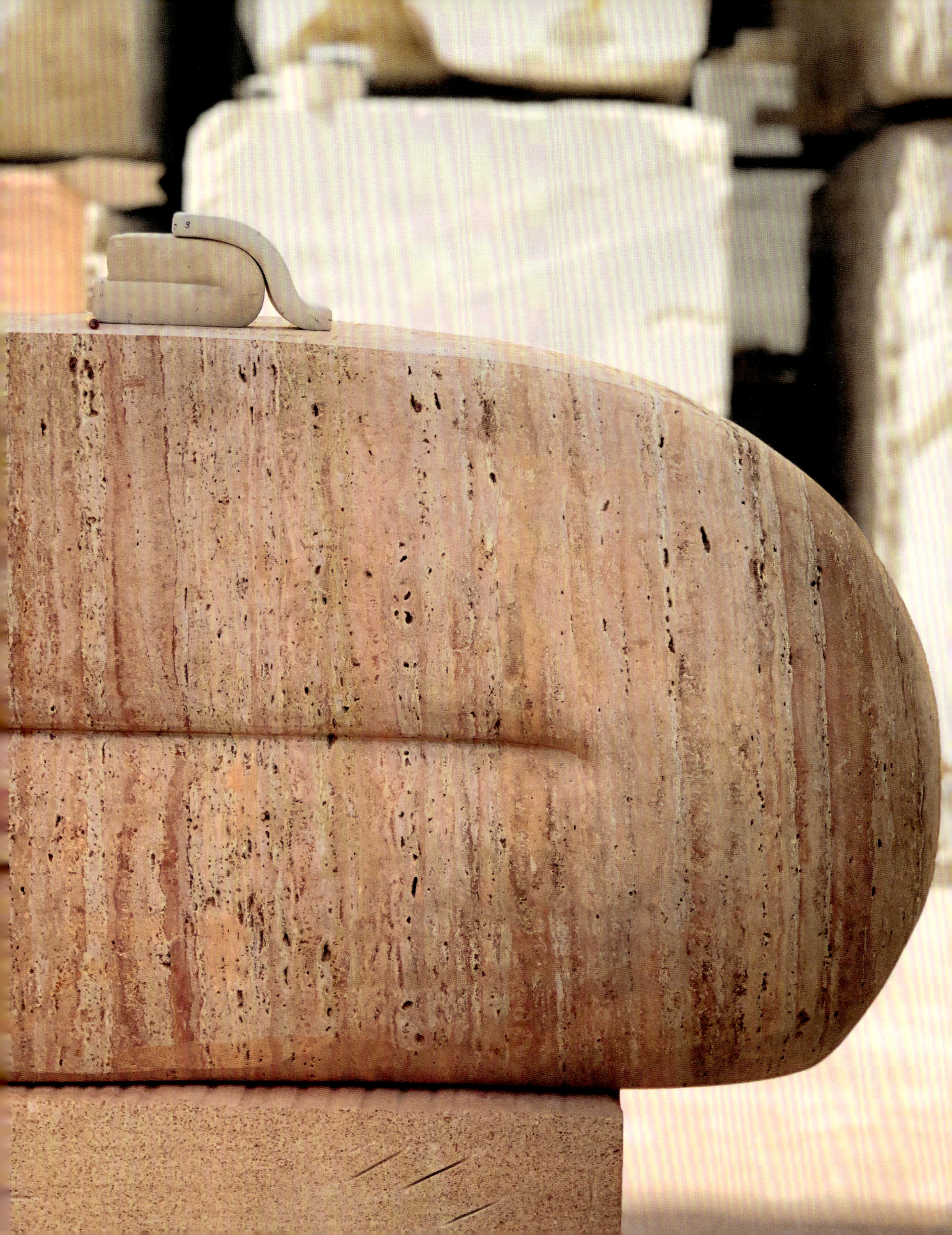

LOOKING BACK

GLENN ADAMSON

Caught you looking. So says Chatsworth, as you tour its magnificent rooms and gardens. At every step, you marvel at wonders of art and design spanning the centuries, and the house looks right back. You appear to yourself again and again: silver-grey in an ancient mirror, a ghostly shape in polished wood, distorted in the graceful curvature of a silver coffeepot, wobbling on the surface of a garden pool. Time seems compressed in these moments. Now and then fuse together into a single fleeting image: a successor to all the others this place has witnessed, of the countless people who have seen these same surfaces, and were seen in return.

Chatsworth is a compelling place, then, to reflect on design, which has been a shaping force here for four centuries. Over that expanse of time, the house and its surroundings have been transformed many times over. What has stayed consistent is the sheer ambition of the architecture and its furnishing, with each generation of the Devonshire family and their many artistic collaborators putting their own distinctive stamp on the property, in a constant pursuit of excellence. The result is a dazzling palimpsest. Each layer is a response to all the previous ones, taking advantage of (and often inaugurating) the latest aesthetic and technological developments. This spirit of exploration has continued unabated right down to the present, as the Devonshires have introduced arrestingly innovative paintings, ceramics, sculptures, and whole art installations into the spaces, to refreshing and resonant effect. This is an old house, with a great many old things in it. Yet it remains an incomparably generative setting for the new.

This is the true generosity of Chatsworth: admittedly a locus of wealth and elite status, it is also a compendium of ideas, free for the taking. In this vast object library, works of design engage in an ongoing cross-century conversation with one another, chairs with chairs, mirrors with mirrors, all thrown into implicit comparison. When something strikingly unexpected is introduced into this milieu—as we made bold to do in *Mirror Mirror*—that ongoing exchange is not interrupted, but extended. Just as visitors to Chatsworth find themselves immediately a part of its multifaceted past, the contemporary works of design we have introduced into the house are implicated in a complex history of contrast and continuity, of back-and-forth glances, of shared ambition.

Chatsworth has been a platform for cutting-edge design for centuries and, in a sense, *Mirror Mirror* is just more of the same. This said, today's designers, at least the ones we have featured here, do approach the past in new ways. What we see in the discipline now is quite distinct from the eighteenth century's reverential attitude towards classical Greece and Rome; the magpie-like eclecticism of the Victorian period; the outright hostility towards precedent that certain modernists felt; or the ironic, appropriation-based strategies adopted by postmodernists in the 1970s and '80s.

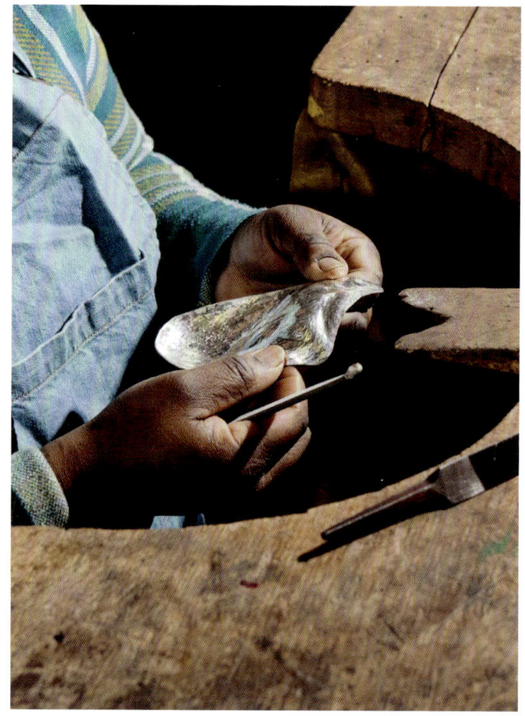

NDIDI EKUBIA

To understand the way that designers encounter design history today, all you need to do is put a term into an internet image search. What you'll get is a mad scramble of stuff, dumped willy-nilly onto the screen: past and present, high and low, real and simulated, all tumbled together like clothes in a dryer. Word-searching 'baroque', for example (at least on my computer, on this particular morning), yields a smattering of seventeenth-century churches and paintings. Also, buildings by Antoni Gaudí, a 2016 jewellery promo from *Vogue*, and a student's AI-generated cathedrals. Keep digging and it keeps going, an endless archaeological site there to be pillaged or carefully sifted by preference. Designers of the calibre of those included in *Mirror Mirror* certainly do their research. They are autodidactic experts in the various subjects that inform their work. But the pervasive simultaneity of digital culture is a working condition for them, just as it is for any creative practitioner today; one of their primary skills is the navigation of formless territory. In practice, this means that they still work within established typologies—chair, vessel, cabinet, mirror—but in an expansive, permissive way, much as a contemporary poet might still work within the sonnet form, or a composer might write a symphony.

Explicit mining of the past was once condemned as an avoidance of design's progressive responsibilities, at best, and at worst, as reprehensible kitsch. Now concerns have shifted. Cross-cultural appropriation is seen, rightly, as problematic. But with that significant exception, history is absolutely fair game. (It's getting hard even to remember the uproar that once raged over postmodern quotation, much less identify with it.) Thus, in *Mirror Mirror*, allusions to the past jostle companionably with the high-tech, the high-craft, and the pop-cultural. It's a wide-open conversation,

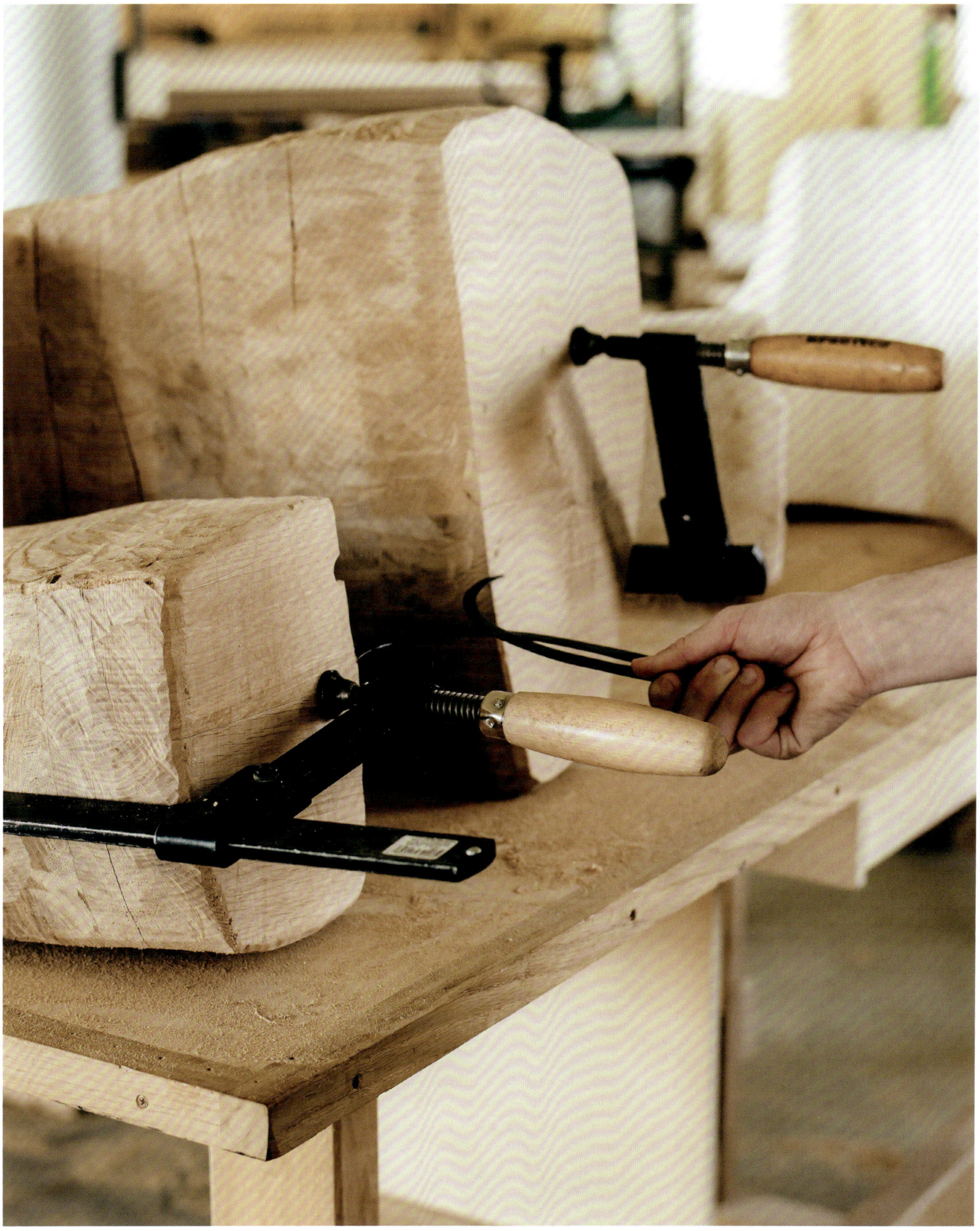

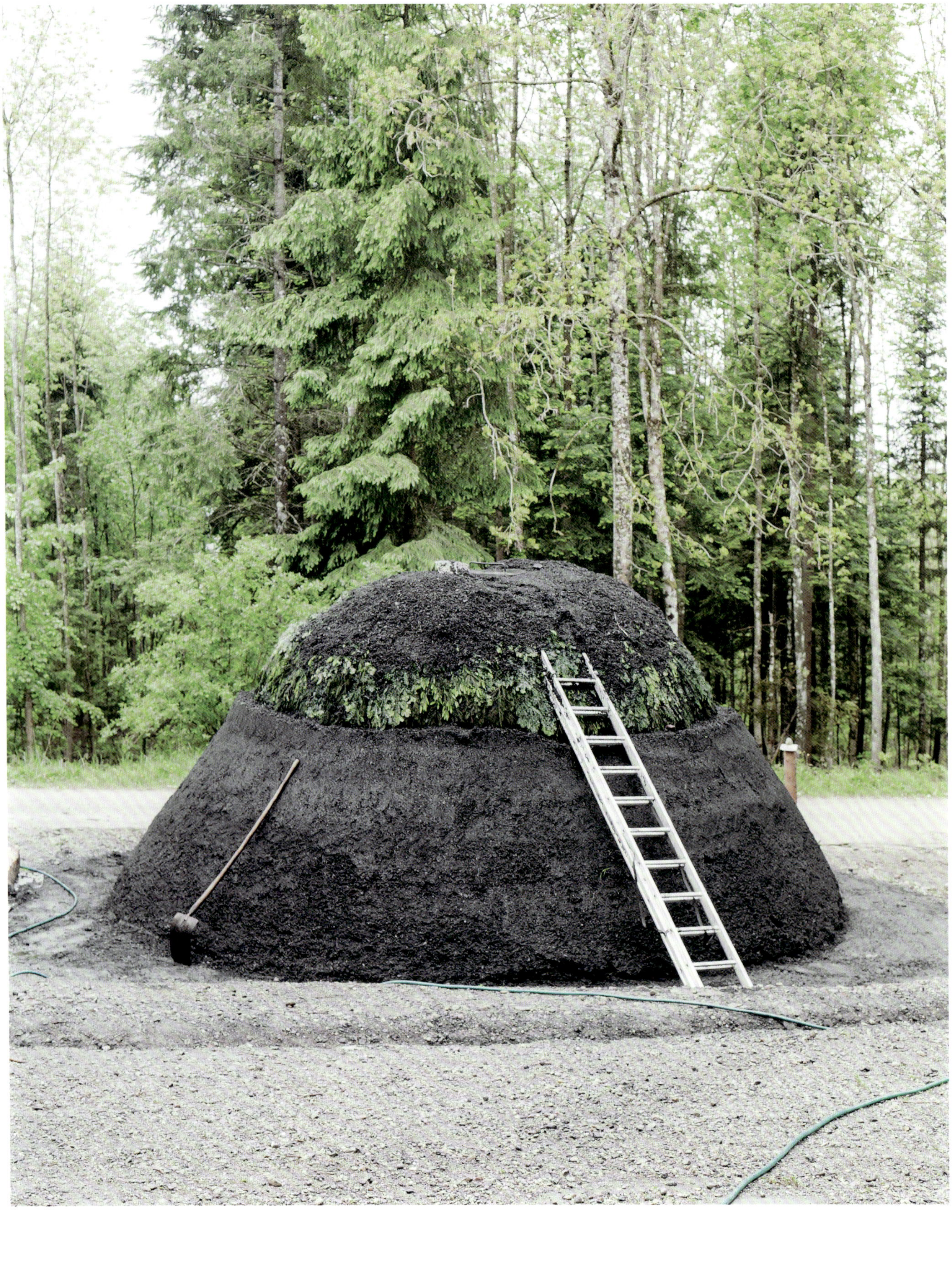

in which things drift unpredictably into connection with one another. The resulting associations may be happenstance or profound, and maybe both at the same time.

Hold the term 'baroque' up to the mirror of the exhibition, for example, and you'll see it reflected everywhere. Jay Sae Jung Oh's Music Room chair has a jumbled composition and seductively enfolded form that could have been abstracted from a Dutch still life, one of those paintings with objects piled high and drapery spilling out from a molasses-dark background. Out in the Chatsworth gardens, bronze seating sculptures by the late Wendell Castle twist and turn upon themselves in a baroque manner; that quasi-figural dynamism is also present, but powerfully compressed, in Najla El Zein's *Seduction, Pair 06*, a coiled carving in red travertine. At Chatsworth, these works seem almost to expand beyond themselves, finding unexpected correspondences with the collection. Yet these same works also teem with other references, other ideas. Oh is operating very much within the forward trajectory from the Duchampian ready-made and postwar assemblage, for example, while Castle's sensibility was informed not just by Bernini but also Henry Moore. El Zein's interpretation of sculpture is notably oblique, having more in common with poetry, perhaps, than anything in the canon of European art history.

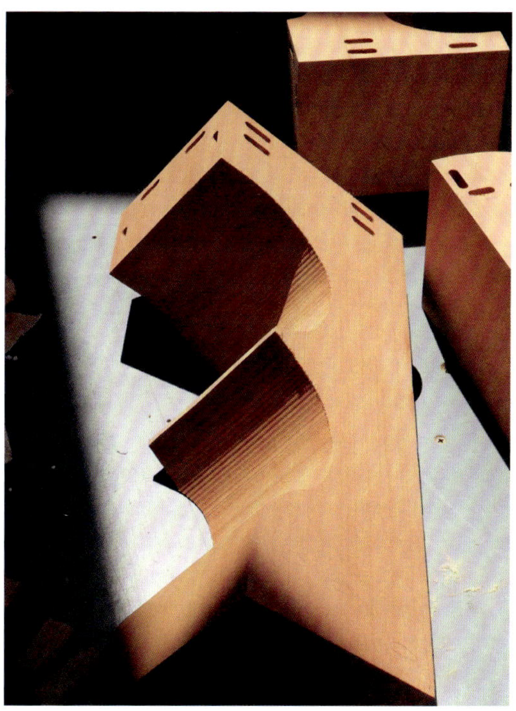

MAX LAMB

Ndidi Ekubia, too, is a master of baroque form, and her work is animated using the same repoussé method that historic smiths employed. Indeed, she is an avid collector and user of antique tools, such as hammers and stakes, the design of which has not substantially changed for several centuries (except, as she points out, that the old ones tend to be better). This continuity points to another important aspect of contemporary design's relationship to the past: its many modes of making, a rich mix of inherited and invented techniques. Ekubia's objects, being made by her own hands, are all unique commissions; this is also the case with most of the works in *Mirror Mirror*, though there are also a few editioned pieces, made in short runs of twelve or so. This limited-seriality approach differs dramatically from the mass production of conventional industrial design, which loses in individuality what it gains in efficiency. It is much more similar, in fact, to the way that artisans worked in the eighteenth century and earlier.

Prior to the industrial revolution, every object was essentially a handmade one-off, though precise repetition was certainly part of a professional tradesman's skill set. The contemporary limited edition finds a historic correspondence, for example, in matched suites of furniture—a template knowingly addressed in Max Lamb's *6×8"* series, in which lengths of cedar are cut and combined into playfully inventive forms, using every bit of the wood. The seating and tables that Lamb derives from this process are ingeniously, entertainingly diverse, yet still could be seen as a "set" by virtue of their common origin and logic. There's a knowing relationship, too, with the tradition of woodcarving, an art form found in its full glory throughout Chatsworth's rooms—a far more elaborate vocabulary of curvature than Lamb's toy-like profiles, to be sure, but likewise a transformation of raw material into aesthetic form.

Some designers featured in *Mirror Mirror* find, in their engagement with craft, a means of building communities as well as objects. Fernando Laposse has assembled a team of indigenous Mayan weavers in the village of Tonahuixtla, in the Yucatán. They work together to realise his characterful furniture, which sports shaggy pelts of sisal, the fibre of the agave plant (and an abundantly available waste product of the tequila industry). His goal is to rebuild the ecosystem of agricultural artisanship that had once flourished in Tonahuixtla but has been massively disrupted by globalism and climate change. Chris Schanck, meanwhile, has accomplished something comparable in diametrically-opposed circumstances, in an economically-ravaged part of Detroit, where he has resurrected a derelict tool-and-die factory as his studio. Here he leads a diverse crew of workers, recruited variously from art schools, the auto industry, and the neighbourhood's Bangladeshi immigrant population. There is a fantastical quality to what Laposse and Schanck are making—they truly allow their imaginations to take flight—yet their work is ultimately grounded in pragmatism, social mission, and a sense of place.

Ini Archibong, similarly, balances a futuristic aesthetic with a craft-focused ethic. He has spent years working with master glassblowers in Switzerland, where he is based, and on the island of Murano in the Venetian lagoon, the celebrated citadel of the discipline. The majestically-proportioned chandeliers he has realised with these skilled makers, gorgeously limned with gradations of hue, are monuments to their own creation. They are all the more intriguing in juxtaposition with earlier work in glass by the late Ettore Sottsass, also included in *Mirror Mirror*, which are more playful, even subversive, in spirit. With their asymmetrical compositions and bold appurtenances (some attached simply with wire), these vases depart radically from the medium's established canons of form. Yet, as usual with Sottsass, their purposeful eccentricity is counterbalanced by a life force, which may be hard to define but is impossible to deny. No less than Archibong's stately sculptural lighting, they are imbued with a potent spiritual presence. Both designers have reasserted the dignity of the glassmaking tradition and the continuing possibilities it offers.

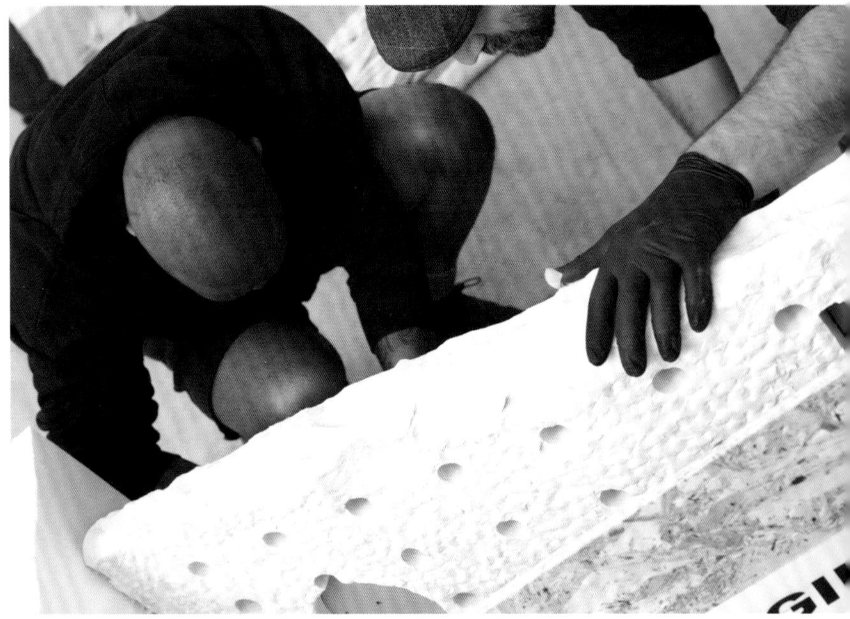

SAMUEL ROSS

There is an undeniable drama to Archibong and Sottsass's glass works; see them in person and you'll likely be surprised at their scale, which is far too large for a standard living space. In Chatsworth's grand rooms, of course, these outsized gestures felt right at home. This points to another aspect of the house's surprising contemporaneity. In design magazines, and more recently, on such digital platforms as Instagram, TikTok, and Zoom, domestic interiors have come to lead a second life, serving as impromptu stages, with the objects in them functioning as props. Chatsworth was not originally intended to be photographed and filmed, obviously (though these days, the house is often used as a shooting location for period dramas). But it was always meant to be theatrical. It is even built along narrative lines, with visitors treated to a carefully choreographed sequence of immersive experiences. Several of the installations in *Mirror Mirror* explicitly exploited this inherent potential for stagecraft. Michael Anastassiades positioned his lighting in the Chatsworth Library, a space that is viewable by visitors only from one end. His slim bamboo fixtures were assembled into a glowing procession within this perspectival rush of space. More flamboyant is Joseph Walsh's *Enignum VIII Bed*, which rises fully six metres, like a drifting whorl of smoke, from the floor to the ceiling. Originally commissioned for an upstairs room, not on Chatsworth's visitor route, we relocated it so that the public could get a front-row seat to the spectacle.

The most magnificent views of all at Chatsworth are those from outside, looking at the house from the gardens. This is by no means a natural setting, though it does a good impression of one; it has been shaped over the course of centuries, partly with an eye to creating ideal vantage points. At one of the prime viewing spots, at the top of a historic meadow, we placed a trio of new seating forms by Joris Laarman. These are intended to become gradually more and more a part of the landscape, as over time, moss and lichen propagate in the channels carved into their surfaces. This idea clearly relates to current concerns about sustainability: the importance of living harmoniously with our surroundings, and the perils of failing to do so. Yet, again, there is a strong continuity with centuries past, when nature's rhythms played a far more powerful role in daily life. Everywhere in Chatsworth's grounds are benches, statues, and architectural features that are alive with a thin layer of growth, surrounded by a pageant that constantly changes with the seasons. One particularly arresting sight is the remnant of the Great Conservatory made of glass and steel, designed by Sir Joseph Paxton, and installed on the property between 1836 and 1840 (making it a significant precursor to the famed Crystal Palace, which Paxton realised for the Great Exhibition of 1851). Demolished following World War I, it now exists as a sort of huge platform for a garden maze—echoed, as it happens, in the meandering lines on Laarman's benches.

The Italian studio Formafantasma, led by Andrea Trimarchi and Simone Farresin, is well known for their explorations at the troubled interface between design and nature. *Mirror Mirror* features a project in which the duo explored the historic practice of charcoal burning. Now largely abandoned as an energy source, in part due to its polluting effects, charcoal was once an integral part of the agricultural economy. Formafantasma looked at it as part of their broader consideration of resource extraction in the past. What did it mean, they wondered, that even basic fuel was once an artisanal industry?

Formafantasma undertook this research-driven exploration fully a decade ago, but it fit well into *Mirror Mirror*, which explores the past primarily as a source of provocation. The same could be said for the contribution of Samuel Ross, whose works enacted a seismic rupture amidst the classical statuary and polychromatic plinths of Chatsworth's sculpture gallery. Compounded of raw chunks of marble juxtaposed with industrial elements, the latter painted a high-alert shade of orange, his designs bespeak a sensibility of collision and distortion. Yet even here, in a body of work that is startlingly new, history looms large. Ross often talks about brutalism, the mid-twentieth century architectural idiom that formed the backdrop of his growing-up years, as an important point of departure. Here at Chatsworth, materiality itself offered a continuity, stone being the stuff from which Ross's works, and this elegant room and its contents, were all hewn.

It's against this geological backdrop, the context of deep time, that Chatsworth has ultimately taken shape. Over the course of centuries, its materials were gathered from nearby quarries and forests; now those contents can be creatively mined in turn. Right across the spectrum of *Mirror Mirror*, designers tune in to this sustained wavelength. Totemic forms predominate—amongst them the aforementioned glass pieces of Sottsass and Archibong, as well as Anastassiades's lighting, and Schanck's *Cryo Cabinet*—all standing proud on their terms, yet implying a connection to an unseen well of the sacred. The final two designers included in the project, Andile Dyalvane and Faye Toogood, similarly access this spring of ancient inspiration; though operating from very different perspectives, they found an unexpected common ground.

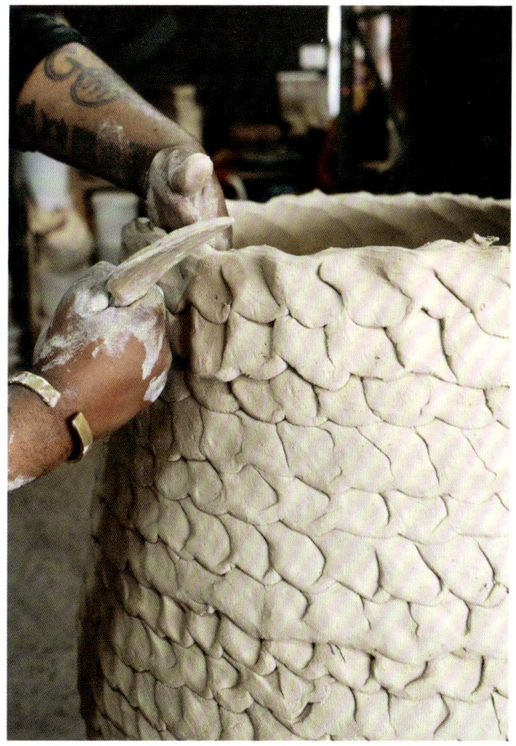

ANDILE DYALVANE

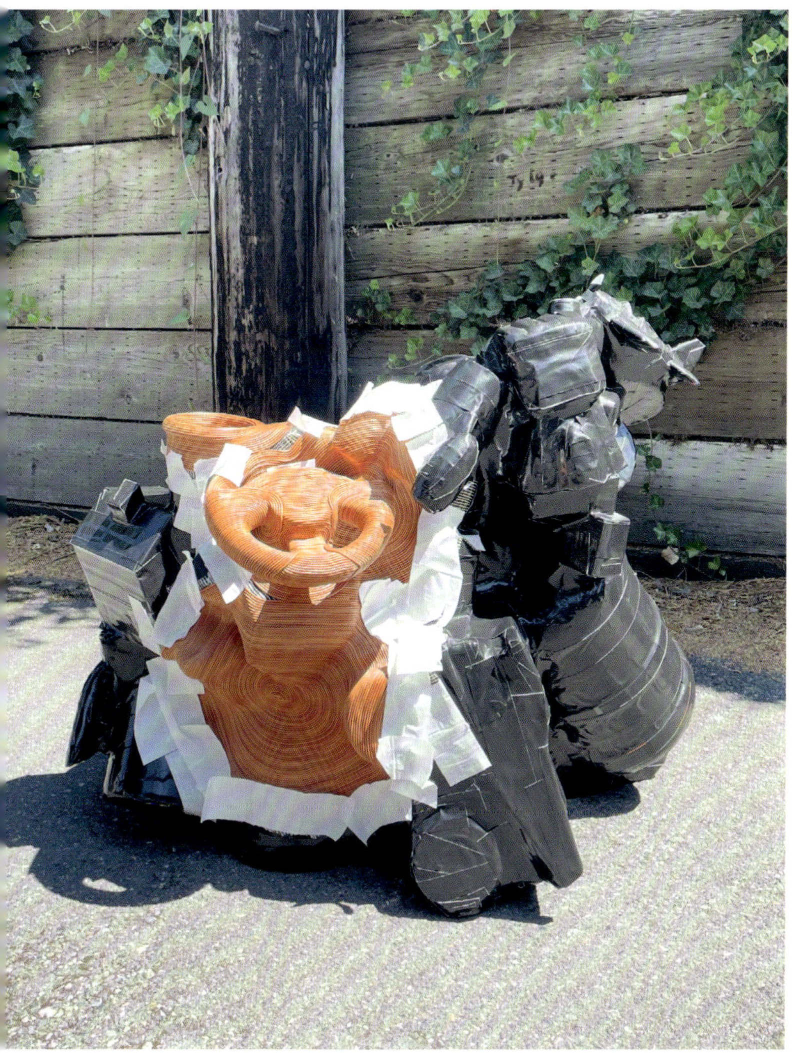

JAY SAE JUNG OH

Dyalvane, who grew up in a village in the Eastern Cape of South Africa, makes vessels (in both the literal and figurative senses of the term) that carry the legacy of his Xhosa ancestry. The motifs and forms of his work allude to this heritage, and they are made of local clay that bears the imprint of former generations' habitation on the land. Yet it would be wrong to see Dyalvane as just an inheritor, pure and simple. He carries his sensitivity to place with him. He thrived, for example, during a recent residency at the Leach Pottery in St. Ives, making work that added a compelling new chapter to that storied site in British ceramic history. The geology of Cornwall, with its sheaves of rock slipping across one another in an immeasurably slow cascade, was beautifully registered in those pots. They in turn have informed the layered vessels he made for *Mirror Mirror*, which can be considered syncretic objects, reflections on multiple temporalities and traditions.

When he arrived in England, Dyalvane was also deeply impressed with Stonehenge and the other sacred circles left on the landscape by its ancient inhabitants. 'I could sense the people that erected these stone', he has said. 'They understood the celebration of rain, the solstice, the harvest, just as my own ancestors did.' These archaic monuments—which predate Britain, and indeed recorded history itself, by many centuries—have also been an inspiration to Faye Toogood. She paid them explicit homage in her installation for Chatsworth's Chapel, an arrangement of austere, menhir-like forms, and in the adjoining Oak Room, set out a massive carved table, a terrain unto itself, with a sculpted top suggesting sloping hills and broad river valleys. While these pieces are anchored firmly in the present (indeed, like everything Toogood makes, instinctively

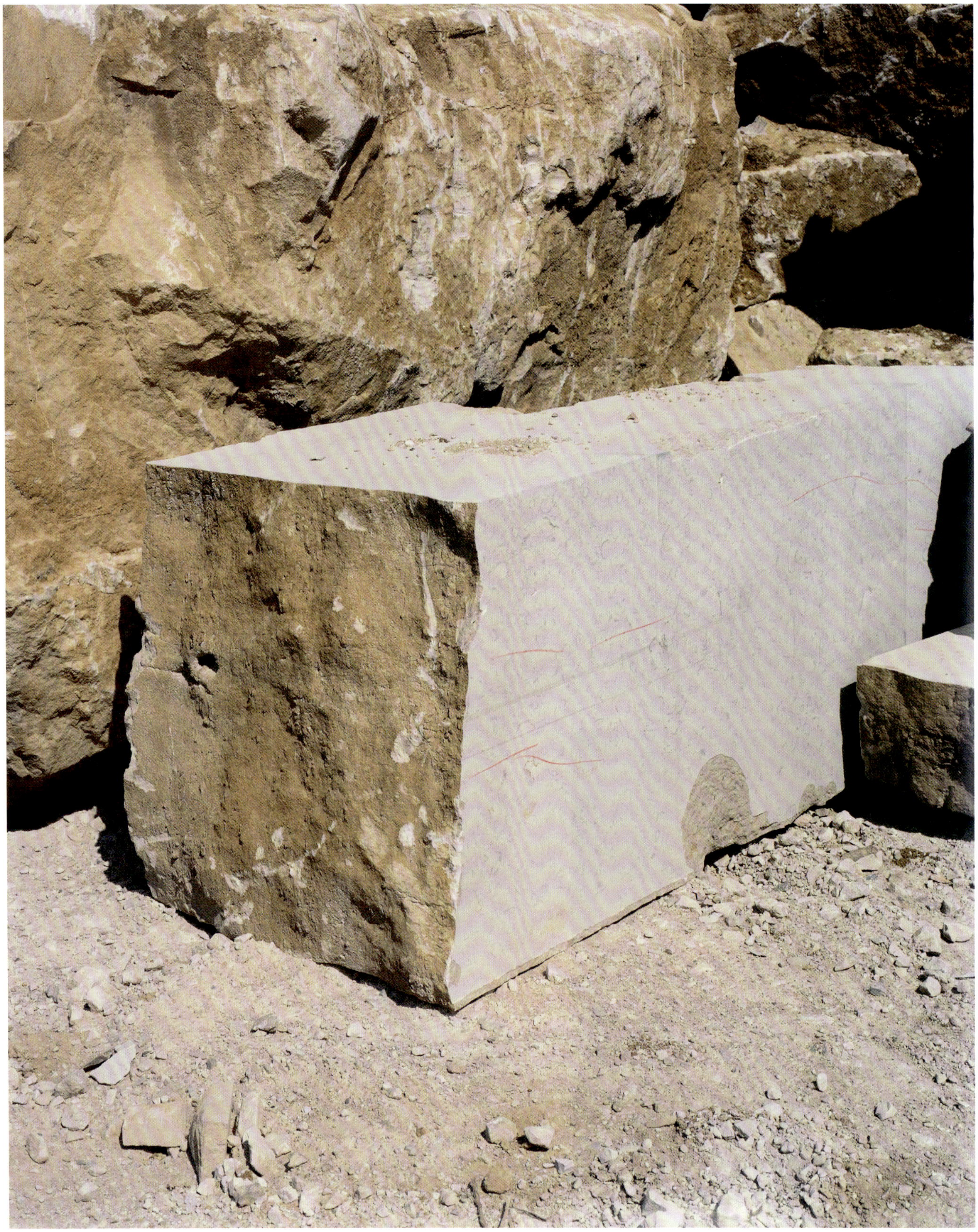

out in front of prevailing taste), they are also elusive, mystical even, evoking an expansive temporality that can never be fully grasped.

Toogood's objects, and *Mirror Mirror* as a whole, serve as reminders—not that they were really needed at a place like Chatsworth—that the past is very big indeed, infinite in its variety and extent. Design itself is a recent arrival. As a profession, it has been around only for a century and a half or so, a brief interval in historical terms, much less within the scope of the cosmic. Strange to say, an awareness of this sublime scale, against which any given object vanishes into insignificance, helps to account for the unprecedented freedom that designers are feeling today. Looking back, we can see a story of enormous dimensions: as industry rose to an initially astonishing, now familiar position of overwhelming dominance, design was empowered alongside, and it became a potent force in shaping society. Designers, the successful ones anyway, laid claim to new forms of authority. The best of them accepted the responsibility that came with it. But that system had its limits and its blind spots. Rather than continually reshaping the natural environment—a way of conquering it—there is a growing collective realisation that we must work in respectful partnership with it. Regularity and efficiency, long watchwords amongst designers, have come to seem less important; instead, they are seeking out meaning and affinity.

These are twenty-first-century values, but they are by no means new. Chatsworth has long fostered them, and *Mirror Mirror* is, above all, an opportunity to explore this symmetry between now and then. It is a chance to see contemporary design in an unusually broad chronological context—to witness it poised, as acts of creation always are, at the fulcrum between a past too huge to encompass and a future we can scarcely guess at. The designers in *Mirror Mirror*, for all their technical, aesthetic, material, and cultural intelligence, may be no wiser than anyone else about what might be coming next. But they have done this: reflect the emergent condition of present, so that it can be clearly seen, illuminated in the sometimes shaded, sometimes radiant light of where we've been before.

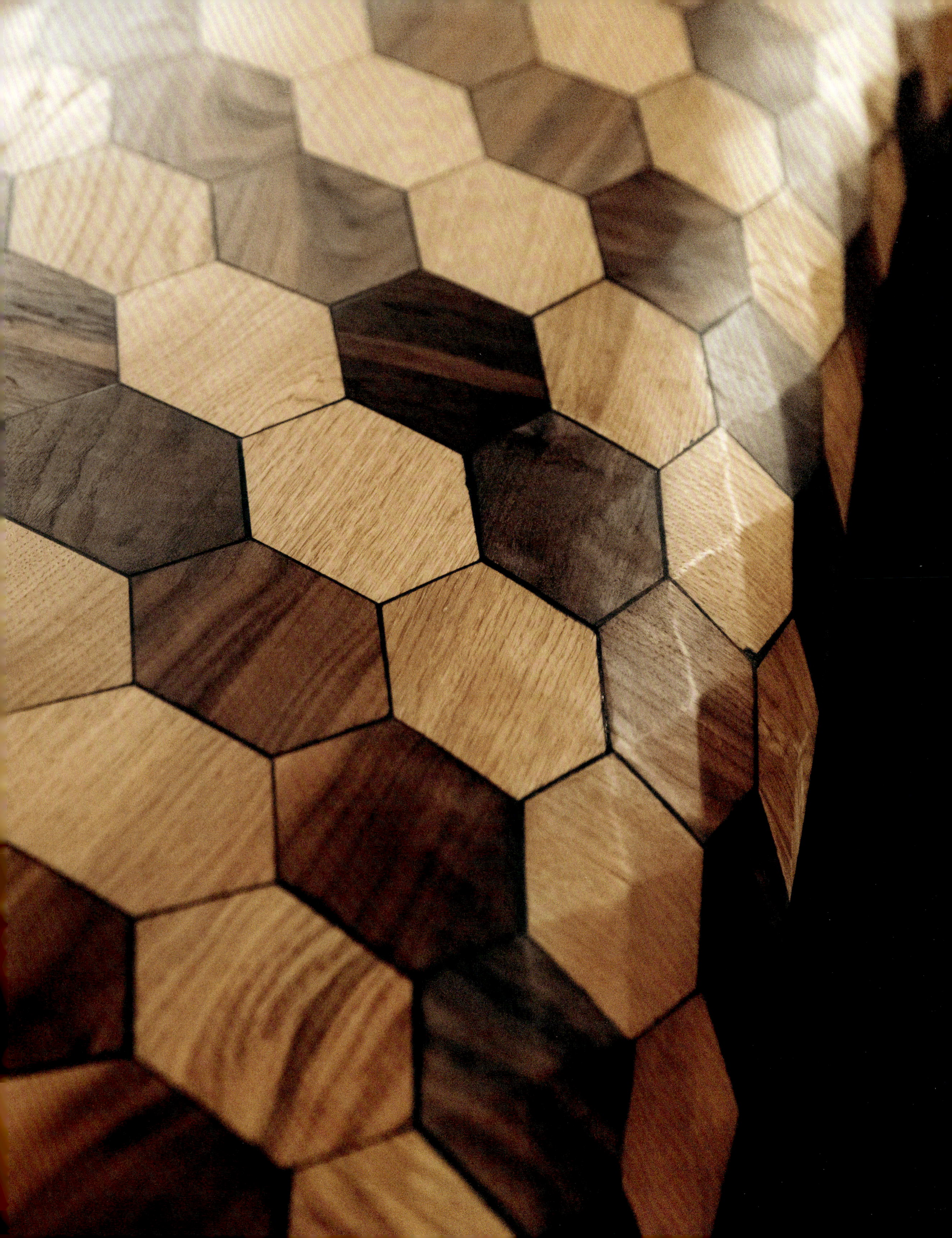

JORIS

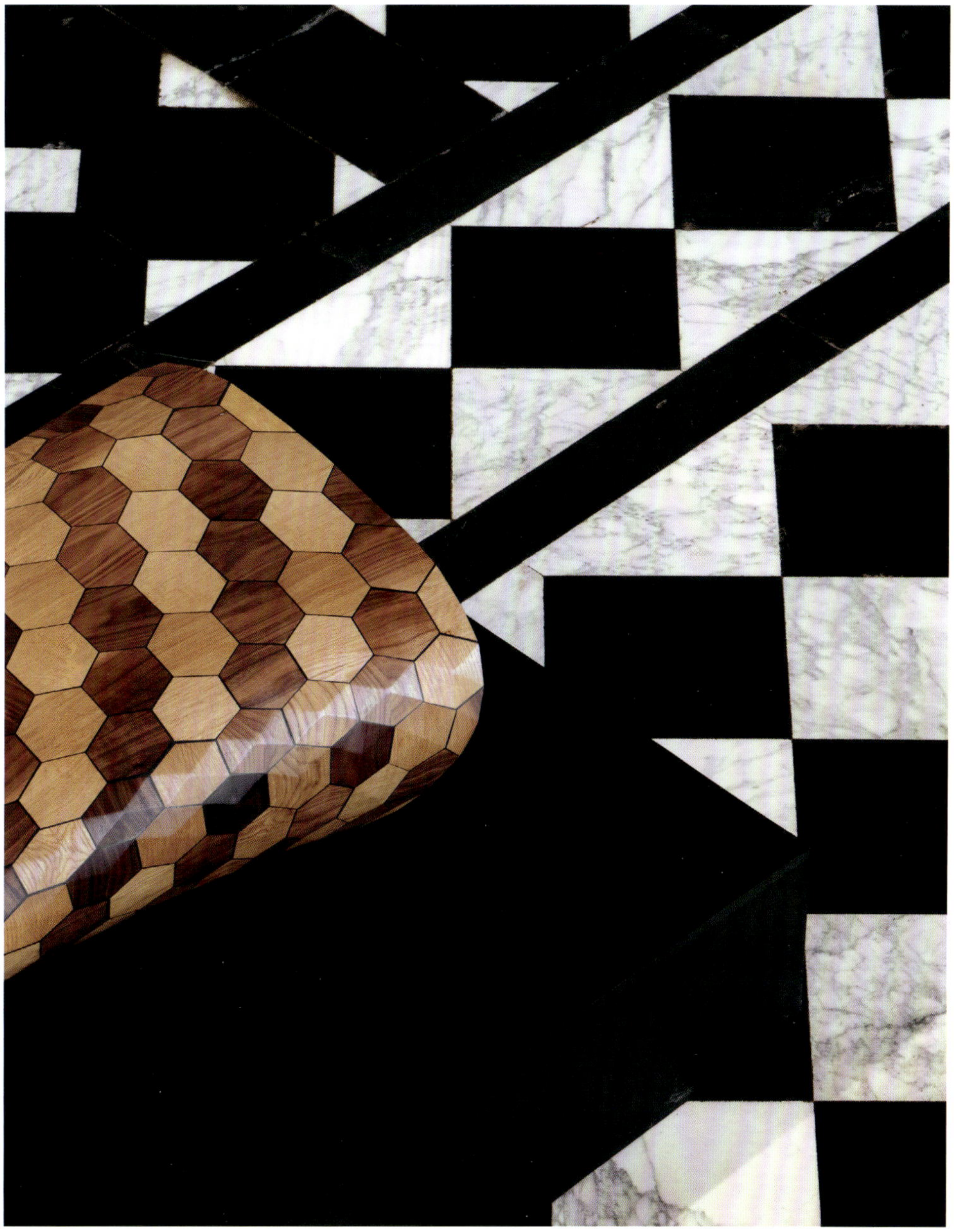

LAARMAN

BETWEEN THE ARTISANAL AND THE ALGORITHMIC

A decade ago, commercially available 3D printers and computer-guided cutters were quite limited in scale. Joris Laarman set out to demonstrate that this limited tooling could be used to create impressive full-sized furniture. He devised an ingenious solution, designing a constructive system comprised of many individual small parts. Each piece is slightly different in shape, but they are engineered to fit together, like a three-dimensional jigsaw puzzle. This mass-customisation approach was one means by which Laarman was exploring the intersection between the artisanal and the algorithmic, seen also in his contemporaneous *Bone* furniture series.

Laarman went on to execute the *Maker* furniture in a range of typologies, using various materials (resin, solid woods, plastics, metals) and differentiated shapes (triangular, hexagonal, figurative, pixilated). In *Mirror Mirror*, we feature two benches from the series, one of which was acquired for Chatsworth in 2020. The forms have the quality of felled tree limbs or human forearms, their taut silhouettes accentuated by a two-tone palette of contrasting oak and walnut. He has elevated the open-source structure of the pieces with extensive hand finishing, so that, for example, along the shoulders of the piece, the hexagons are articulated in facets slightly proud of the surface. The hollow construction admits views into the benches' interiors, torqued tunnels lined with the honeycomb cells of the unit-based carving.

The *Maker* benches are the first objects that visitors encounter in *Mirror Mirror*, in the Painted Hall—one of Chatsworth's most dramatic spaces, with a theatric painted ceiling overhead, and a chequered floor in black and white marble dating to 1779. The objects announce the exhibition theme, in that they mirror each another's twisted forms; one of many advantages of the new digital design is that a complex form can be flipped around 180 degrees. As in historic marquetry furniture, which was often made in pairs, Laarman further exploited the idea of reflection by using offcuts from one *Maker* bench to create the other.

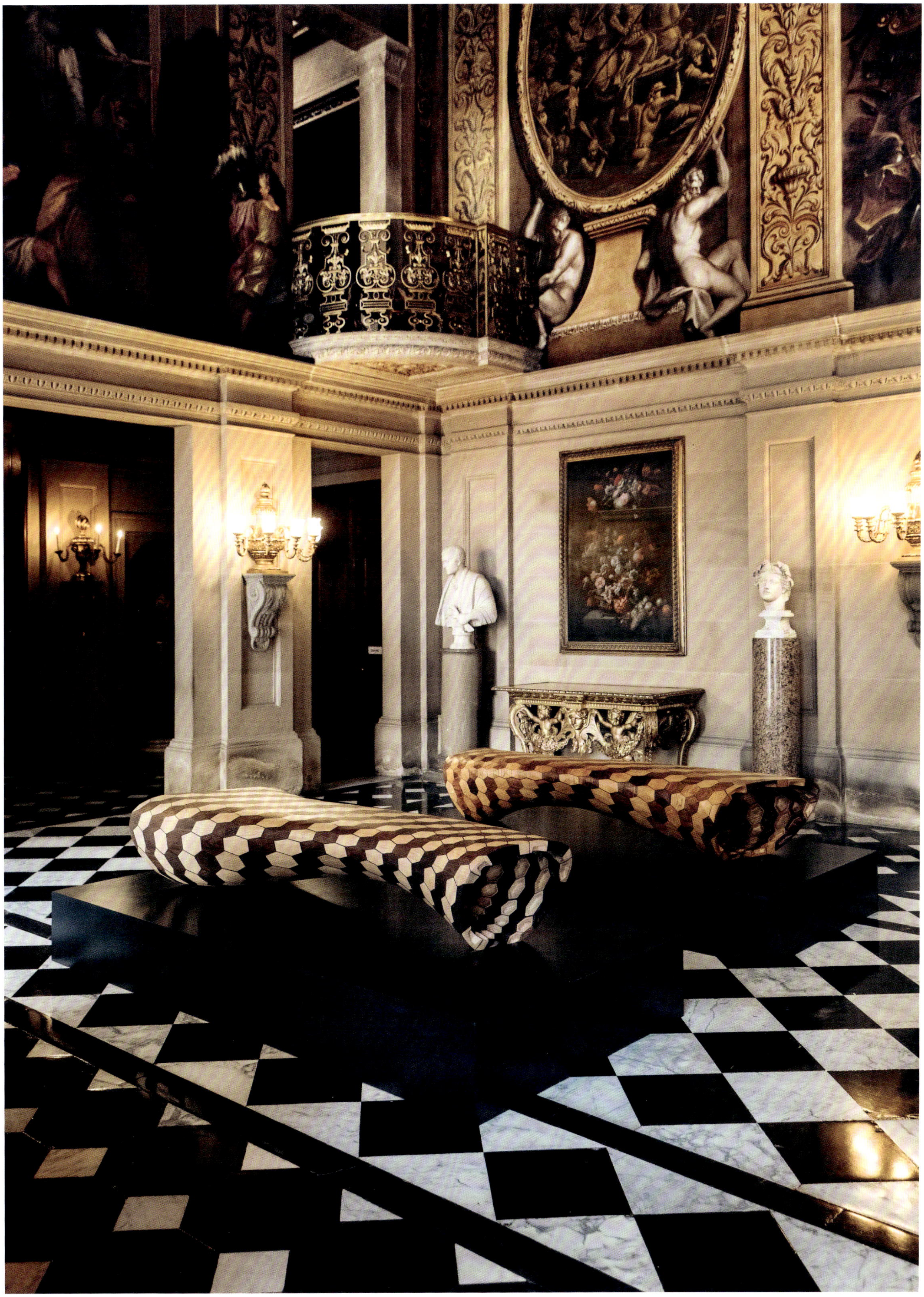

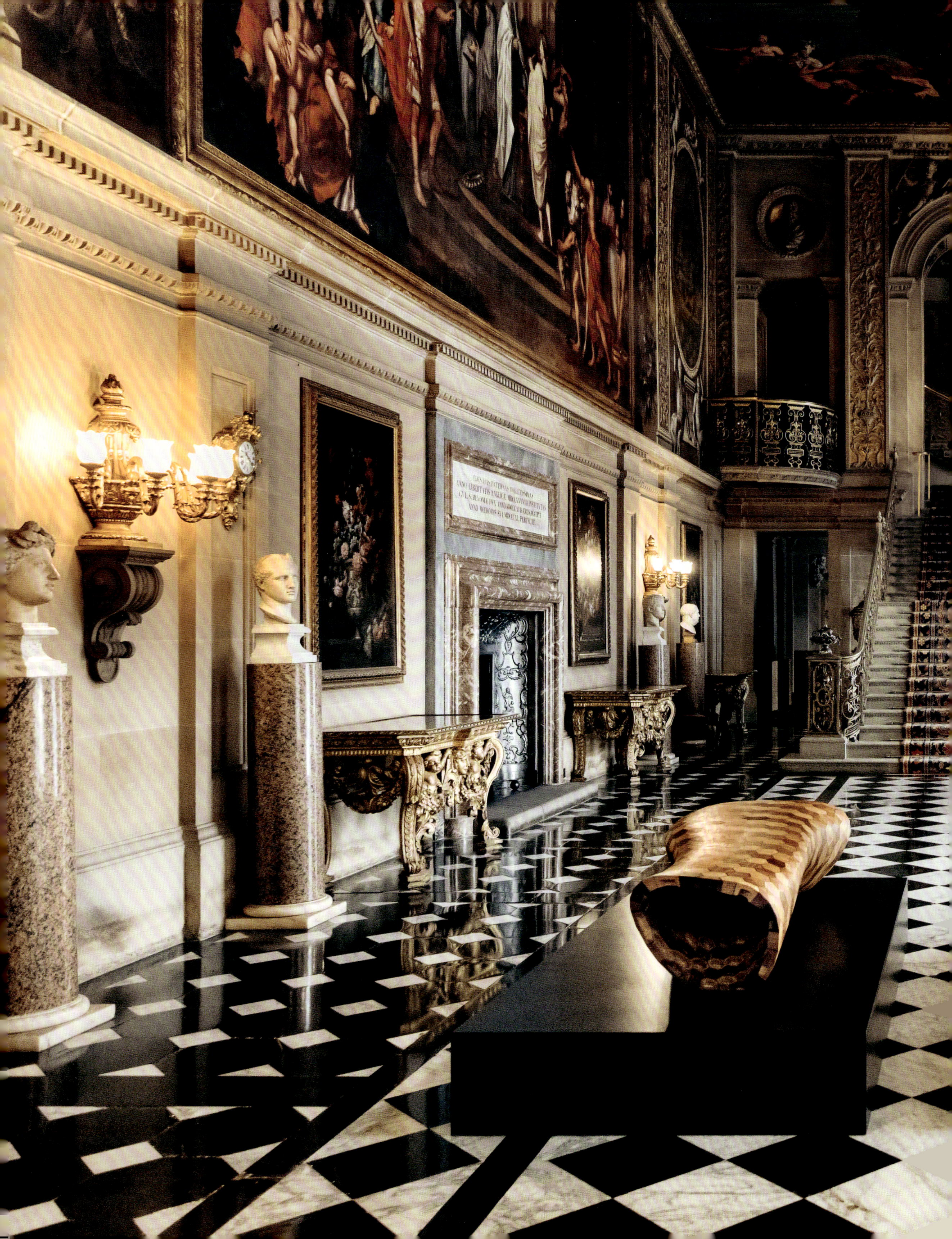

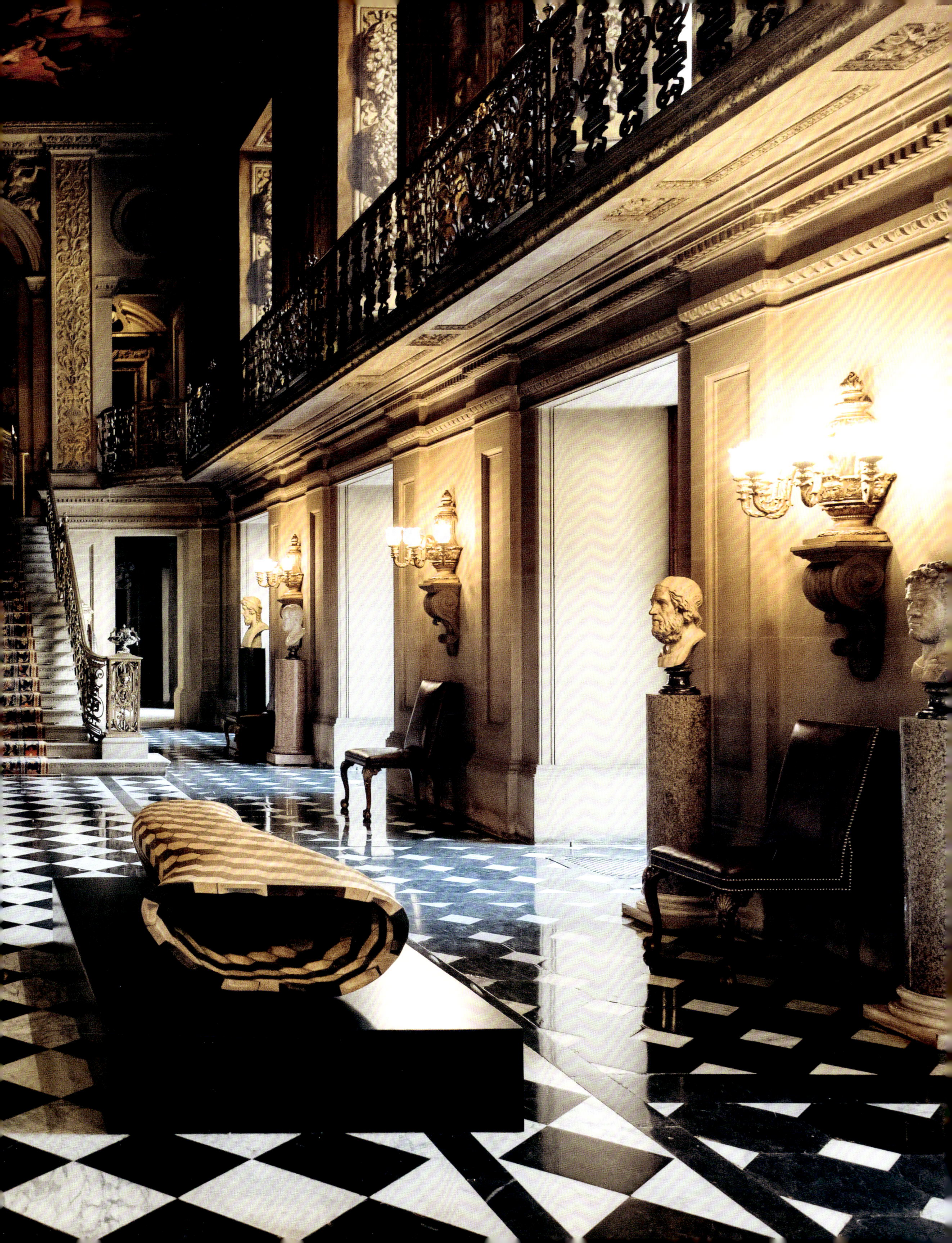

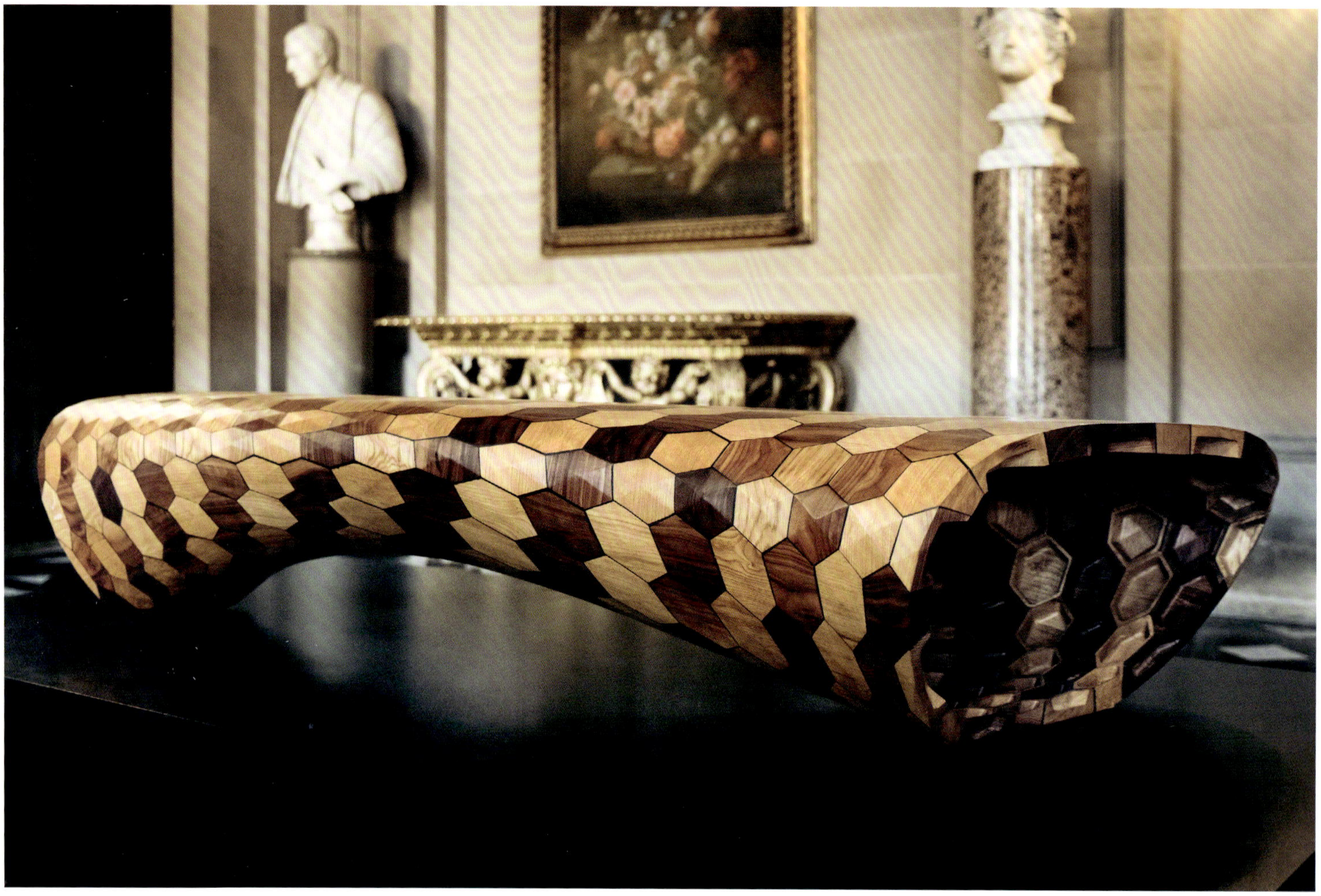

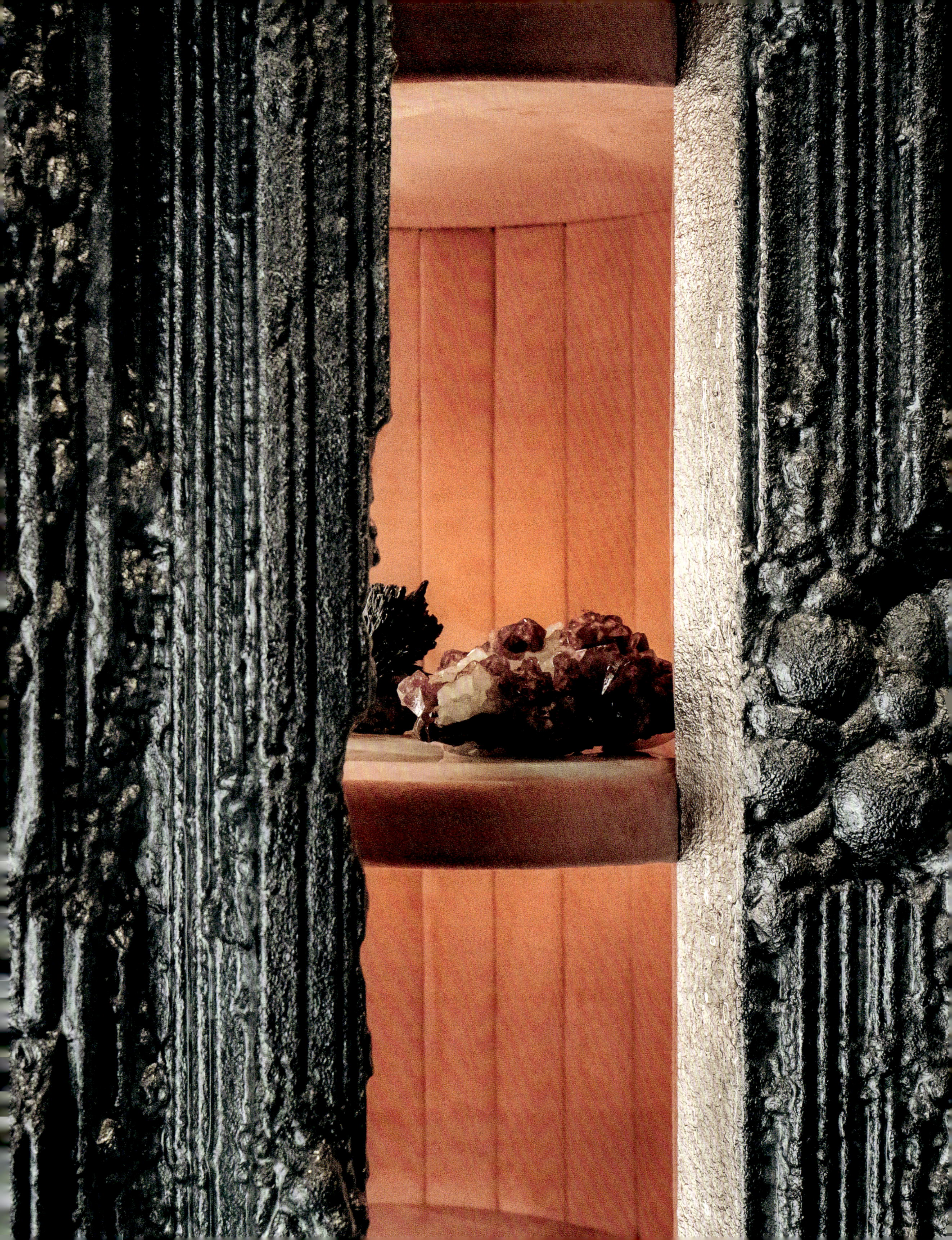

CHRIS

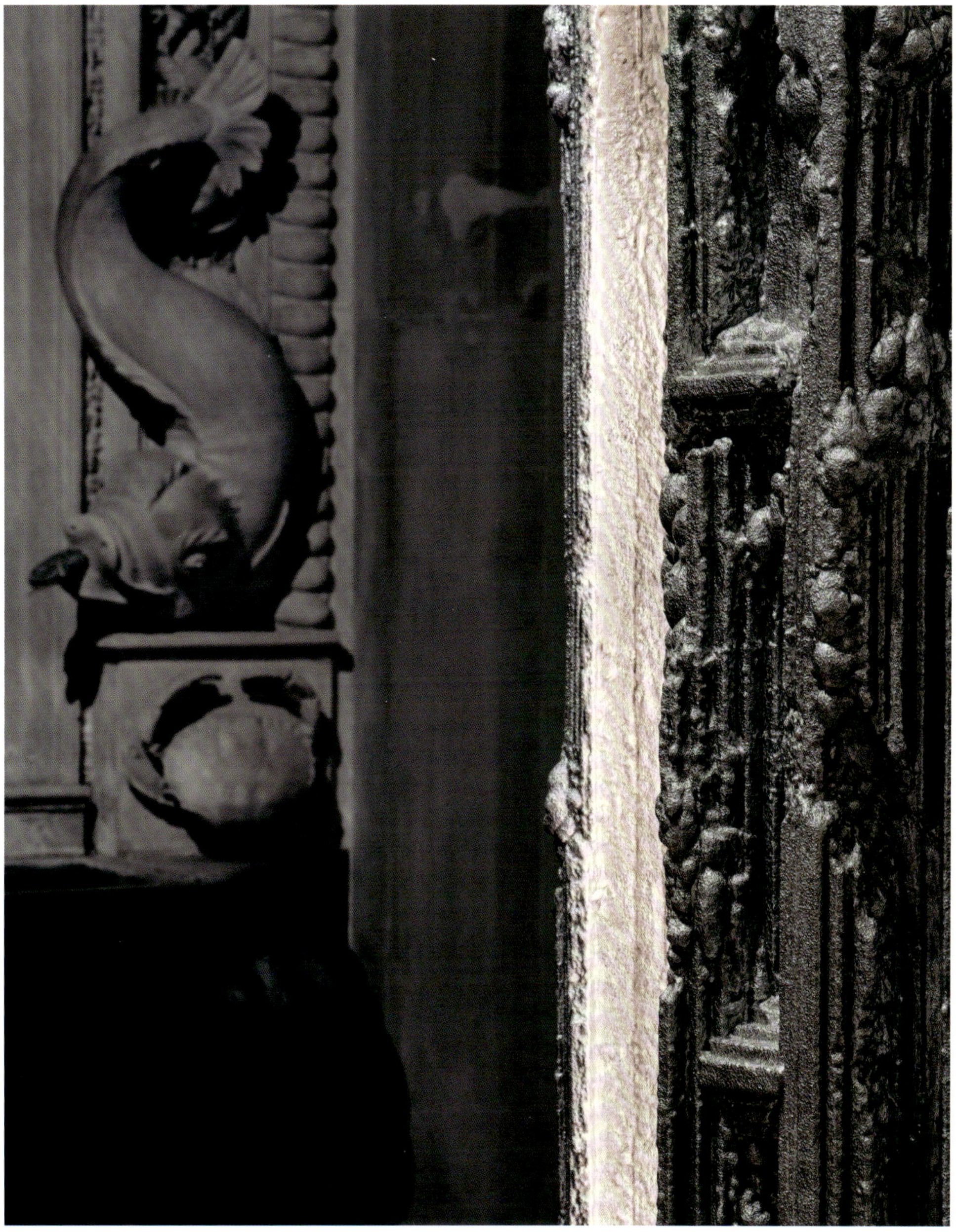

SCHANCK

'THERE IS A FINE GROTTOE ALL STONE PAVEMENT AND SIDES'

CELIA FIENNES

The adventuresome Celia Fiennes (1662–1741) travelled extensively in England, usually on her own, at a time when it was most unusual for women to do so. Her private memoir, which remained unpublished until long after her death, is a valuable document, recording historic details of the many sites she visited, as well as her own subjective impressions. At 'Chattsworth' she took note of a small, dark space on the ground floor, writing: 'There is a fine grottoe all stone pavement and sides. This is designed to supply all the house with water besides severall ffanceyes to make a diversion.' Fiennes was describing one of the newest features of the house, completed in 1692, which supplied hot and cold running water—a luxurious novelty at the time.

The Grotto retains its subterranean feeling to this day, thanks to its position under Chatsworth's grandest stairway. Here Detroit-based designer Chris Schanck has introduced a tall cabinet made in his signature 'alufoil' technique—built from miscellaneous scraps, then sheathed in metallic foil and a clear coat of resin. These materials are purposefully non-precious (Schanck developed the process early in his career, when he had limited resources), but nonetheless combine to majestic effect. The gleaming, thickly encrusted surface speaks eloquently of Detroit's rough-and-tumble creative energies, while also alluding to tropes of fantasy and science fiction. Schanck's *Cryo Cabinet* would look right at home in Superman's frozen retreat, the Fortress of Solitude.

In Chatsworth's Grotto, Shanck has paired the cabinet with a related mirror whose frame is cast in aluminium, an industrial material that stands in nuanced contrast to the alufoil. The liquid surfaces of both pieces reflect the former, aqueous functionality of the space, as well as the carved stone decorations that festoon the walls, by virtuoso sculptor Samuel Watson. We have further enhanced the connections to the house and its history by placing mineral specimens from the collection within Schanck's crystalline cabinet.

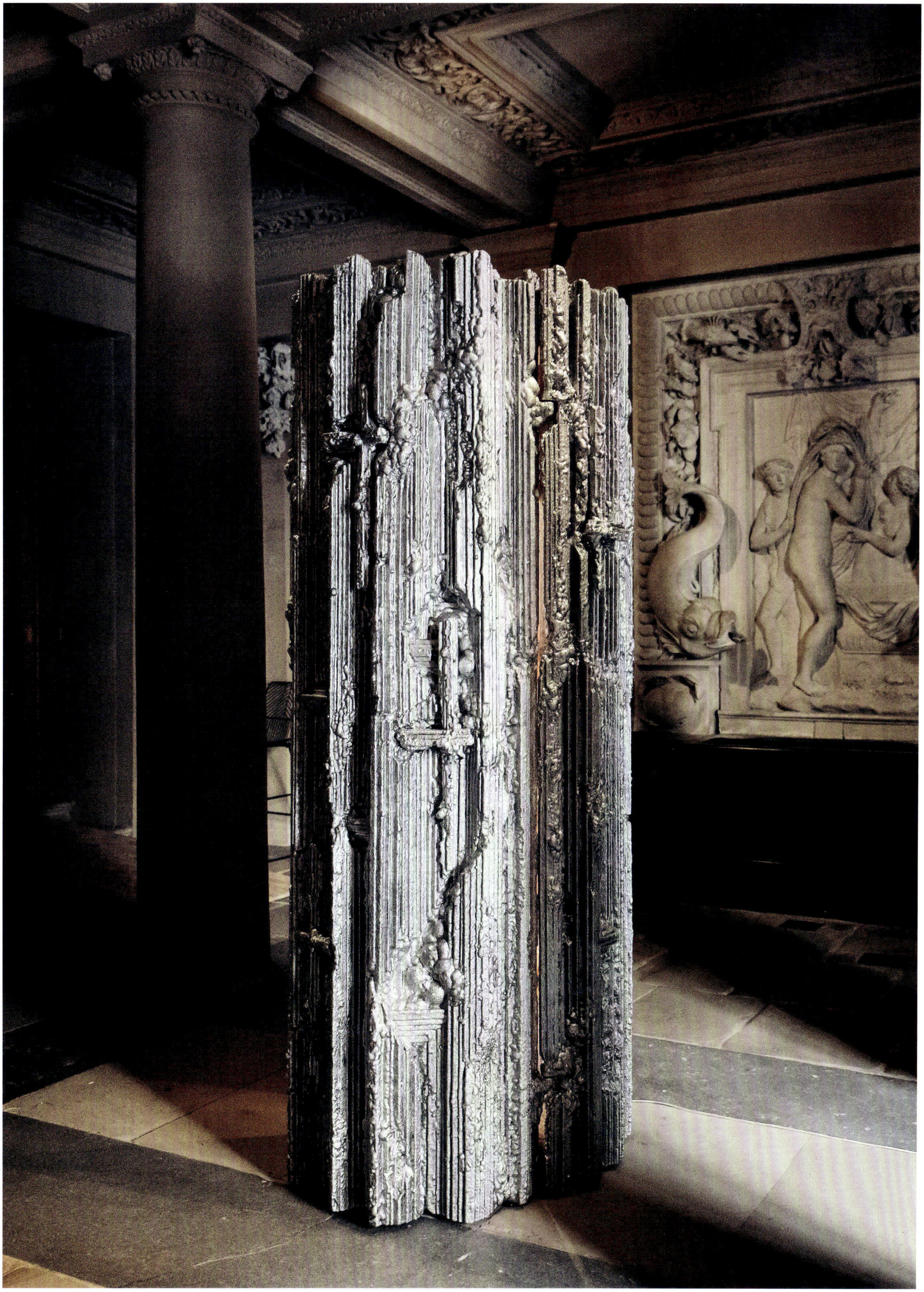

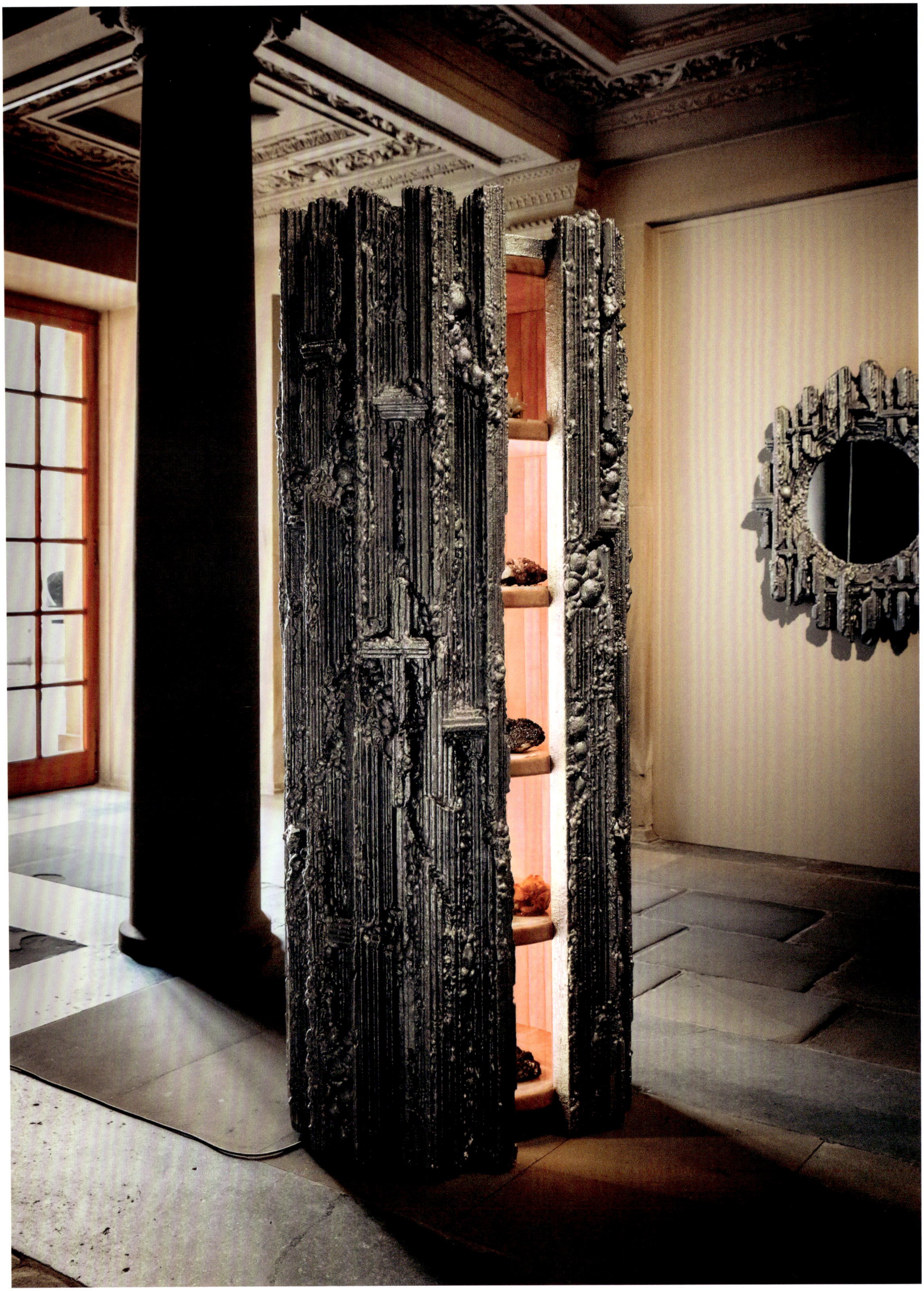

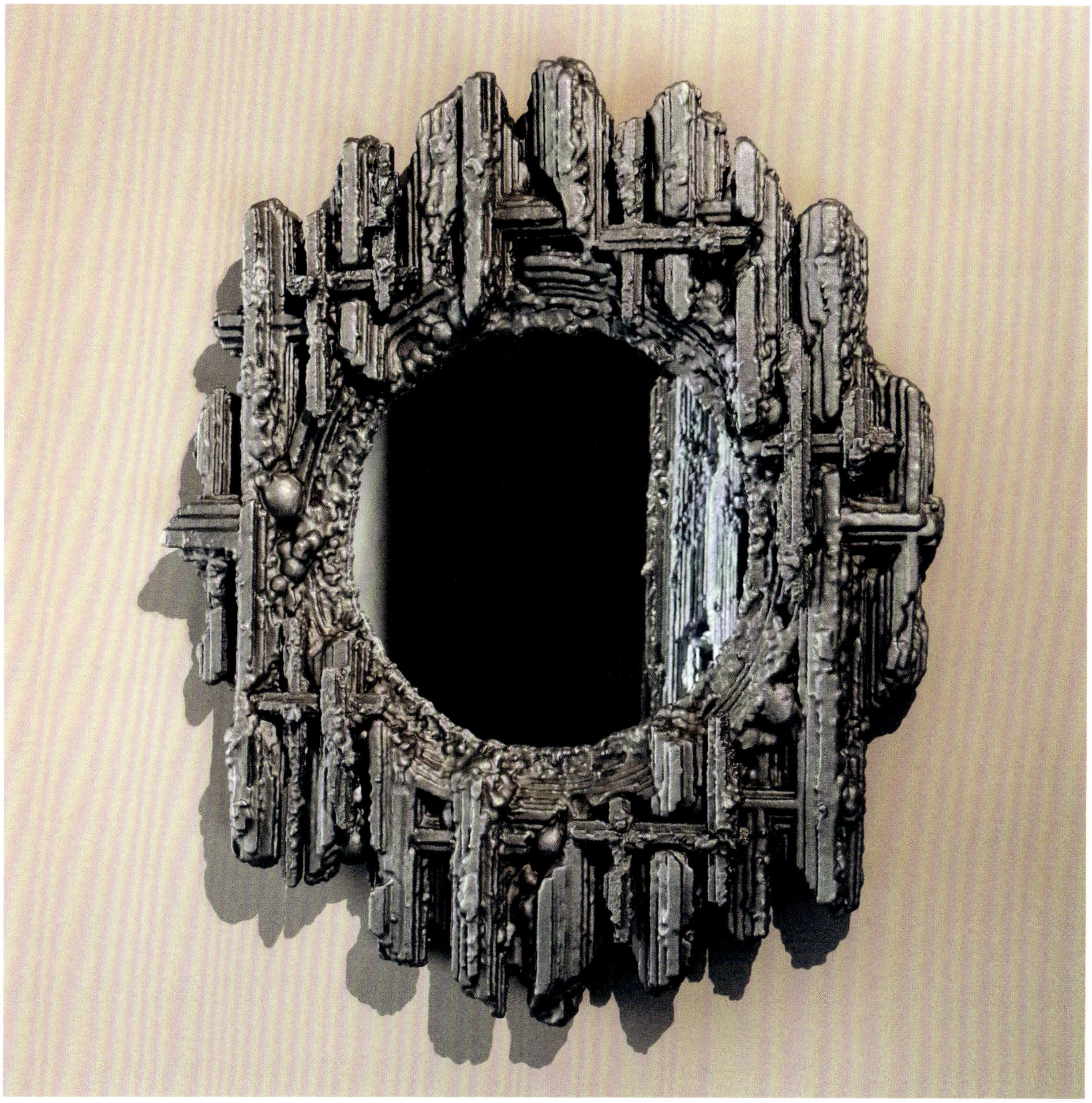

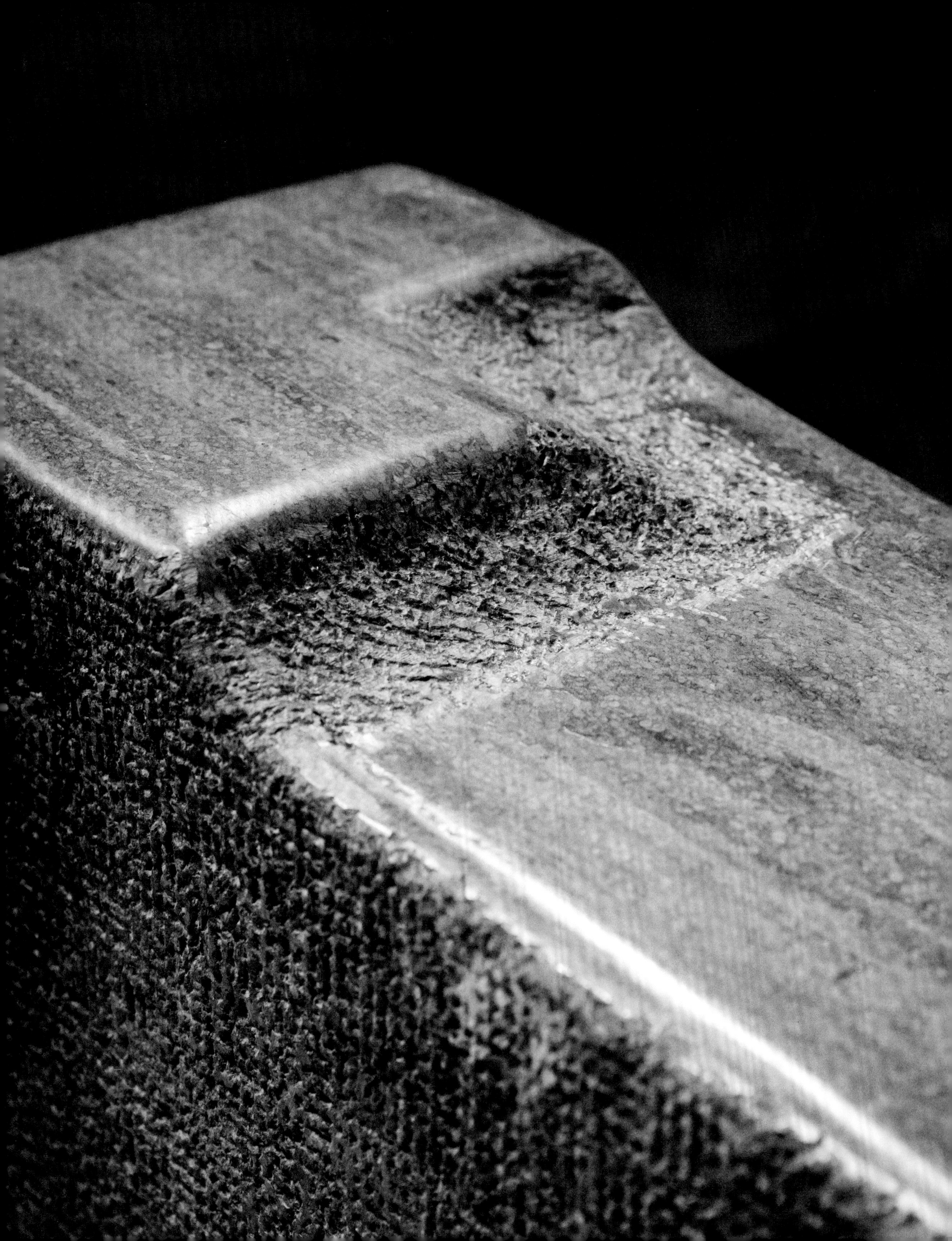

FAYE

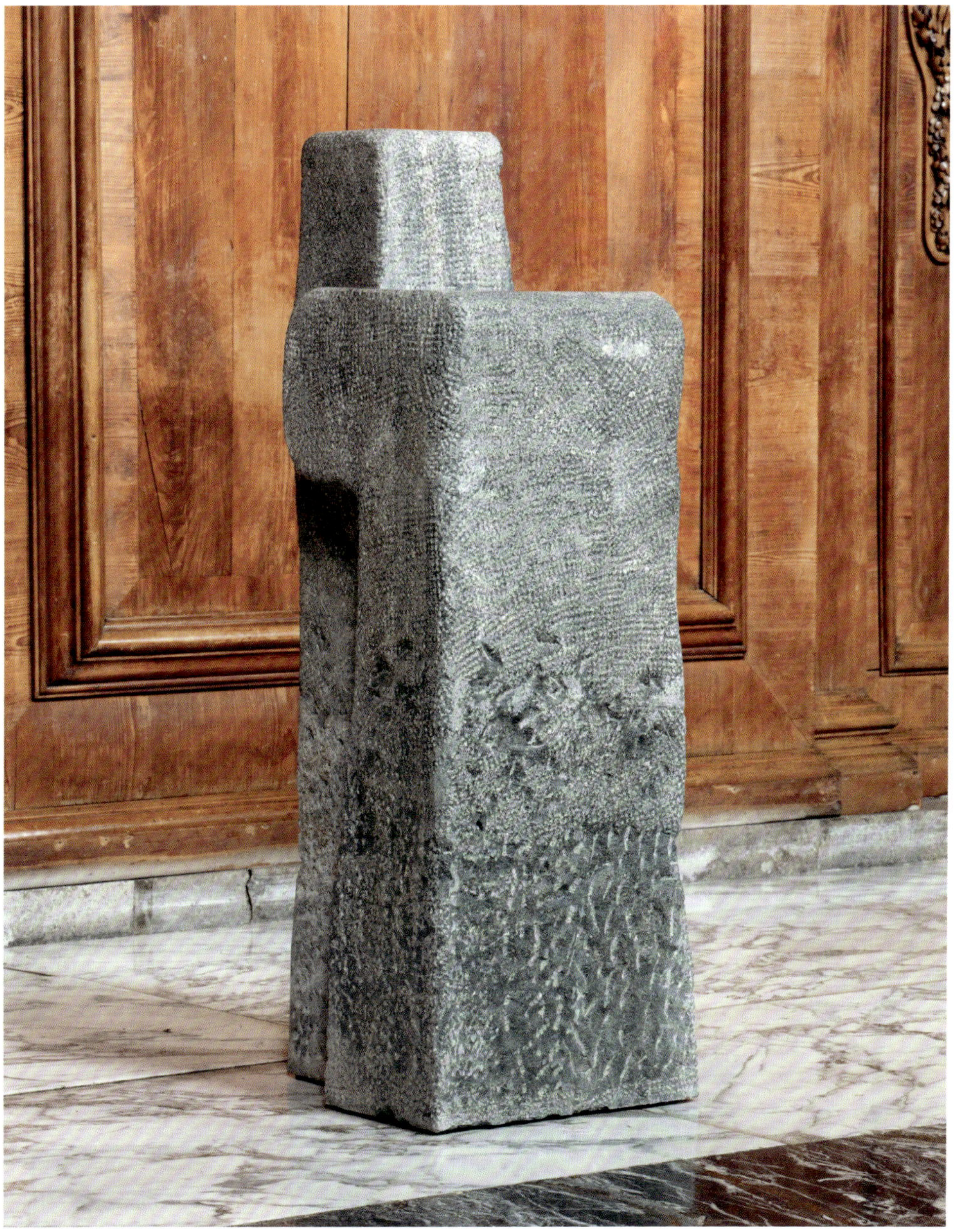

TOOGOOD

'IT WAS MORE A MATTER OF DISCOVERING THAN DESIGNING'

FAYE TOOGOOD

'I felt like I was revealing something that had always been there—something almost prehistoric that had been lost to time, and it was my job to find it again.' This is how Faye Toogood has described the design process for *Assemblage 7*, her latest collection of furniture—though as she indicates, it was more a matter of discovering than designing. Each piece began as a clay model, small enough to fit in two spread hands. The thickly proportioned, sculptural qualities of this quick preparatory study are preserved in the finished works, which are carved in either wood or stone, the final contours found through careful chiseling, like an archaeologist digging on-site.

For *Mirror Mirror*, Toogood and her artisan collaborators realised two parallel expressions of *Assemblage 7*. The first was conceived for Chatsworth's historic baroque chapel: deconsecrated but still glorious, a monumental space with columns 'so bigg that I could not compass one with my arms', as Celia Fiennes noted in her 1702 travel memoir, and elaborate carving in both stone and wood by Samuel Watson. Toogood's *Standing Stones* for the space are executed in so-called Purbeck marble—actually a limestone, quarried in Dorset, in which dense deposits of snail shell are captured. When carved, the material yields a surface pattern of delicate tracery, prized in the Middle Ages as a flooring material. Toogood's interest in the material was inspired by its use at Westminster Abbey; it also can be seen in other English cathedrals.

The elemental forms of Toogood's *Standing Stones* allude to this long history, and still further back, to neolithic monoliths, cairns, and barrows, which can be found across England—including the Nine Ladies, a stone circle on Stanton Moor, not far from Chatsworth in Derbyshire. They have a timeless appearance, as if they occupy multiple centuries at once. They equally suggest functional furniture and sacred forms: a low table at the centre and the two consoles that bracket it all suggest altars; two vertical stele, which appear anthropomorphic from one angle and architectonic from another, could be pulpits to preach from. In acknowledgement of the ecclesiastical setting, and to give visitors with a place to sit and contemplate, Toogood has also provided a *Pew* bench and two chairs, sand-cast in silver nitrate bronze, which are from her earlier *Assemblage 5*—a body of work inspired by Henri Matisse's Chapelle du Rosaire, in Vence, France. Here at Chatsworth, the spooned forms of the chairs tilt back at the perfect angle to appreciate the glorious painted ceiling by Louis Laguerre.

In the Oak Room adjoining the Chapel, Toogood has staged a related presentation of objects from *Assemblage 7*, to which she has given the collective title *Hoard of Oak*. Dominating the space is a carved table, like a miniature landscape, with elevated plateaus at each end and a broad valley between. The topology, wrapping around to the table's underside, is articulated by a texture of varied chisel marks, emphasising the hard-winning of the forms. The composition amounts to a case study in the materiality of oak, the interlocking design throwing end and side grain into direct juxtaposition. Accompanying this monumental work is a pair of small seats, carved from bog oak, which has acquired a dark density from long submersion in a peat bog. The specimens used here are sourced from Ukraine and are thought to be about two thousand years old—an expanse of time in provocative tension with the quick, indeed almost momentary, modeling process from which the table was generated.

The choice of materials, and the typology of a dining table and stools, were all appropriate choices for this room. It is lined in German oak paneling acquired and installed here by the 6th Duke of Devonshire in the nineteenth century. (At that time the room was used for private prayer, and occasionally to host supper, 'like a jolly friar's repast.') The allusion to domesticity makes for an intriguing contrast with the *Standing Stones* that Toogood has placed in the Chapel: within a single form-language, she has staged a conversation between the quotidian and the sacred.

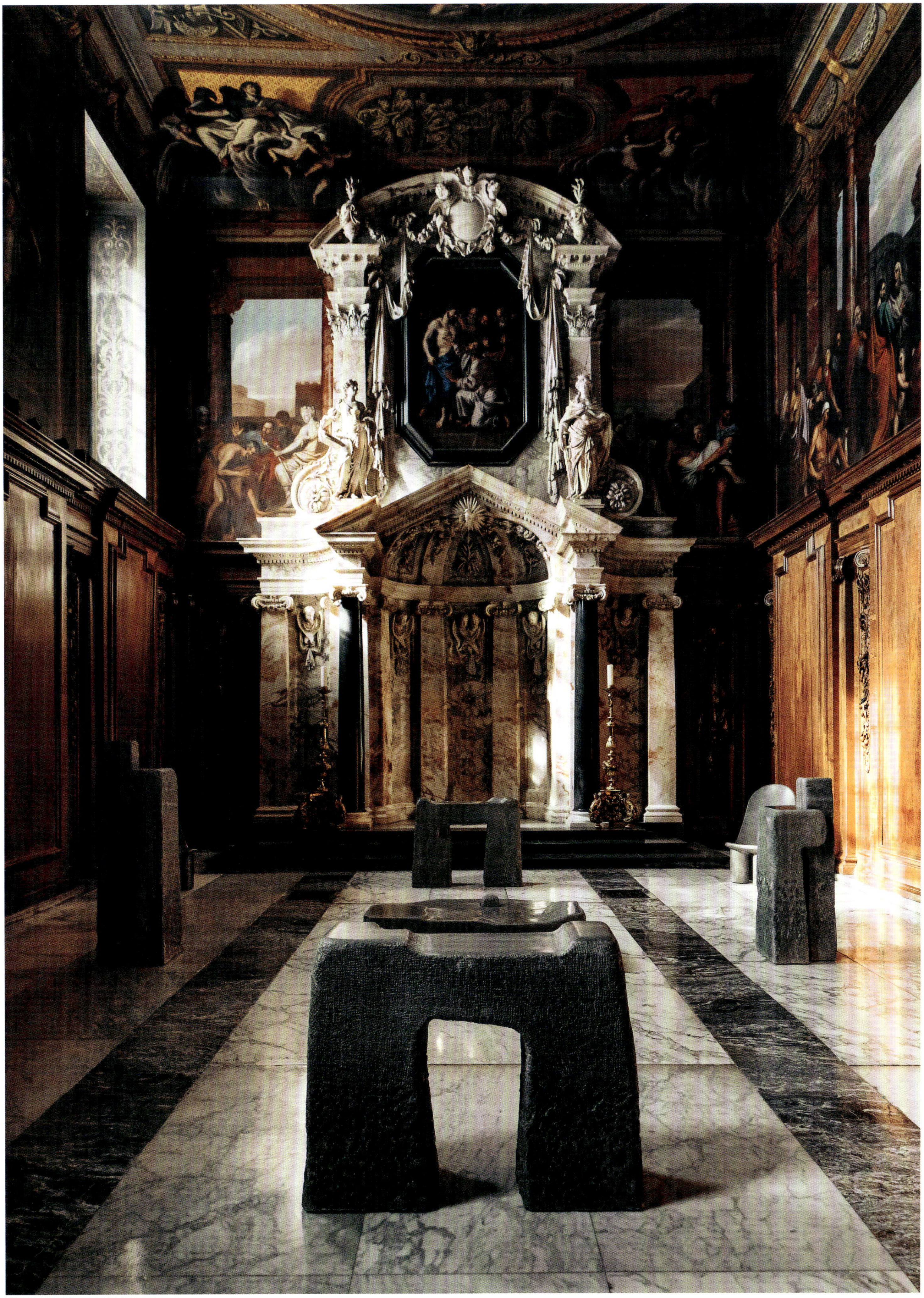

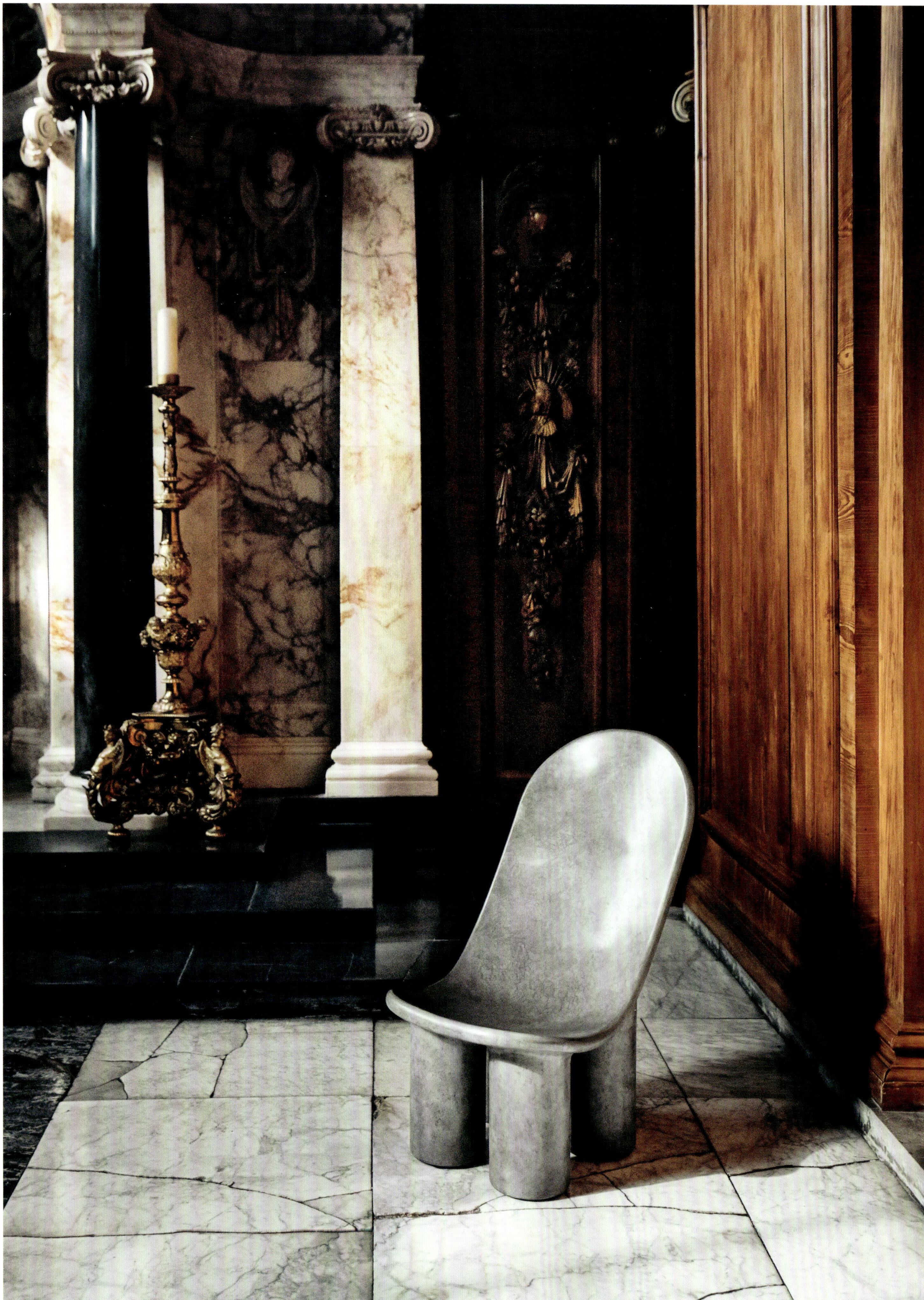

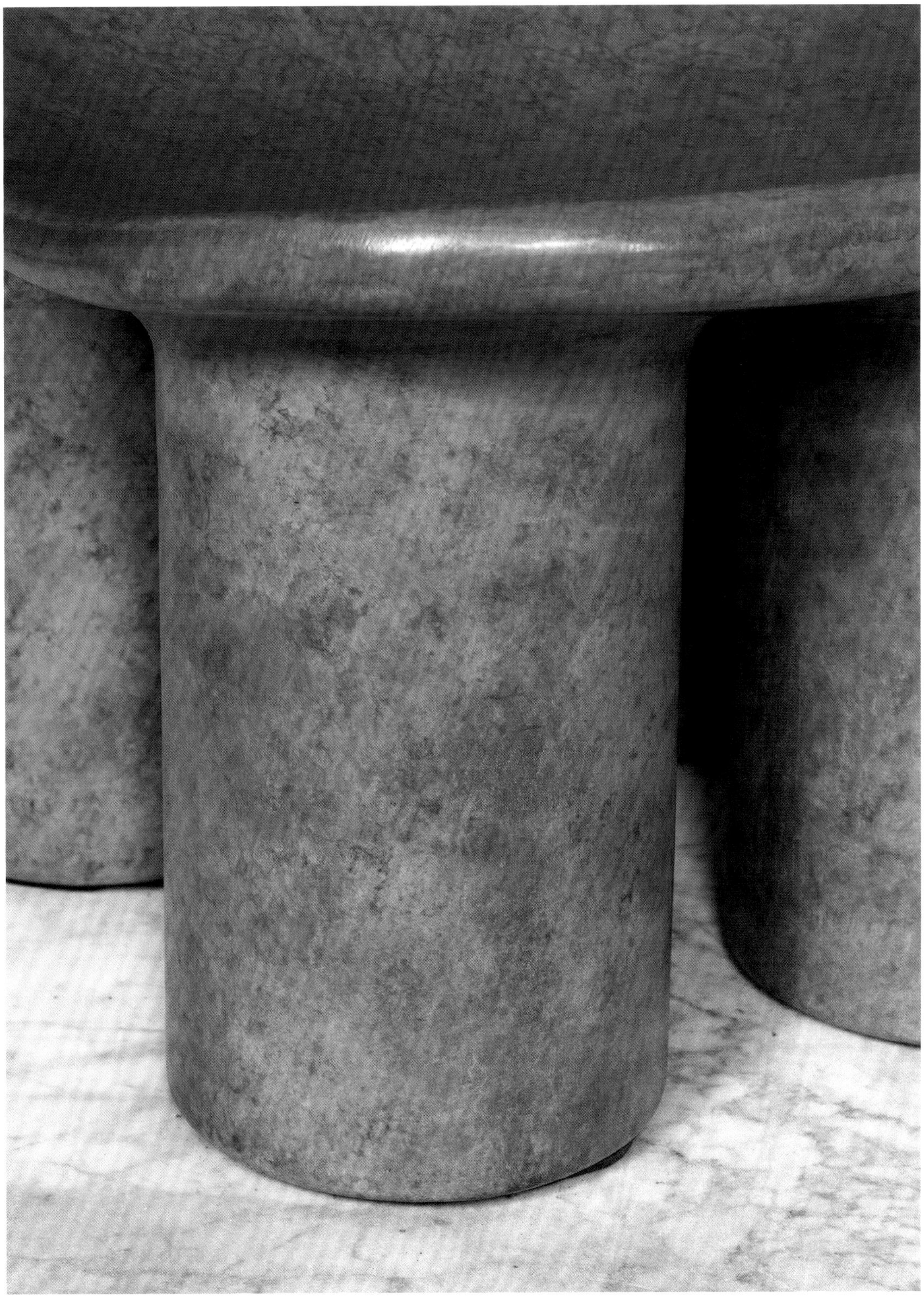

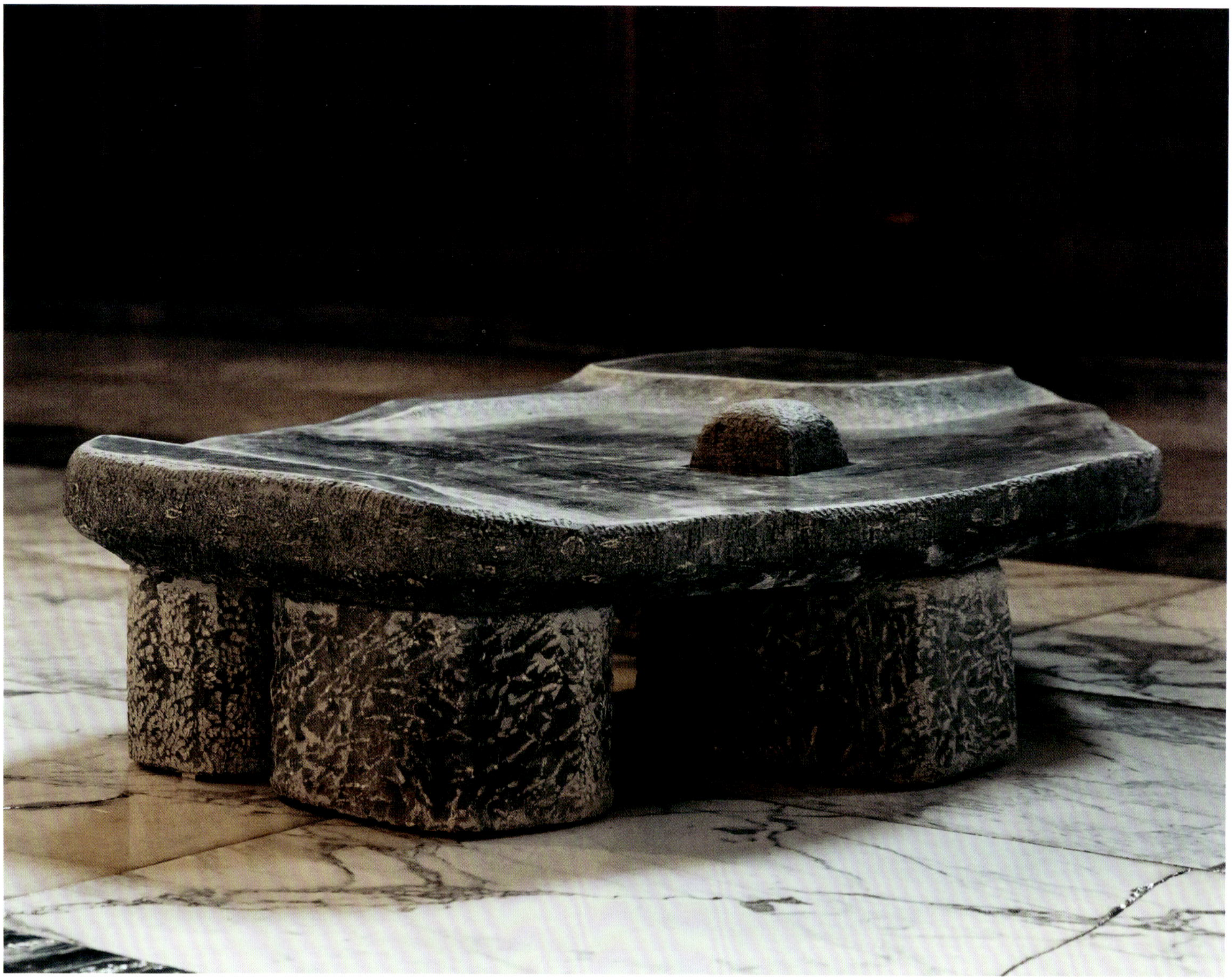

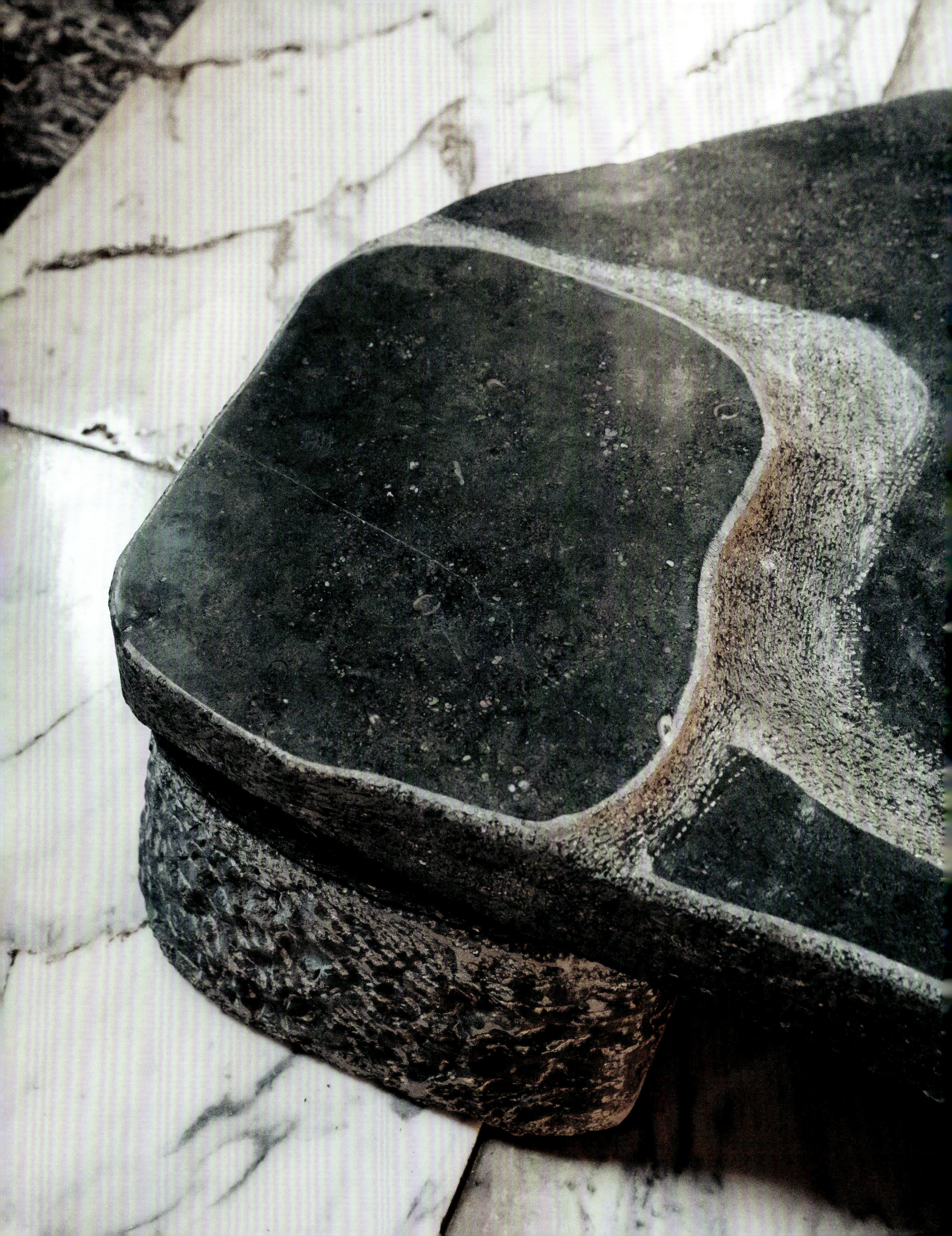

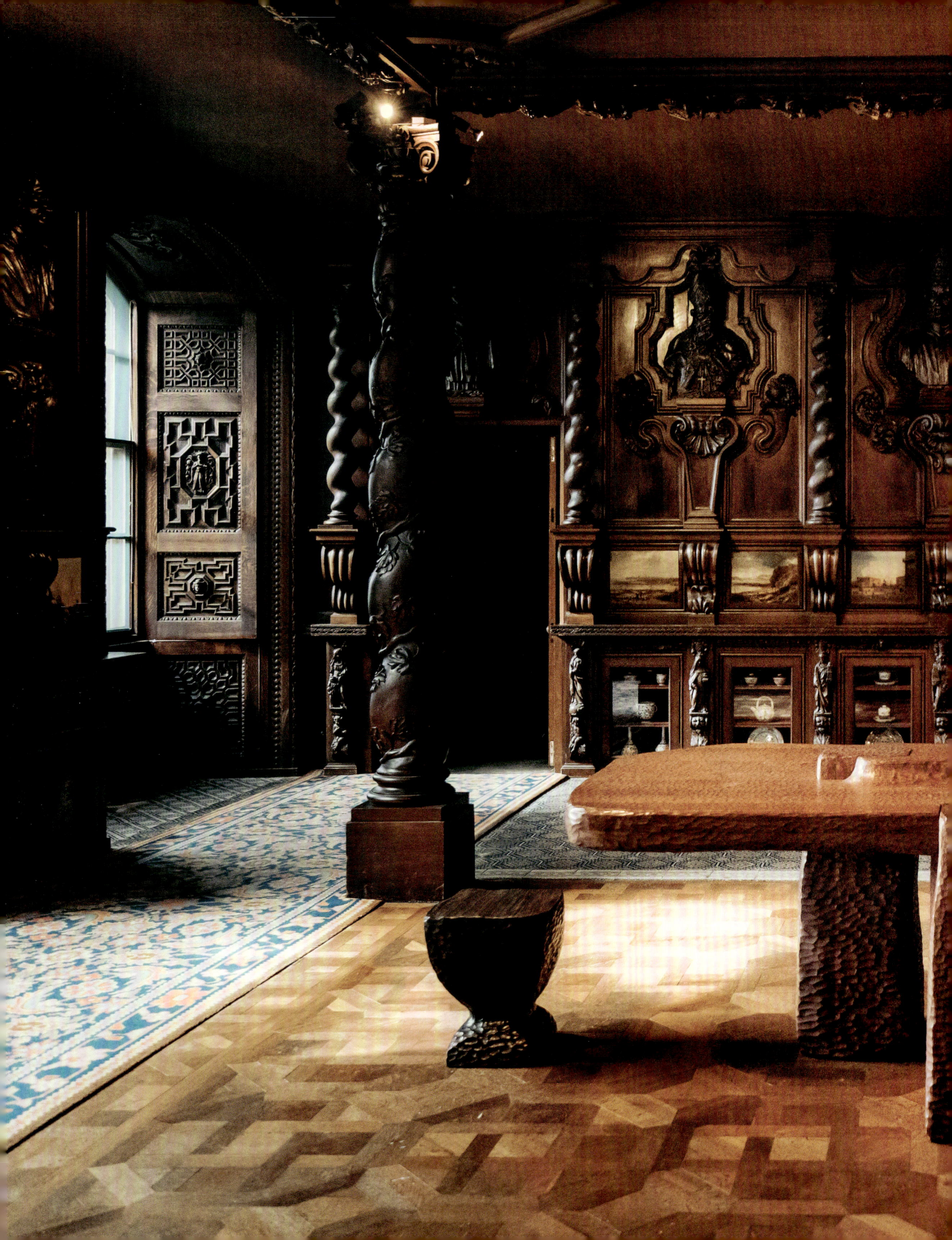

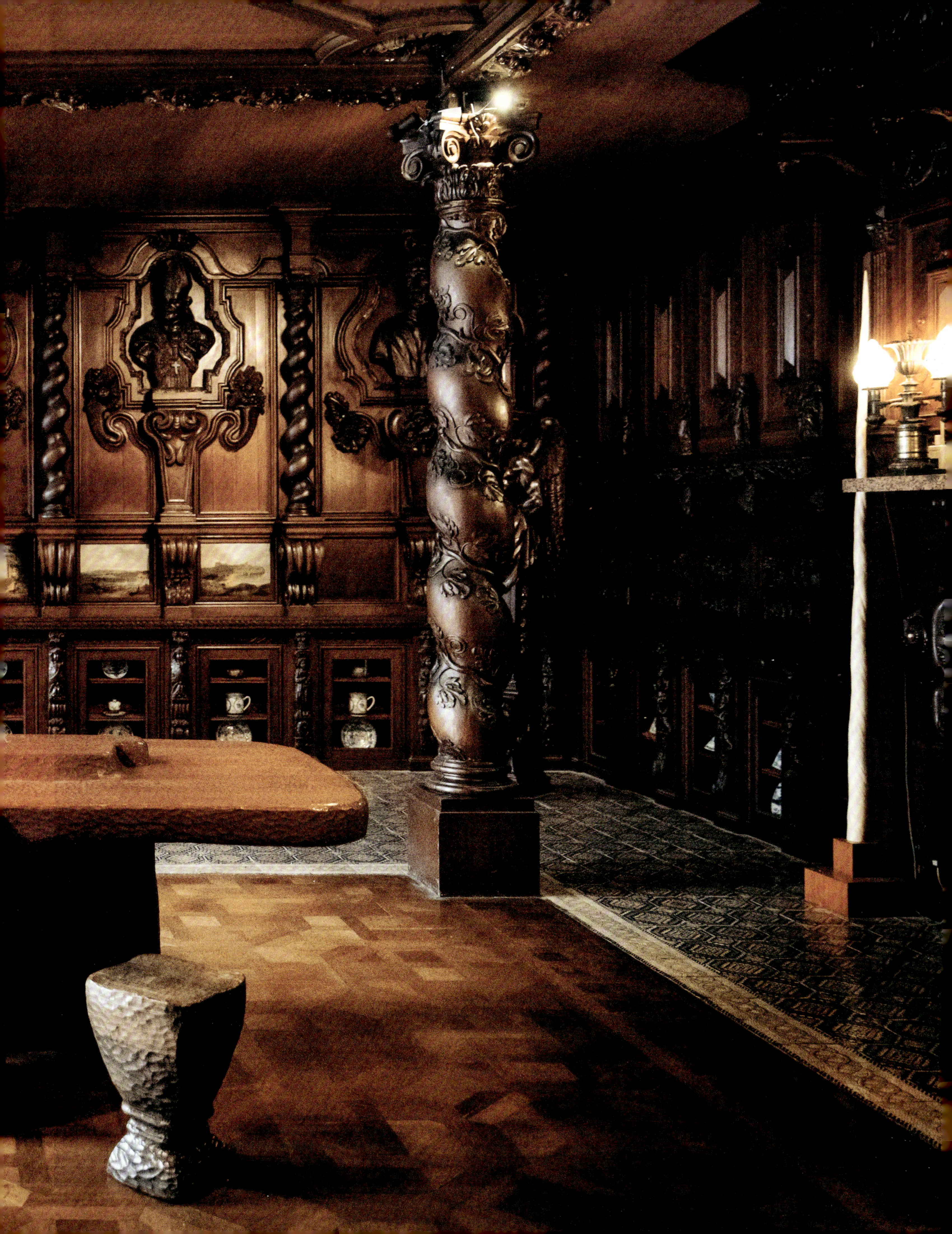

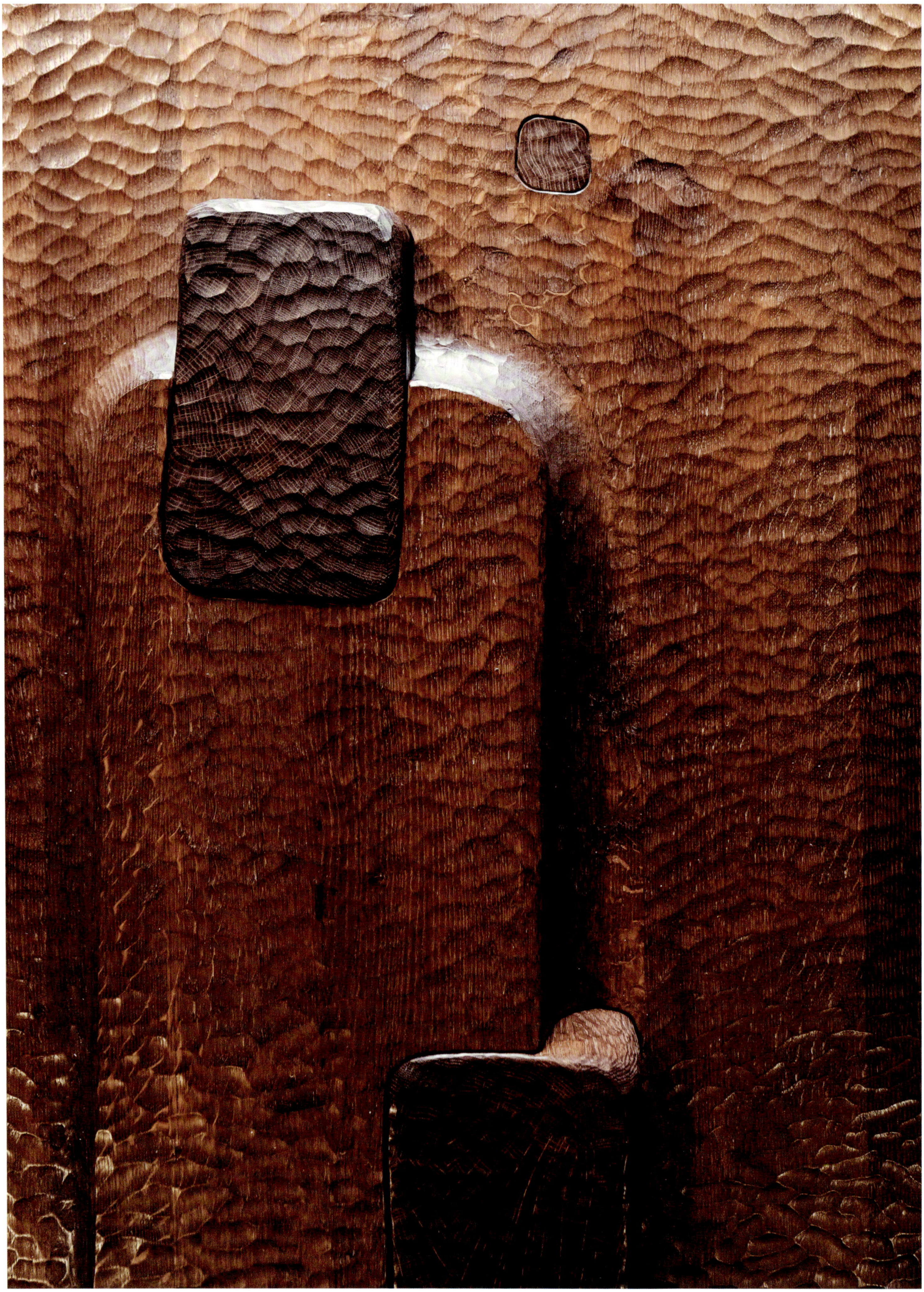

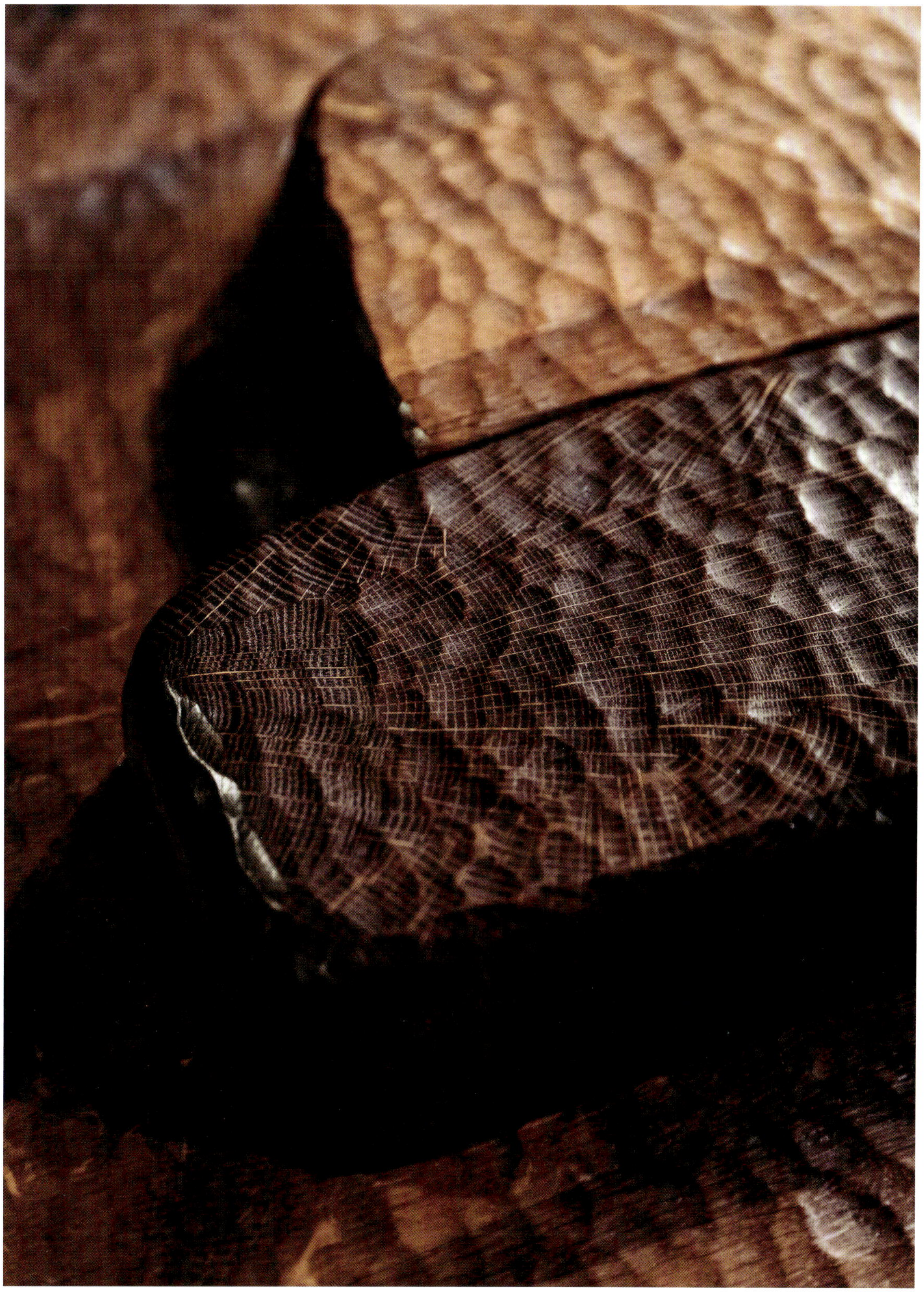

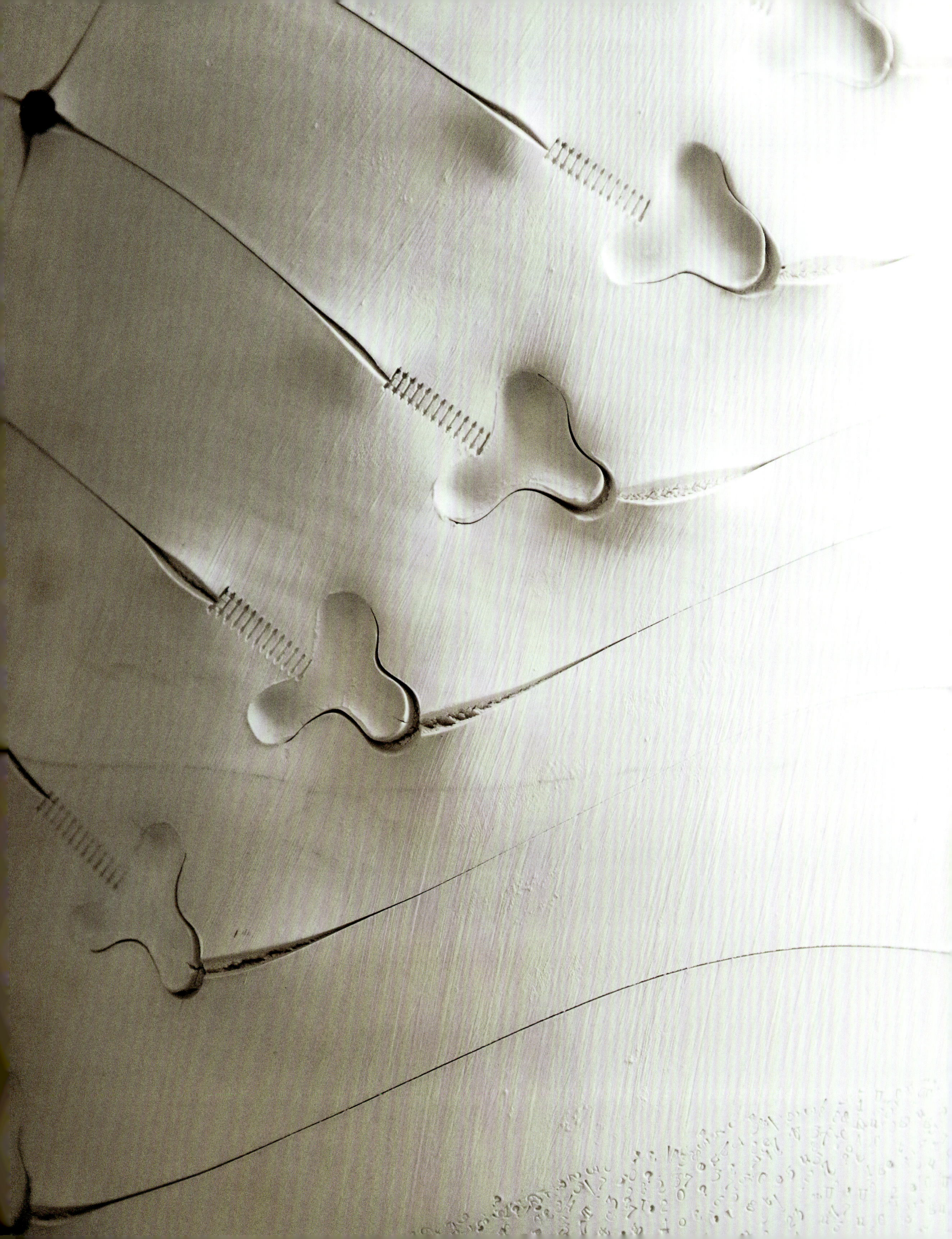

ANDILE

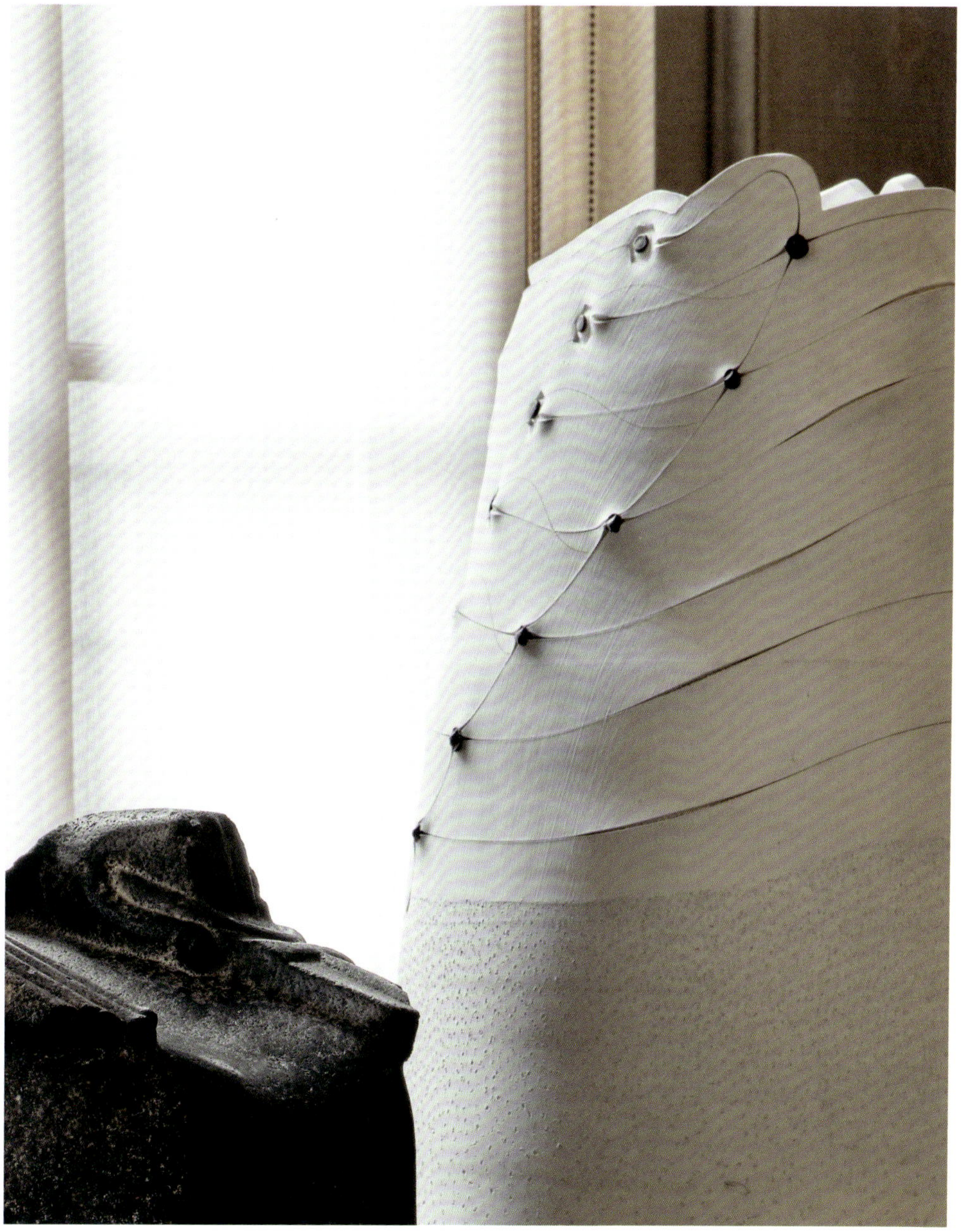

DYALVANE

'HEAR THE WHISPER OF THE ANCESTORS IN THE CLAY'

ANDILE DYALVANE

When he was growing up in the Eastern Cape of South Africa, in a small village called Ngobozana, Andile Dyalvane had little experience of ceramics. The beer pots and other clay vessels traditionally used by his people, the Xhosa, had been replaced by plastic containers. He was taught to observe what was around him, however, and at an early age he discovered deposits of raw clay exposed on the sloping, eroded banks of a nearby river. With this found material, he would shape little figures and herds of cattle, then leave them there to be washed away. Though it would take Dyalvane some years to 'hear the whisper of the ancestors in the clay' in his own lovely phrase, he was already moulding the very soil on which they had walked for generations.

Today, this transcendent inheritance resonates throughout his practice. His complex, large-scale ceramic artworks often feature Xhosa pictograms and patterns, including those from medicinal rituals of body scarification, or *bhaca*. While initially coiled, as is typical of hand-built African pottery, Dyalvane then cuts and reshapes his vessels, giving them sharply defined facets, thus making them literally articulate.

In the pots that Dyalvane has made for *Mirror Mirror*, we see how he has extended his vocabulary through global travel and exchange. One tall, white vessel is made in hand-thrown porcelain, a striking contrast with his usual coiled pieces; it was made in Taipei in collaboration with Master Chan Guo Xiang, a master of large-scale wheel-throwing. Dyalvane enlivened the surface by impressing metal type into the surface, a scatter of numerals and symbols implying some kind of transcultural encoding that exists beyond structured language, but rather in spirit.

Another pot in the group was made during his residency at the famed Leach Pottery, in St. Ives, Cornwall. For two months of 2019 he immersed himself there, adapting his work to the Pottery's clay, glazes, and gas kilns. It would have been elevated still further, had Bernard Leach lived to see the artist working at his former studio, for few contemporary makers are more connected to the cultural 'taproot' that the great British potter saw as necessary to the creation of vital work.

What most fired Dyalvane's imagination during his visit was the Cornish coastline. His pots took on the shapes of the region's geology, the crags defining a ridgeline over the sea. The five pots that Dyalvane made for *Mirror Mirror* continue this geological idiom, while also entering into conversation with the Chapel Corridor at Chatsworth. Ceramics, sculpture, and mineral specimens are plentiful in the space. Many of these pieces were brought to the house long ago, as exemplars of antiquity, but there is also a recent installation by the prominent English potter and writer Edmund de Waal titled *a sounding line* (2007), which measures out an interval of space one cylinder at a time. As it happens, there is quite a bit of commonality here: DeWaal began his career training with a disciple of Leach's, and his work, like Dyalvane's, is a response to Chatsworth's collections, particularly its wealth of porcelain garnitures.

The connections occasioned by Dyalvane's presentation run still deeper and wider, too, right across the divide between times and cultures. Too often, in the past, African art has been treated as a quarry to be mined for inspiration. By so adroitly synthesising influences from his Xhosa ancestry and cosmopolitan experiences, Dyalvane exemplifies the ways in which patterns of artistic exchange may be reconfigured. That sense of possibility is expressed directly in his newest pieces: they feature a huge vocabulary of mark-making, impressed emblems, and running glaze, and each is graced by a vivid blue interior, giving the impression that the sky itself has fallen into the pot and been somehow captured there. Having discovered and mastered his discipline, Dylavane remains dedicated to the memory of its past—all the better to reinvent it.

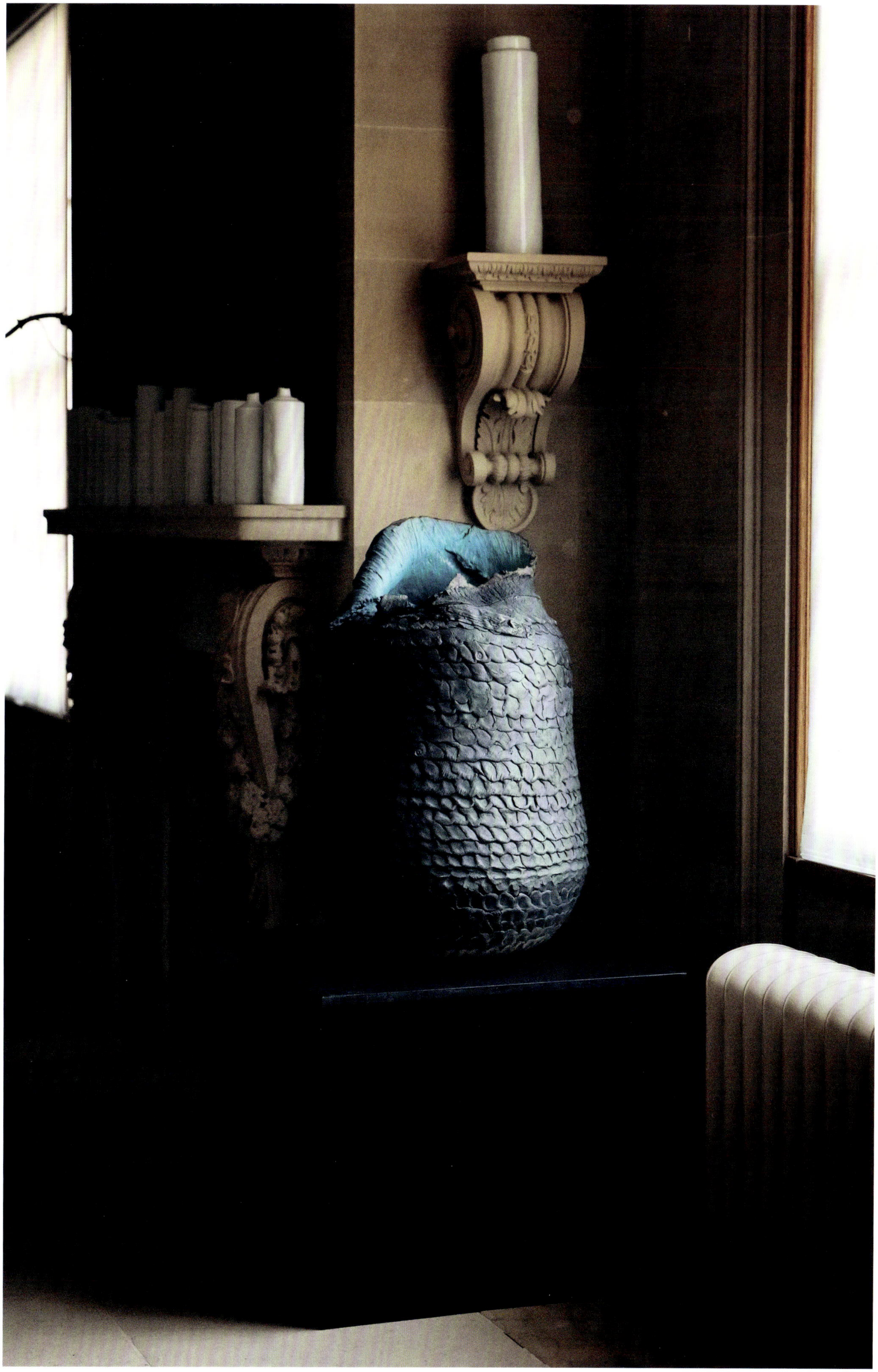

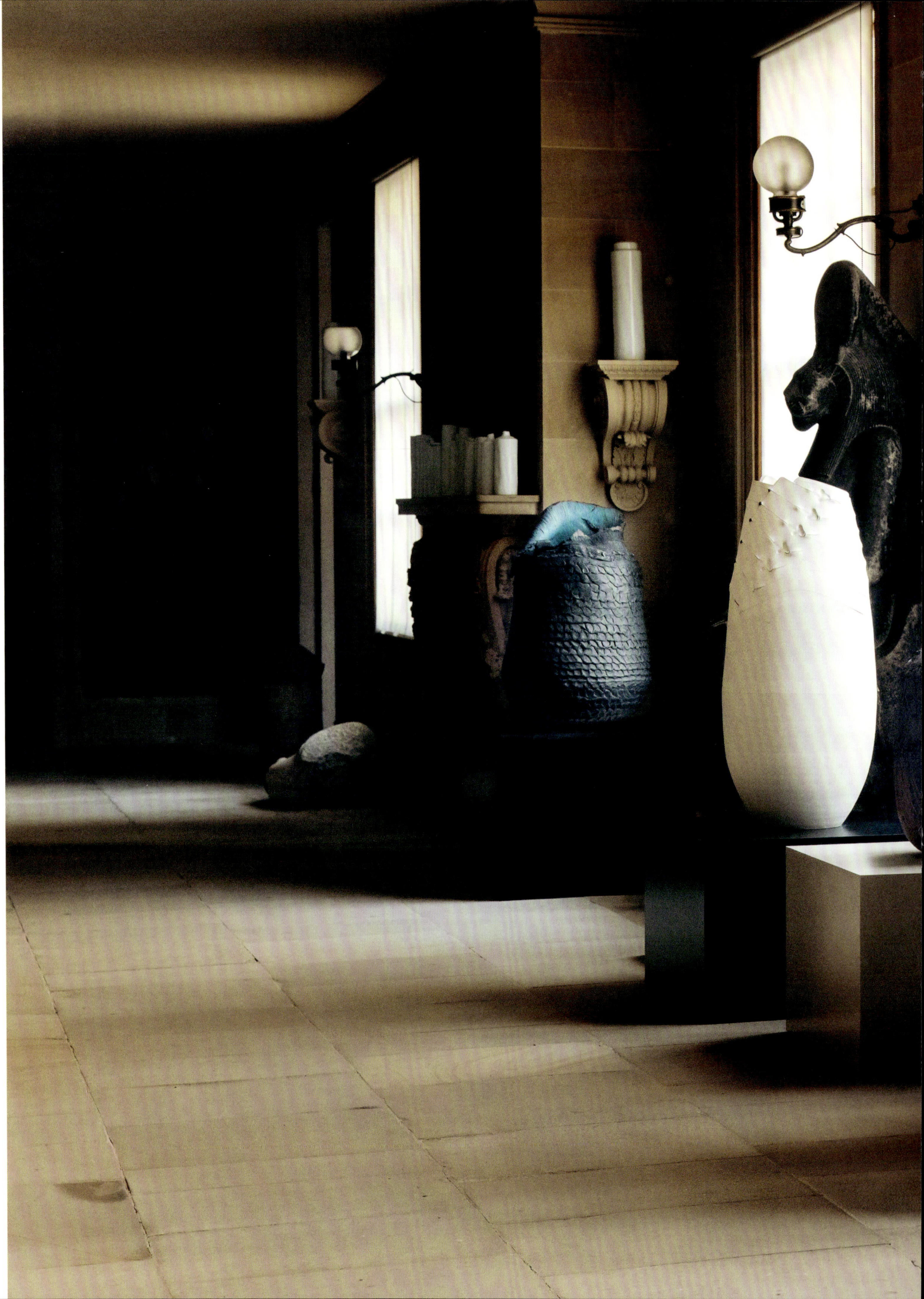

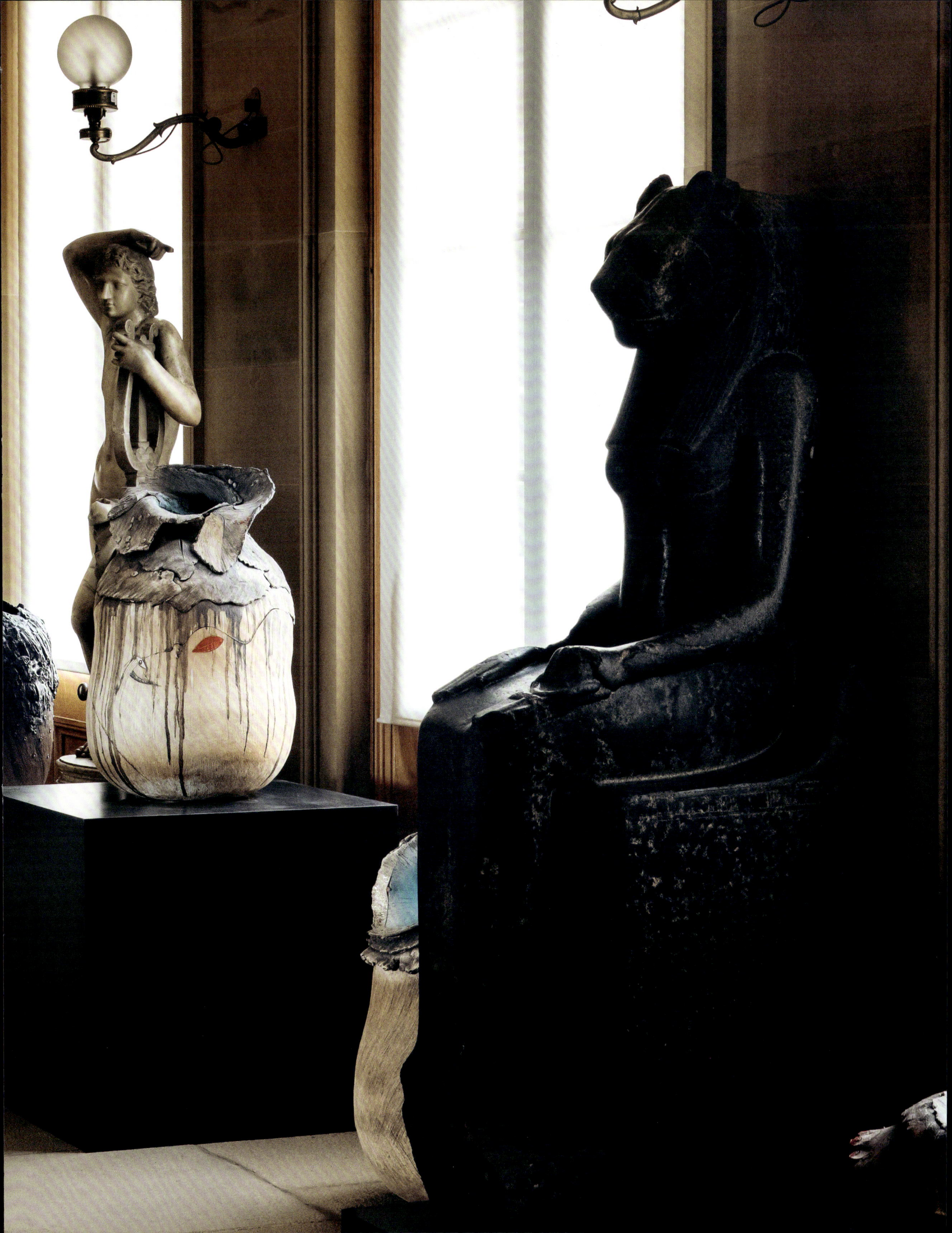

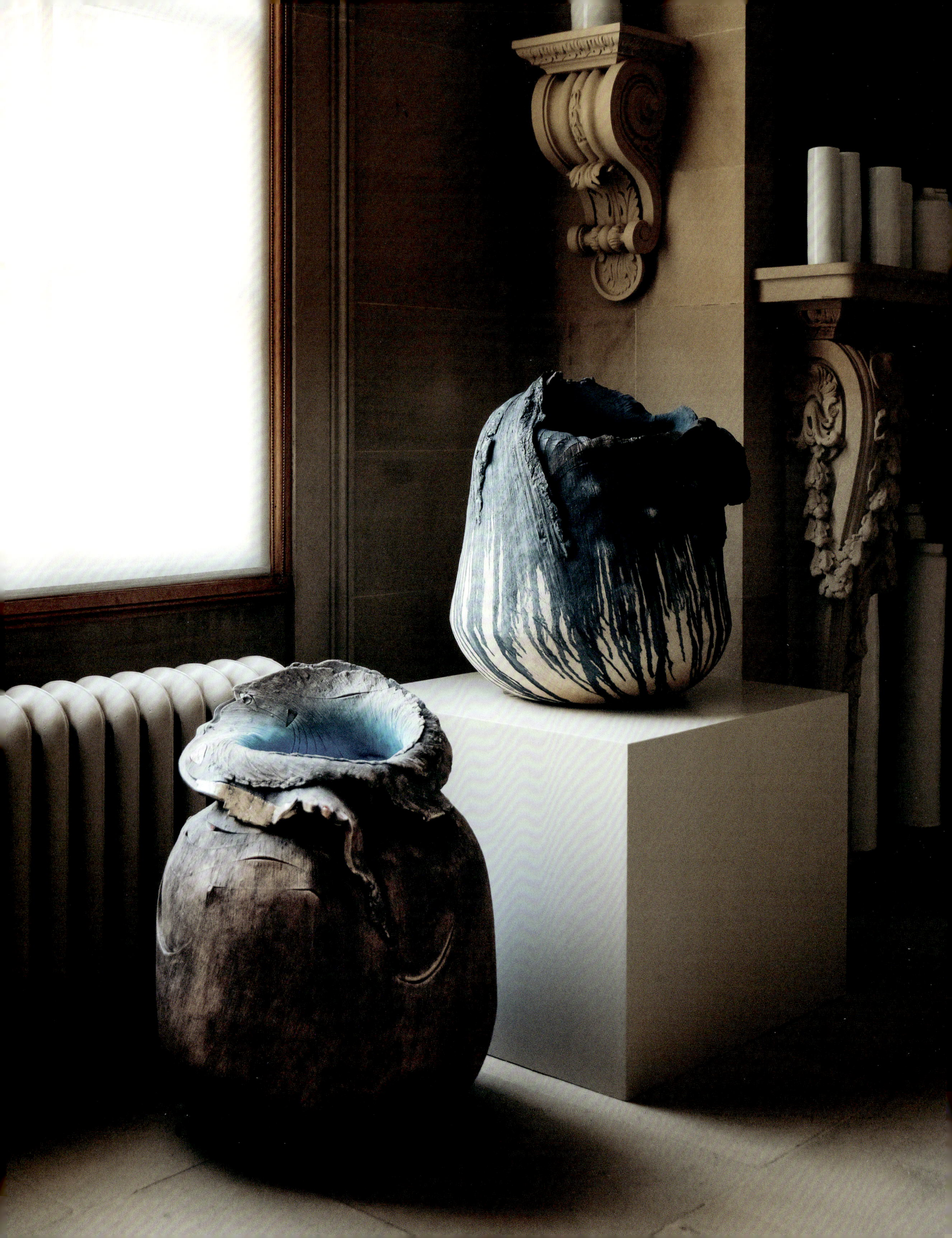

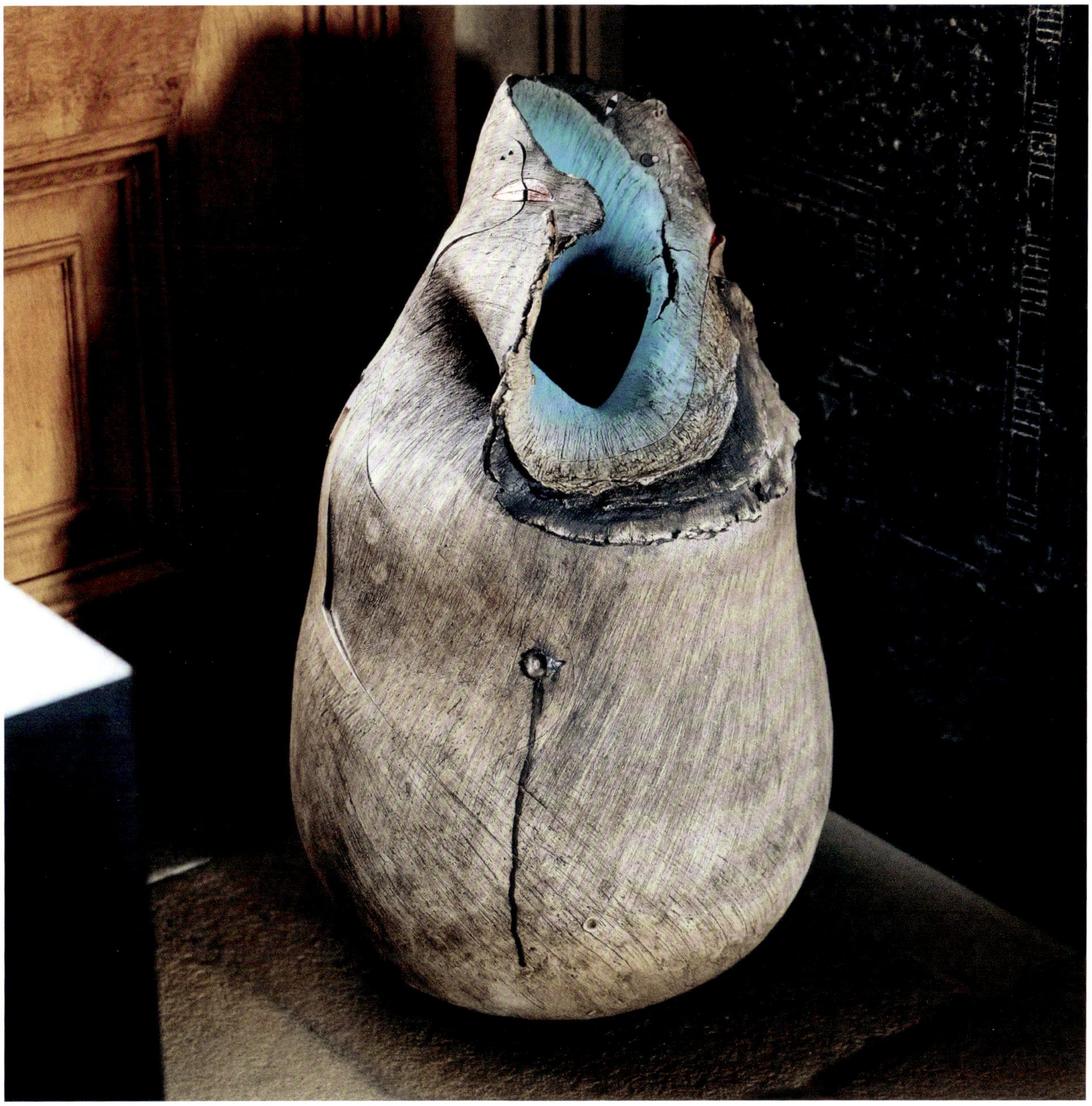

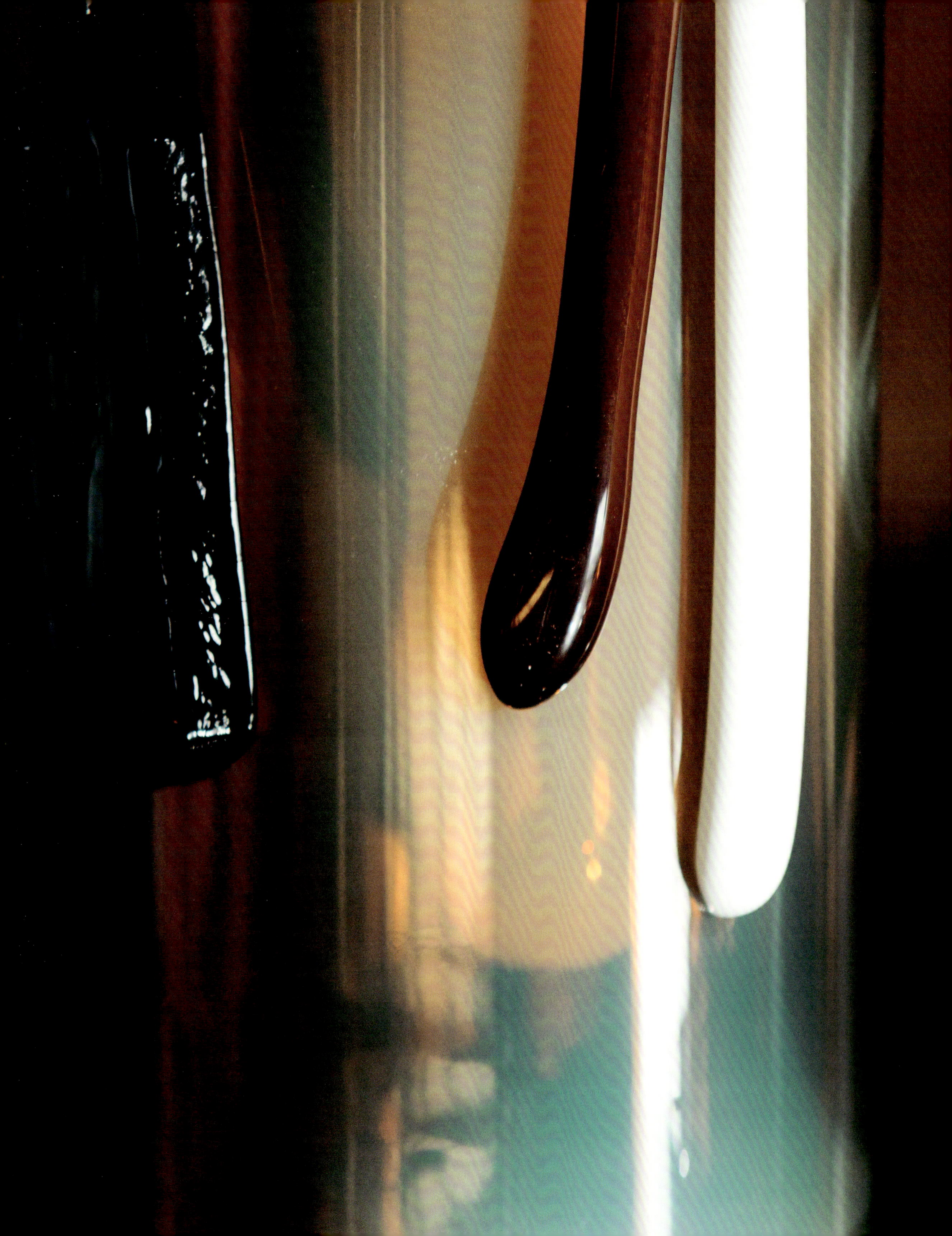

ETTORE

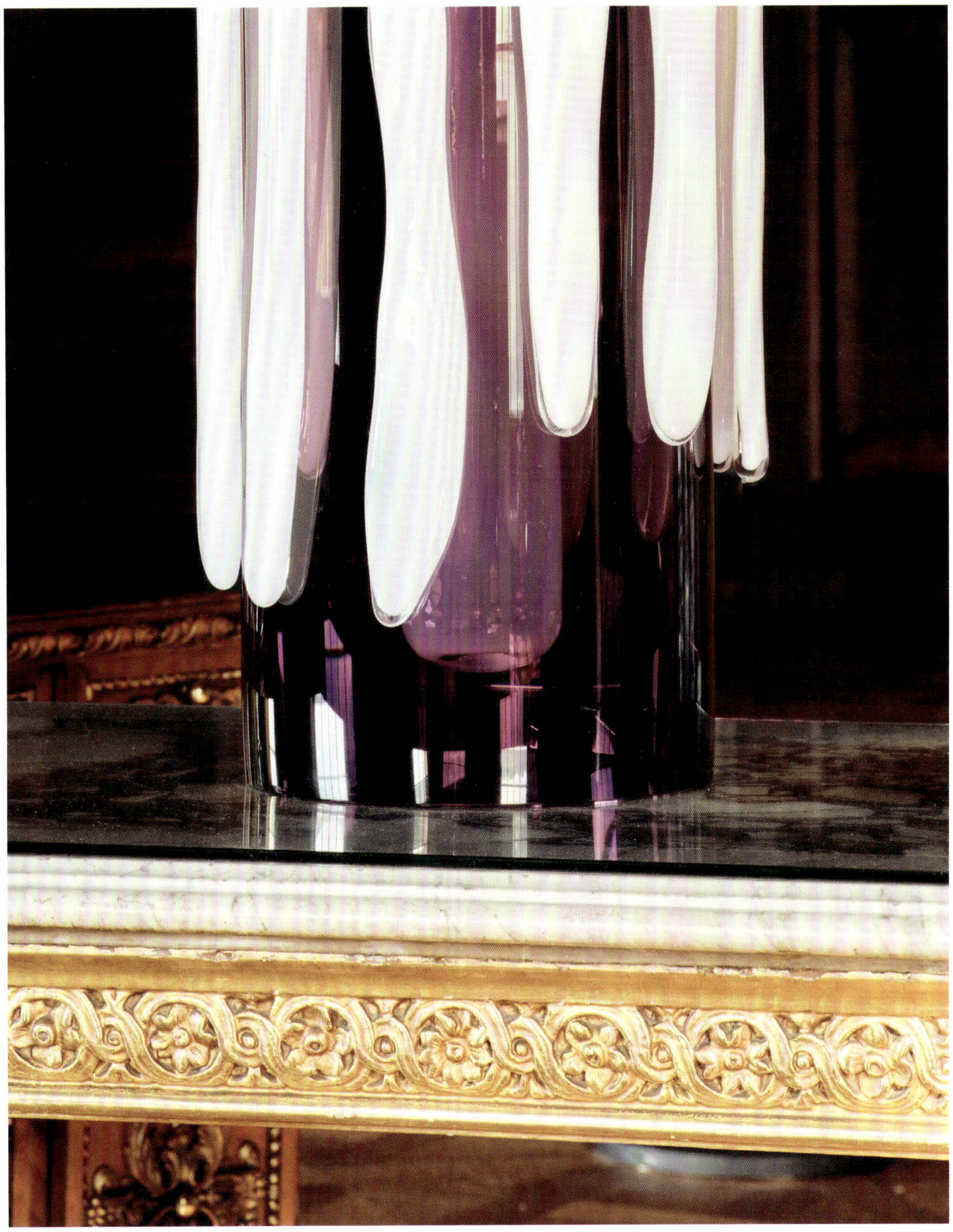

SOTTSASS

'THE SHADOWS OF FIRES DANCING ON THE WALLS'

ETTORE SOTTSASS

Ettore Sottsass (1917–2007) was a vital presence in Italian design for six decades, an avant-gardiste of unique humanity and spiritual depth. He was also, as the saying goes, a true Renaissance man. The scope of his story is enormous, traversing many chapters of art and design history, from the Vienna Secession (which his father, also an architect, experienced firsthand) through postmodernism and beyond. But it was above all Sottsass's restless curiosity that led him to explore so many typologies over the course of his long career: buildings, interiors, industrial design, ceramics, jewellery, painting, photography, and furniture. He unfailingly left each of these disciplines more expansive than he found it. This was certainly true of his intense involvement with hand-blown glass, a medium that charmed him with its alchemical brilliance. Unlike a paper cup, he wrote, a crystal goblet 'has no taste and is fragile, so you know from the beginning that your relationship with this object will have a ritualistic aspect'.

Sottsass's first serious involvement with this quintessentially Italian craft was in 1974, when he designed a series of vessels (closely related to his previous work in ceramic) for Vistosi, one of the fabled glass manufactories on the island of Murano. A few years later, during his leadership of the short-lived but sensational design collective Memphis, he produced further work in Murano, in collaboration with a newly-formed progressive studio called Toso Vetri d'Arte. Here Sottsass departed from accepted practice by using adhesives to join components of his vessels together. While scandalous from a traditional point of view (and nobody has greater pride in their traditions than Italian glassmakers), this simple expediency dramatically expanded the possibilities of shape. With typical nonchalance, Sottsass remarked, 'What difference does it make? Isn't the culture of glue an invention just like the culture of glass?'

Sottsass's most sustained engagement with glass came in the last decade of his career, initially through a collaboration with CIRVA (Centre International sur le Verre et les Arts Plastiques) in Marseille. Many luminaries have had residencies there—amongst them Sottsass's fellow Italian designers Andrea Branzi and Gaetano Pesce, as well as sculptors Anish Kapoor and Richard Deacon—and in most cases, they enjoy working closely with CIRVA's skilled fabricators. This was not Sottsass's approach. Though he was entranced by the theatre of the hotshop—'When I go into those big white very hot rooms, with the shadows of fires dancing on the walls, and the men's eyes folded onto the idea that a piece of glass must be made, I gape'—he also had very precise ideas about what he wanted. As Françoise Guichon, the artistic director of CIRVA, recalled, 'Everyone could tell that this little man, with his long grey ponytail, his heavy eyes and his distant gaze, would impose his own law ... his expectations were clear: the drawings were there and there was nothing else to say.'

This purposeful distance from the processes of making can be felt in the pieces Sottsass made at CIRVA and in the years following. They are abstract, intuitive essays in shape and colour, sometimes incorporating other materials like marble, wood, metal, and Corian. In *Mirror Mirror*, we include examples from two collections, both originally made with the support of Ernest Mourmans, a key ally of Sottsass's and today the custodian of his archive, who has also lent them to the exhibition. The first collection was fabricated by Pabel Cajethamel at CIRVA in 1999, the second at Gino Cenedese e Figlio in Murano in 2007. They are Sottsass's final creations in glass.

The latter are again unconventional in their manner of assembly, with hanging elements attached with wire, suggesting an improvisatory or transient attitude to form. At Chatsworth, we have placed them atop three historic tables—including designs by the imaginative early exponent of English neoclassicism, William Kent. Monumental pieces of early Delftware stand nearby in a fireplace, their bulbous forms echoing those in Sottsass's glass. By introducing his avant-garde objects into the space, we hope to remind visitors that these works in decorative art were, in their own time, just as bold, just as contemporary.

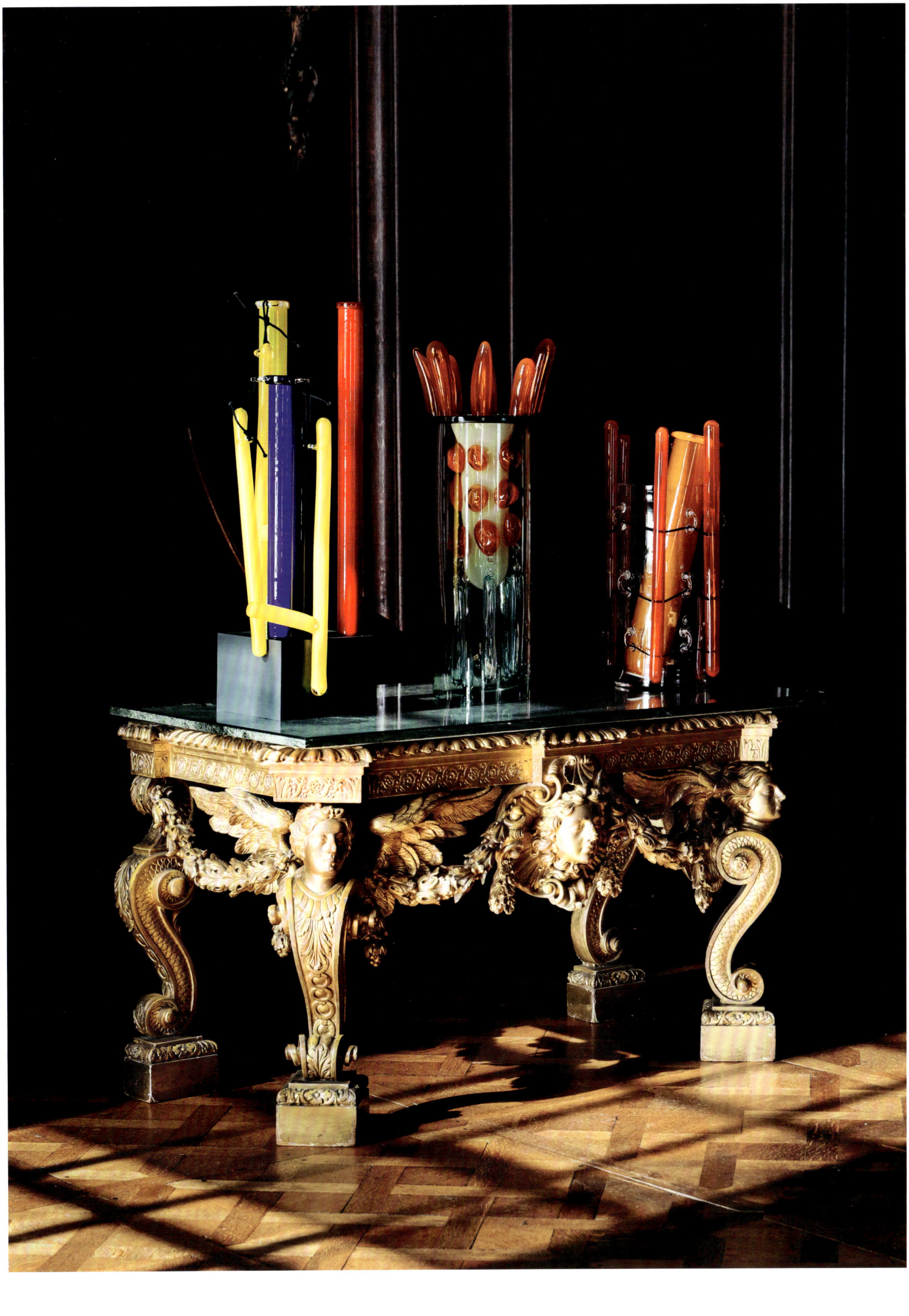

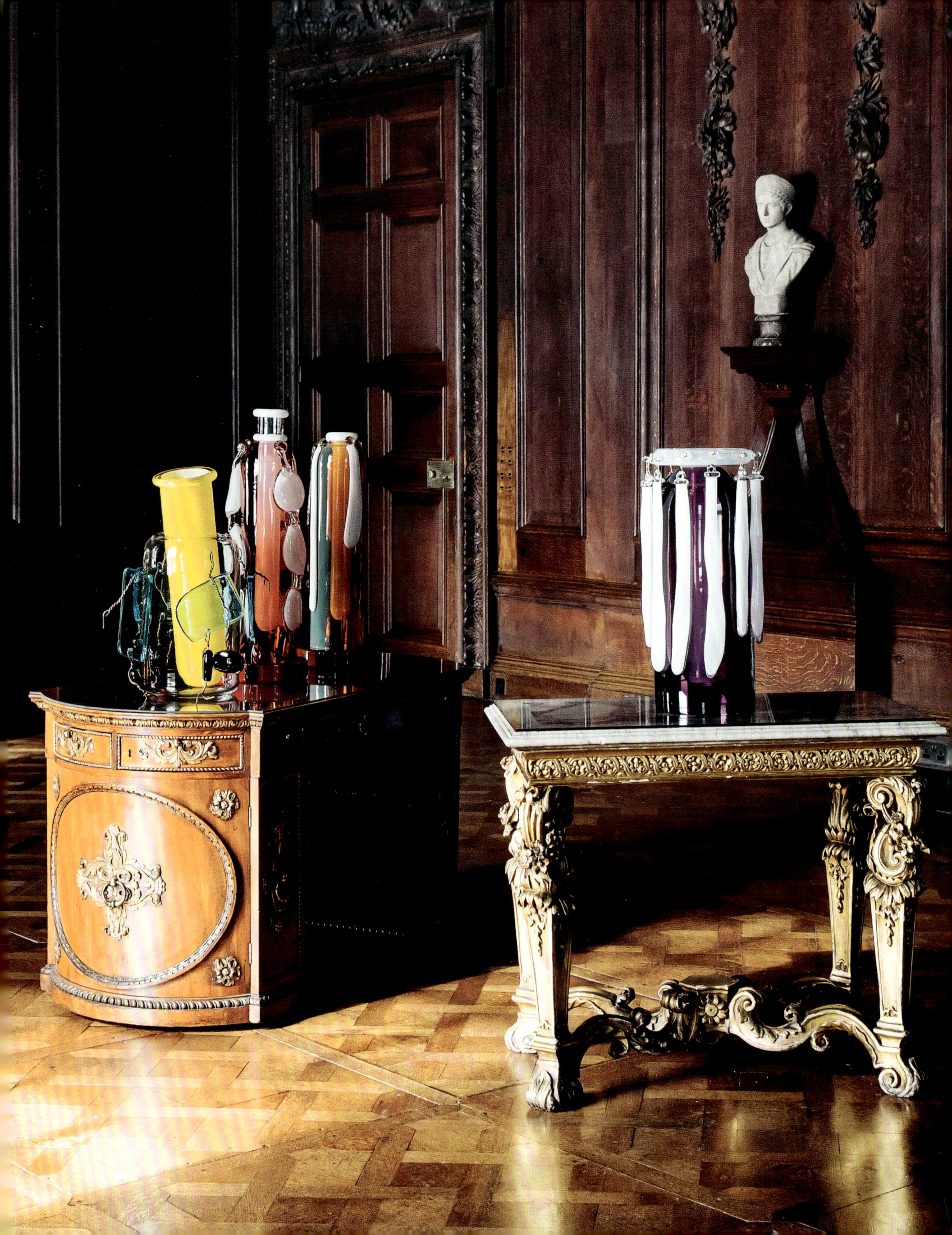

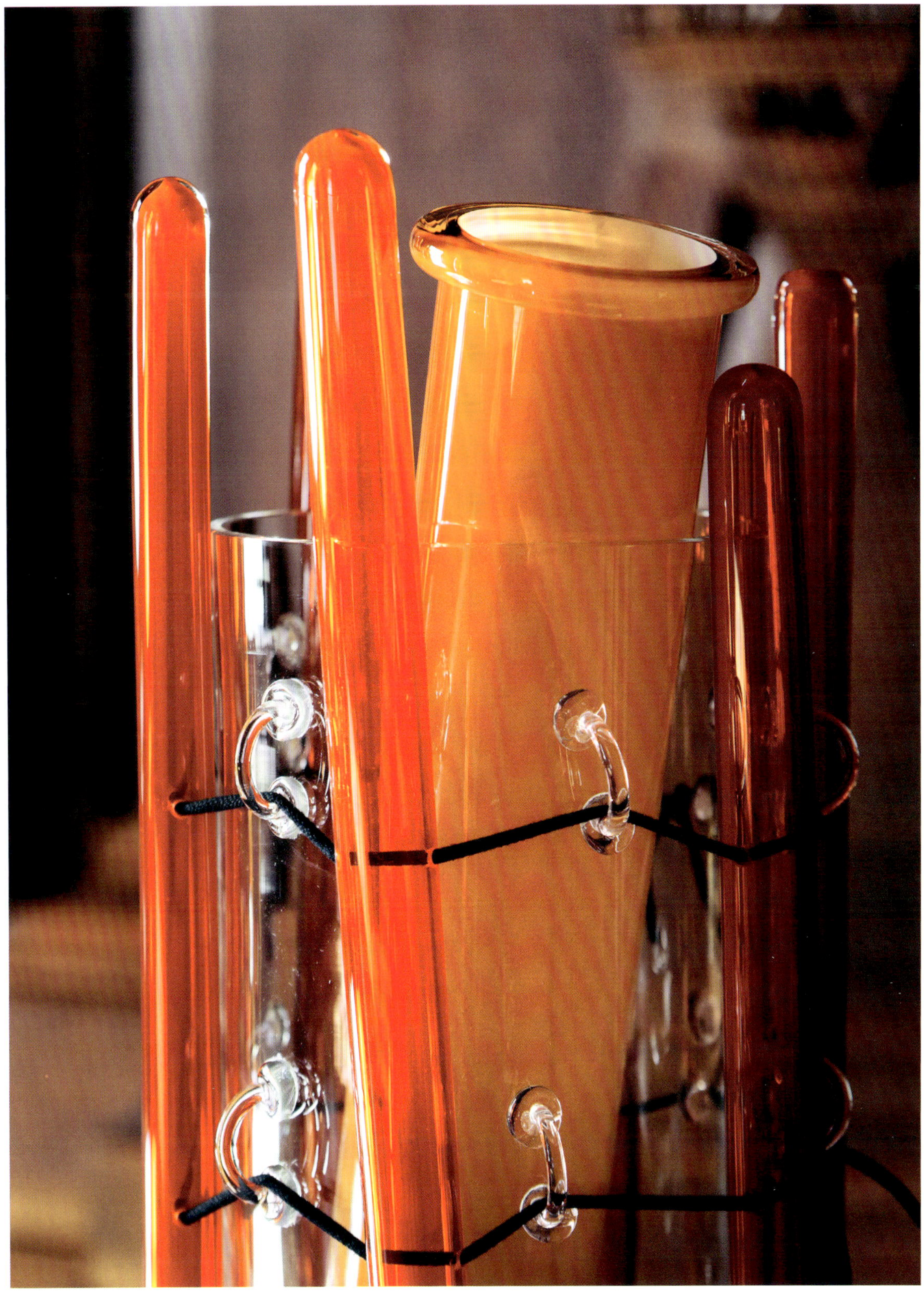

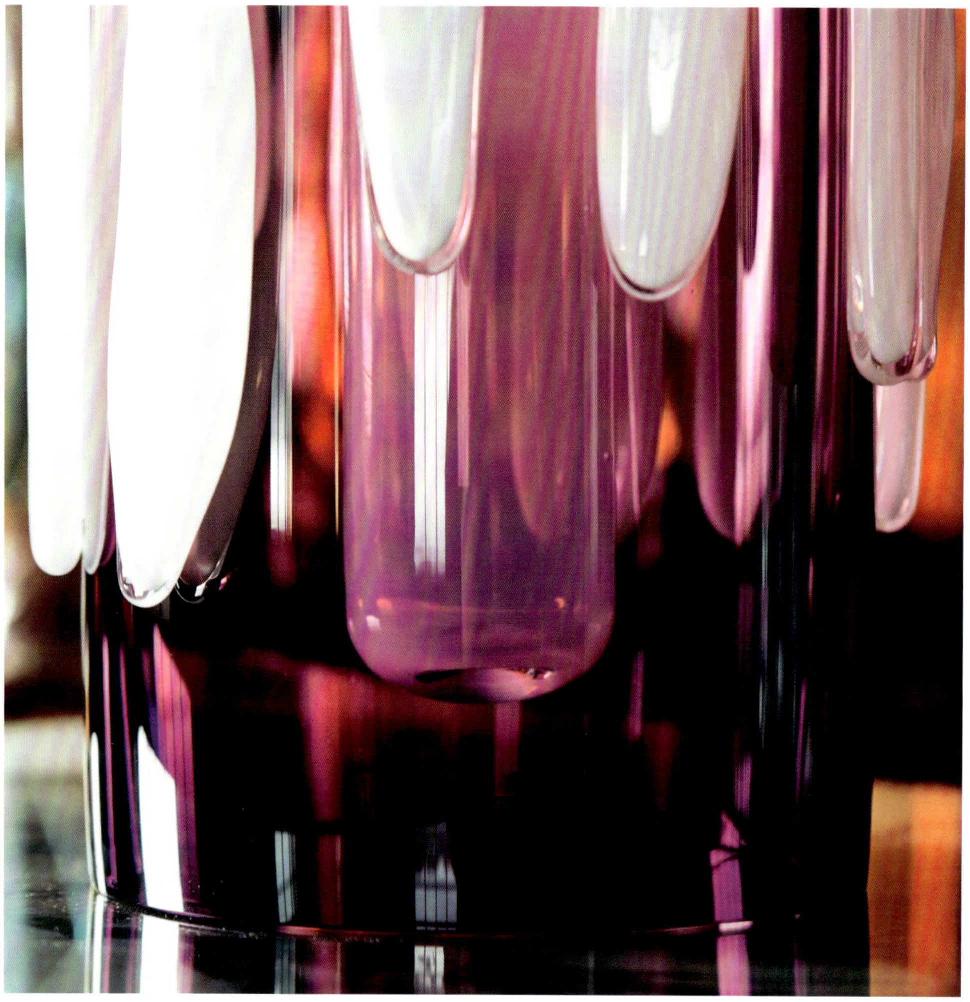

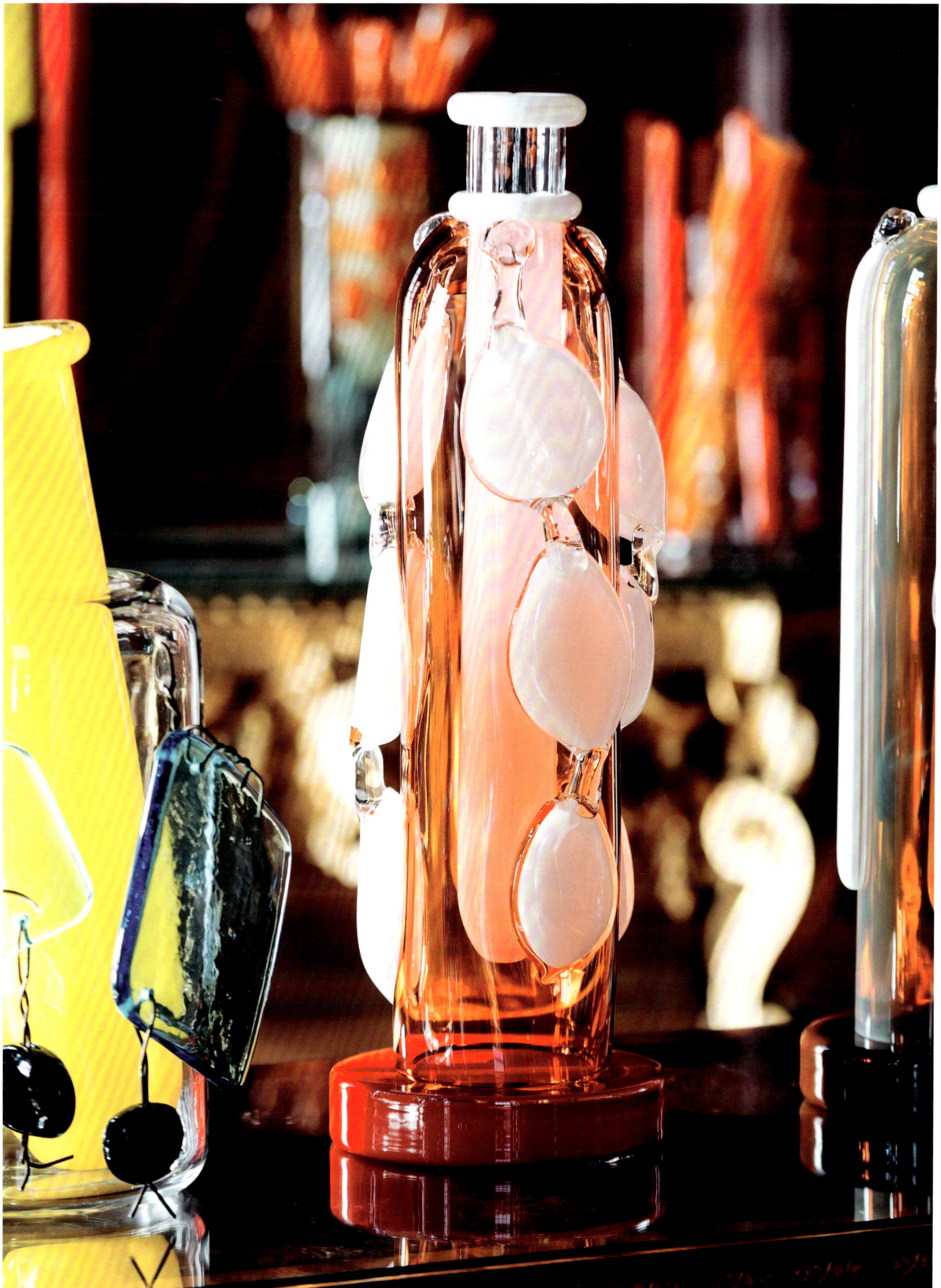

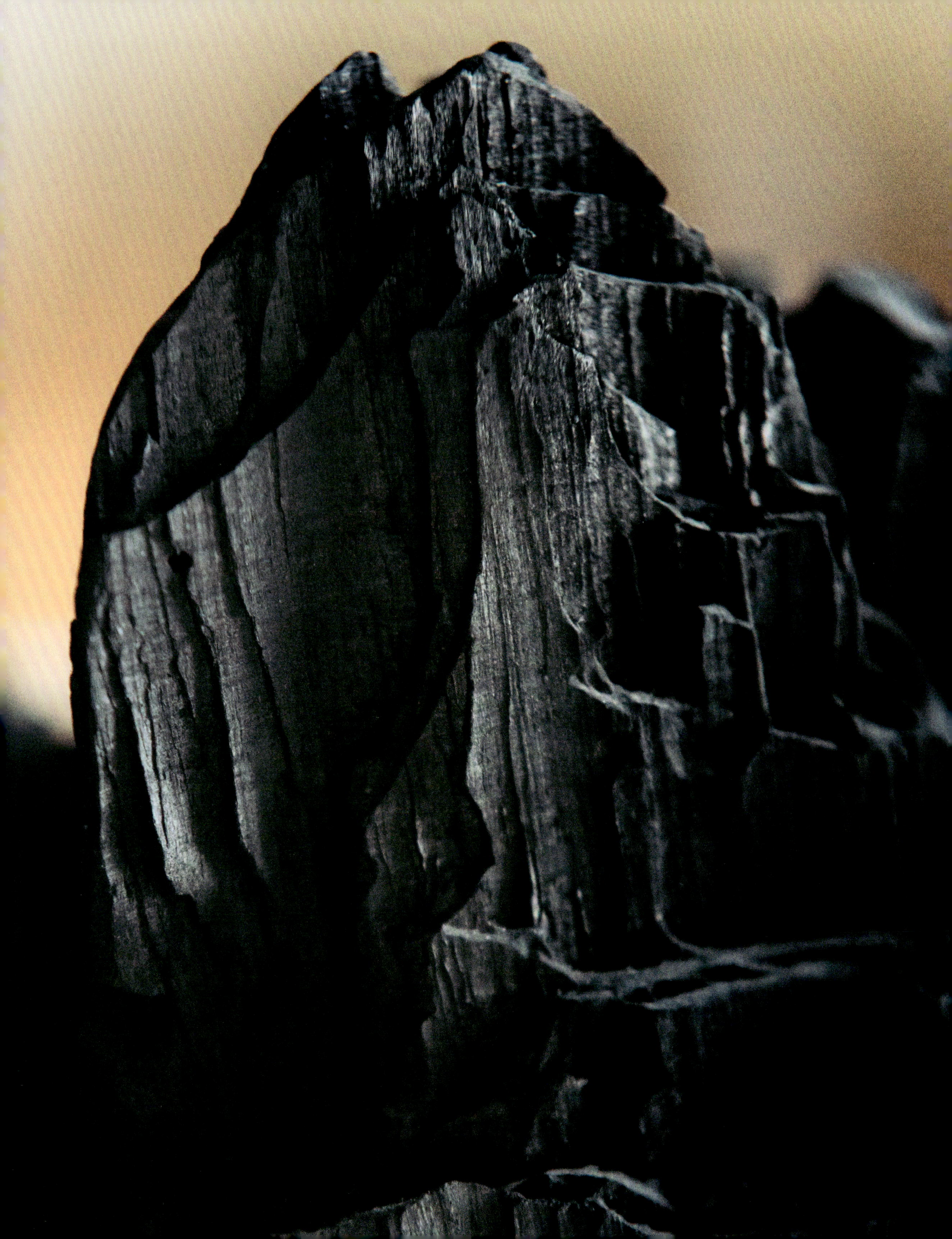

FORMA

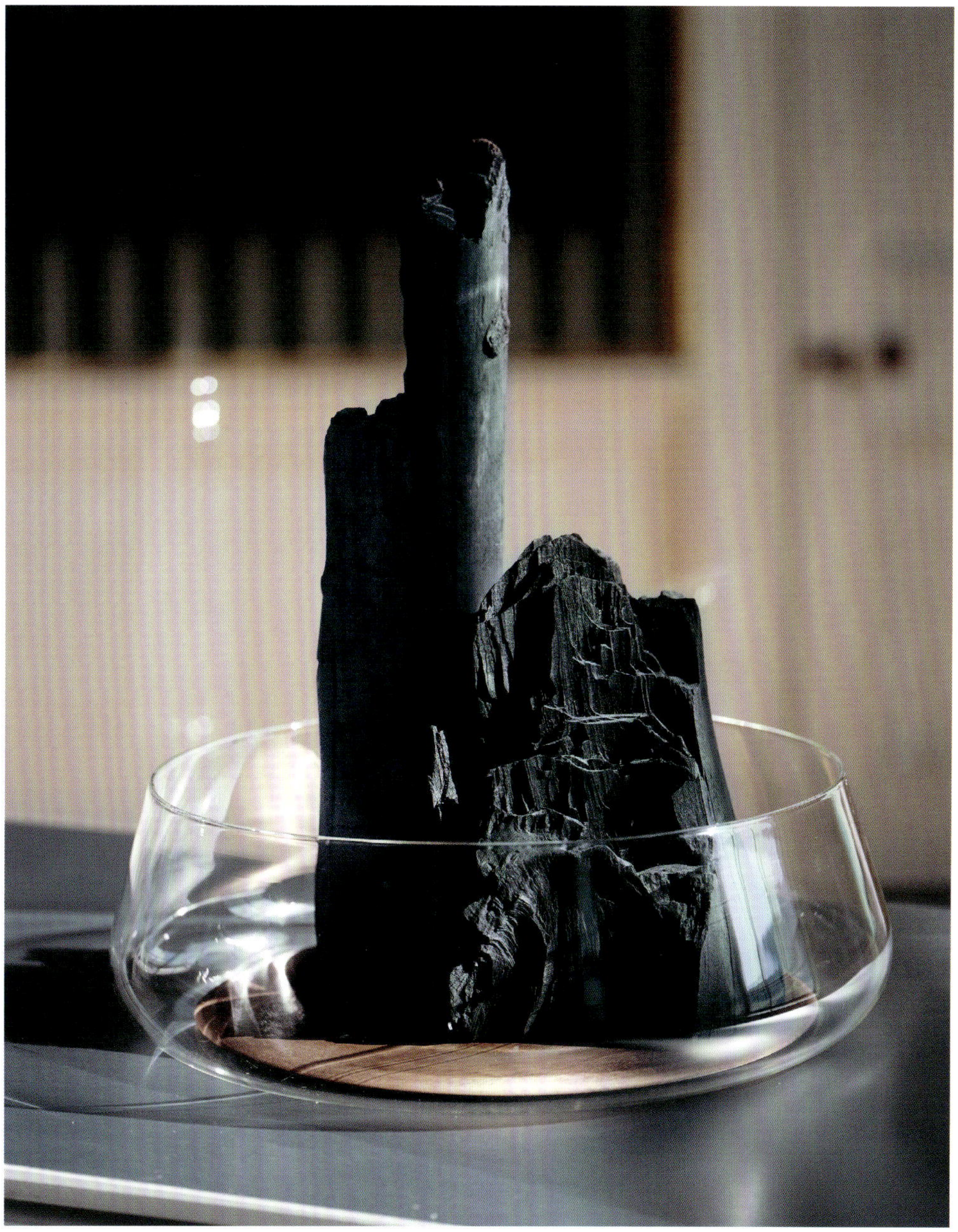

FANTASMA

PART SCULPTURAL, PART FUNCTIONAL, ALL POETIC

Many designers have responded to the reality of climate change by looking to new technologies, which might help us to find more sustainable solutions. The Italian studio Formafantasma—founded by Andrea Trimarchi and Simone Farresin in 2009—shares this motivation, but their approach is just the opposite: they look back into history, searching out abandoned pathways that may still have something to teach us.

In *Mirror Mirror* we feature one of their earliest projects, commissioned by the Vitra Design Museum in 2012, which focuses on the all-but-forgotten craft of charcoal burning. At first, given concerns about releasing carbon into the atmosphere, this might seem like the least promising of artisan traditions. But as Formafantasma discovered, through a collaboration with the Swiss charcoal specialist Doris Wicki, it could be an important part of living lightly, and rightly, on the land. By slowly heating naturally-fallen timber over the course of several days, it's possible to create a local energy source, without any need for fossil fuels.

Charcoal is also an excellent means of water filtration, a property that inspired Formafantasma to make a series of objects, made in collaboration with Wicki, in which charcoal is combined with wood and glass. In *Mirror Mirror*, we have presented these talismanic artefacts alongside historic paintings of Chatsworth and the surrounding property; charcoal burning was once practised here, too, just one of the many ways that value was extracted from the land.

This history is summoned in the Green Satin Room by a group of paintings, dating from 1703 to today, which depict the estate and show its evolution. The largest and earliest, by Jan Siberechts, is a recent acquisition at Chatsworth; it shows the formal, French-style gardens that were first laid across the land, as if a gigantic paper plan had been unrolled flat. It's almost shocking to see the extent of later changes, particularly the reversion to the picturesque mode enacted by the famous landscape designer Lancelot 'Capability' Brown in the eighteenth century. His seemingly naturalistic scheme was in fact completely artificial, even involving the displacement of a river and a small village.

Part sculptural, part functional, all poetic, Formafantasma's charcoal filters stand in silent witness to this history of ongoing transformation in the landscape, which of course is still happening. In 2022, as *Mirror Mirror* was in preparation, an unprecedented heat wave blasted the gardens, exposing previously unseen contours of earlier building schemes normally hidden under the grass. Formafantasma does not intend their works as literal remedies to climate change. Rather, they embody the key questions of our moment. Will our world continue to be darkened by pollution? Or will we find a cleaner, healthier way forward? Both of these alternative futures are suggested by the artefacts; they sit at the intersection of dystopian fear and utopian optimism.

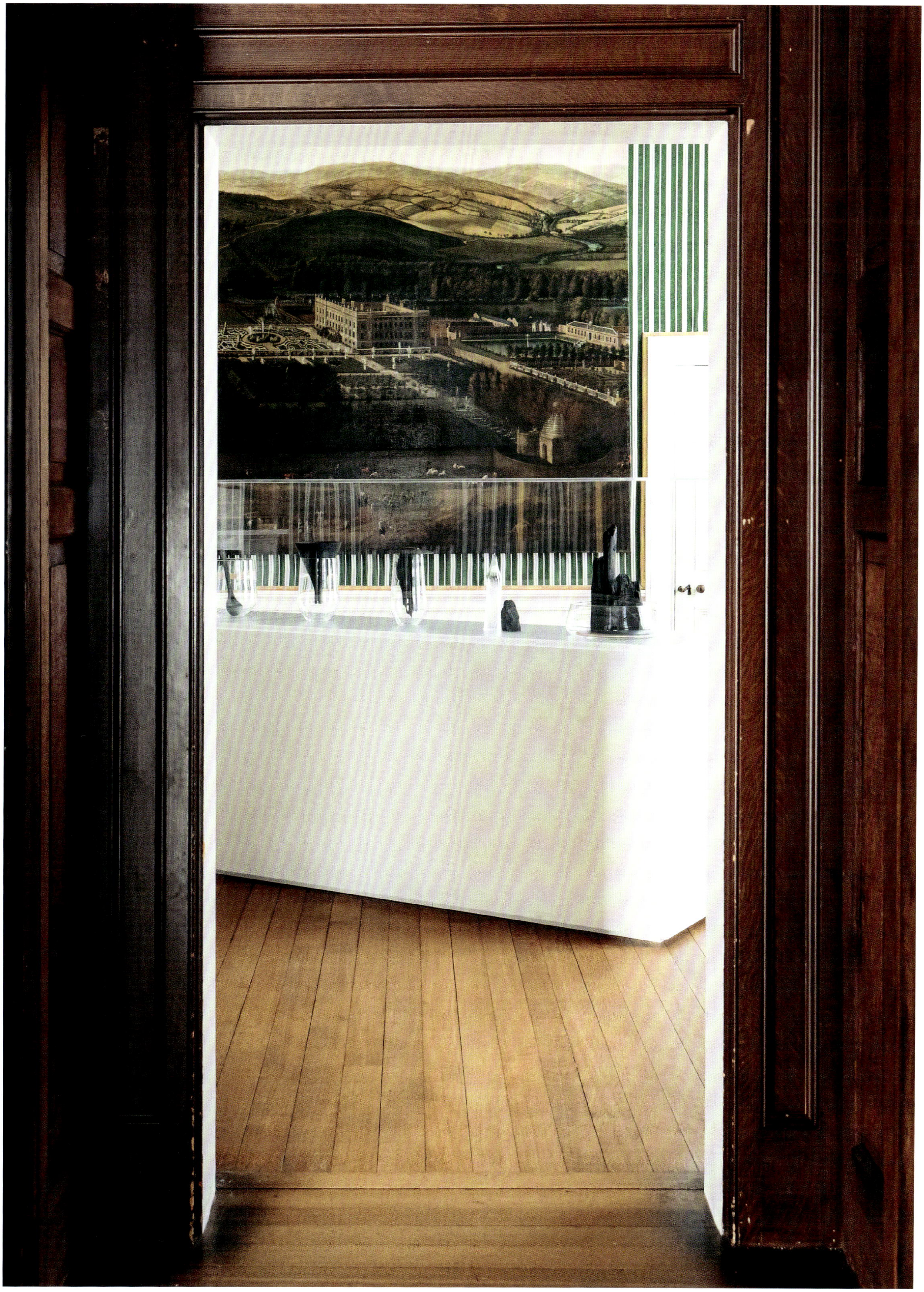

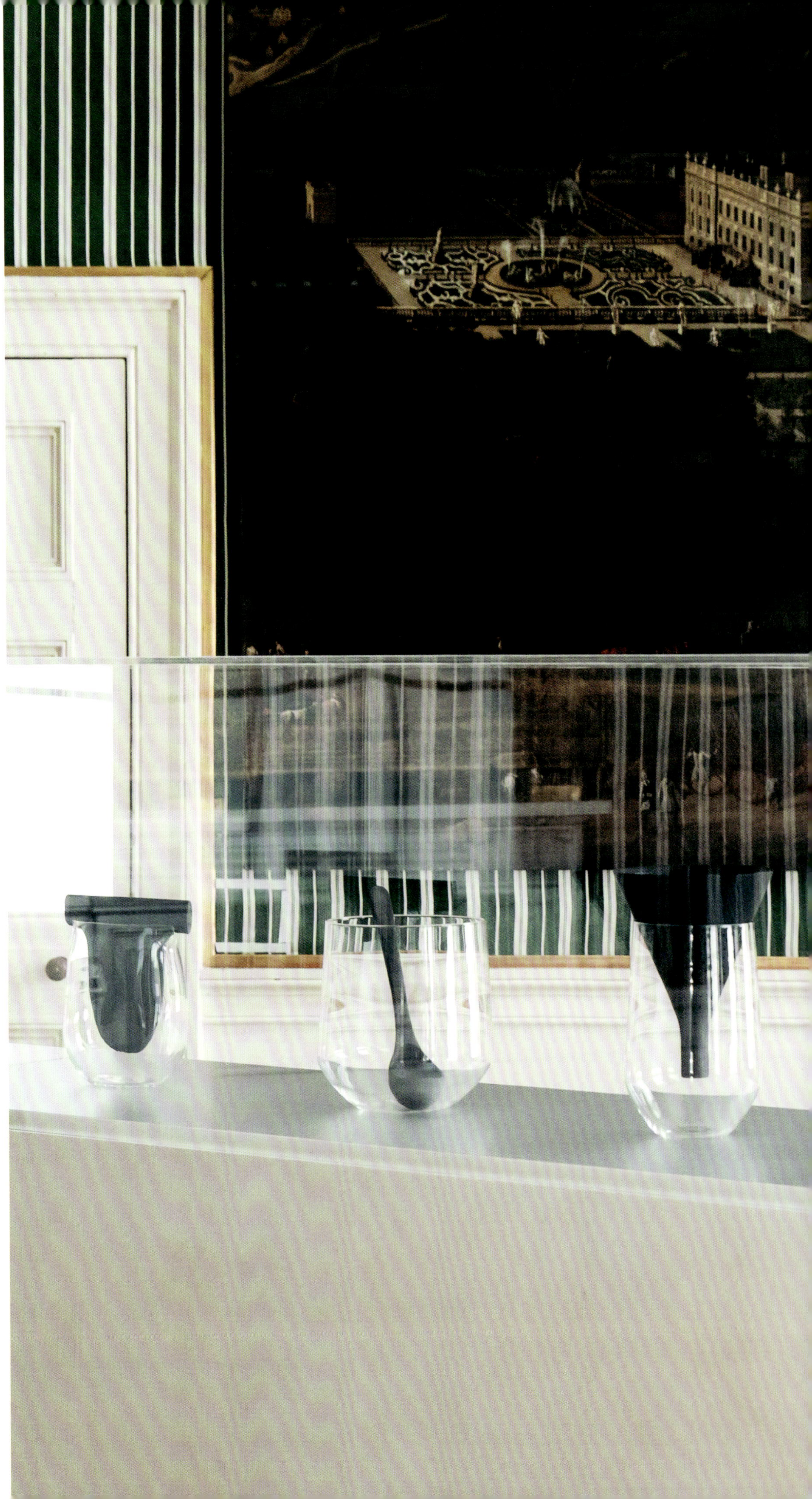

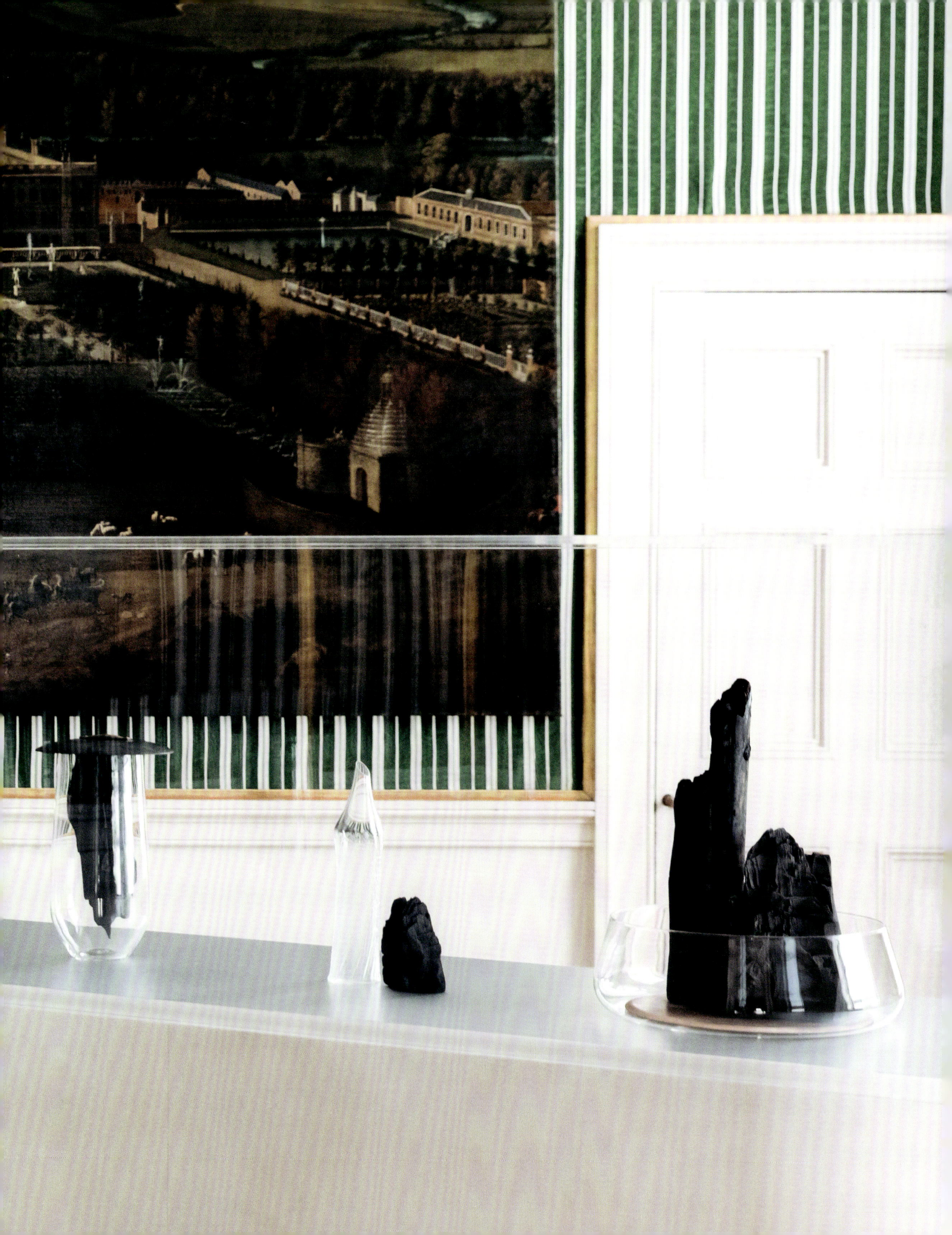

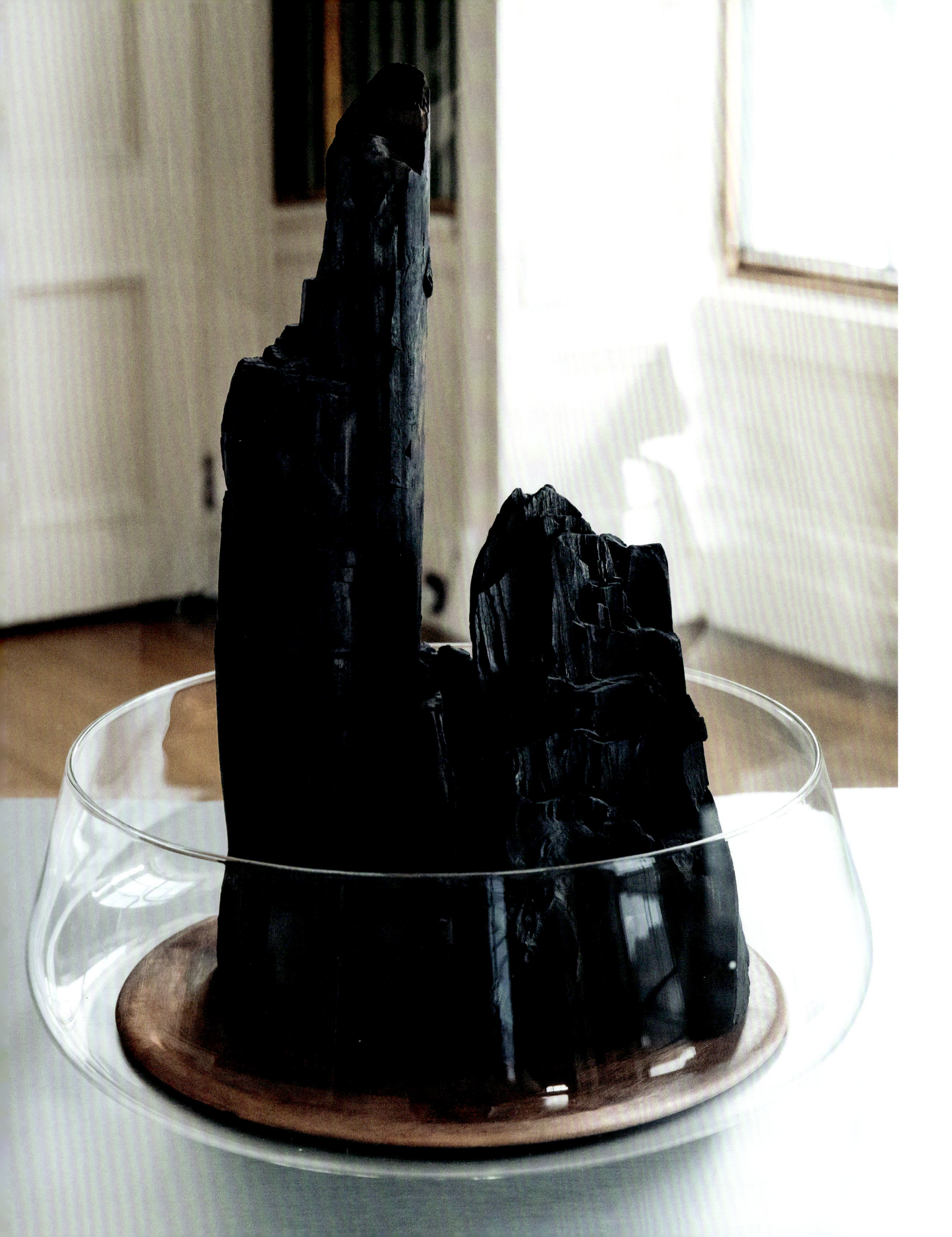

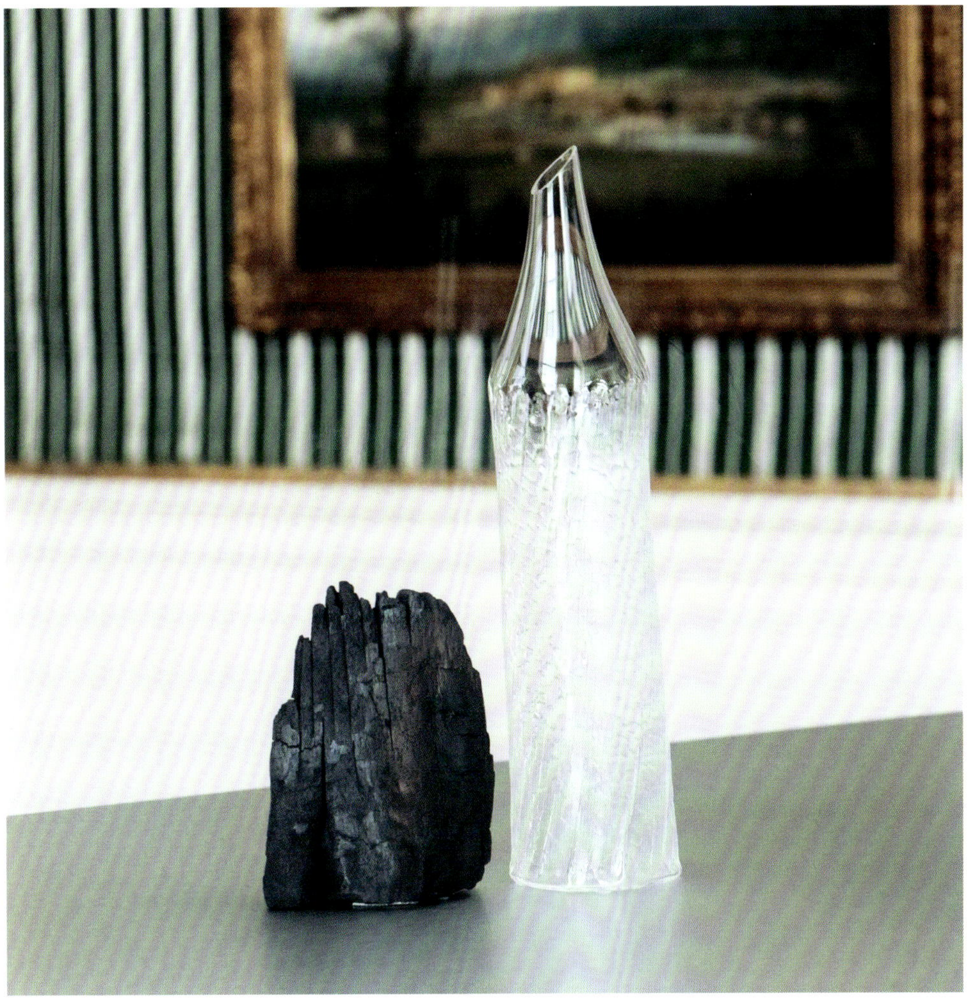

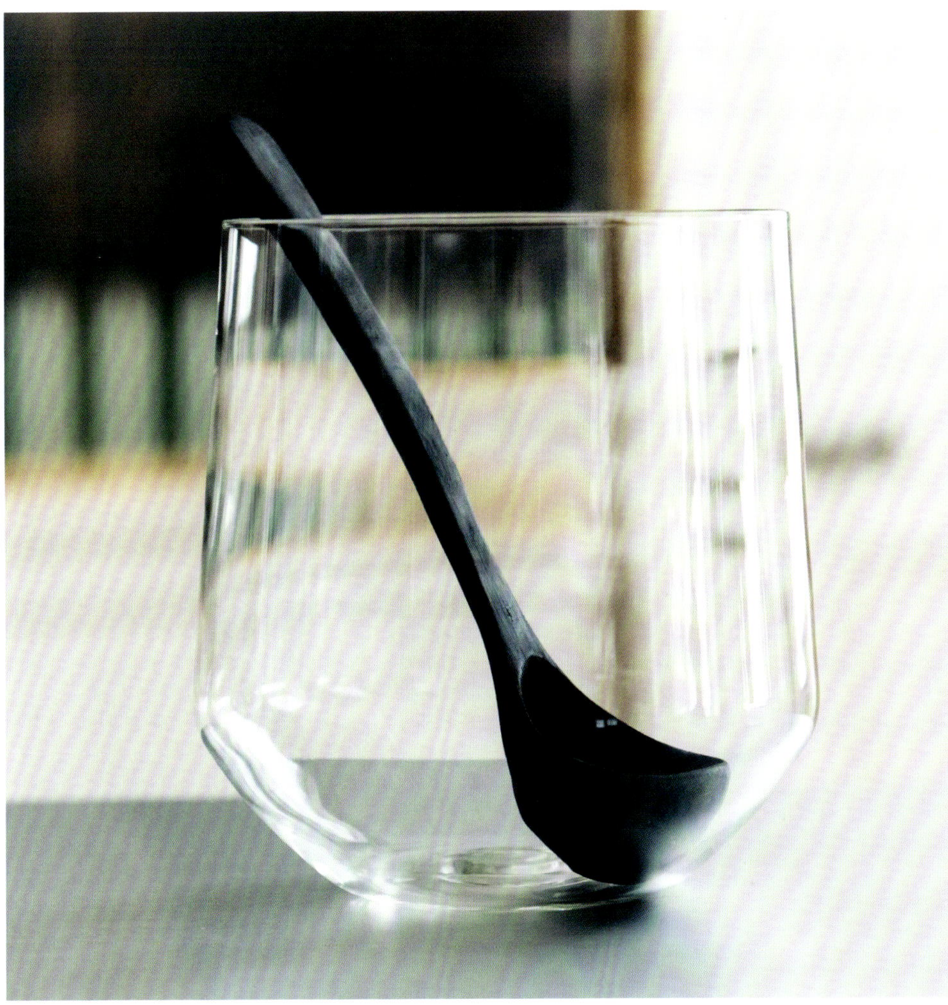

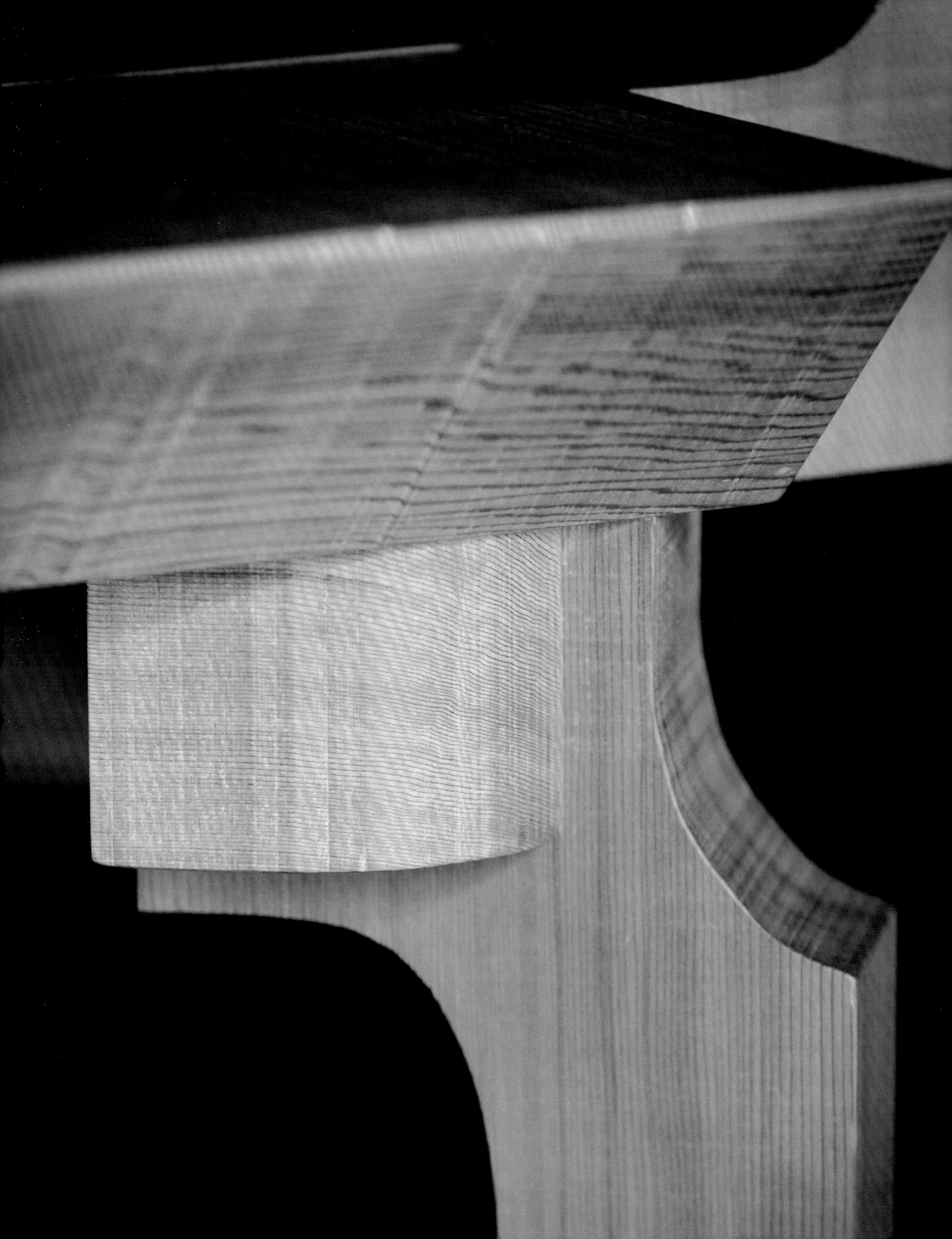

MAX

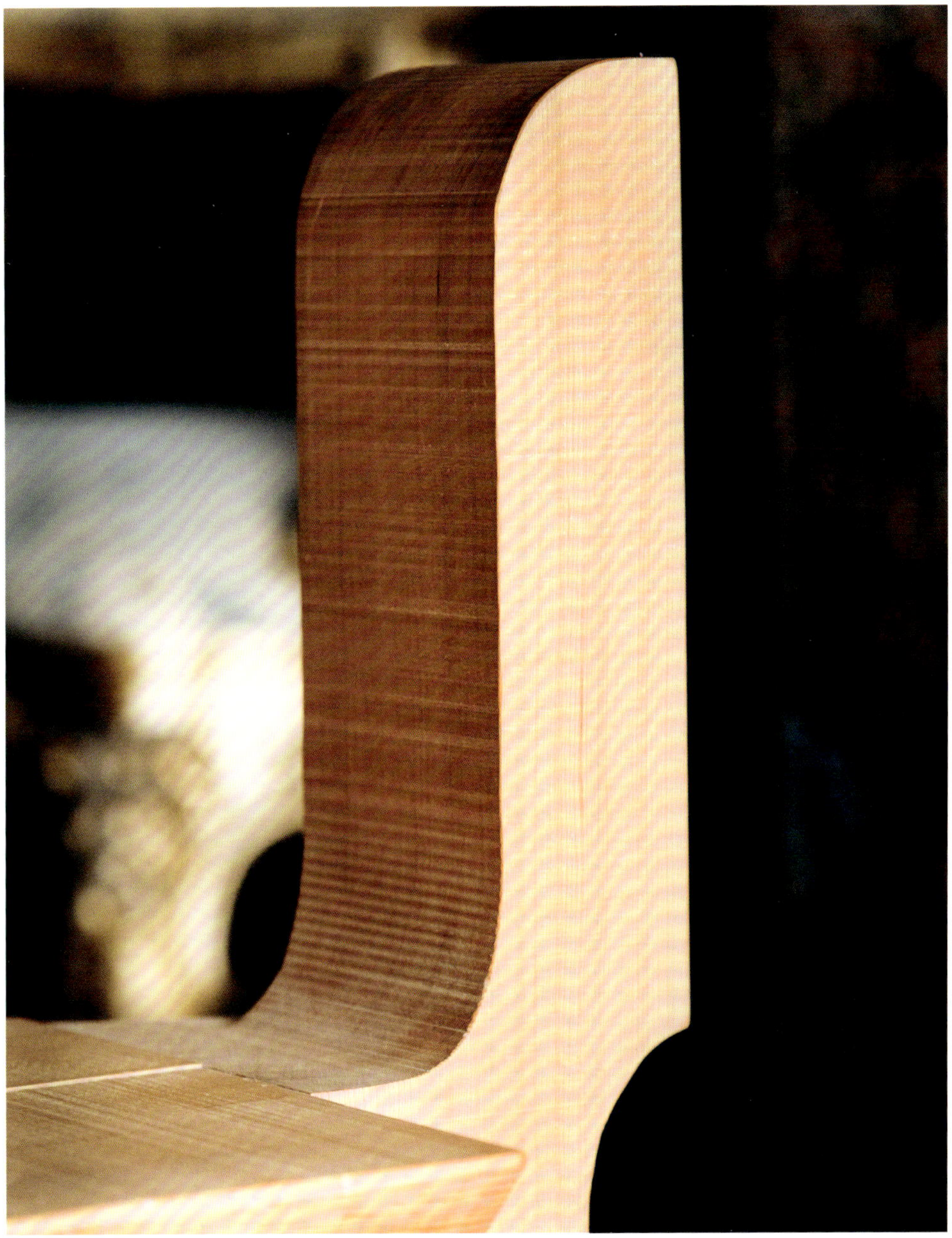

LAMB

EXPERIMENTS WITH THE BUILDING BLOCKS OF DESIGN

British designer Max Lamb likes to start at square one. His works tend to focus on the initial moment of transformation in which a raw material becomes something else—something useful, beautiful, expressive of human intention. In one early project, he made furniture simply by pouring molten pewter into object-shaped holes dug into sand at the beach. His more recent *Cleft* chairs are fashioned from seasoned wood, each component shaped with just a few decisive cuts of an axe.

In *6 × 8"*, Lamb puts a particularly playful spin on this back-to-basics approach. Each design is made from a single length of Western red cedar, whose section measures six by eight inches. Wasting none of this wood whatsoever, Lamb reconfigures each of the beams into furniture by cutting them into pieces on a bandsaw, which he then reassembles into typological forms: bench, chair, table. For *Mirror Mirror* we introduced two chairs into the grand space, so small as to seem almost toy-like. With their slim backs and jaunty stance, they have the quality of animated characters who have landed in the space and are having a look around.

The pieces are ingeniously simple, experiments with the literal building blocks of design. They are also very quick, still retaining bandsaw kerf marks along their curves. At the same time, in their intricacy and precision, they allude to the painstaking art of historic woodcarving. This art form is spectacularly exemplified at Chatsworth by the work of Samuel Watson—so skilled at his trade that his handiwork has often been mistaken for that of the great Grinling Gibbons—which embellishes many of the rooms of the house. The State Drawing Room is also where visitors encounter two majestic thrones with matching footstools, provided for the coronation of George III and Queen Charlotte in 1761 by Katherine Naish, one of the few female master carvers known from the eighteenth century. The *6 × 8"* chairs sit at their feet, a little comically, while also echoing their curves.

Lamb sees himself as offering 'a polite nod of respect' to his illustrious precursors, but instead of skilful ornamentation, he emphasises the potential that is latent in each piece of wood. The viewer is tacitly invited to imagine the process, reassembling the squared-off timber in their mind—not easy, given the cleverness of Lamb's cutting, but possible.

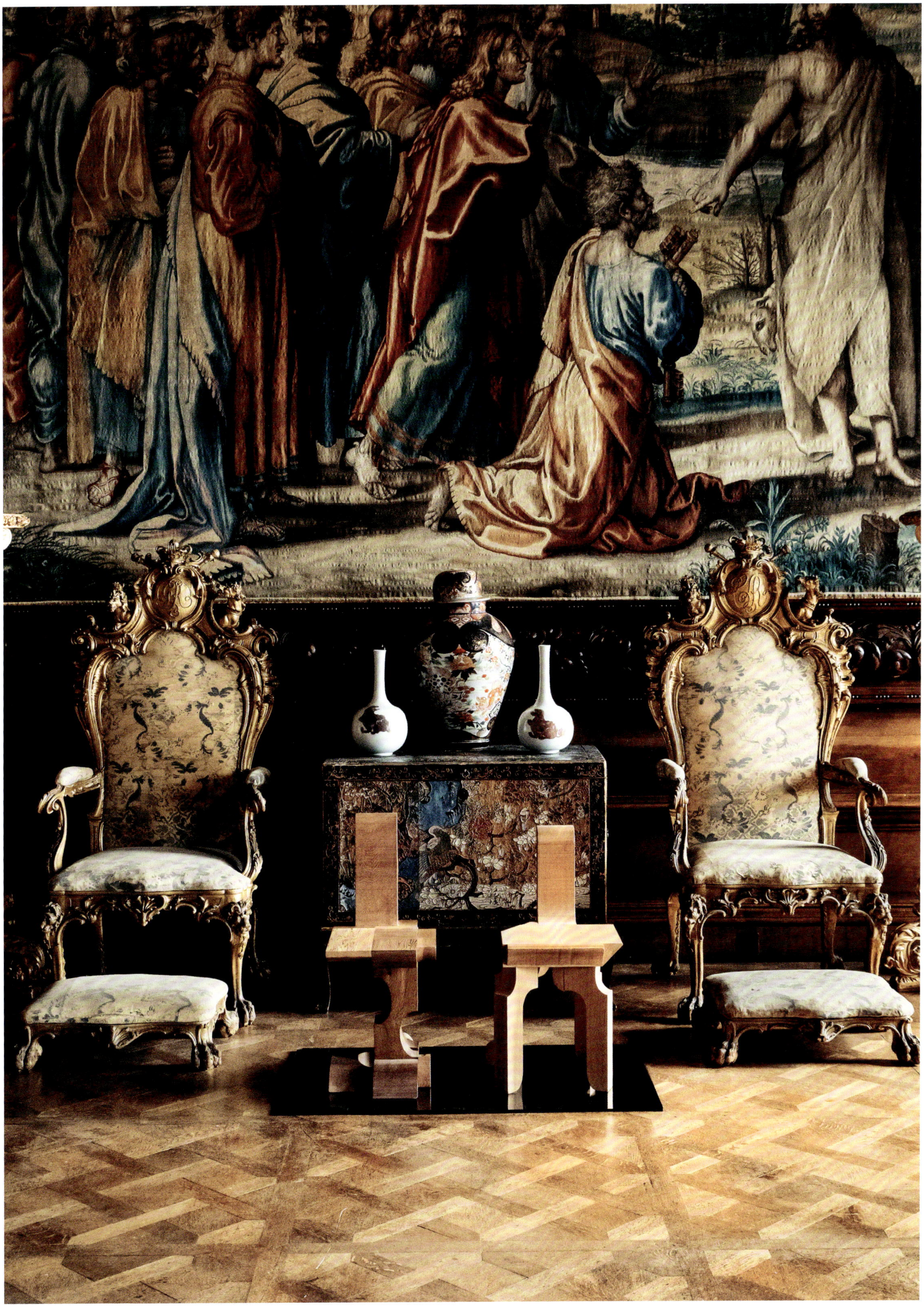

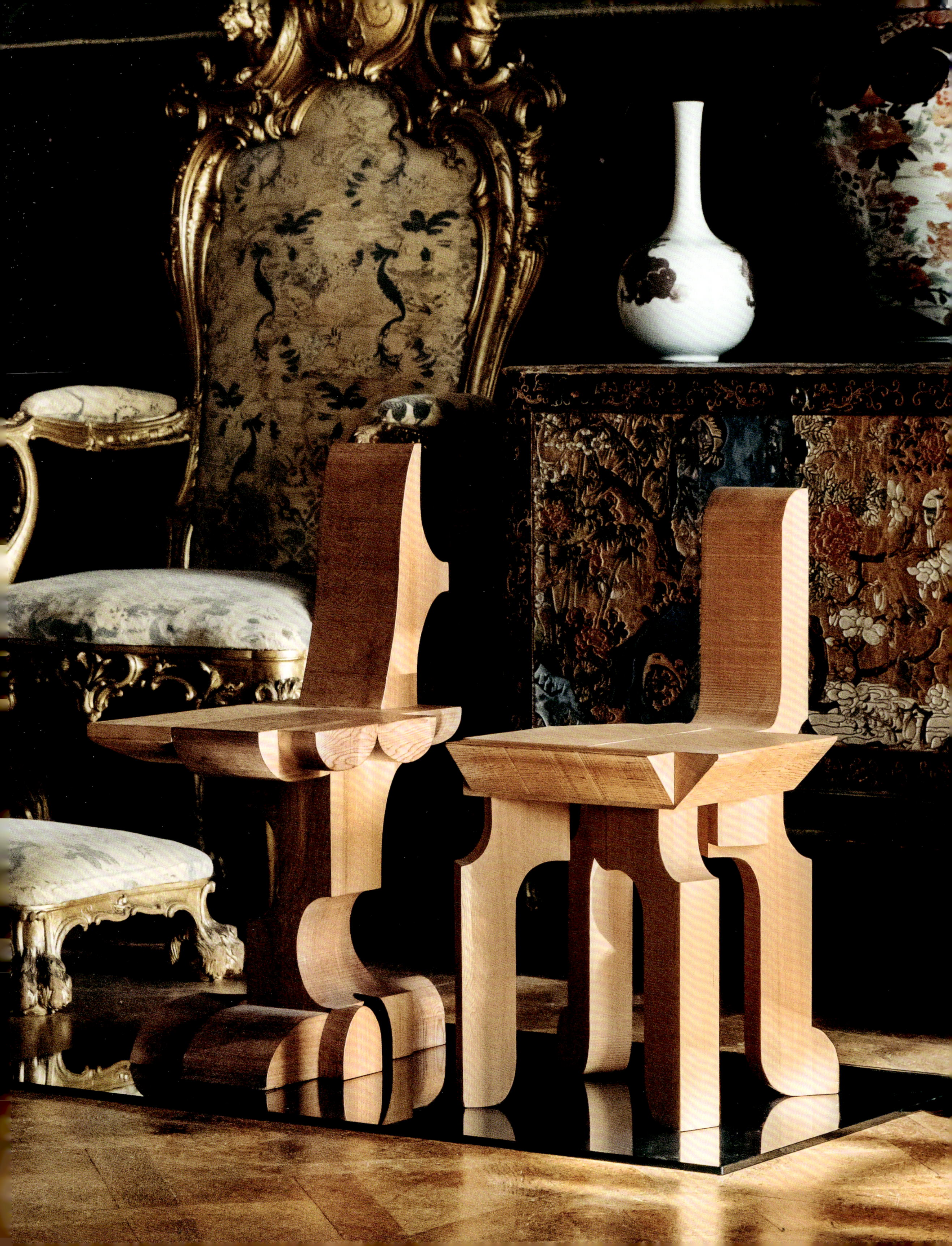

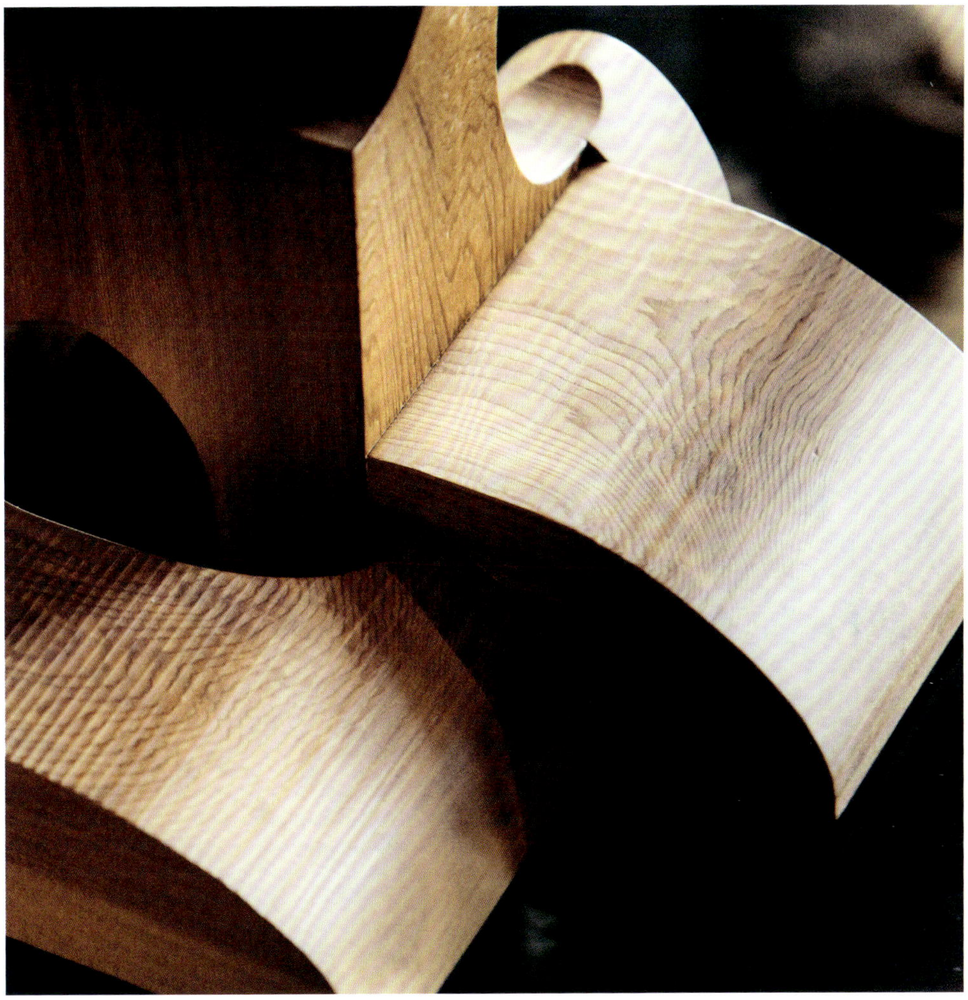

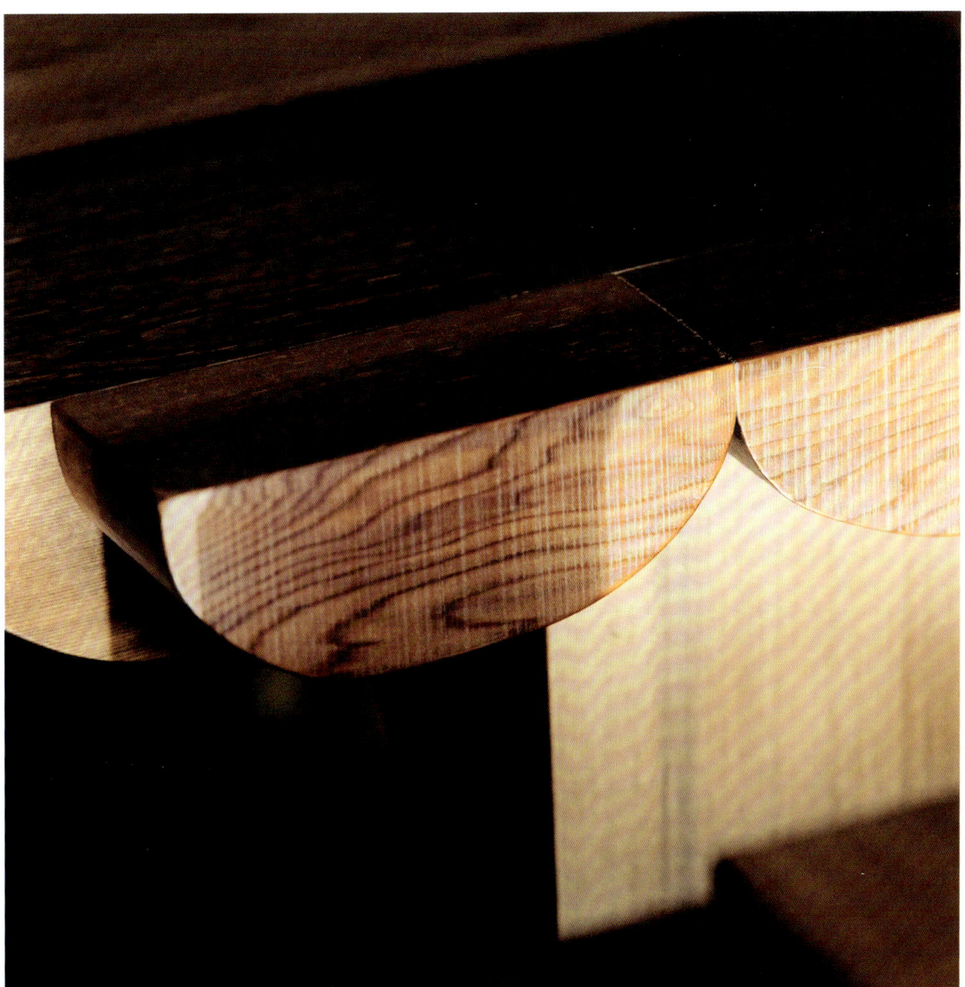

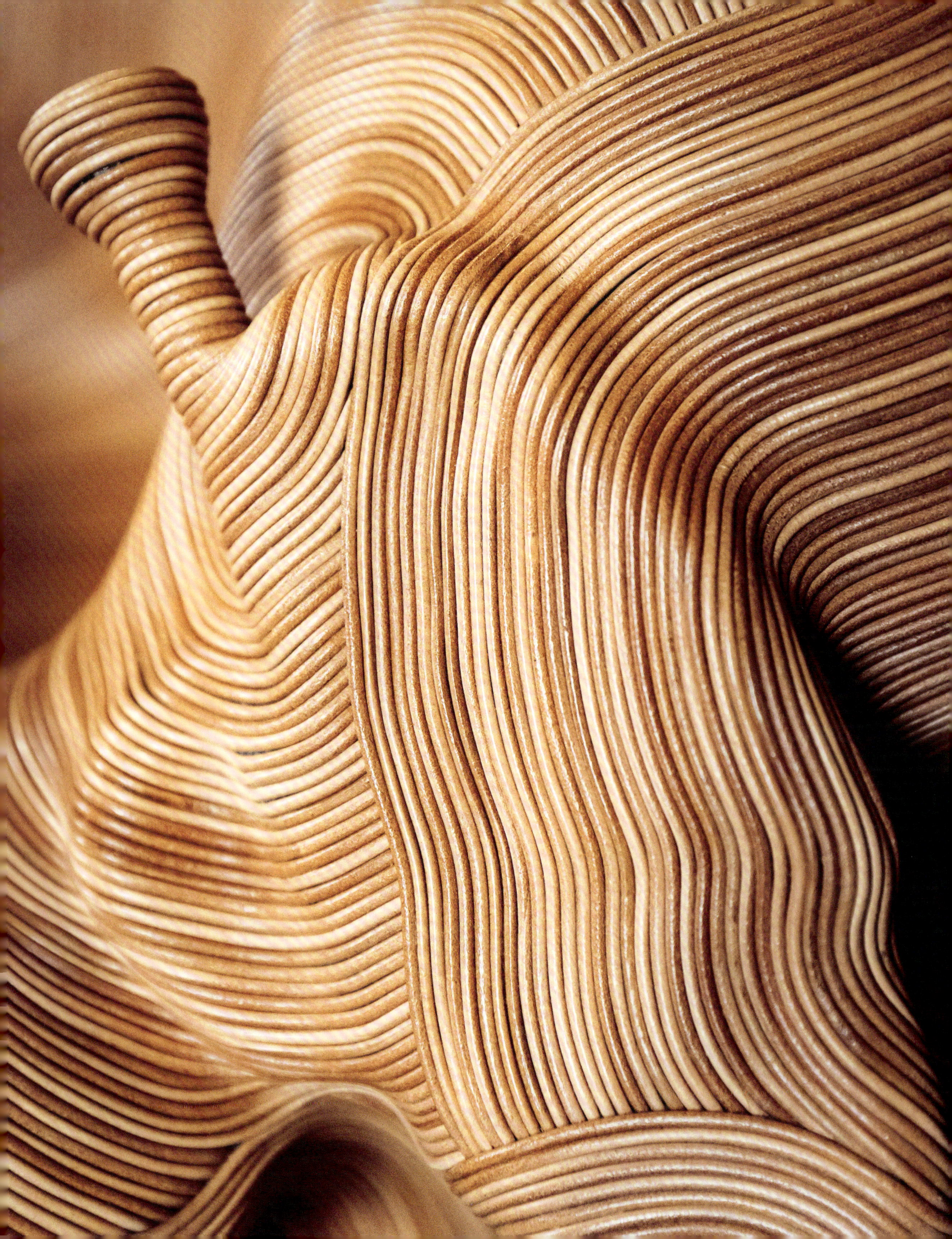

JAY SAE JUNG

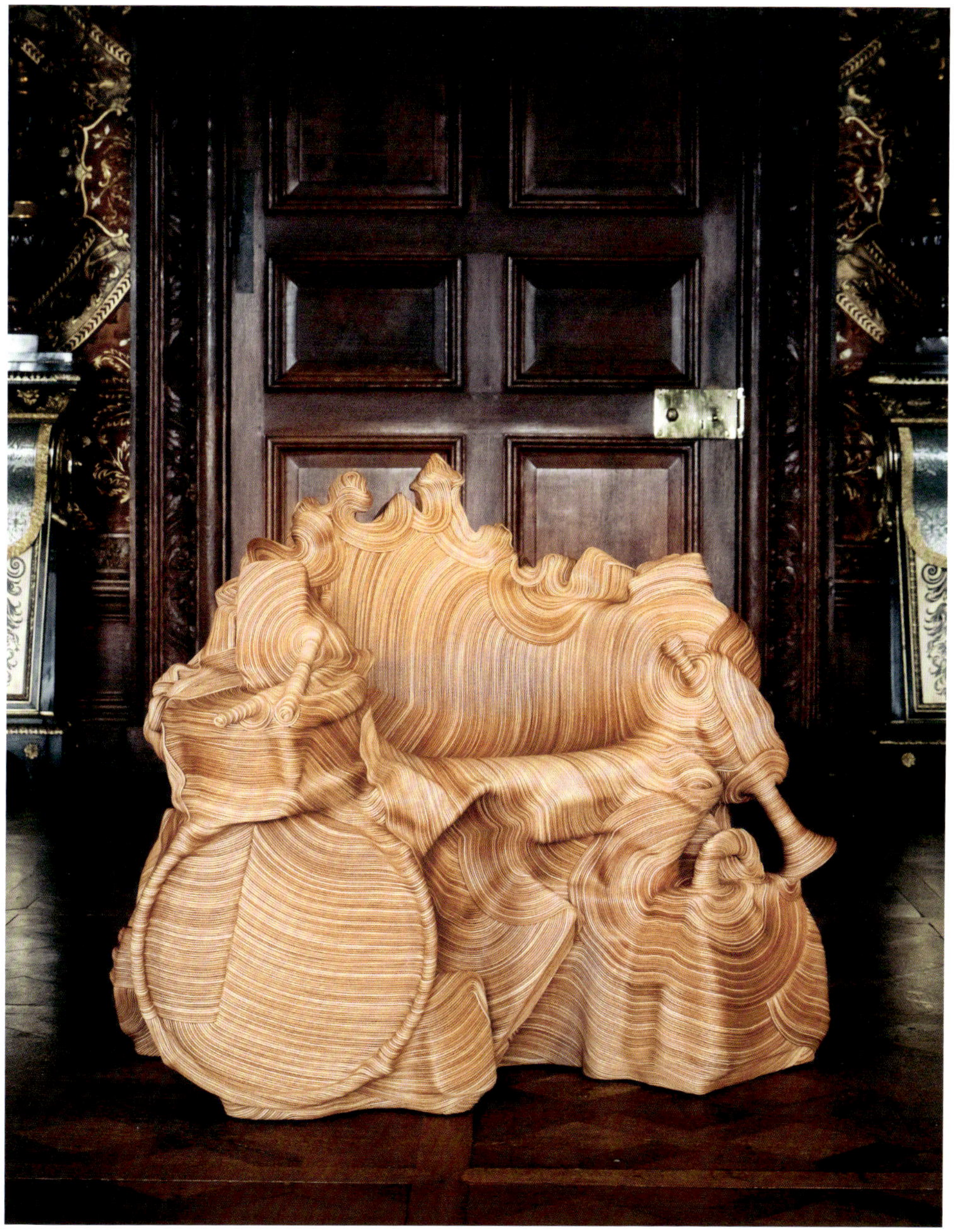

OH

IMPECCABLY CRAFTED, CONTINUOUS BINDING

The world is full. Now what? This is a question many people have been asking themselves—especially designers, who are normally in the business of making the brand-new. Few have come up with an answer as simple and elegant as Jay Sae Jung Oh. Born in Seoul and currently based in Seattle, she responds to the prevailing conditions of disposable culture by making her work almost entirely of salvaged materials. Oh builds her found objects into elaborate assemblages, which she then wraps tightly with fine cord. Occasionally, they peek out—one memorable side table features a partly exposed iron skillet for a top. But for the most part, the shapes of the detritus are translated into topology, thanks to Oh's impeccably-crafted, continuous binding. Beyond their compelling sculptural quality, these works serve as physical metaphors of how we might better relate to a world teeming with waste, given sufficient imagination and care.

For *Mirror Mirror*, Oh was invited to create a work for the State Music Room, one of the grand apartments that form an enfilade on the house's second floor. The decorations include one of Chatsworth's most convivial notes—Jan Van Der Vaardt's trompe l'oeil of a violin hung from a ribbon, painted directly on the rear door of the room (which was moved here from Devonshire House) three hundred years ago, in 1723. A real peg, made of gilt metal, adds to the trickery.

In response to the room's theme, Oh has made a suitably majestic throne, containing a trove of derelict musical instruments. Distinguishable are a French horn, a snare with drumsticks, a large tambourine, and an electric guitar: this is the instrumentation of today, not the eighteenth century. Yet Oh does engage in a fascinating duet with Van Der Vaardt. Just as his painted violin remains silent and untouchable, her decommissioned instruments forever await the moment when they will be played, rendered into mere impressions of their former selves.

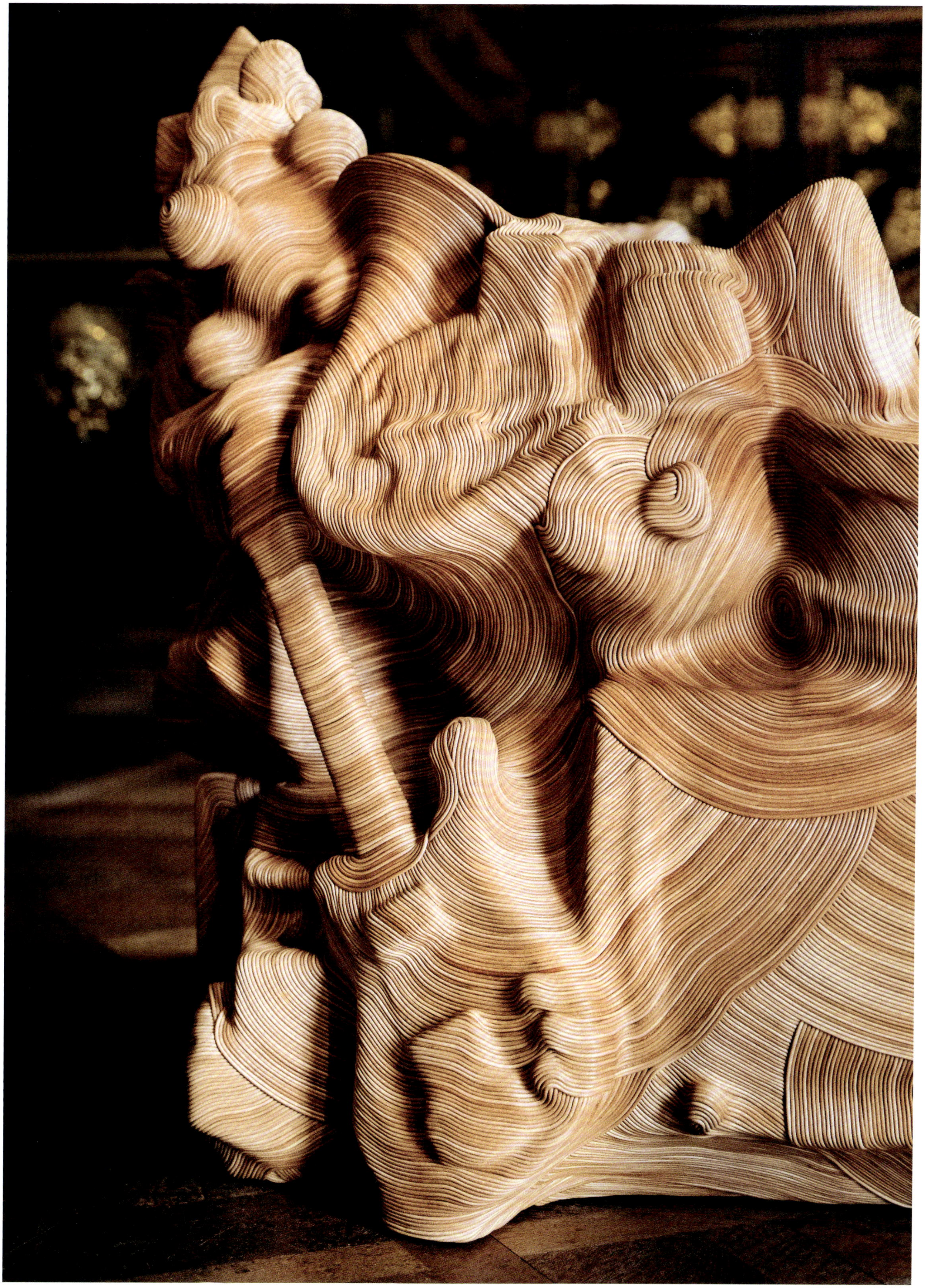

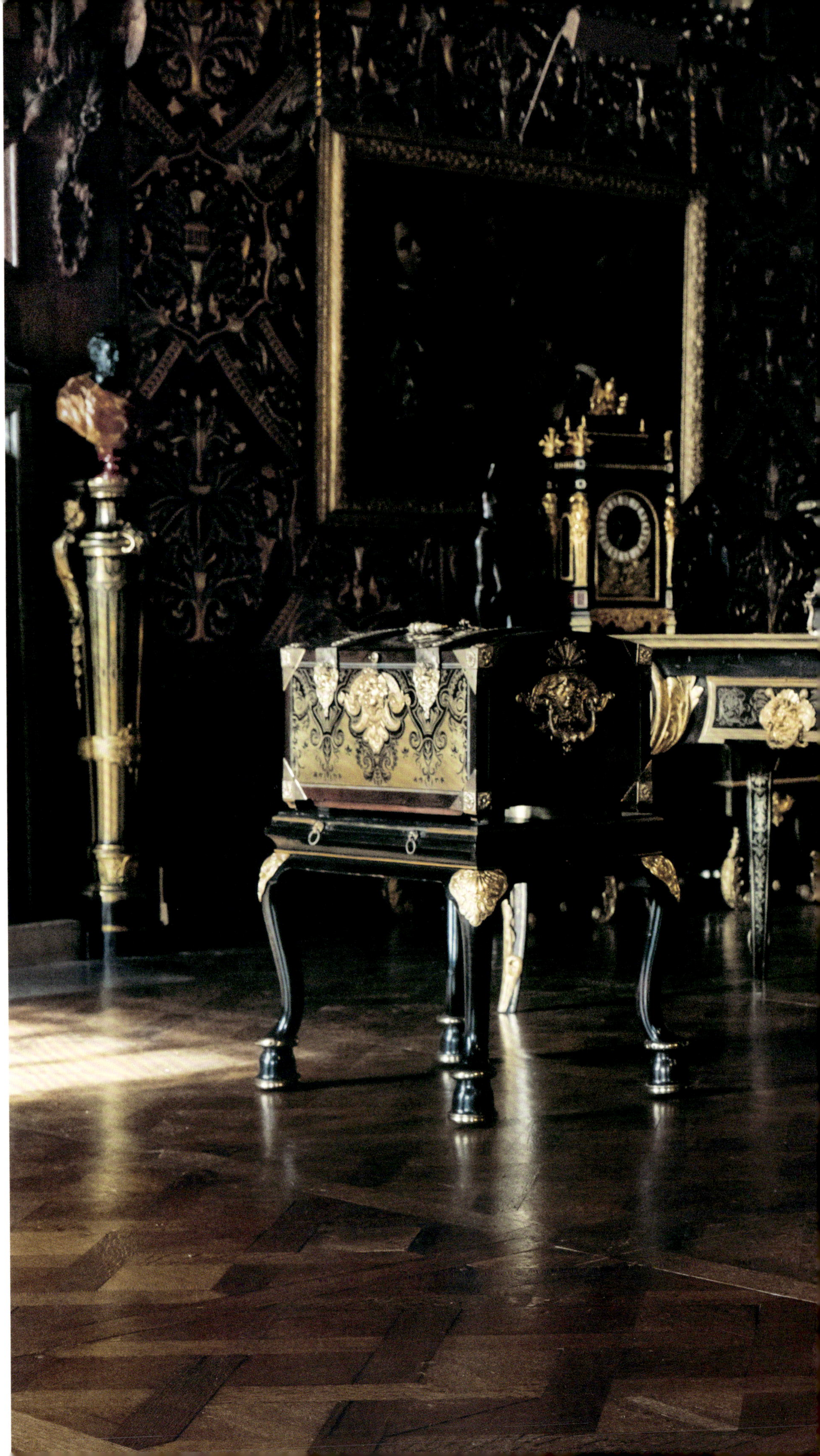

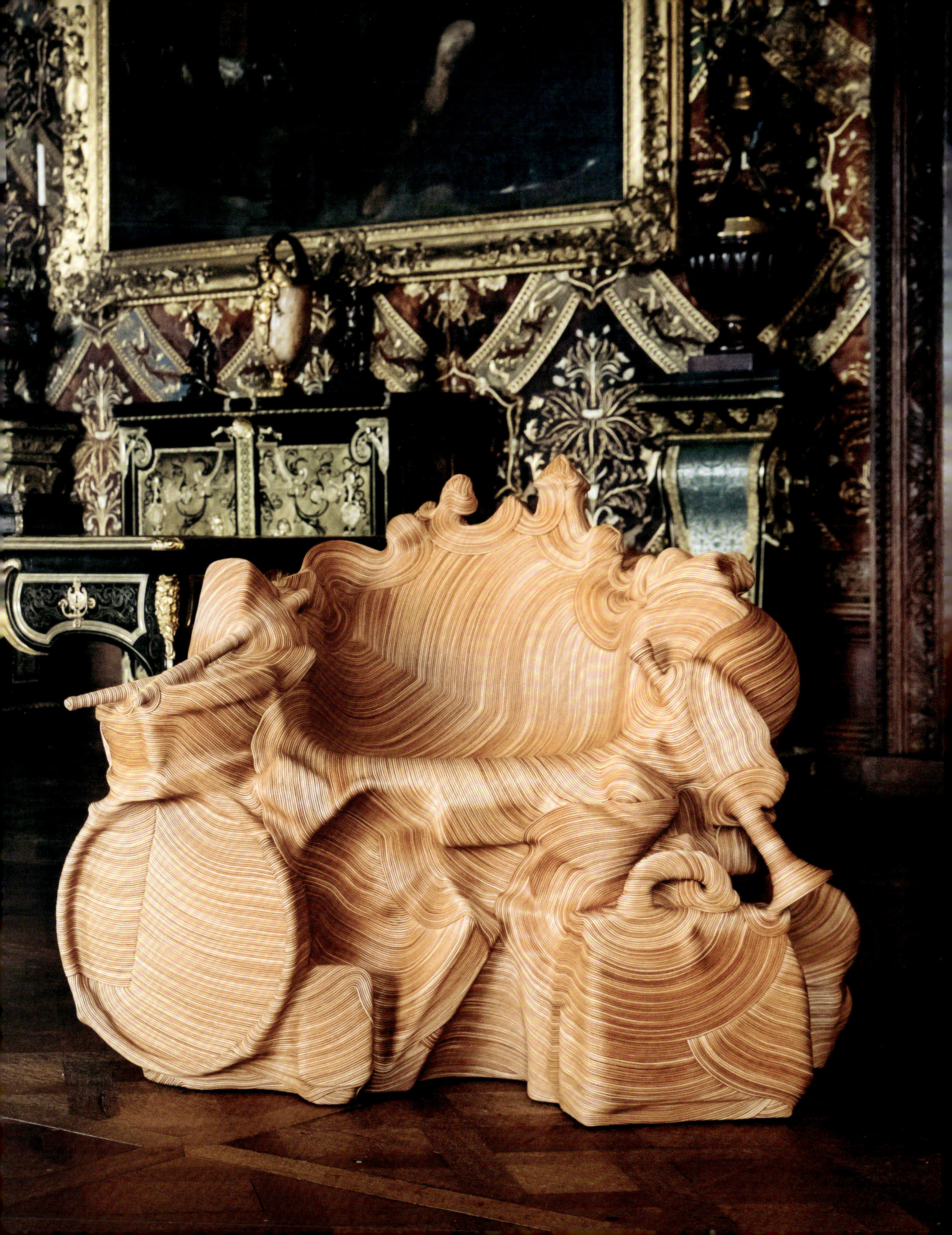

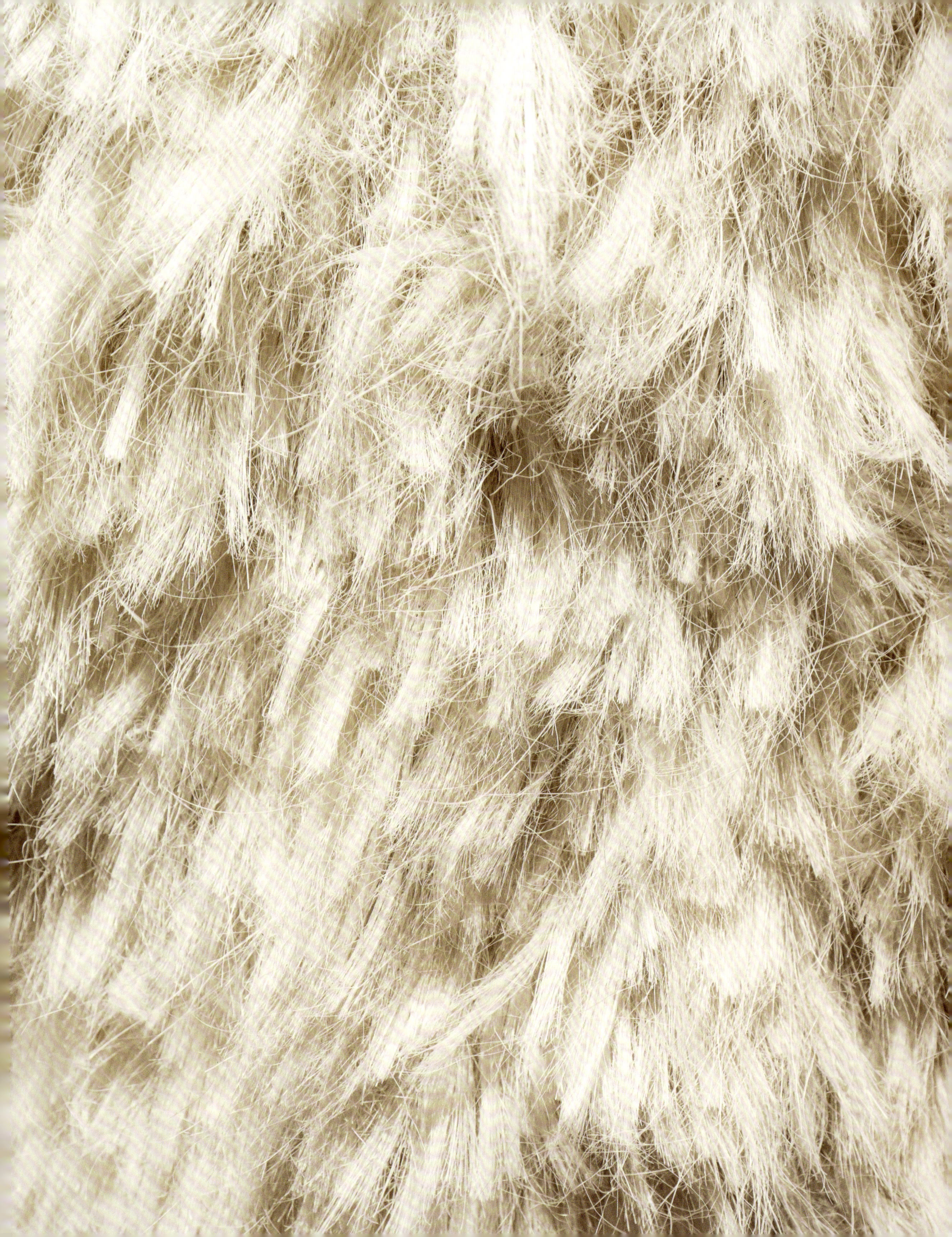

FERNANDO

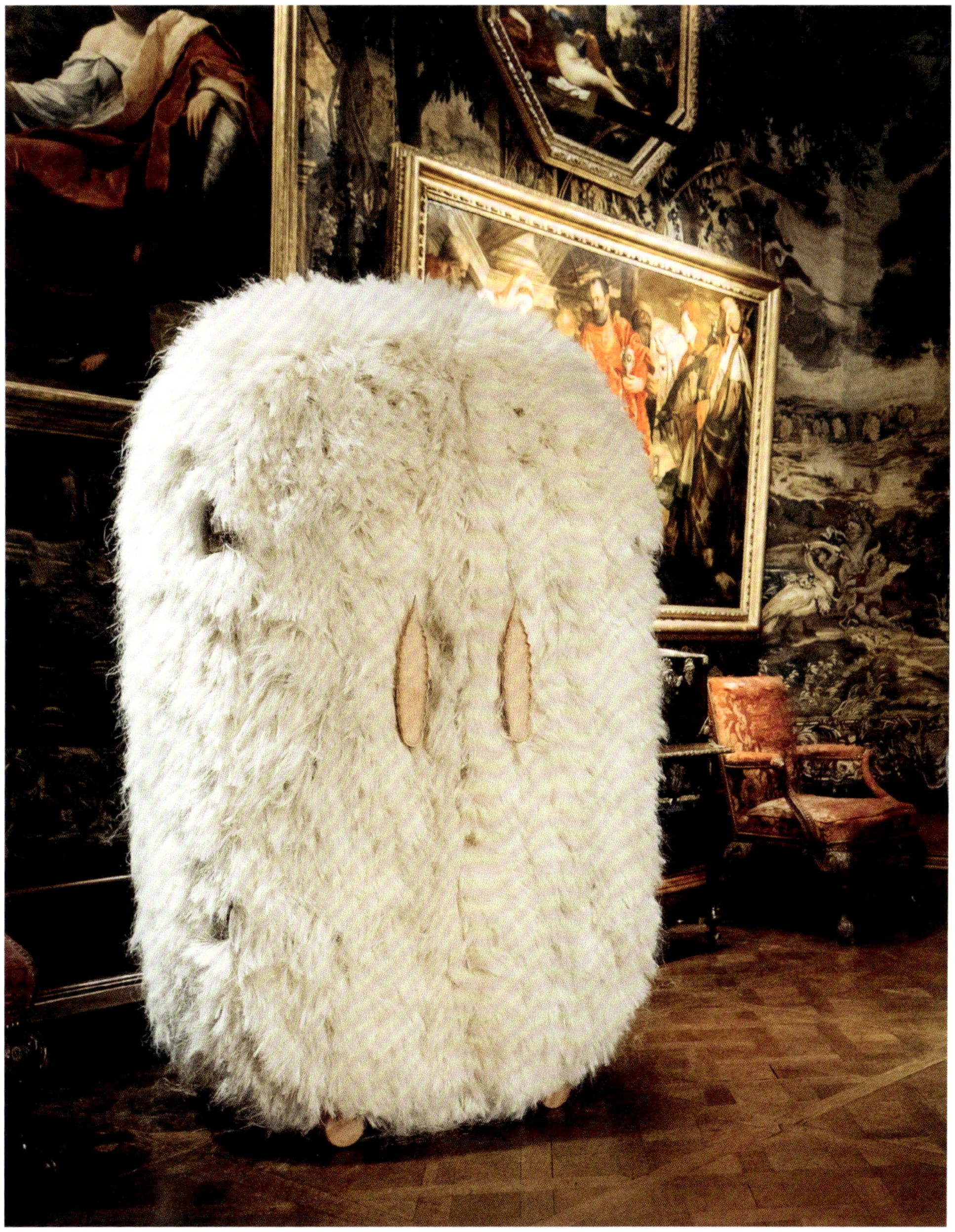

LAPOSSE

LAND, CRAFT AND PEOPLE

With their endearing shapes and long, shaggy pelts, the cabinet and chair that Fernando Laposse has contributed to *Mirror Mirror* are like something out of a fairy tale: objects that one can imagine befriending. The pieces take on their full meaning, however, only when you know how they are made. Laposse creates them in a Mexican village called Tonahuixtla, whose agricultural way of life has been disrupted by global competition. At the same time, its landscape has been devastated by climate change, resulting in wildfires and erosion. As farming communities have become gradually less sustainable, they have been depopulated by economically-motivated out-migration.

Laposse, who was raised in Mexico and trained as a designer in London (he worked in Faye Toogood's studio for a time), asked himself how he could empower the indigenous people of Tonahuixtla through his own work. He wanted to contest the 'parachuting' strategy so common in contemporary design—anchored on a salable product line, here today, gone tomorrow—and instead invest in communities holistically. The idea was not just to create employment, but to restore a biodiverse ecosystem of land, craft, and people.

He originally began by using multicoloured corn husks to make marquetry veneer for furniture. Concurrently, he was developing ways of working with the fibres of the agave plant, the succulent used in the production of tequila and mezcal. Its leaves, which are typically discarded in the distilling industry, yield the resilient sisal fibre. Laposse pioneered the craft use of this material in Tonahuixtla, where he is also organising an extensive planting of agave. The goal is to fight erosion, both natural and cultural, restoring a viable economic base to the community. Today, his work involves members of about fifteen families, providing financial support for forty or fifty people. This is impressive enough, but it's also important to Laposse that his work is scalable; his methodology, built from the ground up rather than imposed from above, could and should be replicated elsewhere.

Despite their large scale, the pieces that result from this research project have an air of vulnerability about them—it's as if they were members of a rare endangered species. At Chatsworth, their palette mirrors that of the elaborate painted ceiling above, which shows the sky divided between the dawn, represented allegorically by Aurora, and the night, represented by the goddess of the hunt, Diana. In reflecting this temporal transit from day to night, there is perhaps a subtle message of universalism expressed by Laposse's installation: rural Mexico and the north of England may seem culturally distant, but they shelter under the same shared sky.

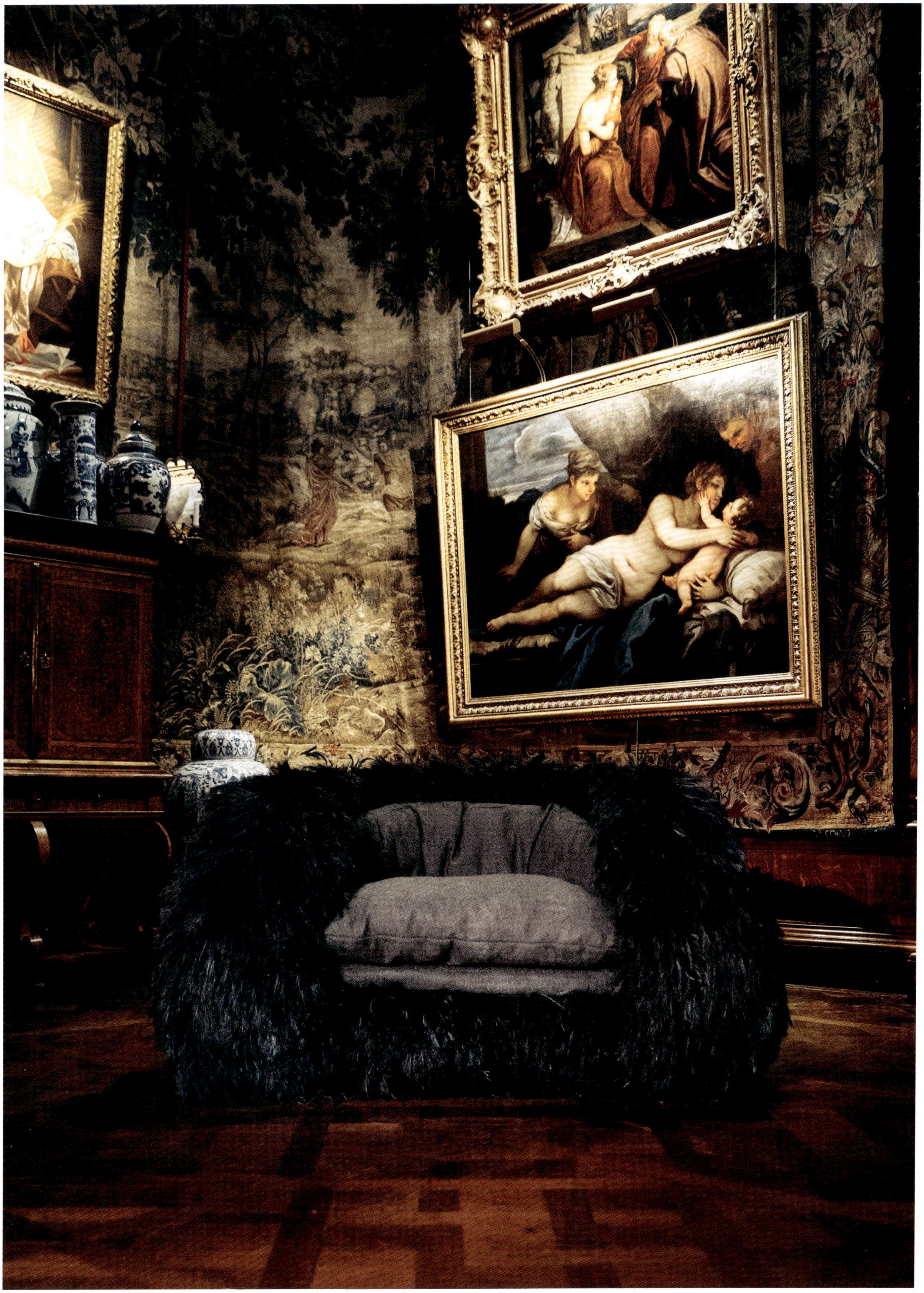

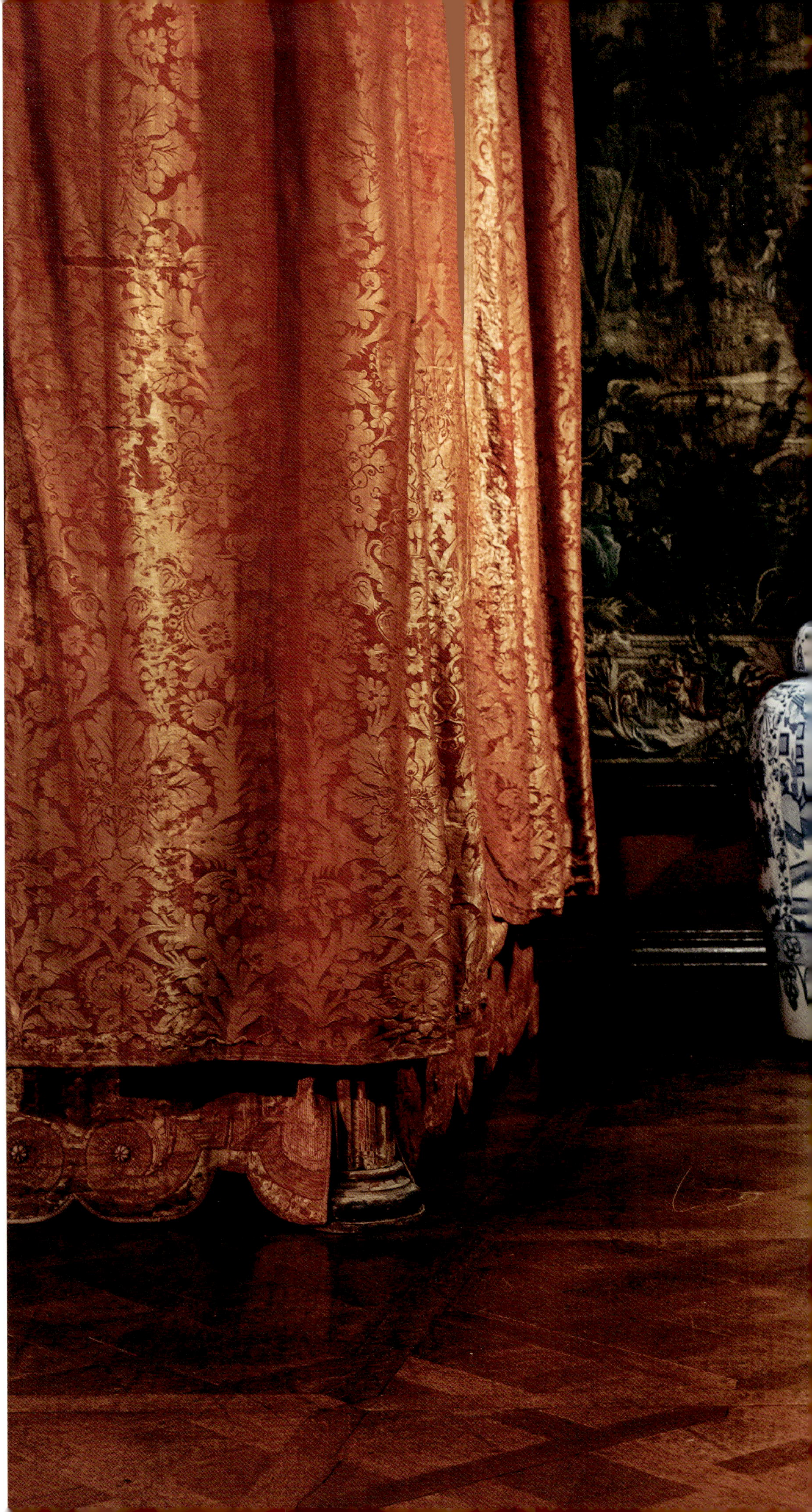

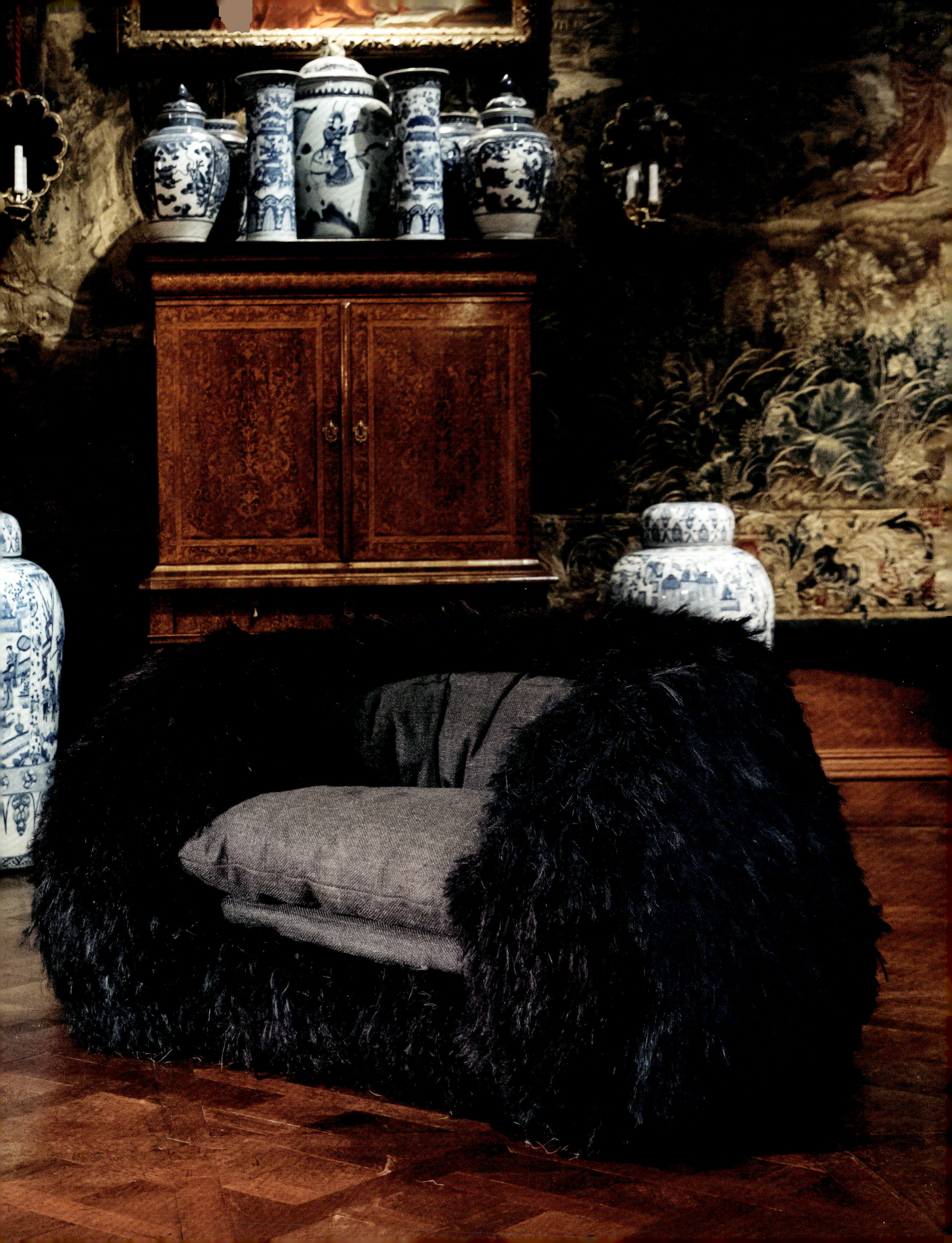

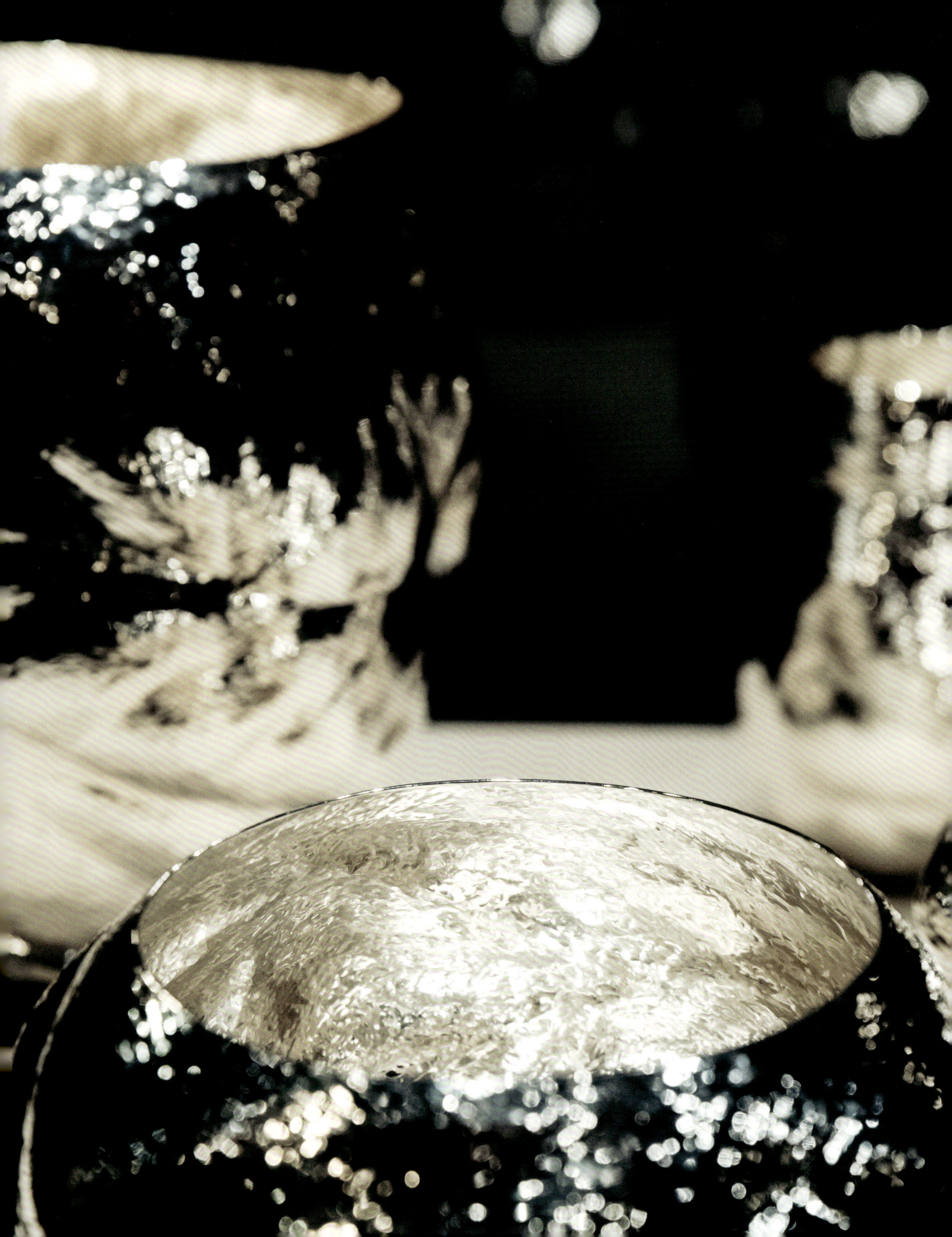

NDIDI

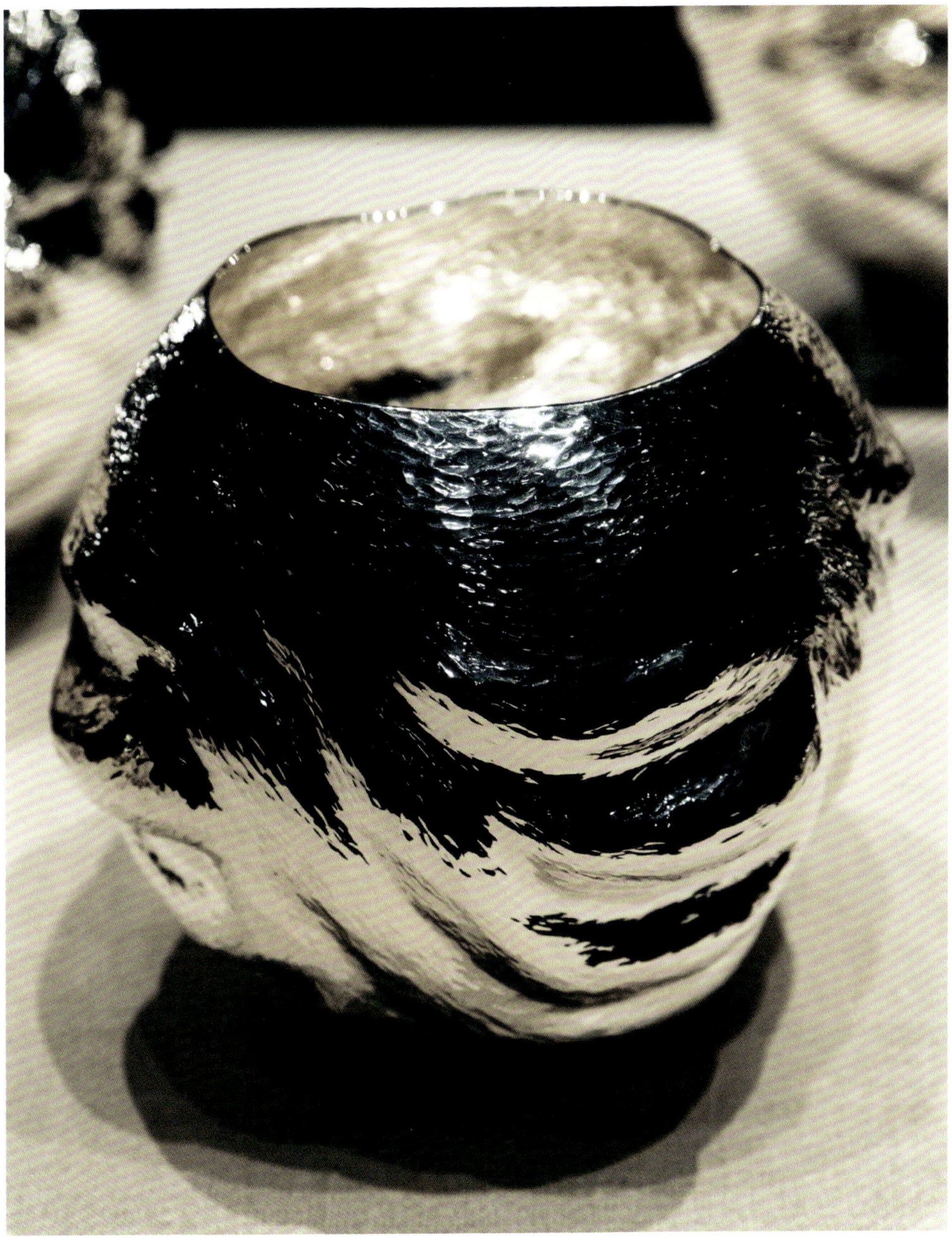

EKUBIA

‘TWO BLOWS ON AIR, ONE ON METAL’

NDIDI EKUBIA

Melt silver, and it pours like milk. Hammer it, and it still moves—if much more slowly. The work of the British silversmith Ndidi Ekubia is both inspired by and made possible by this malleability, this possibility of inner flow. Unlike traditional silverware, which tends to feature mirror-smooth expanses interrupted by cast or chased decoration, her abstract vessels feature an all-over texture of hammered marks, coursing over tapered swells.

Ekubia begins each piece by drawing its principal lines on paper. Then the template is raised from a flat sheet of the metal, working through each course of hammering in a steady rhythm (‘two blows on air, one on metal’) as she rotates the piece in her hand. The object gradually rises from a two-dimensional idea into something purely volumetric, curves swerving and converging. The effect is that of rippling waves, as if a liquid were actually caught in the act of transmuting into a vessel.

There’s nothing quite like these works in the history of metalsmithing—though the still-astonishing auricular (‘ear-like’) designs made by Dutch masters in the seventeenth century come close. In *Mirror Mirror*, Ekubia’s originality is brought into still higher relief. She has created a custom suite of works, which have the graduated sizes of a historic garniture, for the State Dressing Room, or Closet. Though compact by Chatsworth standards, the space features an extraordinary array of decorative arts, including a number of porcelains, two large looking glasses (supplied by one John Gumley in 1703, they bear his signature), and an impressive silver chandelier in the heavily strap-worked style of Daniel Marot. Ekubia’s gleaming vessels match the grace of these surroundings, while also introducing a note of pure, surging vitality.

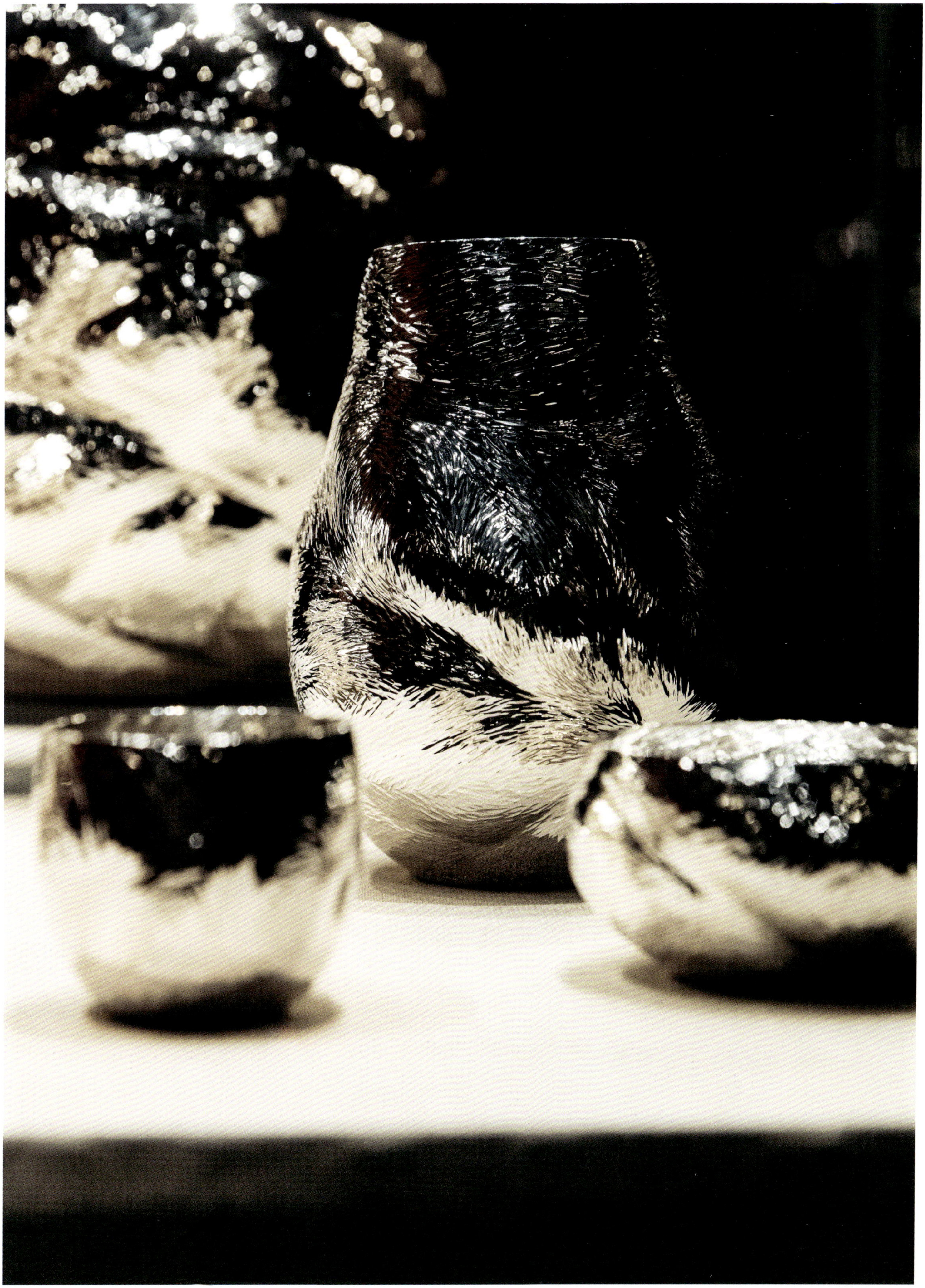

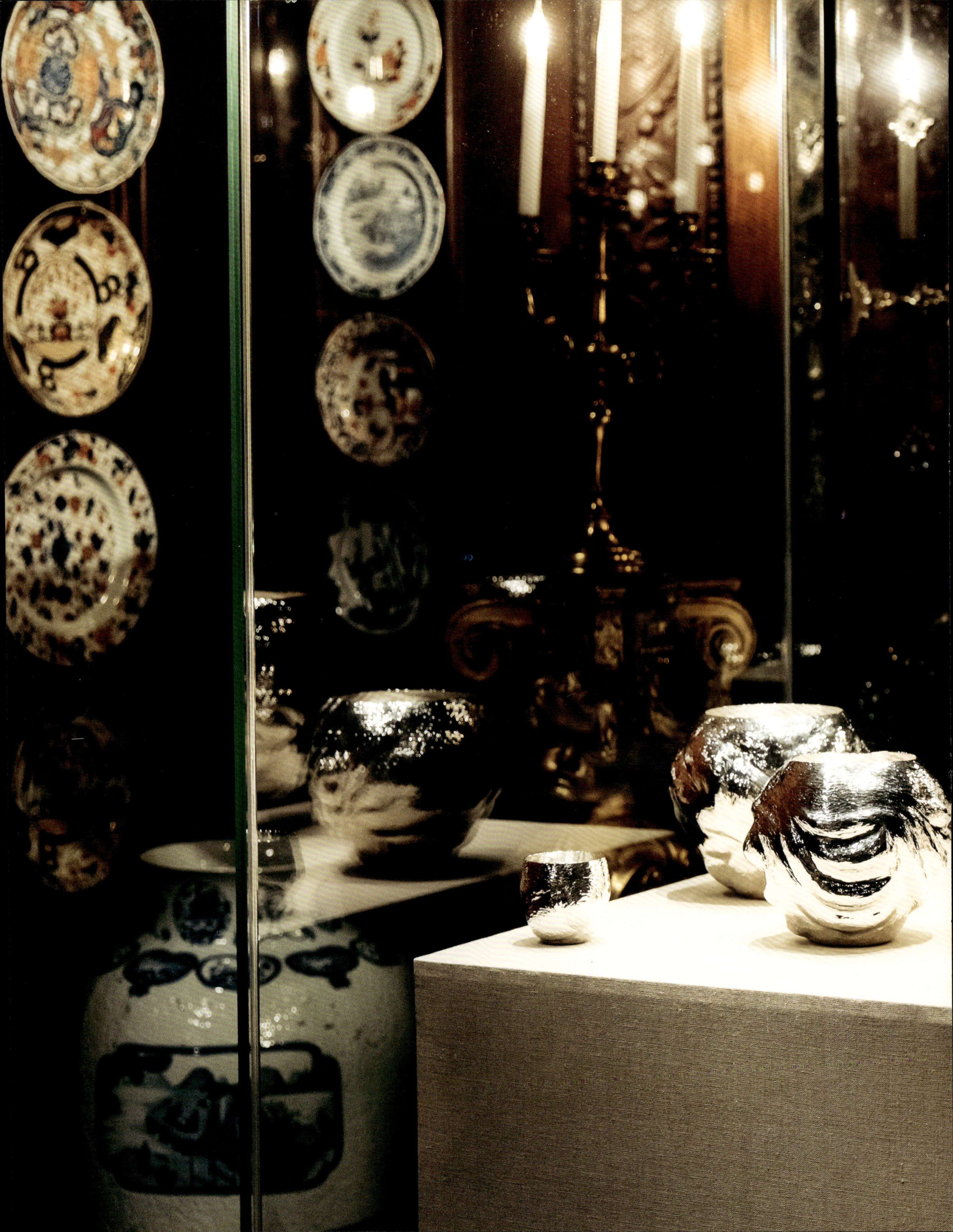

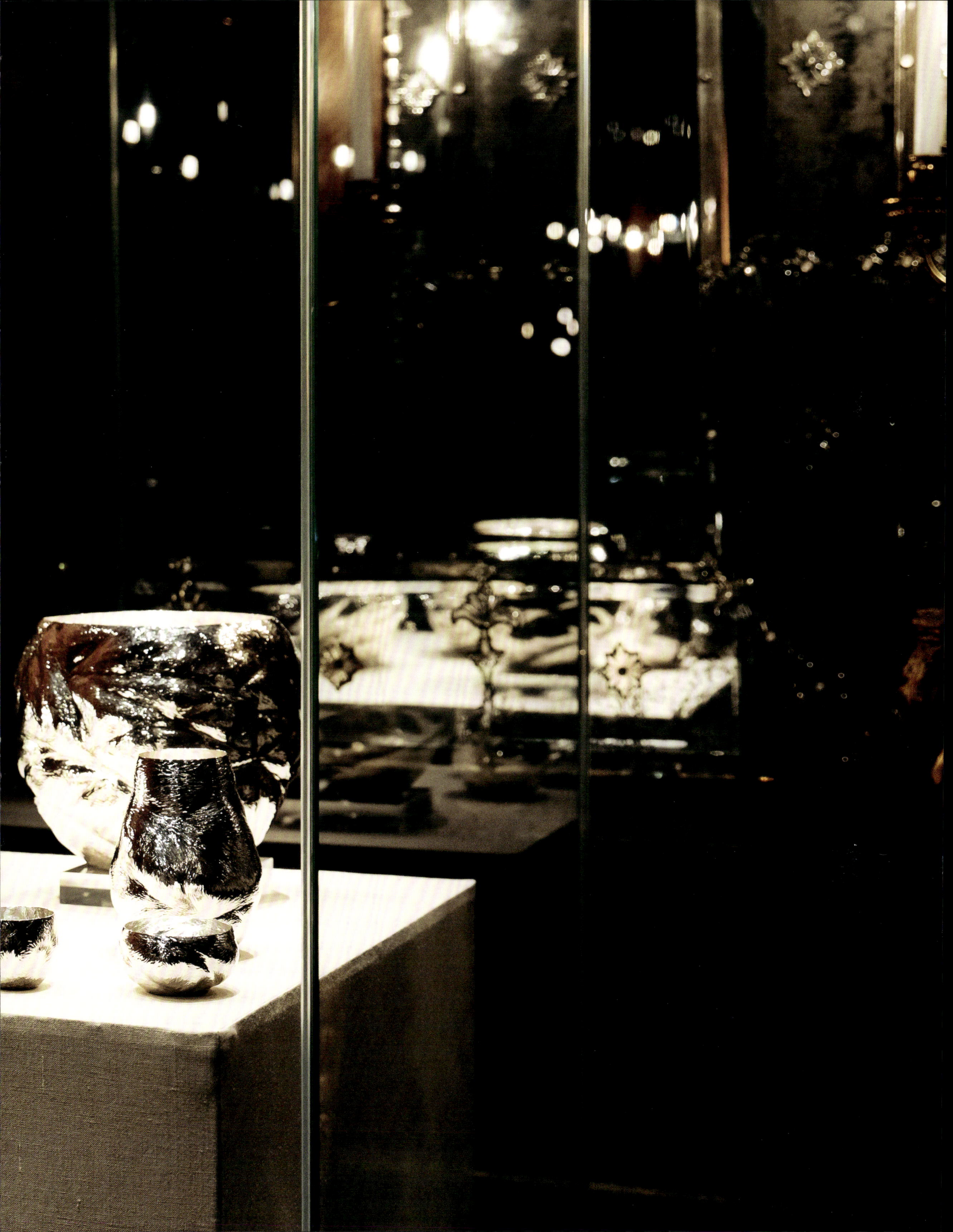

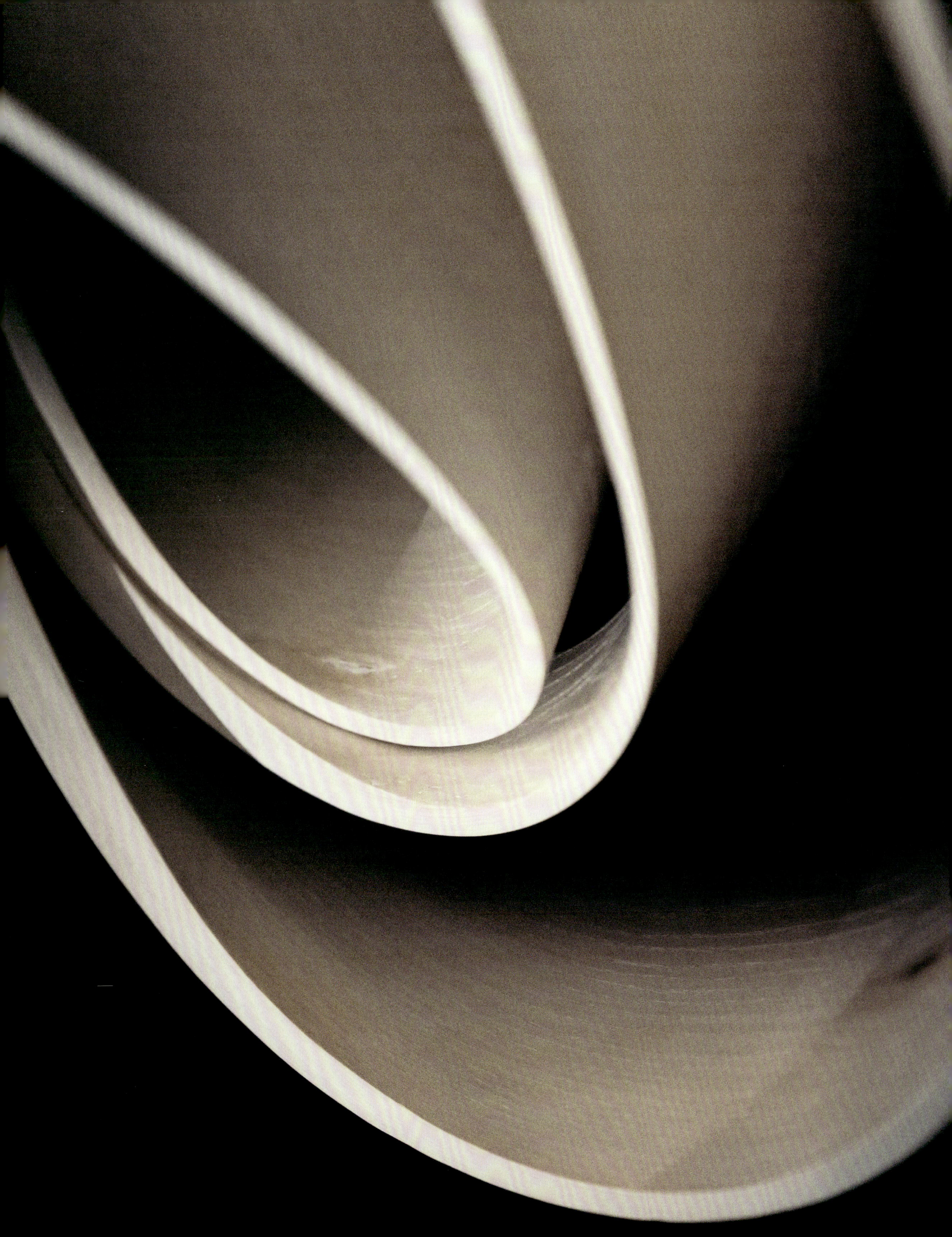

JOSEPH

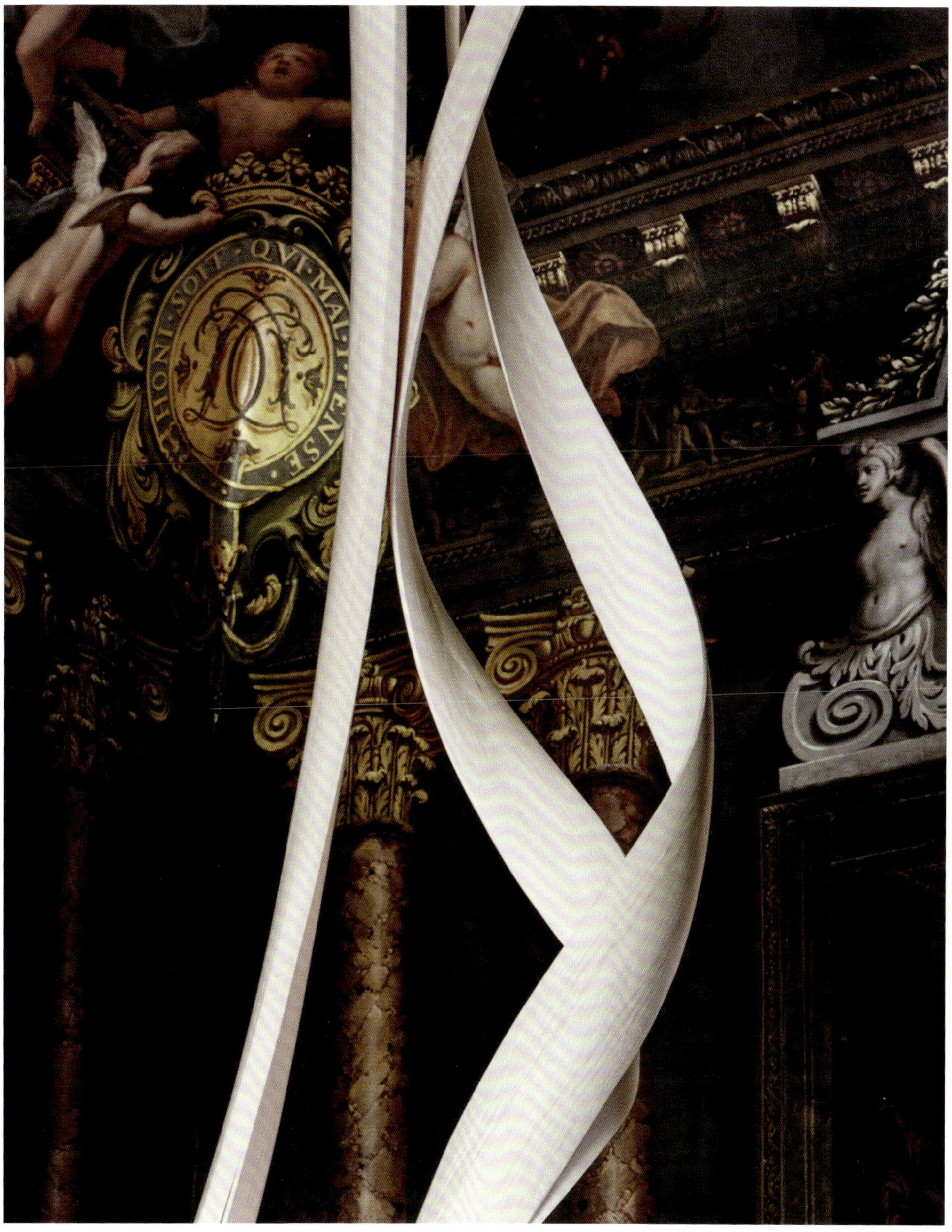

WALSH

POETRY IN IMPLIED MOTION

If Ireland, like Japan, had a Living National Treasure program to recognise stewardship of tradition and innovation, there is little doubt that furniture maker and sculptor Joseph Walsh would top the list. A leading advocate for the contemporary value of making—the deep connections to place that only intact artisan cultures can provide—he has a unique stature in *Mirror Mirror*, having already completed several major works for Chatsworth before the exhibition was conceived.

Walsh's studio, located on his family's farm in County Cork, is near Lismore Castle, the Irish residence of the Devonshires. So it was only natural that they should have thought of him when they wanted to commission a new set of chairs. He responded with a design he called *Enignum I*, a neologism suggestive both of some mystery to be solved and a wholly new substance, both of which the chairs indeed seem to be. Walsh eventually completed many works for Chatsworth, including a set of no less than twenty-four dining chairs, which call to mind the exquisite whiplash forms of art nouveau, as well as the graphic economy of East Asian calligraphy. More recently, for Chatsworth's South Sketch Gallery, Walsh completed an equally sinuous set of ribbon-like sconces, which can support other objects from the collection, but are also sculptures in their own right.

For *Mirror Mirror* we have relocated the final and most spectacular of Walsh's commissions for Chatsworth, the *Enignum VIII Bed*—a composition in bentwood originally installed in the View Room, in the upper reaches of the house, in 2017—to the Sabine Room, named for its painted decorations. Completed in 1707, the scheme is the work of Sir James Thornhill, and depicts the ancient story of the abduction of the Sabine women—a strangely violent subject for a bedroom. Against this turbulent backdrop, Walsh's bed is a beatific presence. Poetry in implied motion, its choreography of curves rise high above a sleeper's head, like a dream realised.

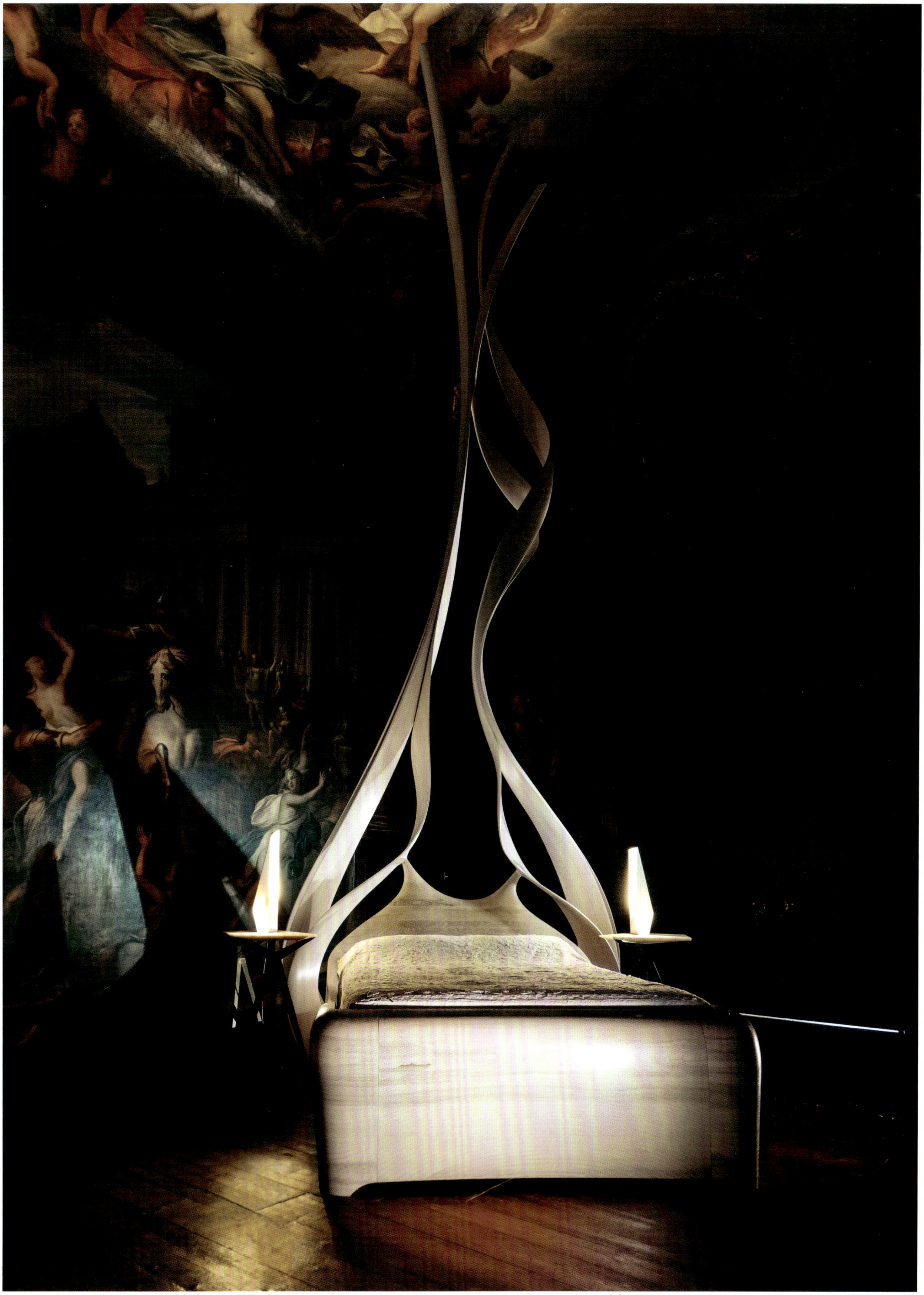

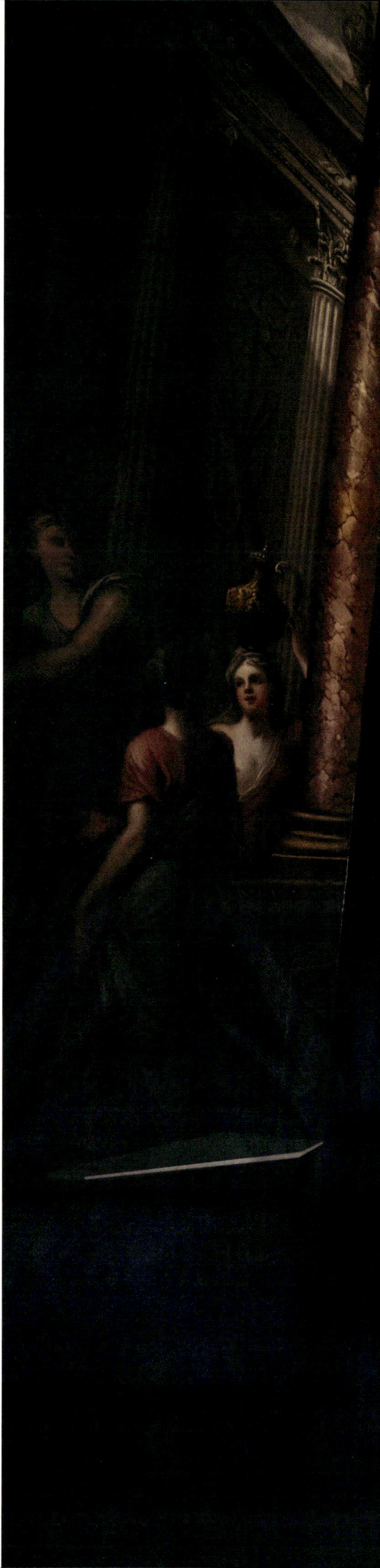

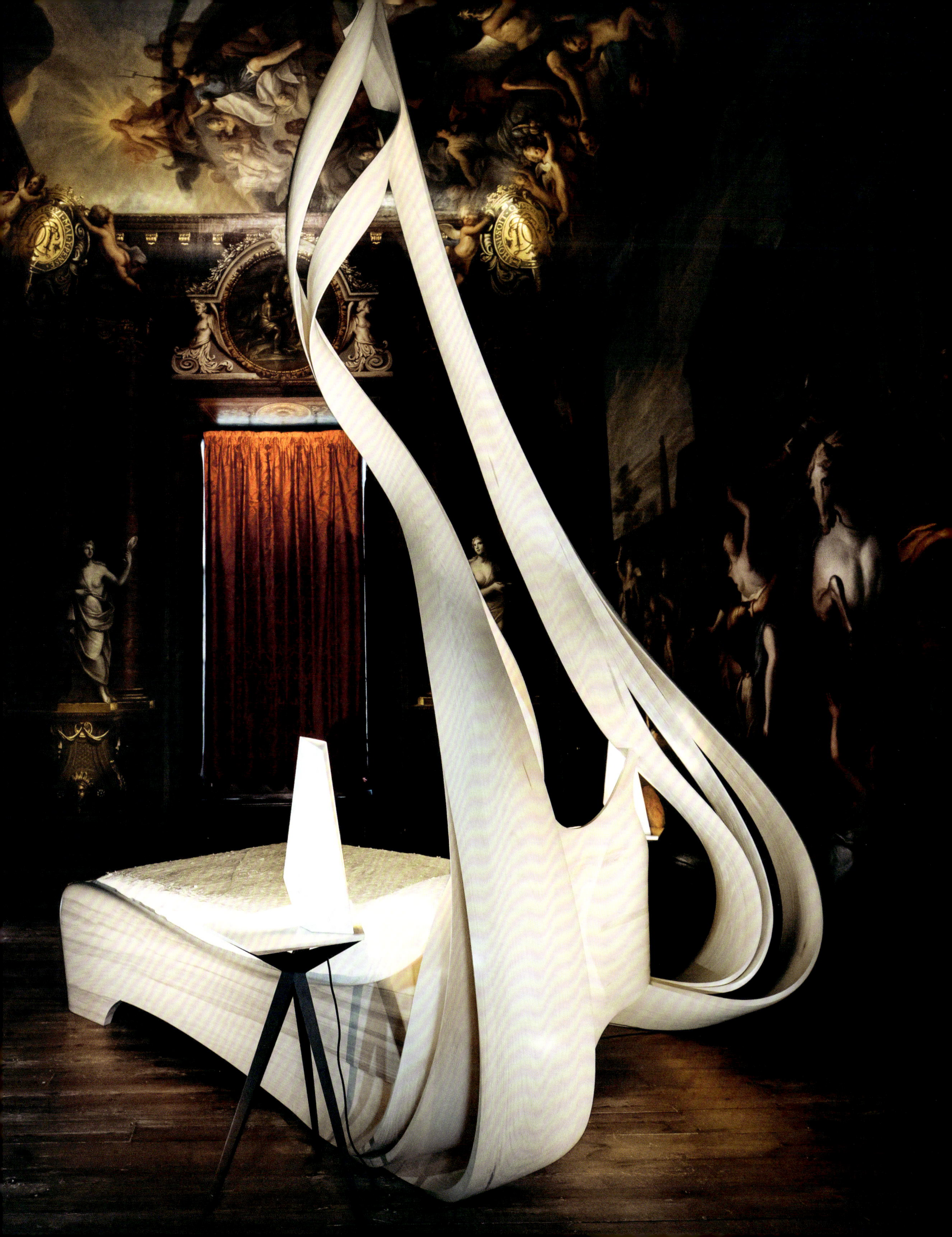

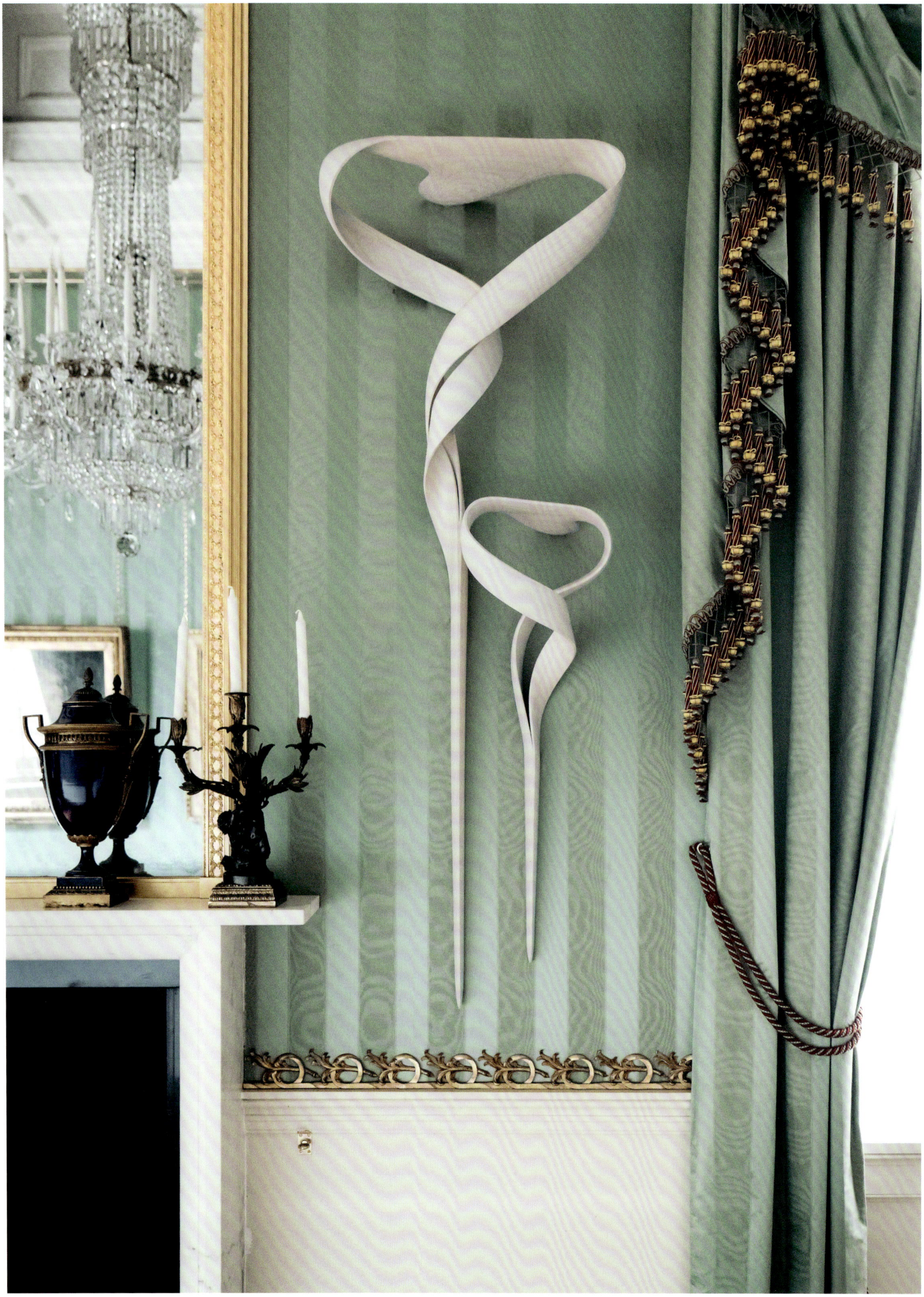

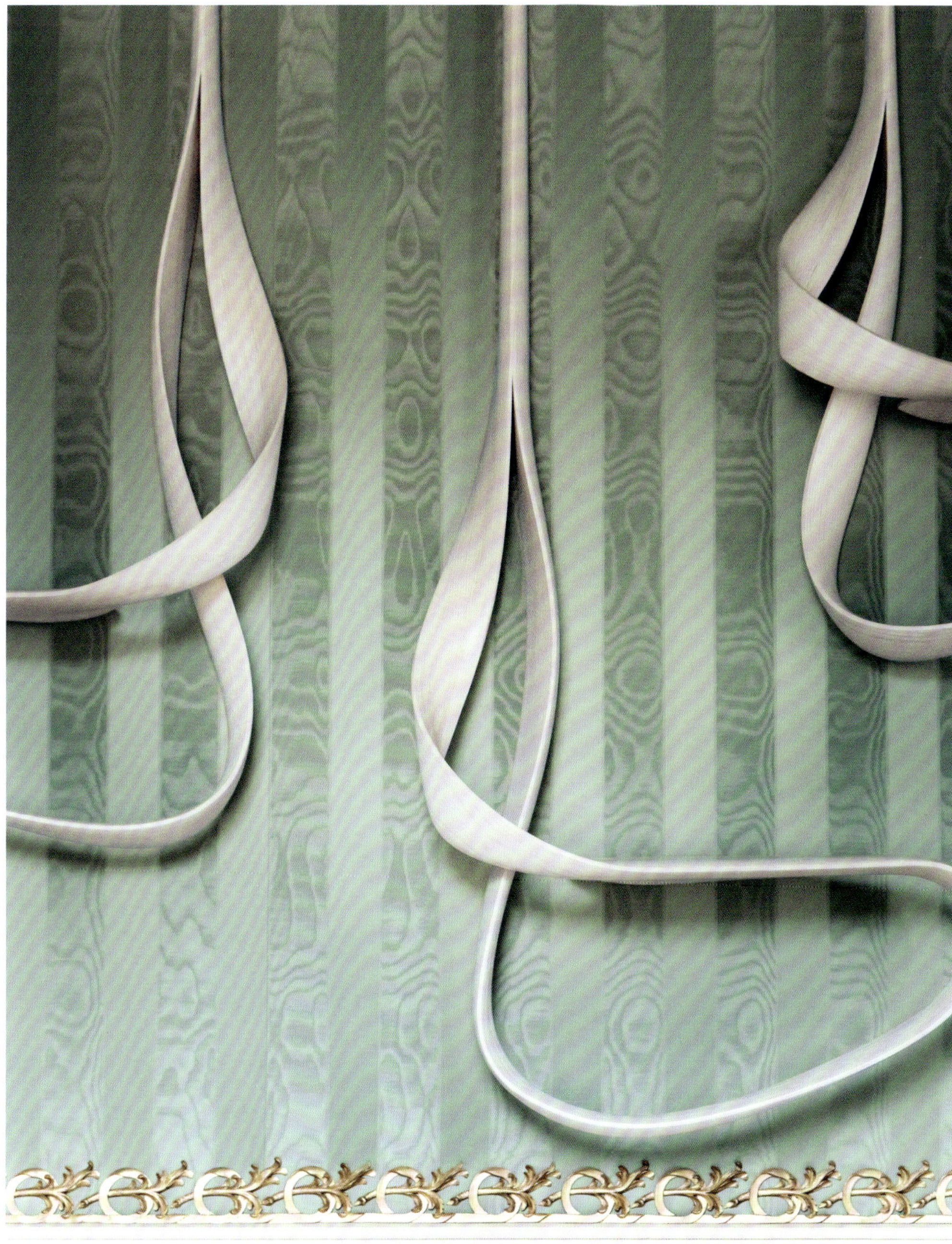

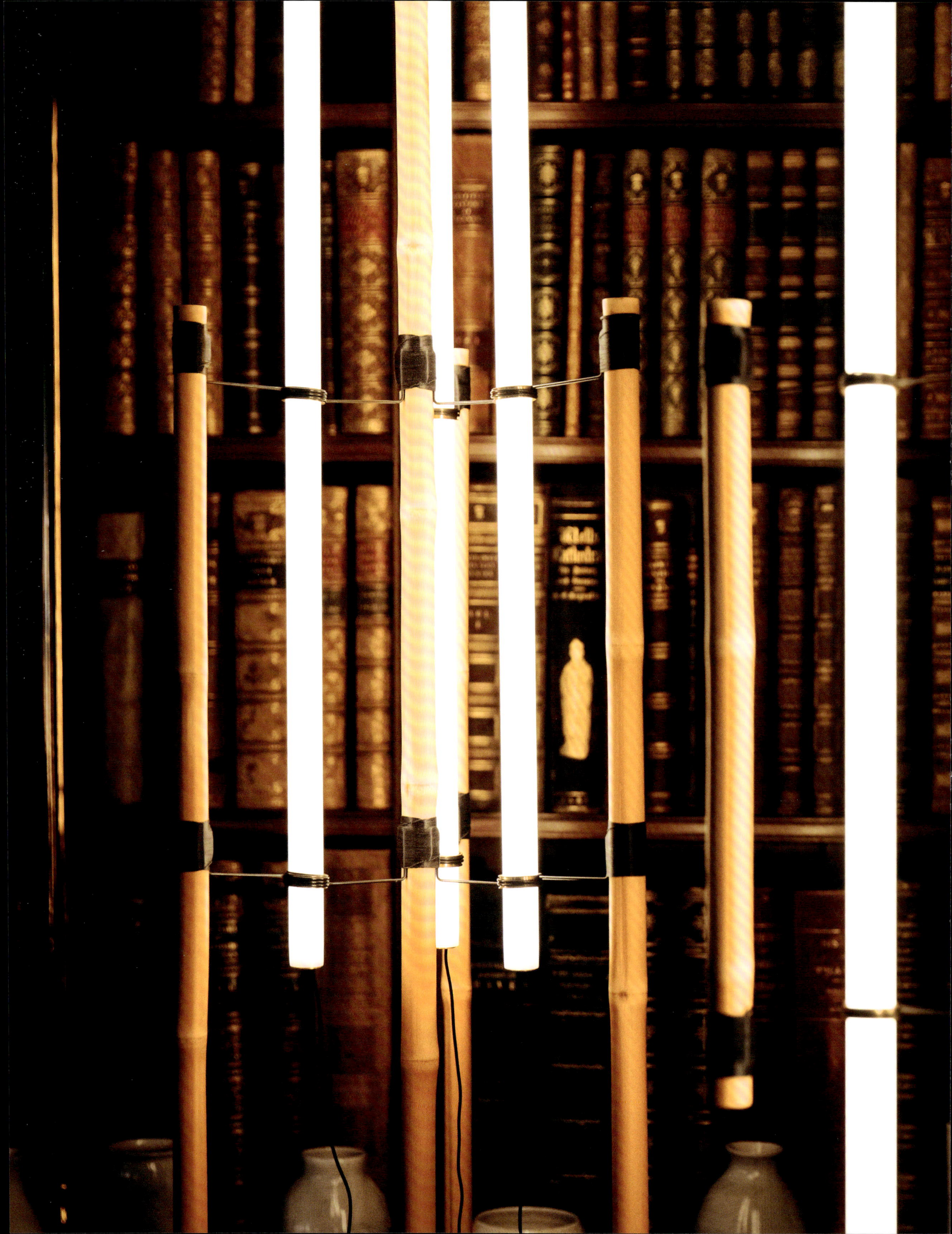

MICHAEL

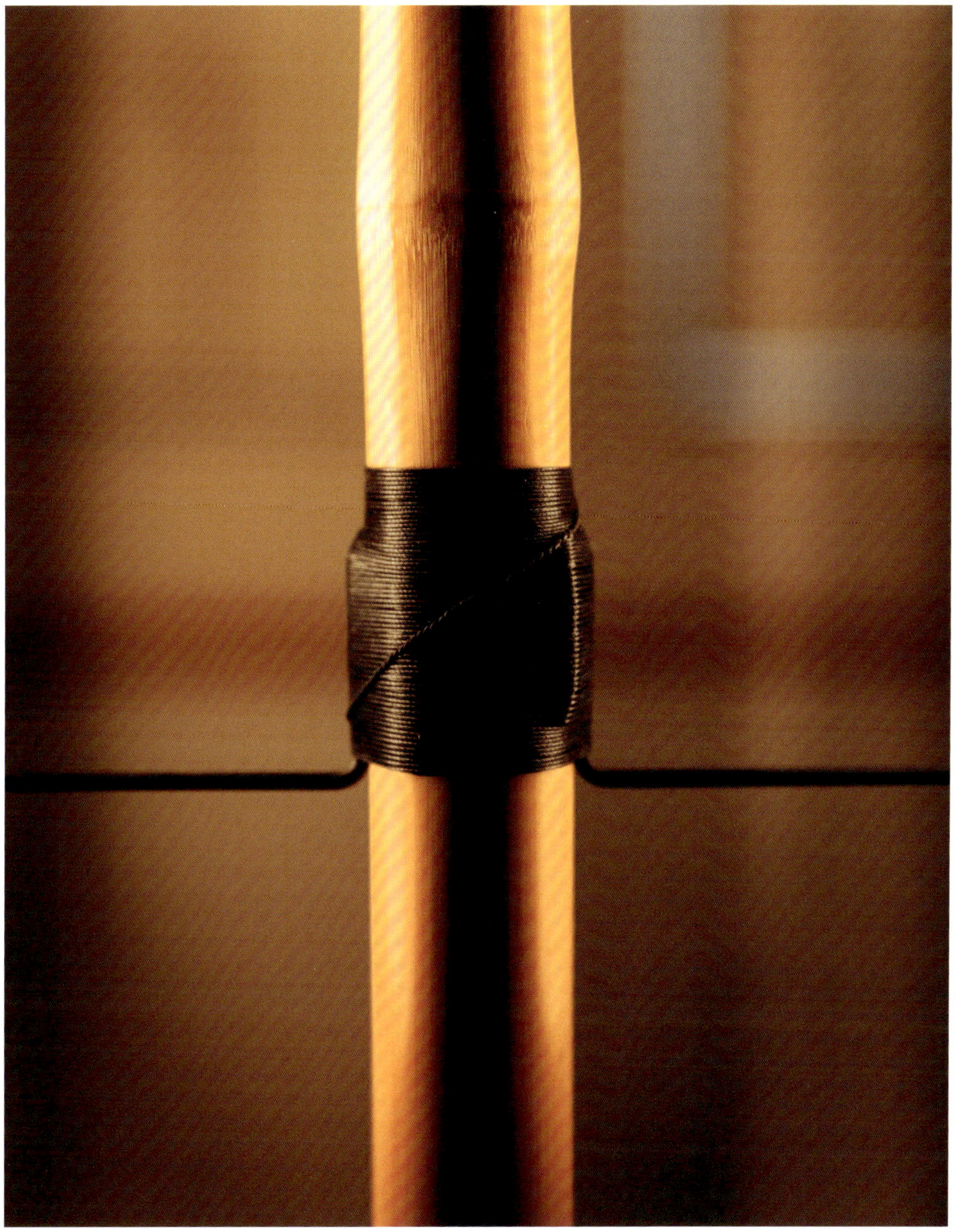

ANASTASSIADES

LIGHTLY BUT FIRMLY ANCHORED IN SPACE

The peerless lighting designer Michael Anastassiades, now based in London, grew up on the ancient island of Cyprus. His experiences there infused him with a deep affinity for light—ever present and ever beautiful in that part of the world—and also to ancient civilisations, which deposited their fragmentary remains across the Cypriot landscape. These early influences help to explain the uncommon serenity of Anastassiades's work. His fixtures are always poised, precise, and self-possessed. Particularly when grouped into an installation, they have the expressive intensity of minimalist sculpture.

Anastassiades's installation for *Mirror Mirror,* conceived for the Chatsworth Library, exemplifies these qualities. Comprising twelve fixtures in all, it is an organic rearticulation of the space. Half of the fixtures establish a line along the left-hand side of the room, while the other half are positioned in a choreography extending all the way to the back wall, leading the eye down the perspectival rush of the room. This indoor grove is made principally of bamboo. The stems have been carefully hand-finished—scraped, sanded, and waxed, according to a traditional Japanese method—resulting in a surface that gleams softly in the fixtures' own light. Each length tops out at a chopped node, revealing the plant's concentric inner structure. The circular bases are made of pewter, chosen for its low melting point, which was pooled around the bottom ends of the bamboo without scorching the surface. Once cooled, the metal forms a perfectly-fitted stand.

To provide attachment points for the bulbs—standard LED tubes, an allusion to the work of American artist Dan Flavin, particularly his *Monuments to V. Tatlin*—Anastassiades used waxed linen thread, wound tightly around the bamboo. Spring steel connectors are inserted into this binding, a method inspired by the construction of historic fishing rods. He has described this as 'a simple gesture of attachment', a phrase that conveys the whole attitude of these designs. They are lightly but firmly anchored in space, essays in deftness and discretion.

The Chatsworth Library was originally the house's Long Gallery, and was lined with paintings rather than books. It was converted to its present use in the nineteenth century by the 6th Duke of Devonshire, who was both a moderniser and a bibliophile. He also introduced the spectacular and enormous Axminster carpet, one of the great glories of the house, which reflects the composition of the ceiling above. Until the electrification of the house, the space had to be used mainly by day, though family members could have read by the light of candles or oil lamps in the evening. Anastassiades's installation evokes this past moment in the space, when artificial illumination could not be taken for granted, but had to be actively tended. The vertical compositions of bamboo and bulbs, from pairings to dense clusters, echo the vertical lines of the library with its abundance of leather-bound gilt volumes, warming the whole space with a golden glow.

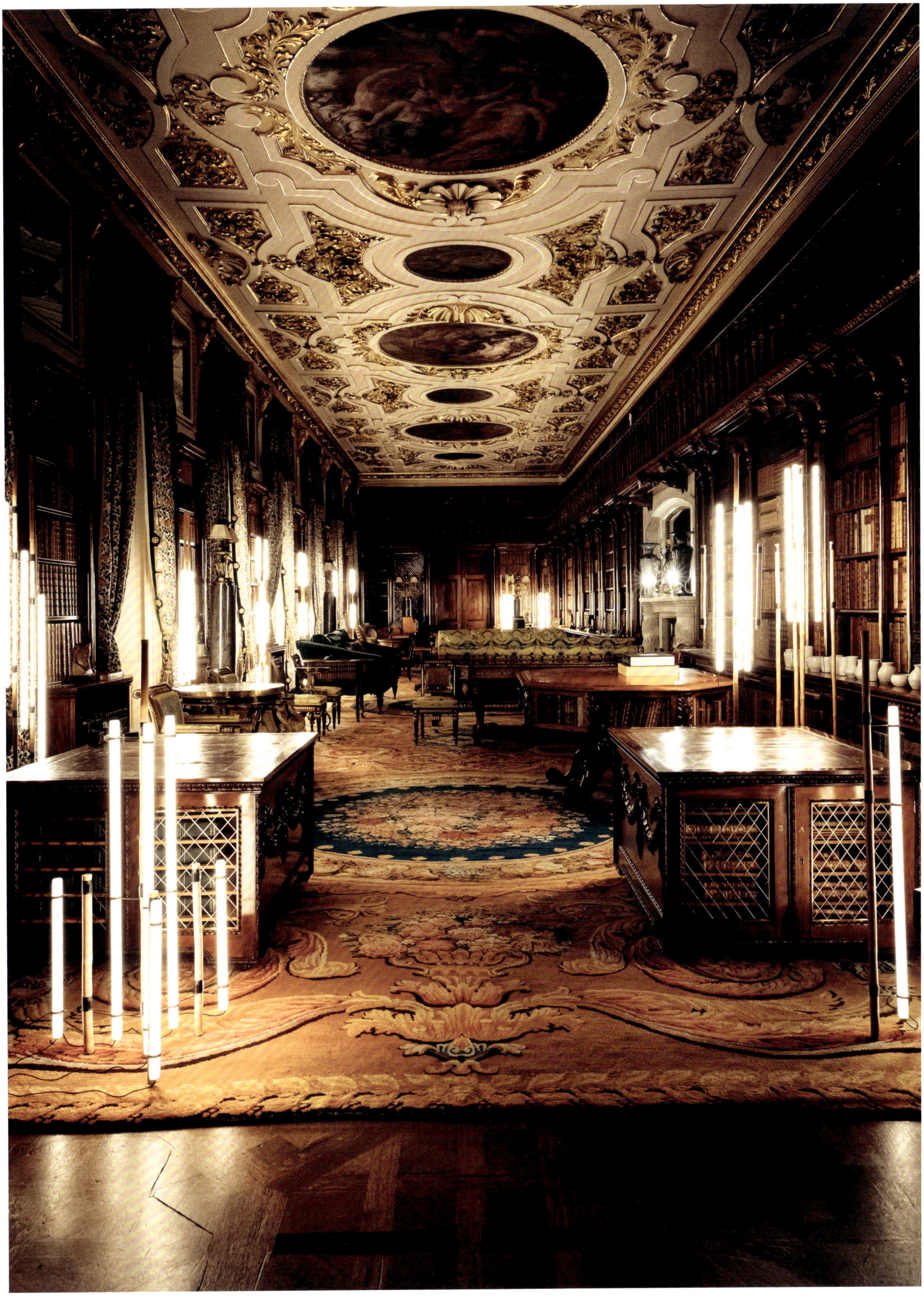

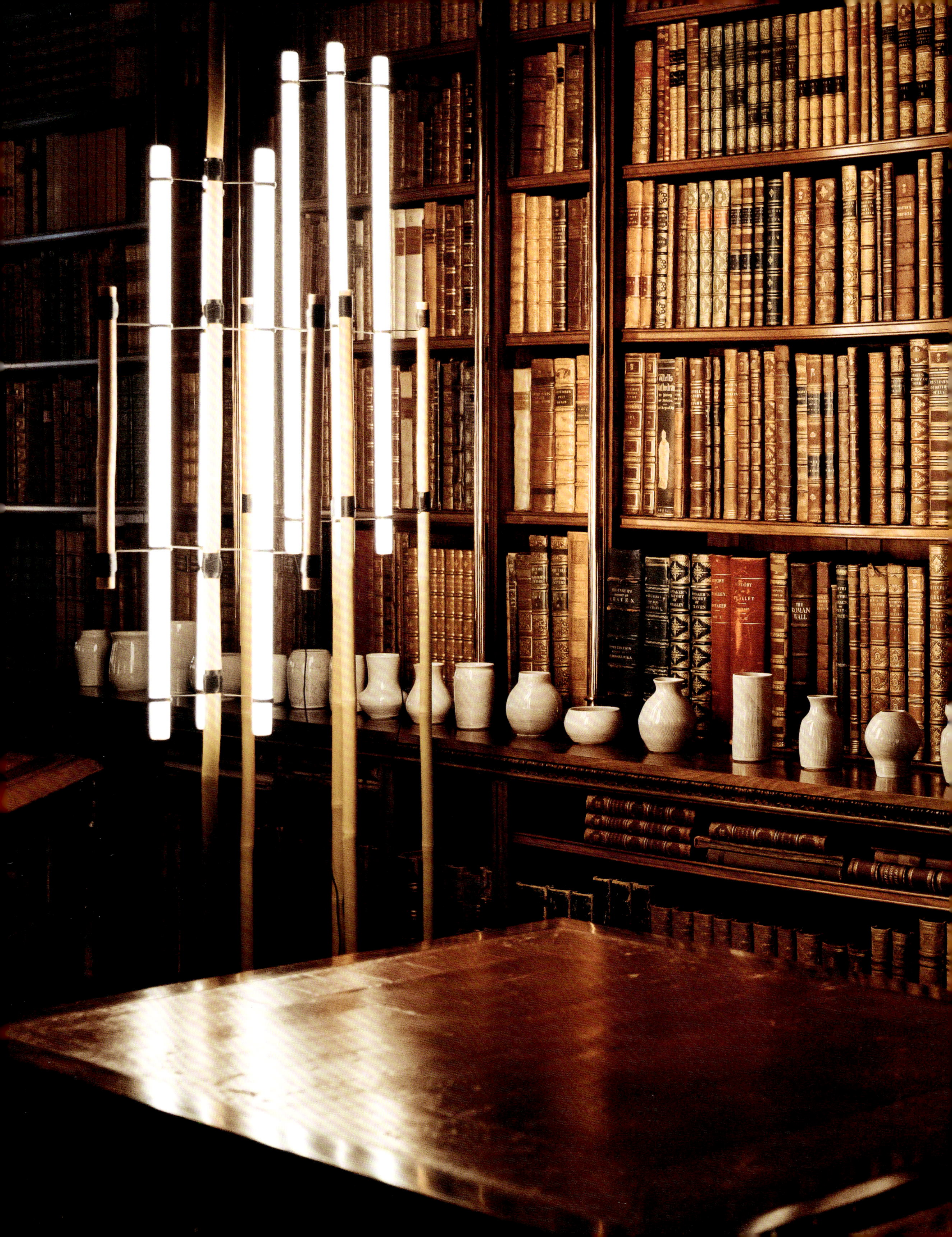

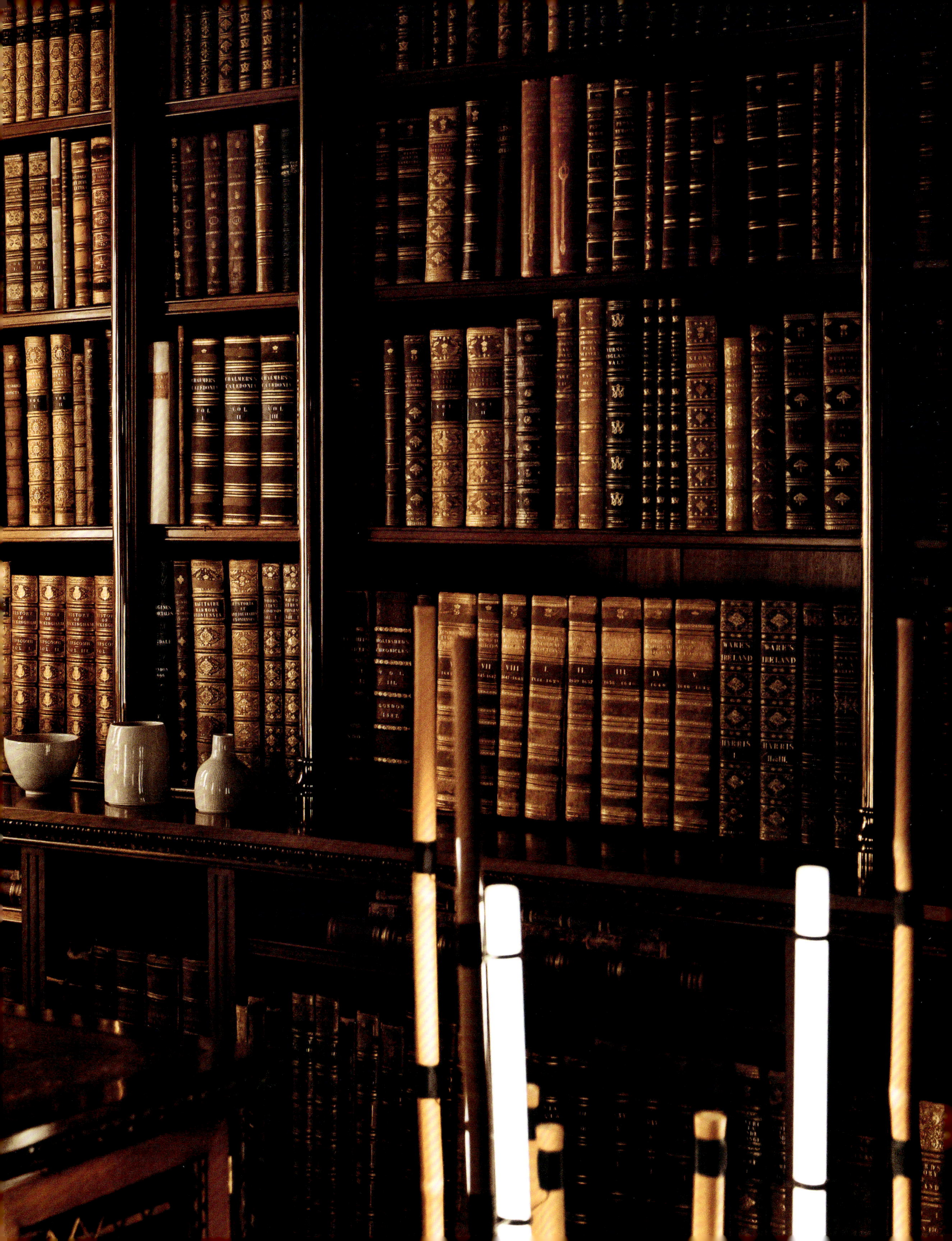
CHALMERS'S CALEDONIA
VOL I
CHALMERS'S CALEDONIA
VOL II
CHALMERS'S CALEDONIA
VOL III
WARE'S IRELAND
HARRIS
WARE'S IRELAND
HARRIS

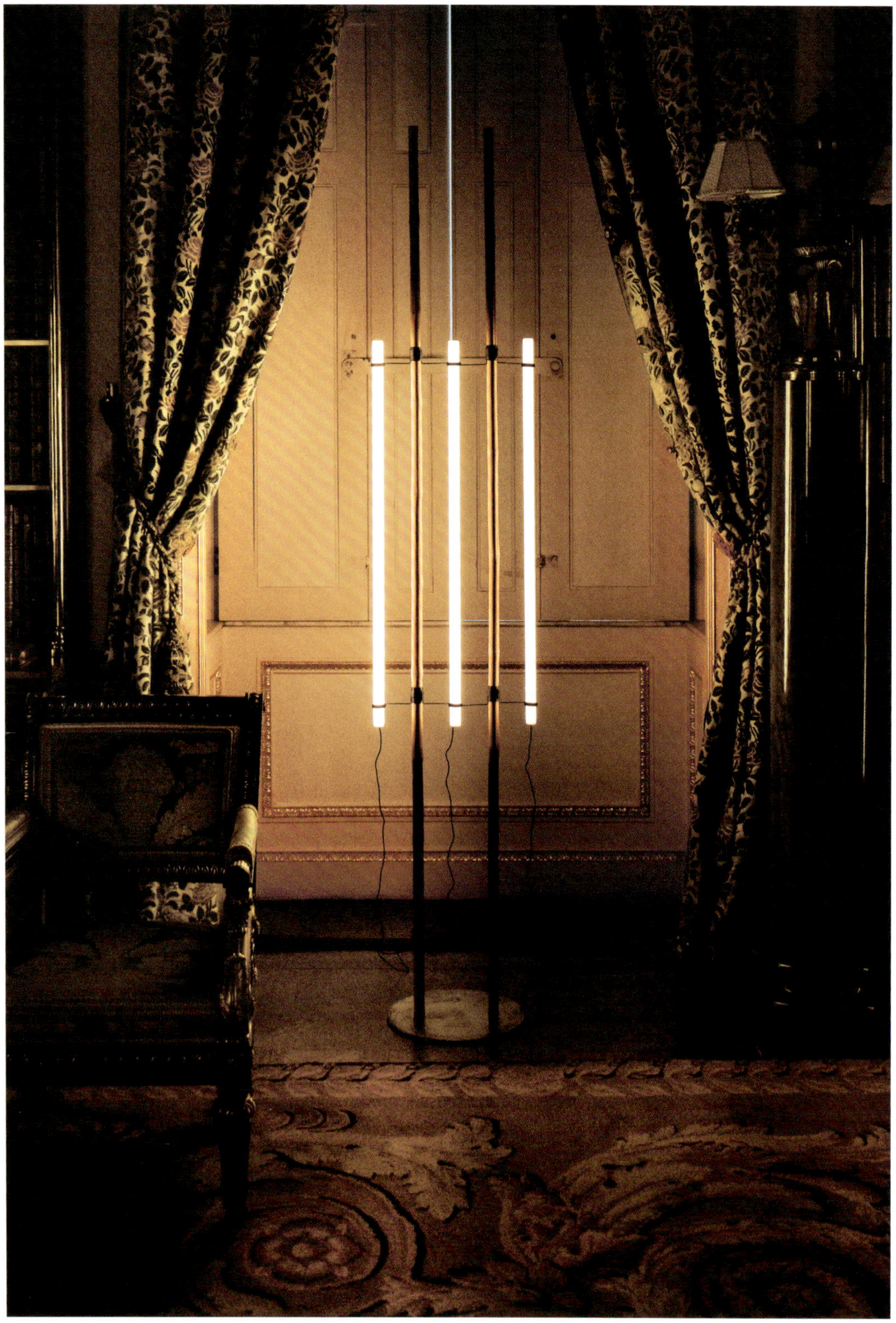

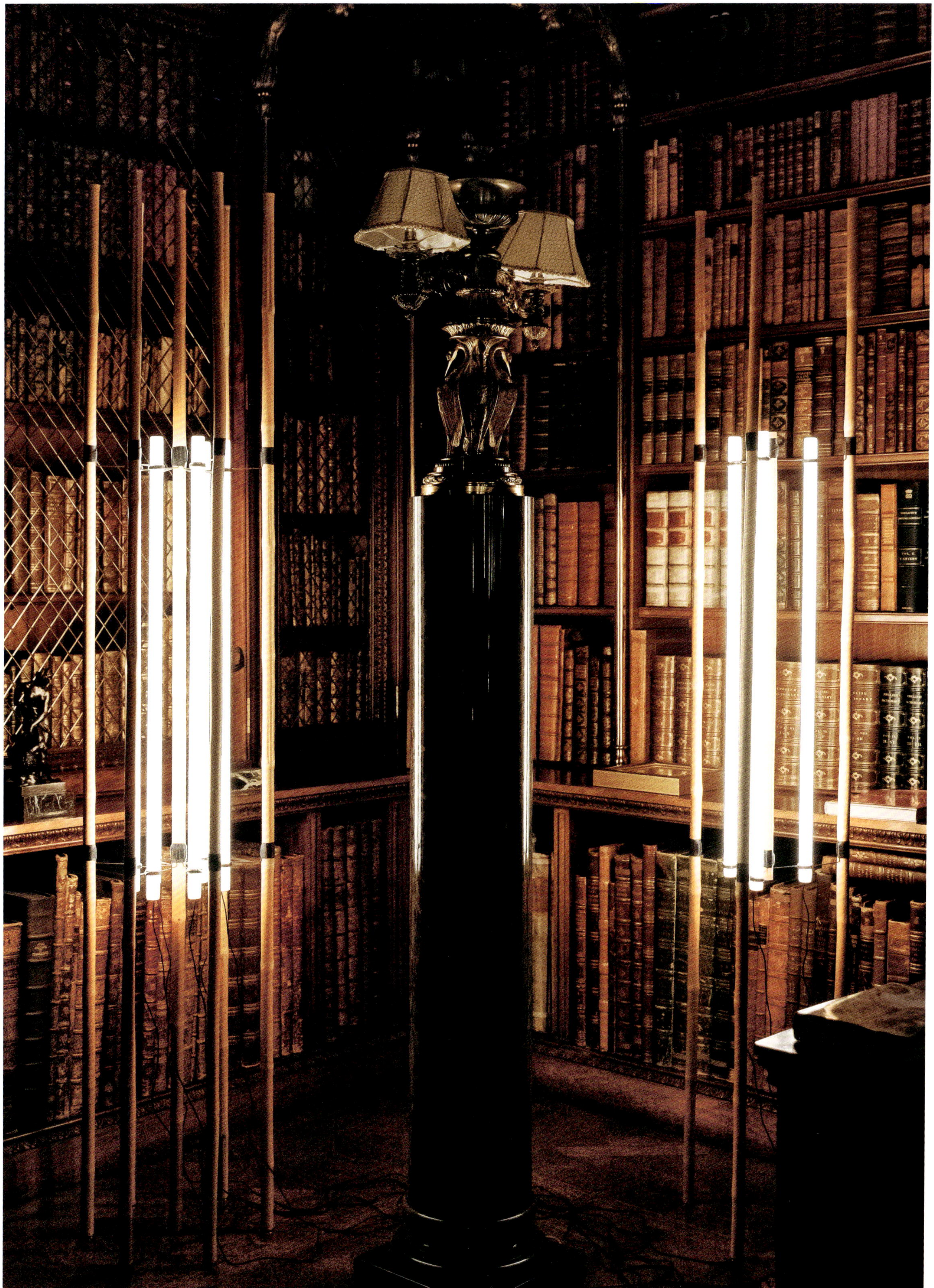

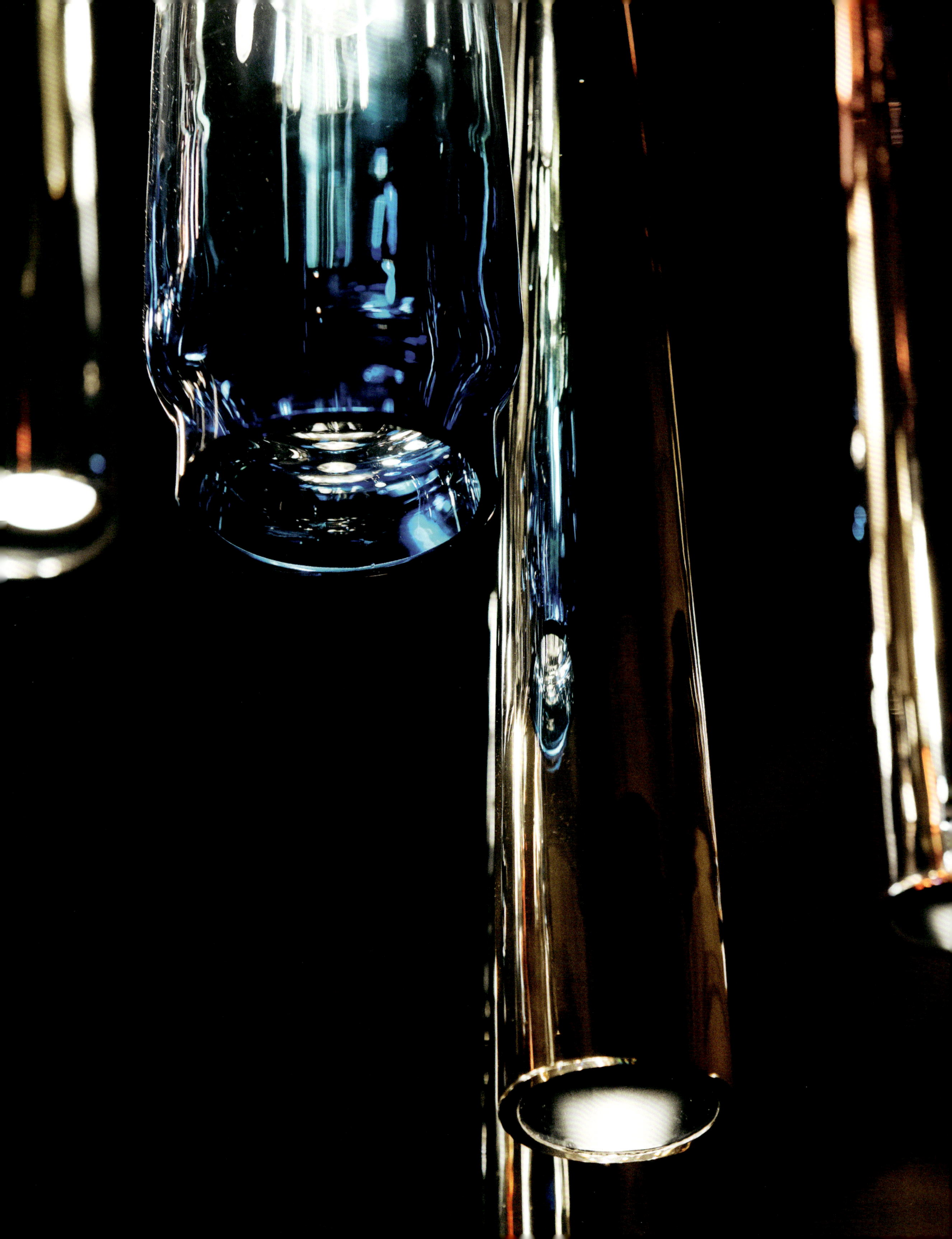

INI

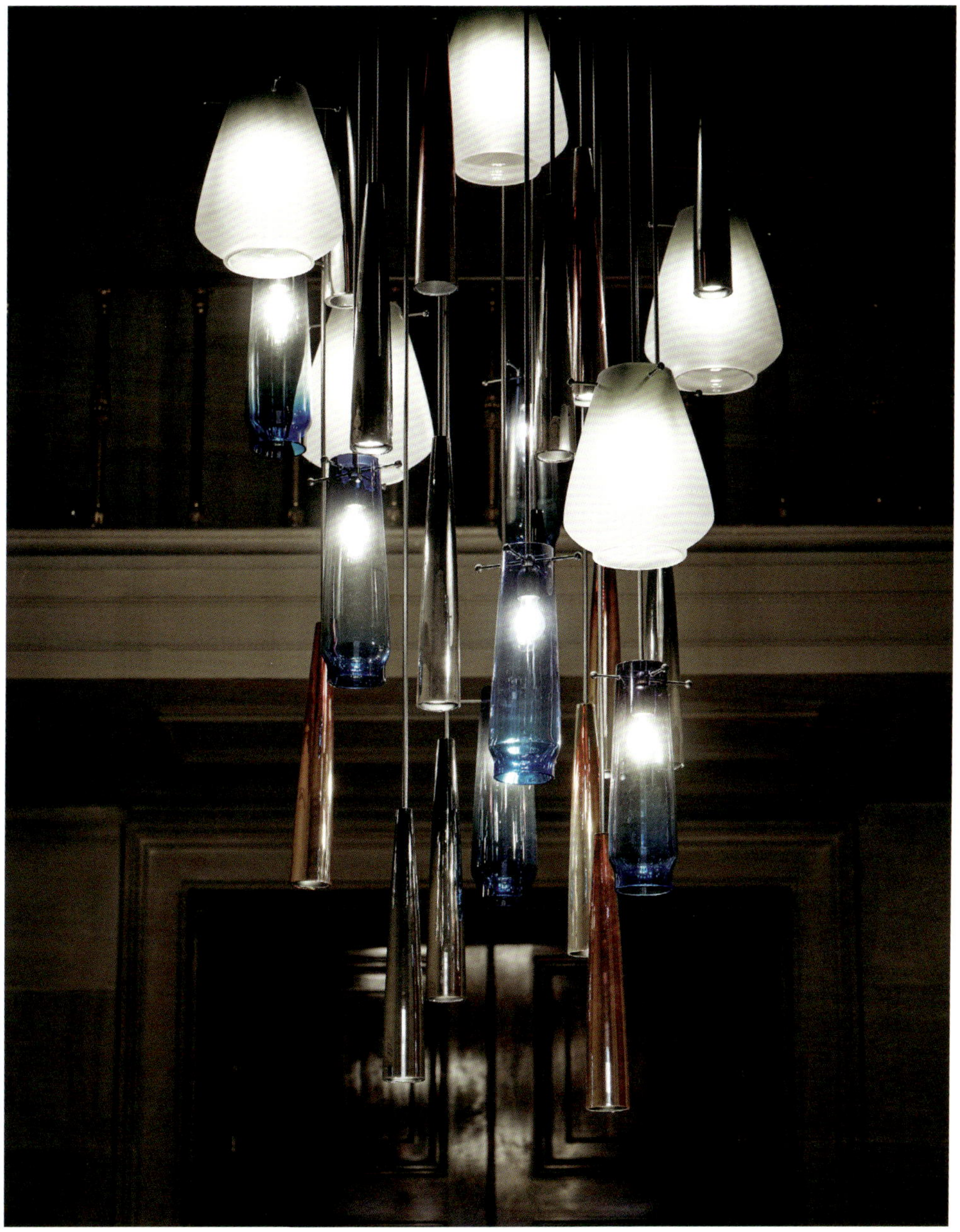

ARCHIBONG

A SATURNINE ENERGY FIELD, SUGGESTIVE OF RAIN, OR WEEPING

The versatile Ini Archibong, who grew up in California and is now based in Switzerland, traverses an uncommonly wide spectrum of design. In 2016, having already established himself in the luxury sector, he began collaborating with skilled glassblowers to realise furniture and lighting. Especially emblematic of his vision are his monumental chandeliers, suspended gatherings of vessel-like forms with a powerful spiritual presence.

Dark Vernus—the title incorporates the Latin word for 'spring'—is typical of Archibong's way of breaking down the apparent oppositions that surround us, pointing to a holistic unity of all things. The piece comes from a group of related chandeliers, expressive of different aspects of such transformation; this is the most melancholy of the series. With its palette of blood reds and deep indigos, descending from a circle of solid black, it emits a saturnine energy field, suggestive of rain, or weeping. The fixture's glass shades are themselves shaded, with subtle gradients of hue and value along their lengths. Their collective effect is both refined and transcendent; Archibong has spoken of making 'objects that point at the moon', that is, tangible things that invoke the all-encompassing, higher significance of the intangible.

At Chatsworth, *Dark Vernus* is suspended above visitors' heads as they pass from the Great Dining Room to the Sculpture Gallery. In this vestibule are also displayed two nineteenth-century bronze busts by the French artist Charles-Henri-Joseph Cordier. While the depictions are arrestingly beautiful, even idealised, Cordier was also clearly exoticizing his subjects, showing them as ethnographic 'types'. One figure portrays a man called Seïd Enkess, who is thought to have been born in Ethiopia or Sudan, and lived in Paris, where he worked as an artist's model. The identity of the female sitter is unknown, but her likeness eventually became known as the *Venus Africaine*, indicating that despite her dignified bearing, she was subjected to a stereotypical, sexualised interpretation.

Archibong chose not to address these problematic representations directly, instead literally rising above them by hanging his chandelier within the vaulted space. To this pre-existing work, he also added music, cascading down from a mezzanine balcony historically used by musicians to serenade guests. The soundtrack is his own composition. It describes a transcendental journey across the history of Black voices. A spacious echoing void is gradually populated by rhythmic sounds, which are then suddenly disrupted by the cries of bagpipes, representing the arrival of colonisers on the African continent. Then the subtle interplay resumes, with music from Eddie Kendricks, Tony Allen, Sun Ra, amongst others—all sampled from vinyl, and subtly interwoven—leading up to the ecstatic climax of celestial jazz on the harp, played by Alice Coltrane. This complex sonic fabric makes for an ideal accompaniment to *Dark Vernus*; like the chandelier and the illumination it radiates, the soundscape is epic, abstract, and inspiring.

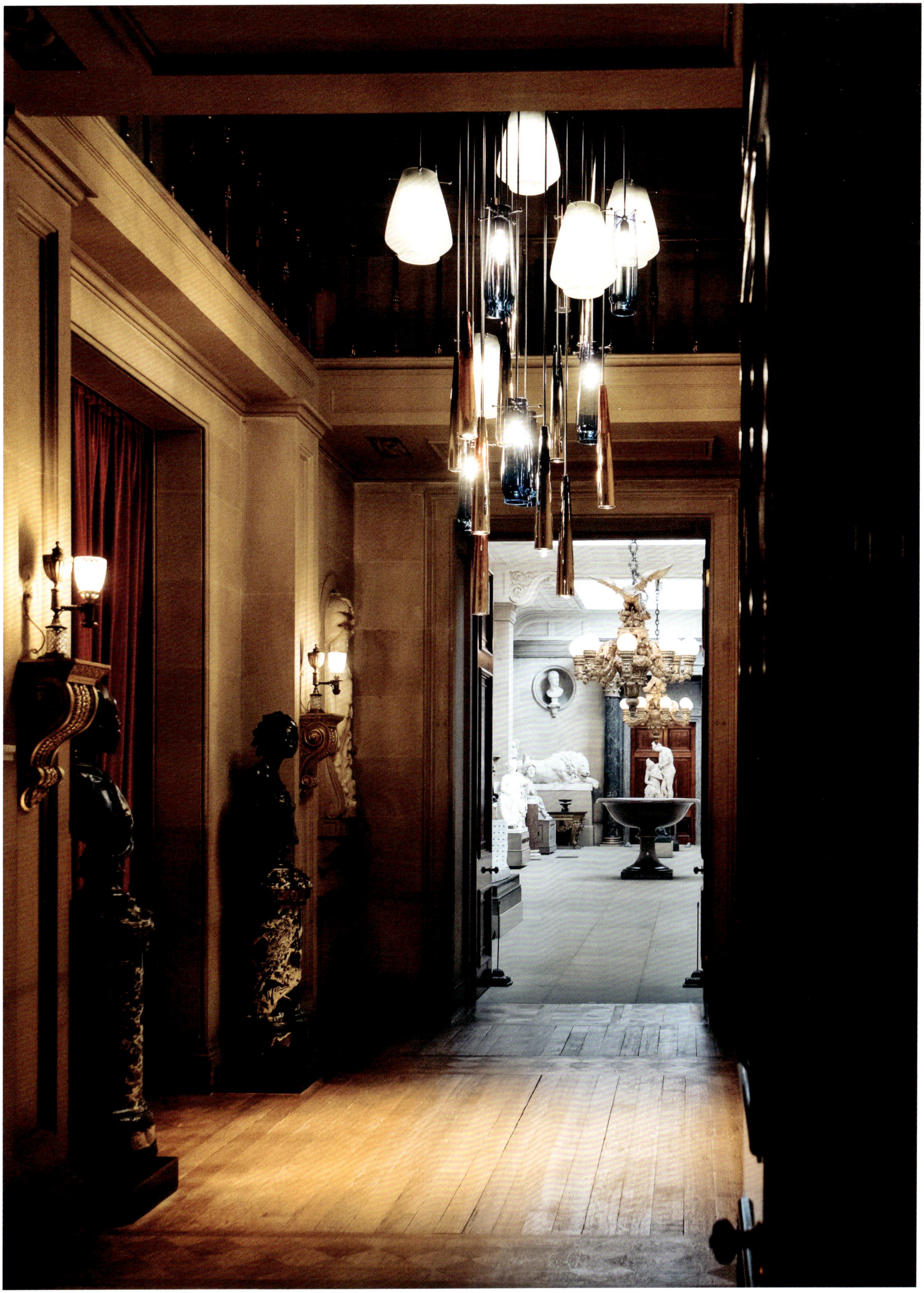

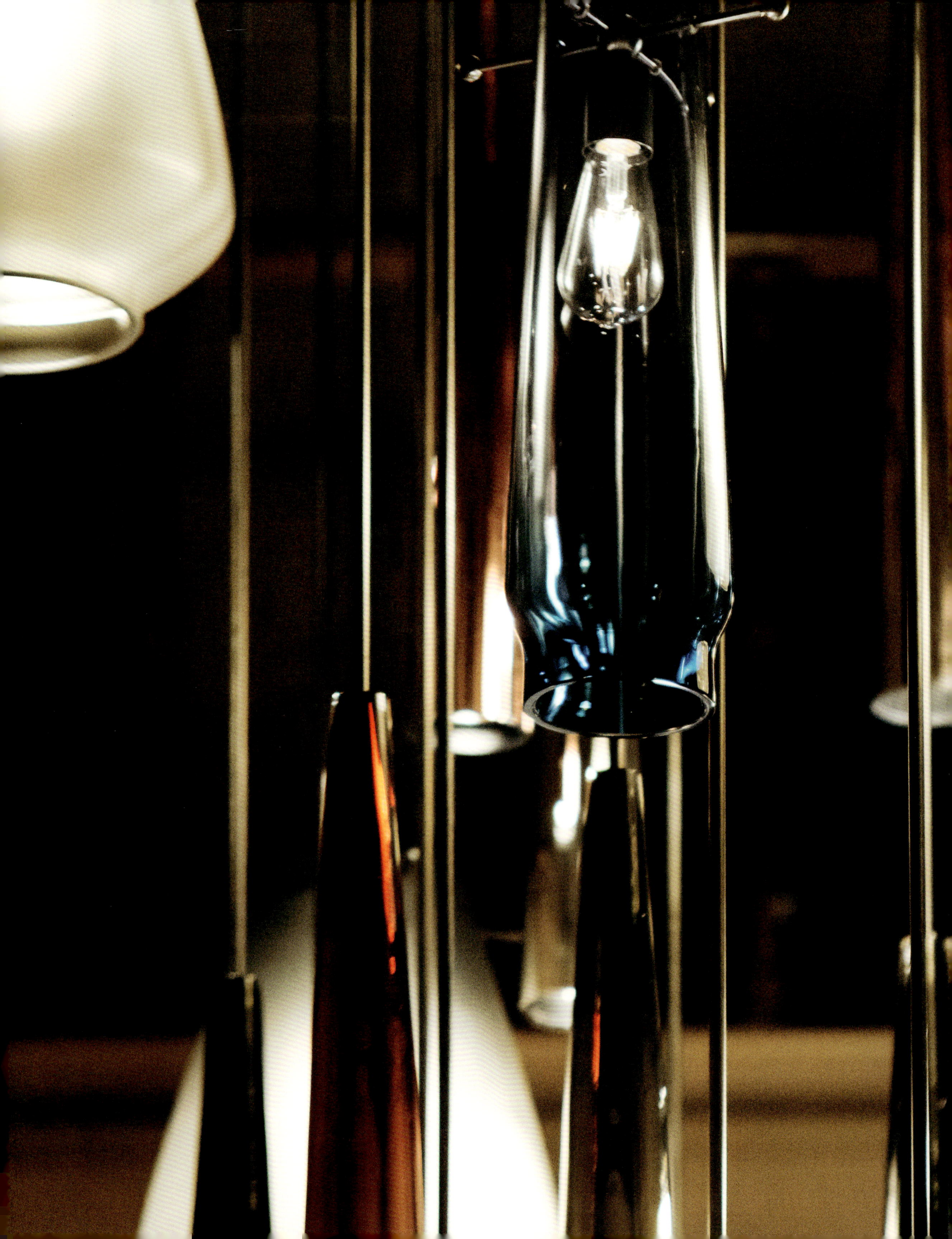

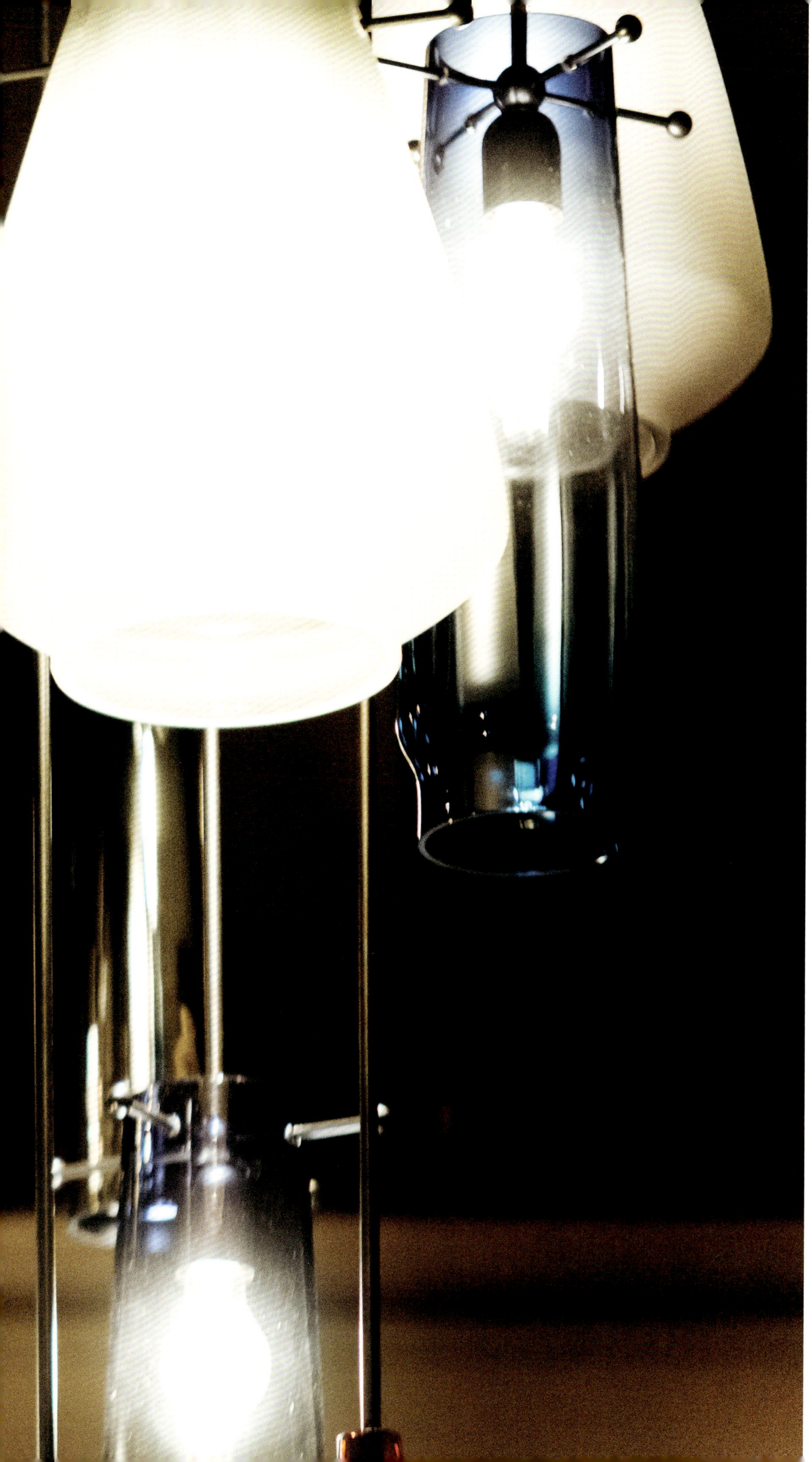

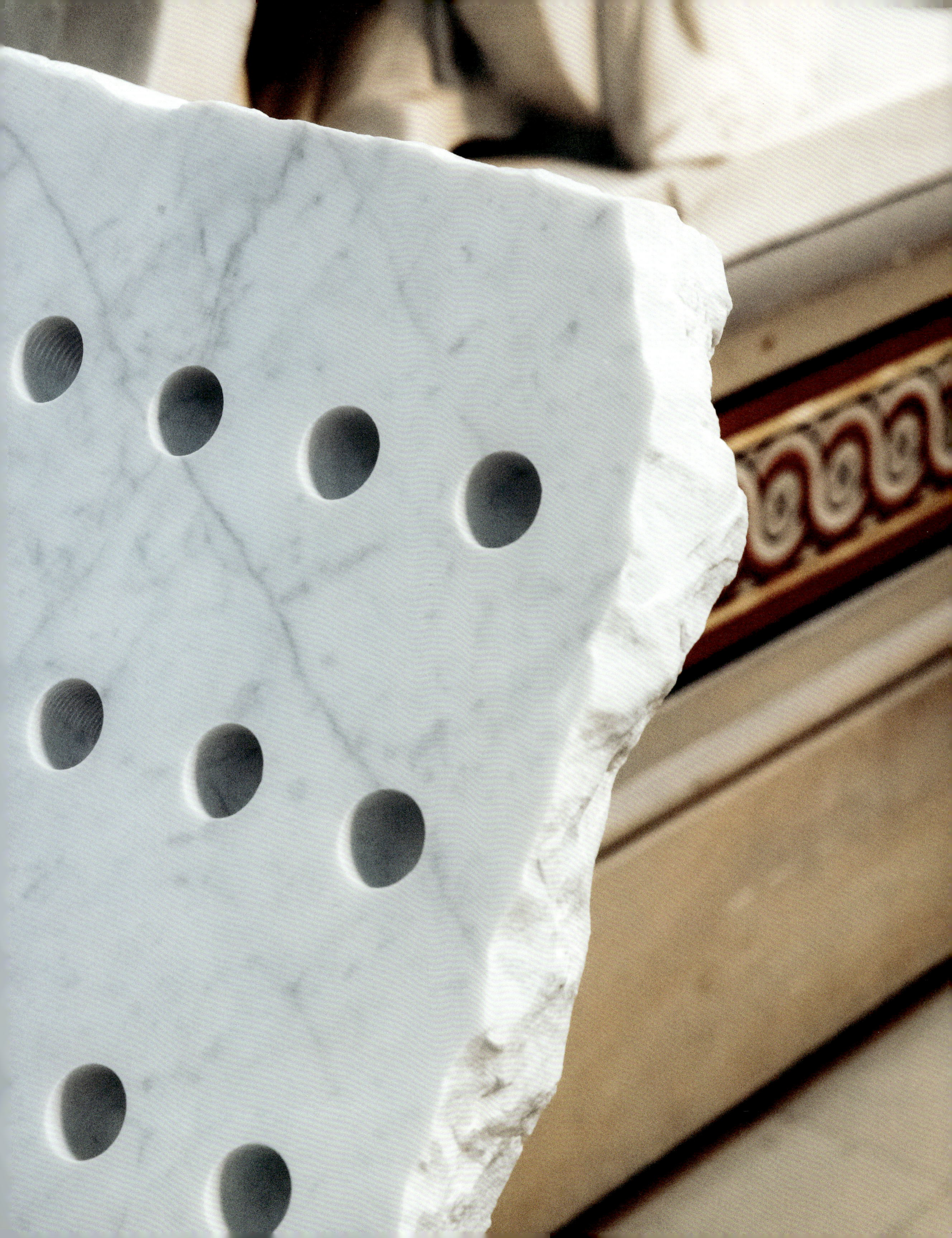

SAMUEL

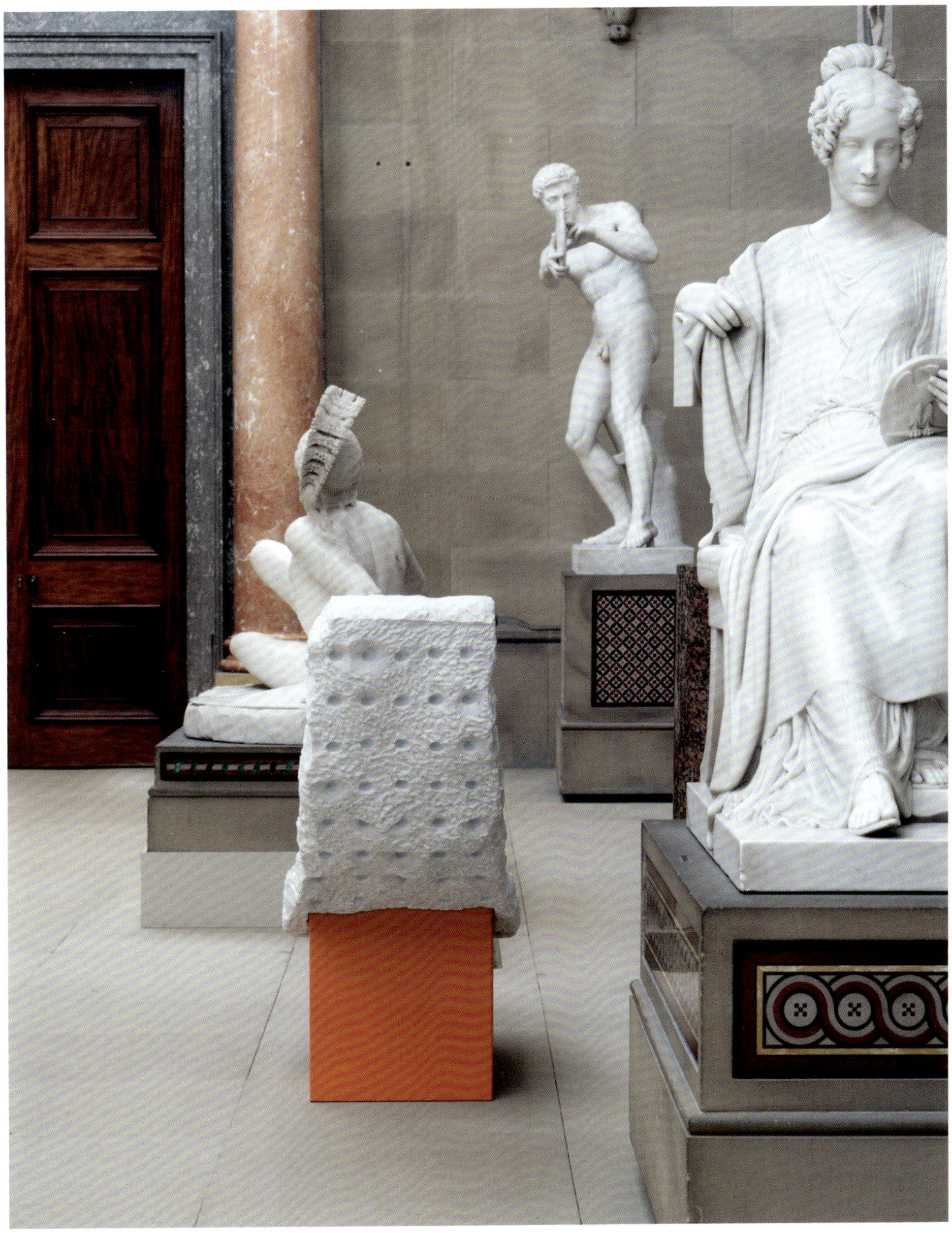

ROSS

A FRICTIONLESS PLANE IN WHICH ALL IDIOMS CAN CIRCULATE

No space at Chatsworth is grander, or more replete with cultural prestige, than the Sculpture Gallery. Created by the 6th Duke of Devonshire in the nineteenth century, the hall holds a virtual catalogue of classical ideals—one white marble figure after another, many supported by plinths that are artworks in their own right, geometries of exquisitely figured stone. Two of the sculptures represent reclining male figures from ancient mythology, Filippo Albacini's *The Wounded Achilles* (1825) and Antonio Canova's *The Sleeping Endymion* (1819–22). They are beautiful, elegant, and emotive—exactly the sort of works that are esteemed in the art historical canon.

Against this backdrop, we have placed four works by Samuel Ross, an explosive new star in the art and design firmament. After swerving smoothly into the cultural fast lane through his fashion label A-COLD-WALL*, founded in 2015, Ross has demonstrated a polymathic ability to move into other disciplines, including furniture design, which he creates through his studio SR_A. *Mirror Mirror* features four works from this output, one of which was made for the exhibition. They are made partly of marble, reiterating the Sculpture Gallery's primary art material, and partly of steel, powder-coated in his vivid signature colour, Volt Orange.

Ross has referred to himself as an 'atypical protagonist' in the elevated field of the arts. He grew up in the housing estates of Brixton and the East Midlands, navigating an architectural fabric of postwar brutalism. That aesthetic has stayed with him, both as a stylistic influence and a conceptual matrix. He is fascinated by the utopian promise of modernism, but also its blind spots, which he relentlessly illuminates. In modernism, there was a preference for the industrial over the antique, and the abstract over the figurative. In the Sculpture Gallery, of course, the priority is the other way around. What Ross proposes, however, is that all of these hierarchies are invalid. He instead treats the terrain of art and design as flat, a frictionless plane in which all idioms can circulate. Thereby much energy is generated, and in the unexpected company of Ross's futuristic objects, *Achilles* and *Endymion*, those inert, nude bodies cloaked in veneration, are stirred into lively correspondence. They are suddenly, newly relevant—as everything potentially is, in Ross's omnivorous imagination.

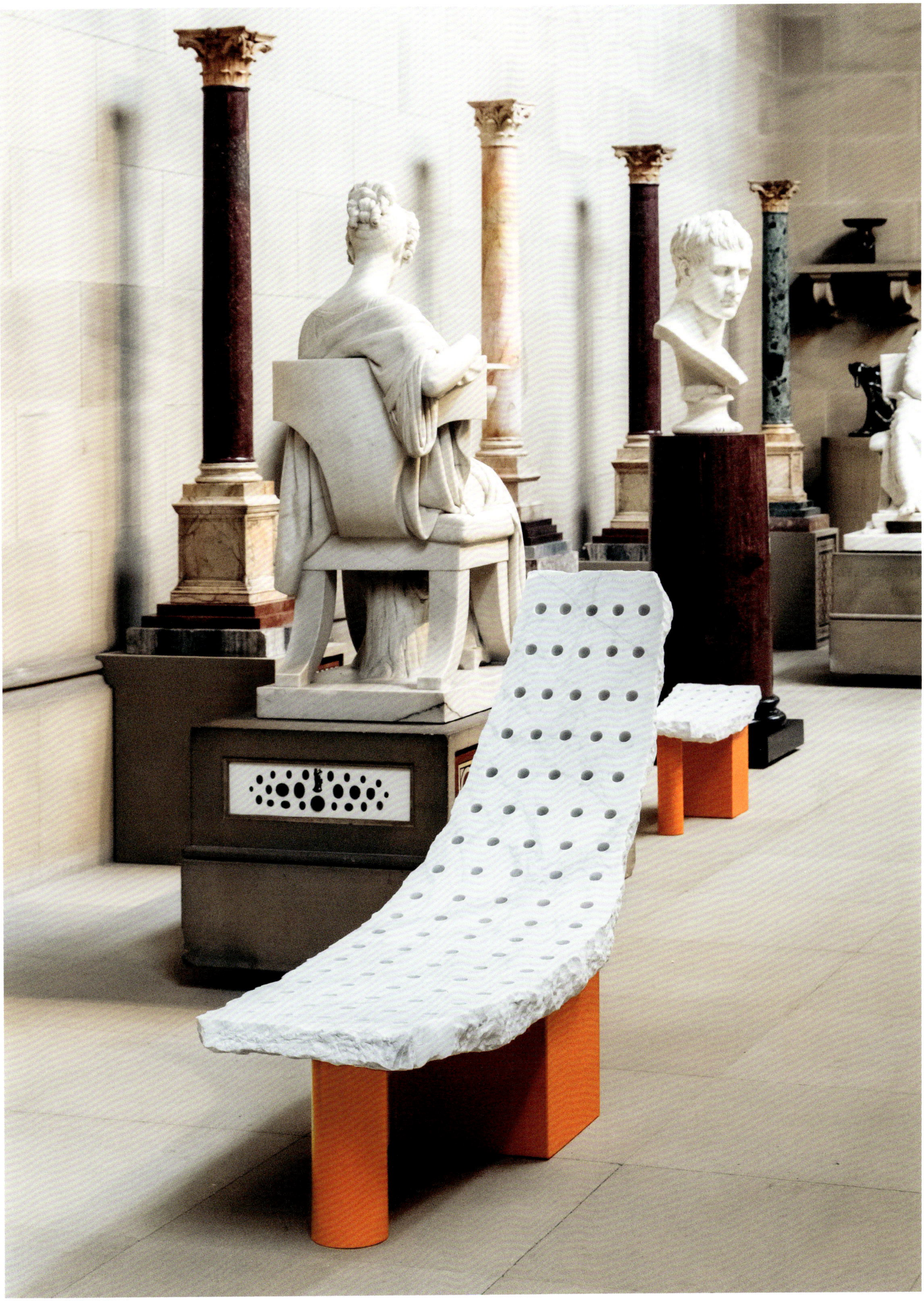

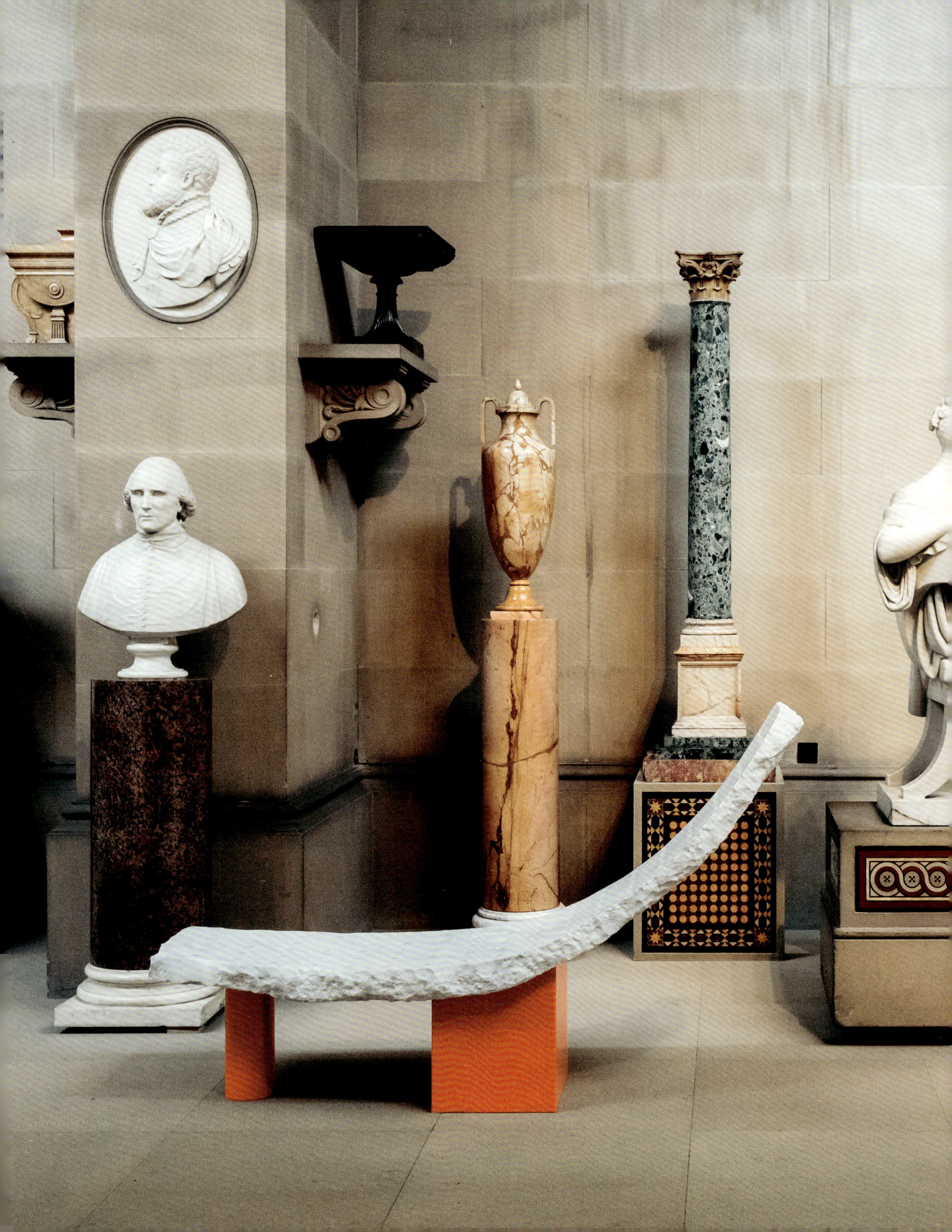

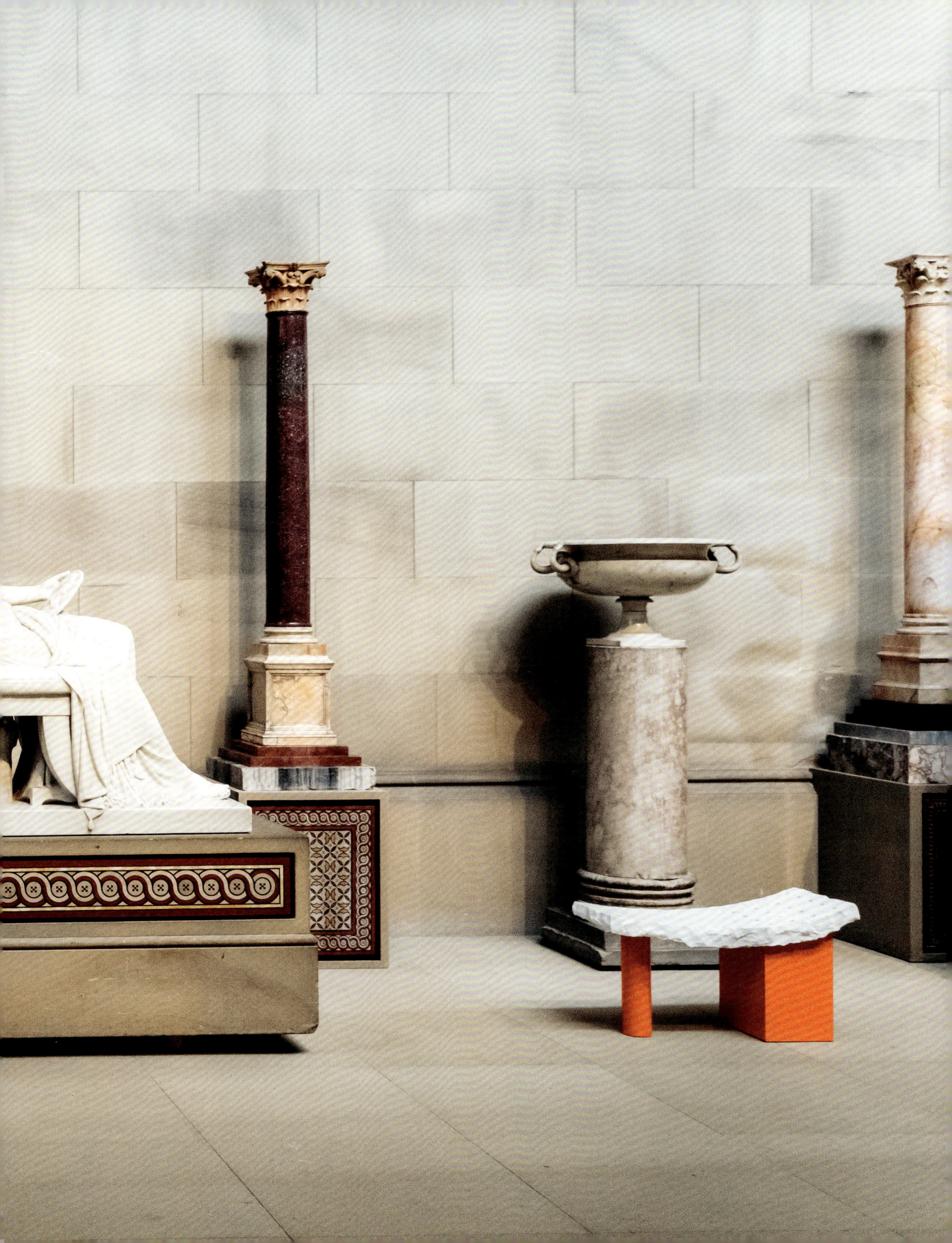

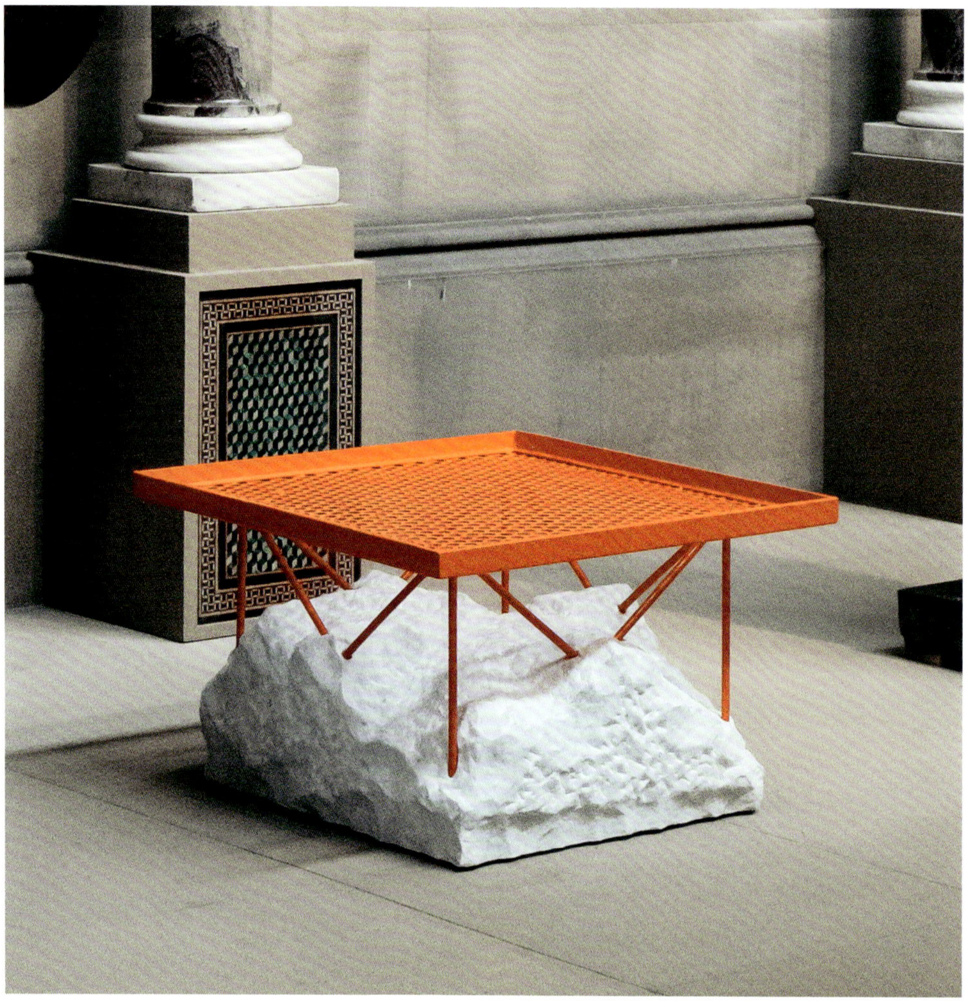

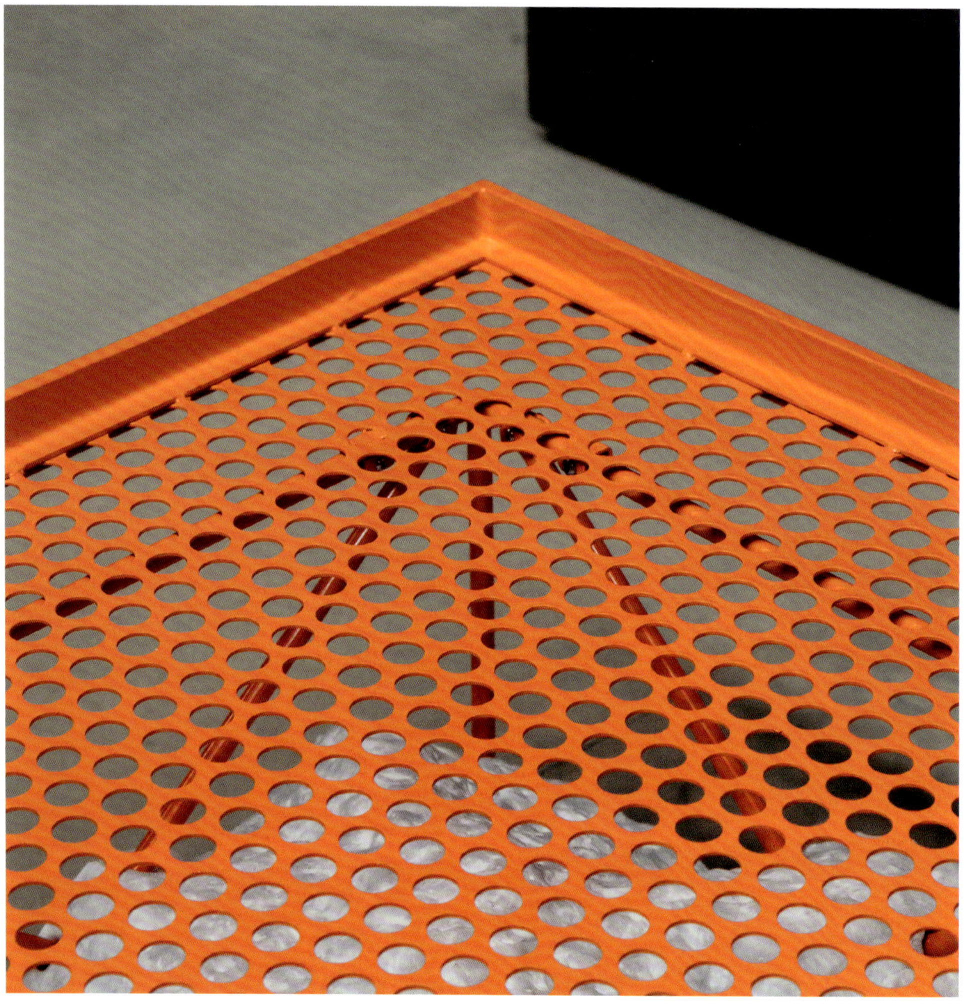

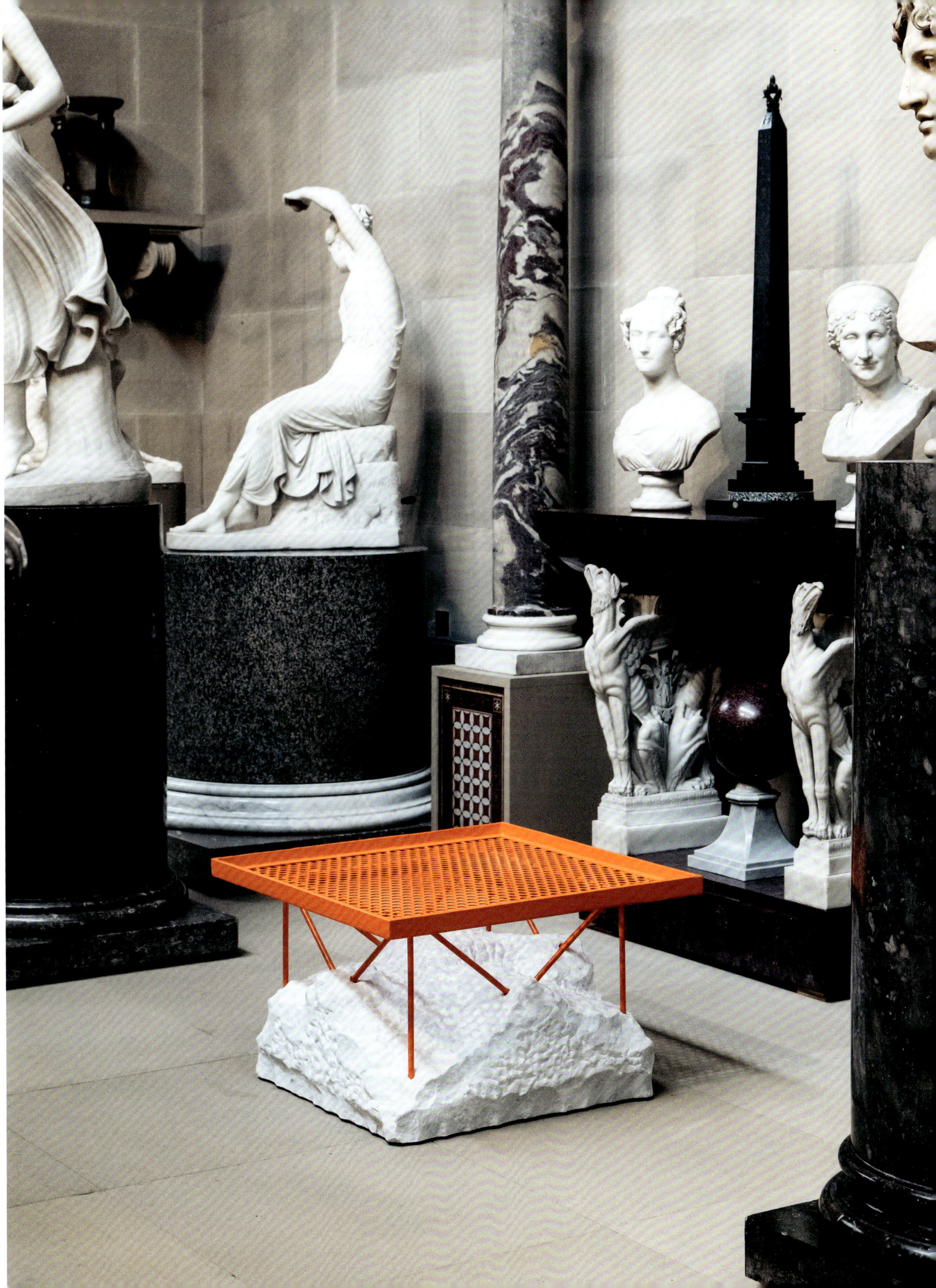

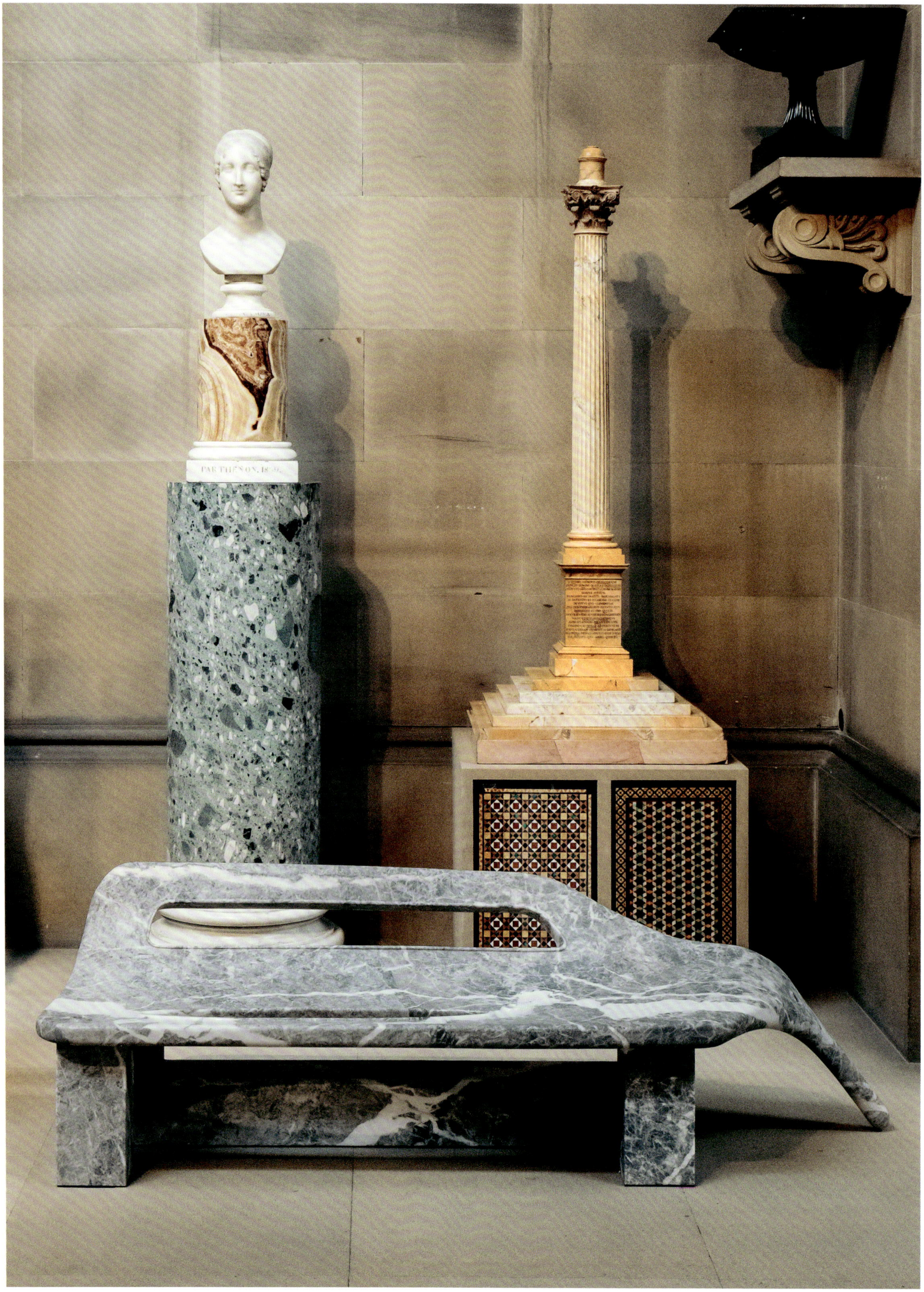

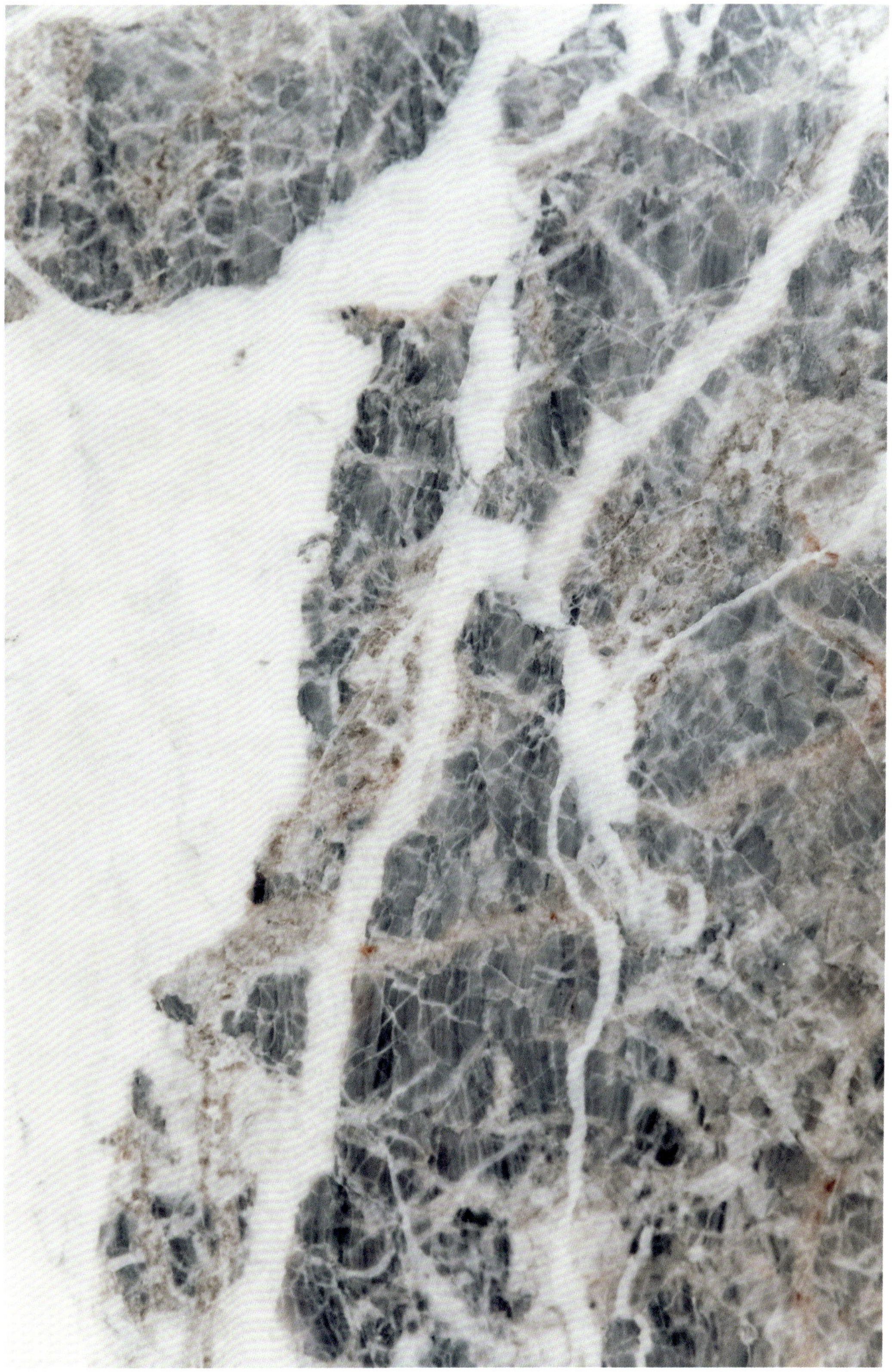

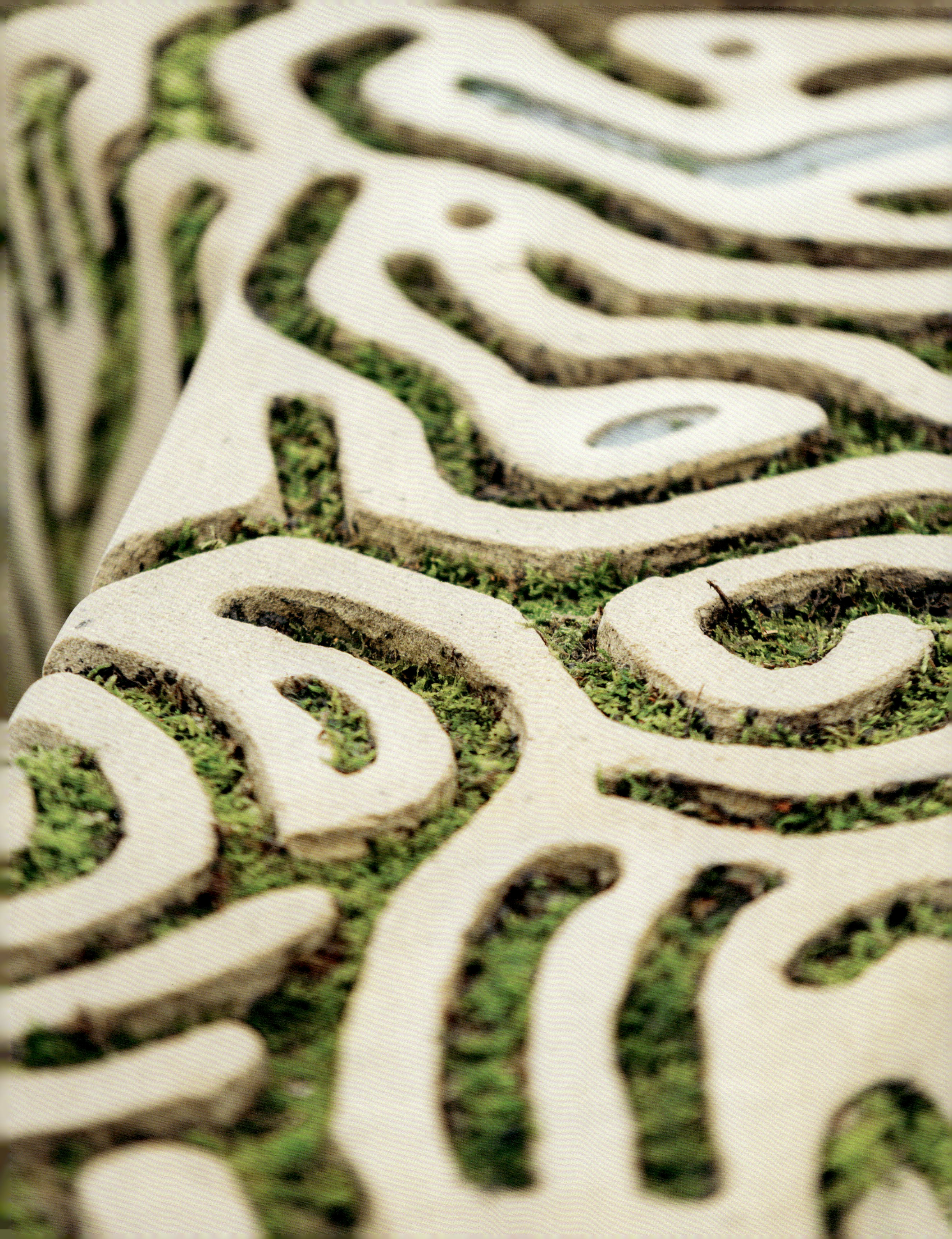

JORIS

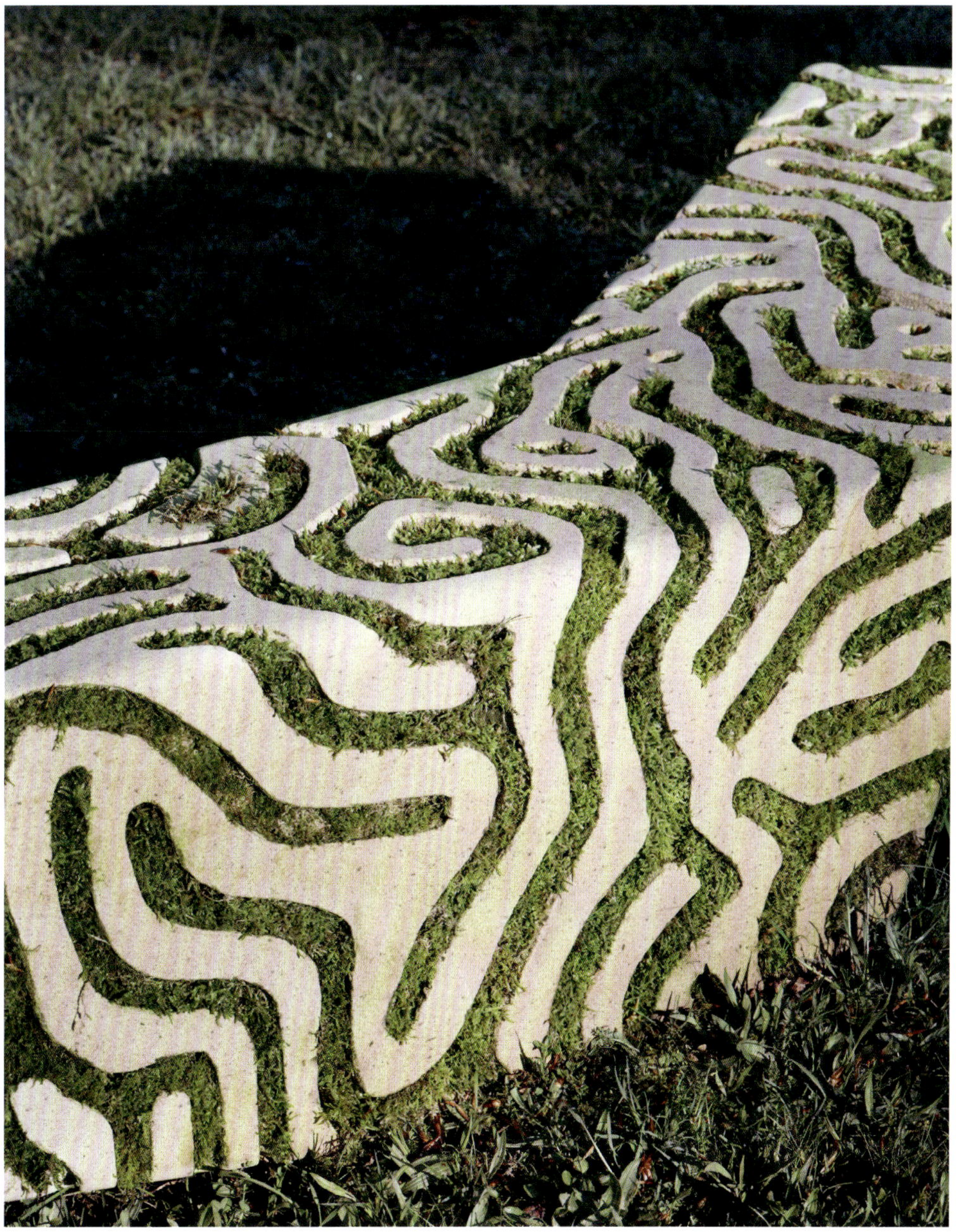

LAARMAN

‘A RADICALLY DIFFERENT TIME SCALE THAN MODERN LIFE’S HASTINESS’

JORIS LAARMAN

Many contemporary designers are thinking about how to design in a more environmentally sustainable manner. Joris Laarman is going one step further. Having already explored the relationship between the analogue and the digital in his earlier career—as in the *Maker* benches, which welcome visitors at the start of the *Mirror Mirror* exhibition—he is now bridging the divide between the artificial and the organic. His goal is to make his pieces in actual collaboration with nature, allowing living things to take an active part in the making of the work. This is the intention behind *Symbio,* a ‘bio-receptive’ furniture project intended to accommodate organic life. The pieces have channels cut into them in a computer-generated maze pattern inspired by the theories of pioneering mathematician Alan Turing. (This motif often appears in Laarman’s work.) The recessed areas are lined with a phosphate-rich cement, or ‘mosscrete’, which encourages plant growth by providing water retention and frost resistance, as well as elementary fertiliser. The rest of the surface, conversely, is treated with an eco-friendly water-repellent coating. As a result, mosses and lichens—‘pioneer organisms that exist in a radically different time scale than modern life’s hastiness’, as Laarman notes—slowly but surely populate the pieces, but only in the carved recesses, completing a graphic image that traverses their shapes. Rather than keeping nature at a safe distance, as industrial design tends to do, here it is welcomed and nurtured.

The project has been executed in the most ecologically sensitive way possible. The stone used is from Chatsworth’s own quarry—the same distinctive figure, with its swirls of pale mineral brown, can be seen throughout the house’s facade and interiors. It was hand-carved by a local mason, based on Laarman’s 3D digital models. The plant life that is propagated on the pieces is more local yet, coming as it does from the ground just underneath, gaining nutrients from the sky above. Laarman has considered making a similar piece that would support a tree, its roots finding secure purchase in the channels. He reckons it would take about fifteen years to realise—a very long time in design, but just a fleeting moment in the story of life on earth.

We have positioned the *Symbio* benches on the upper reaches of a lawn that has been in continuous hand-mowing for about two centuries, which is untouched by modern fertilisers or pesticides, and consequently has an abundant and diverse ecosystem. Move Laarman’s works even a few hundred feet away, and they might end up looking quite different. No matter their location, however, they will serve a long-term diagnostic function—the healthier the environment around them, the more pronounced their surface pattern will become, as it is continually painted by the hand of nature.

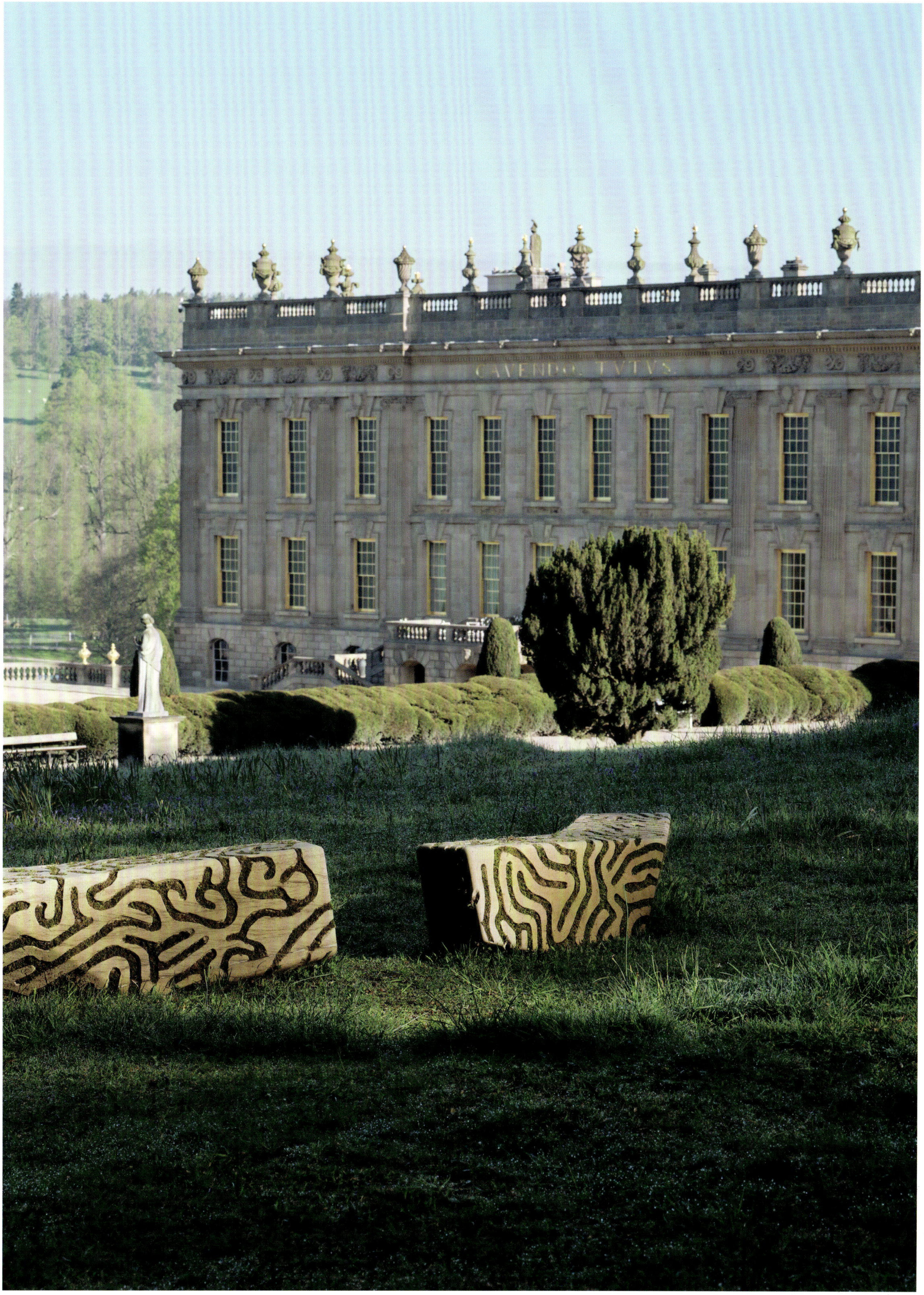

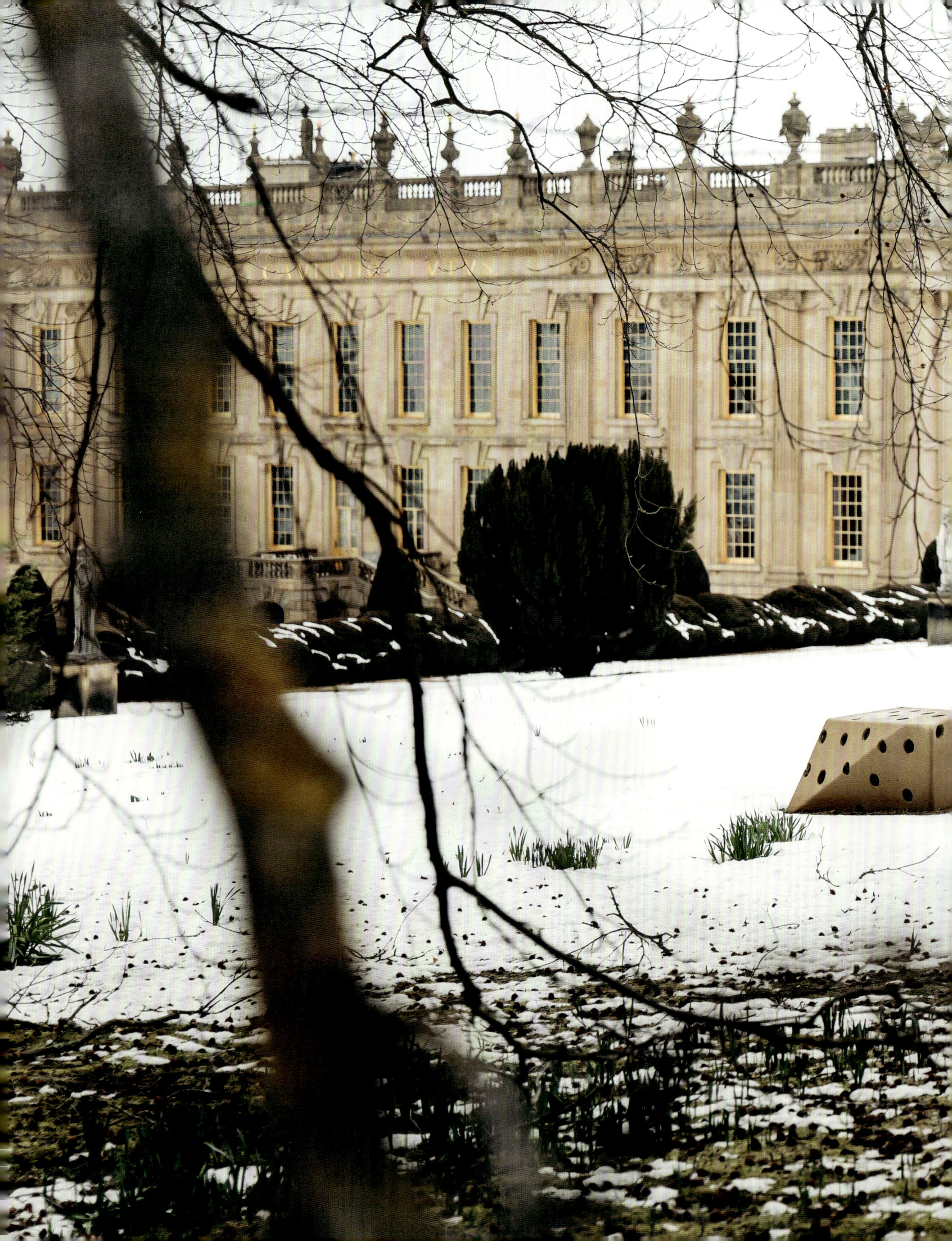

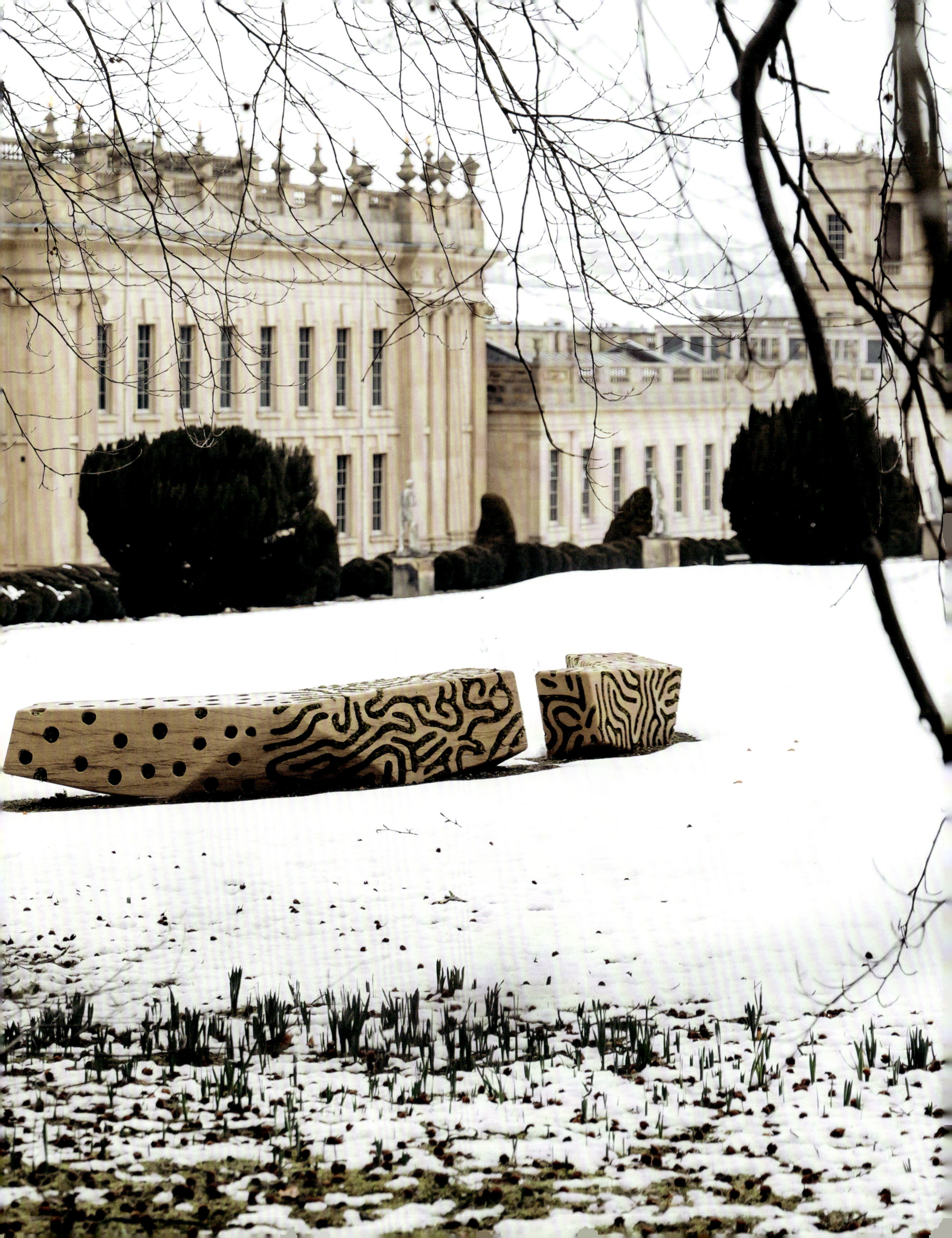

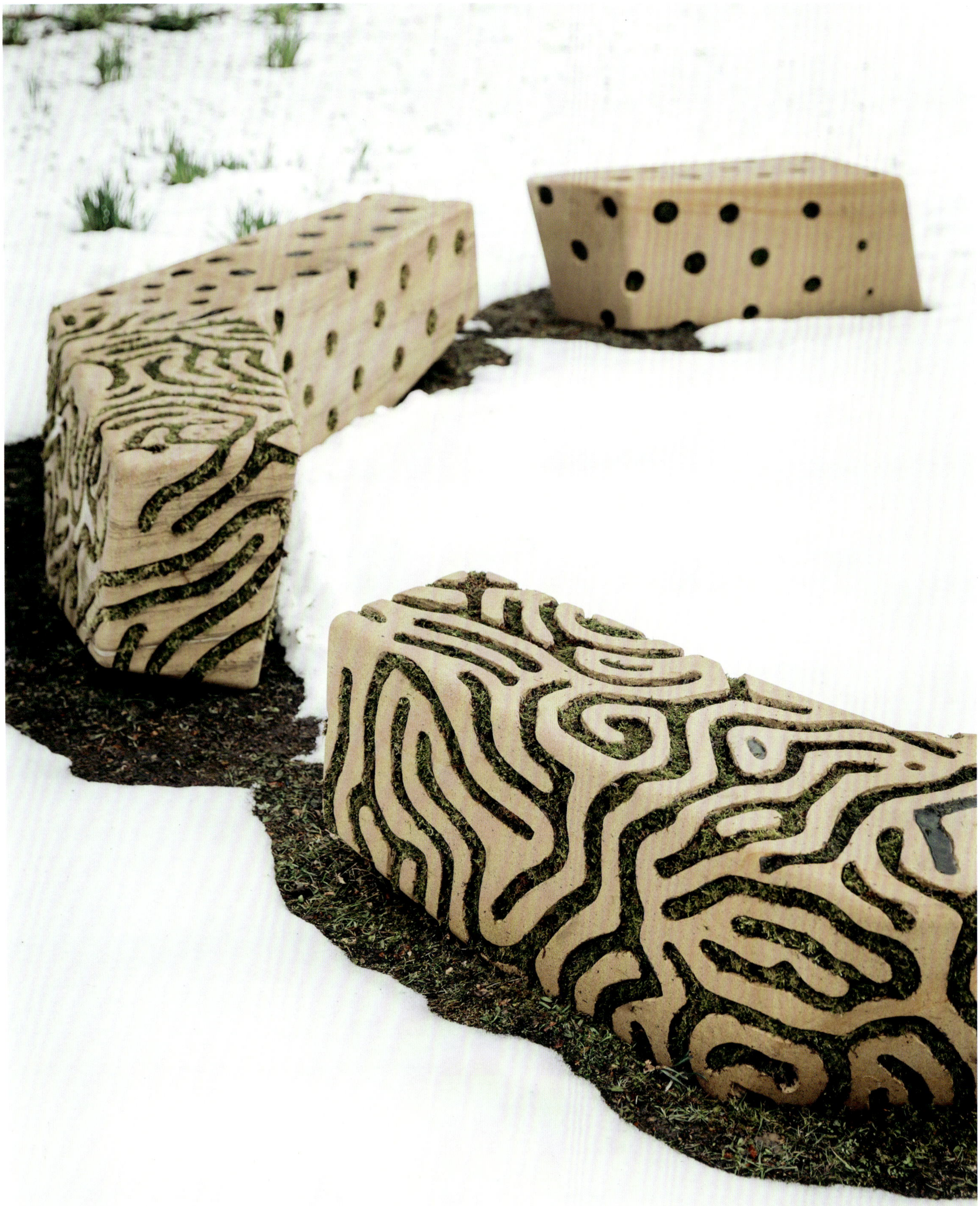

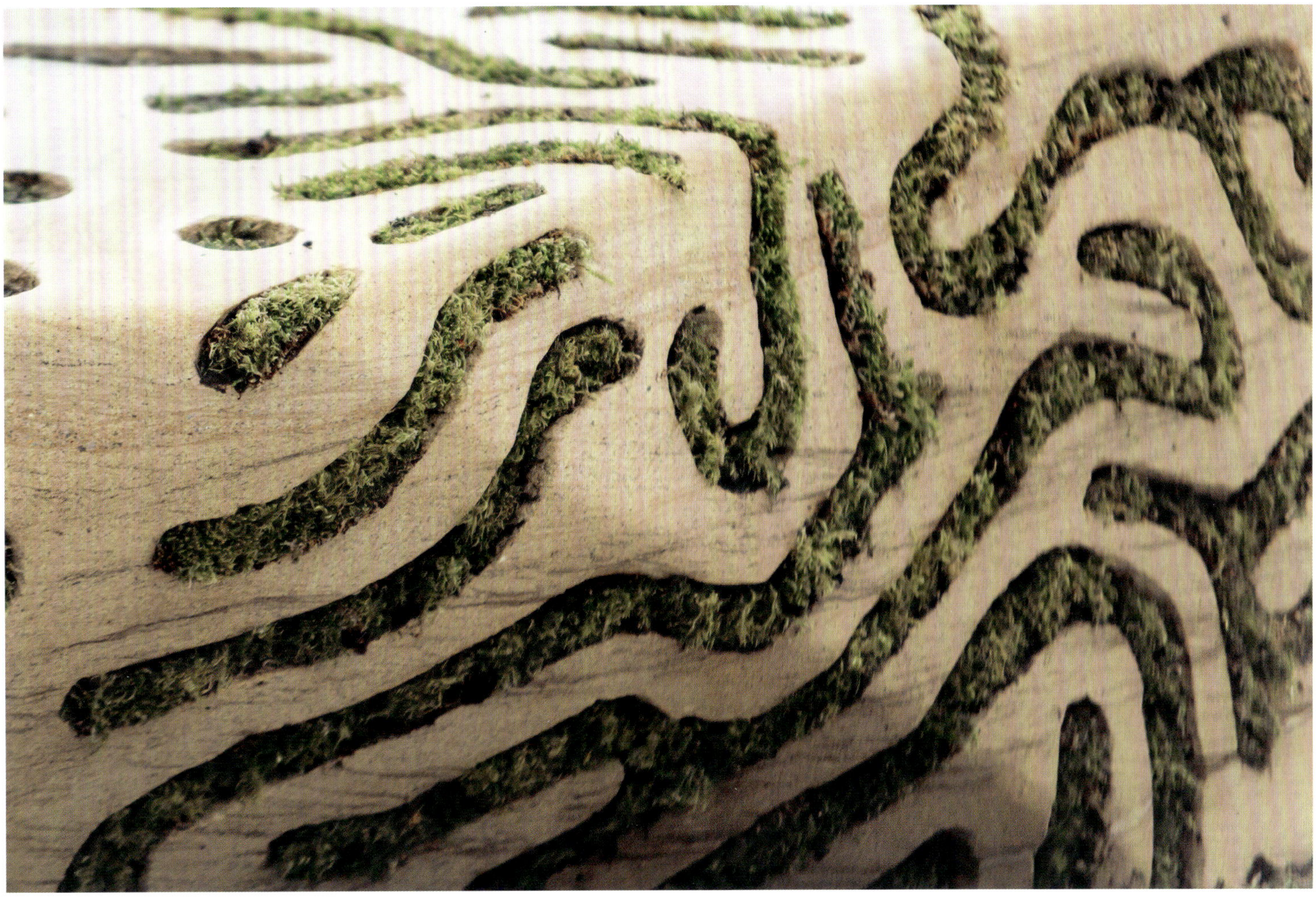

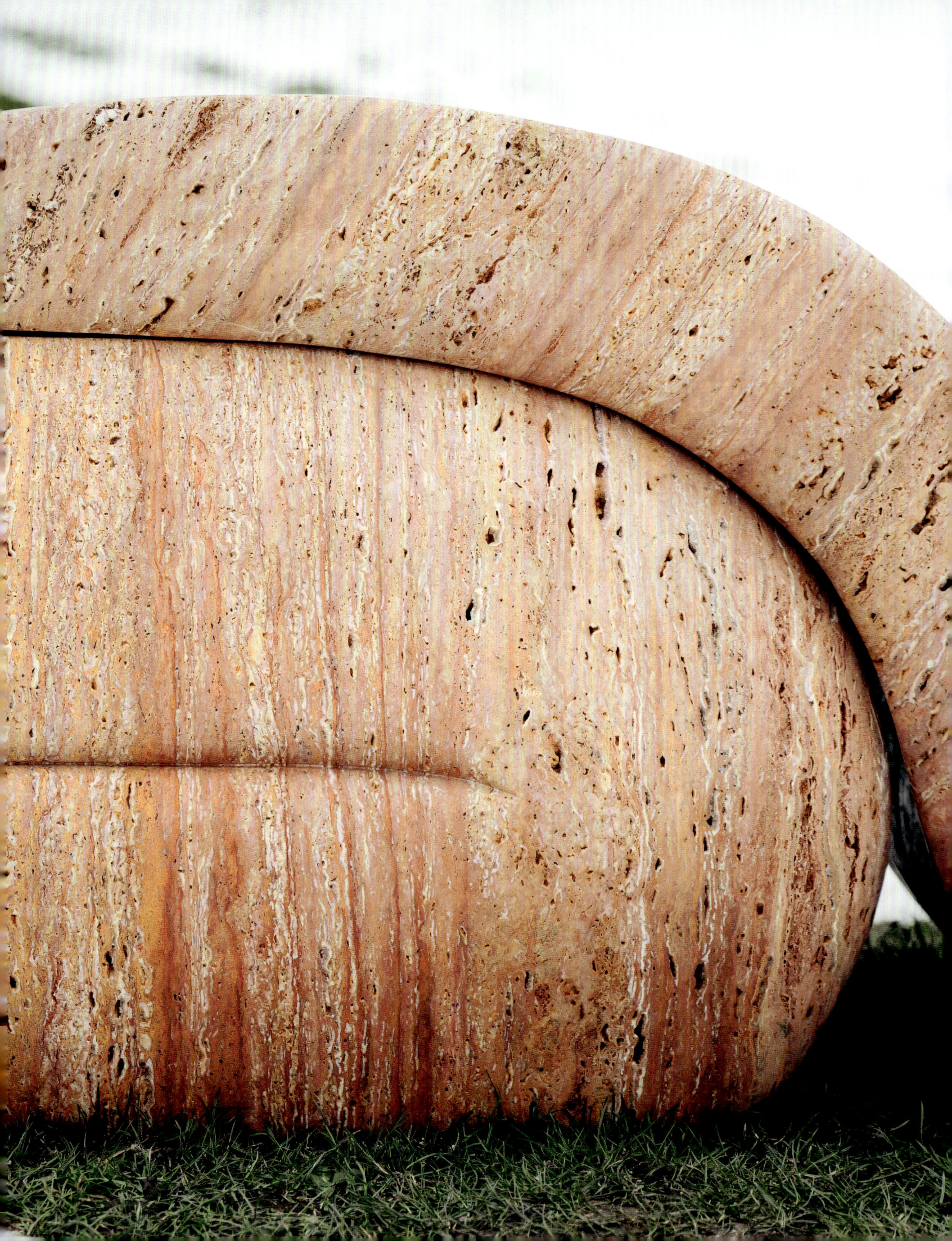

NAJLA

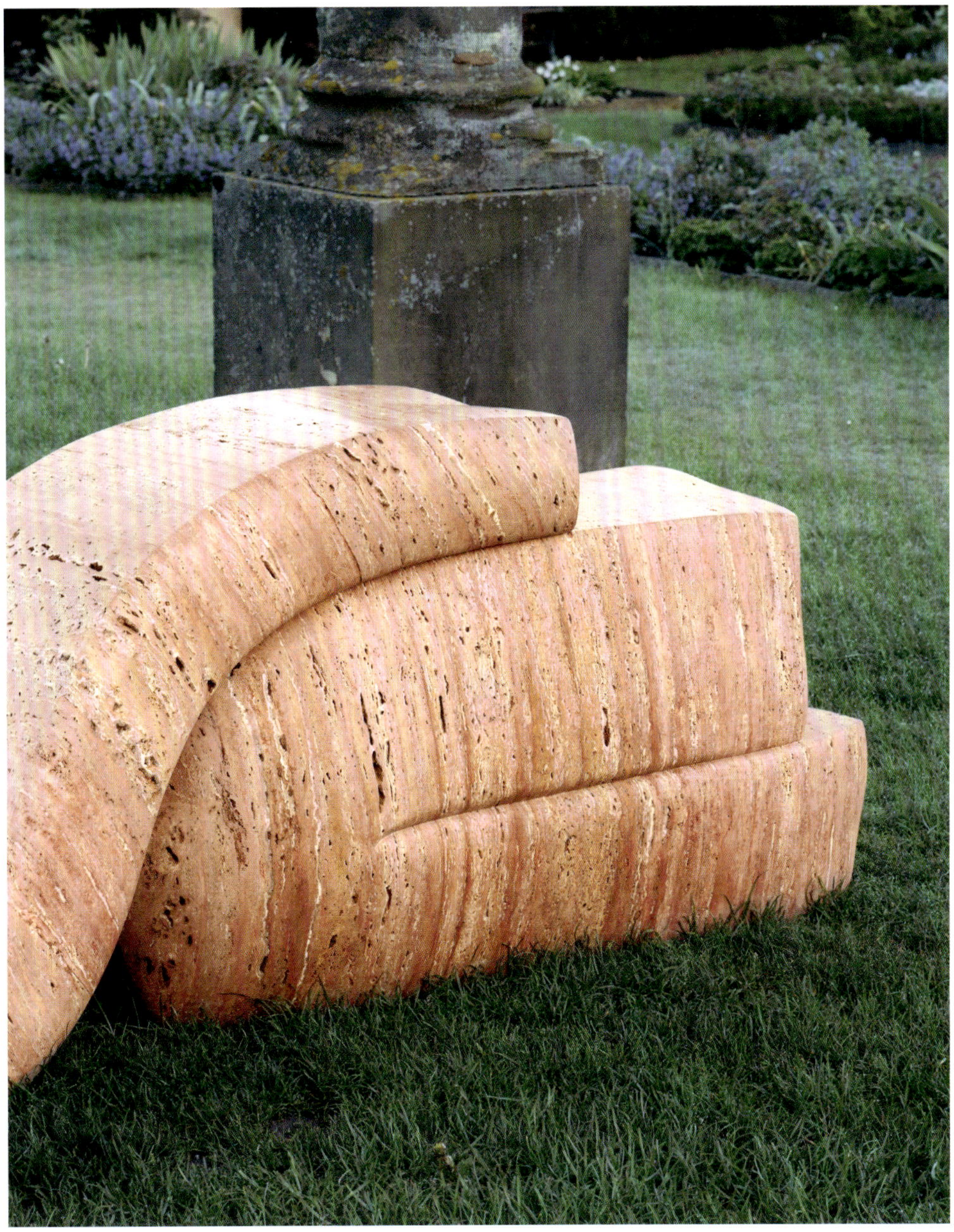

EL ZEIN

SHAPES TOO ESSENTIAL TO BE SIMPLY READ

Najla El Zein tells stories through her objects—but not in any straightforward way. She creates (she might say 'finds') shapes that resemble those of human bodies and convey the emotional complexity of our relationships to one another. Yet the narrative thrust that one might expect from such an exploration, in her hands, is quieted down to a murmur. Like sculptures by Barbara Hepworth or Isamu Noguchi, the shapes are too essential to be simply read; El Zein wants them to remain open to interpretation.

Seduction, Pair 06 is a perfect example of this approach. Initially modelled in clay, the shape was hand carved to El Zein's specifications, retaining the pliancy of the original maquette. It is one work from a series that traces the interactions of two abstract, changeable forms. One might be legible as male, the other female, though even this is hard to know for sure. What's certain is that there is a sensuous connection between the two. Each work in the series is carved in a particular type of stone, appropriate to the mood of that piece. Thus, *Seduction, Pair 06*, which seems to depict a moment of intimacy or affection, is executed in an Iranian red travertine, which gives the piece an all-over warm flush.

In *Mirror Mirror*, we placed the work in Chatsworth's gardens, setting it near the house against the backdrop of a colonnade, each pillar topped with a bust. This context highlights the degree to which El Zein does, and does not, follow the norms of figural sculpture. Most important, perhaps, is the offer she extends to interact with the work, perhaps just by sitting on it; perhaps caressing its cool, smooth surface; perhaps recalling moments that felt something like this. Either way, you're adding the work's story to your own.

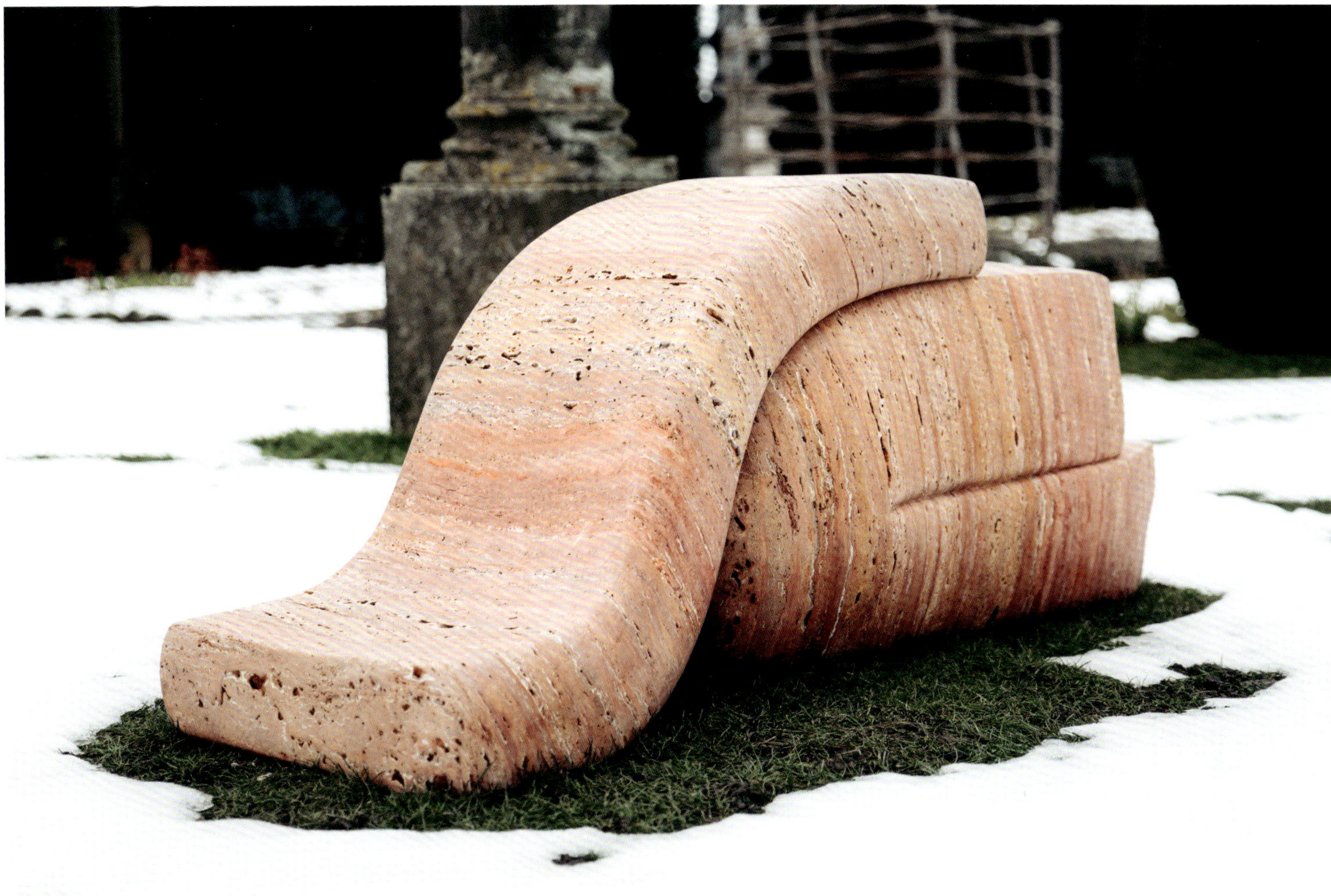

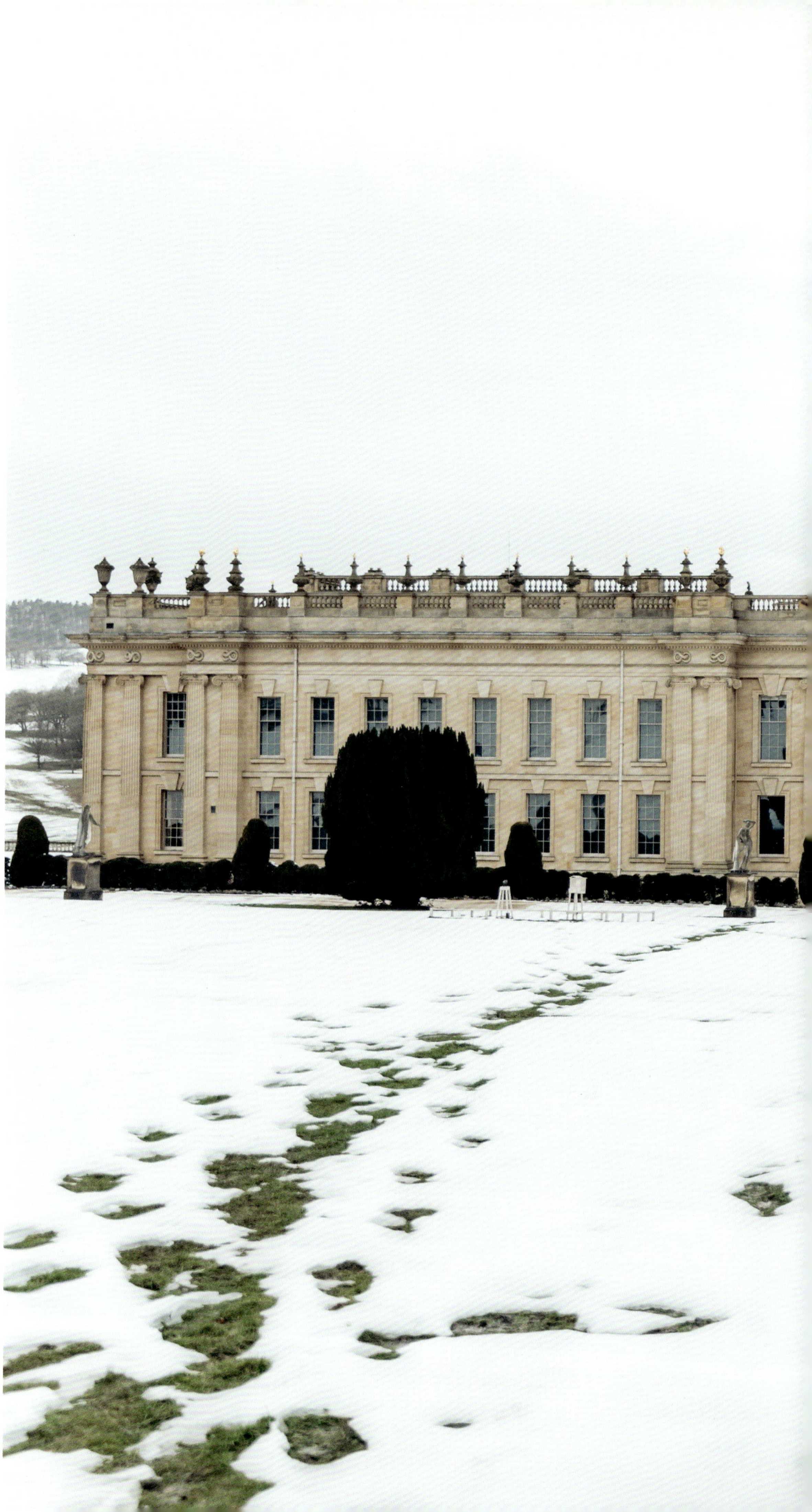

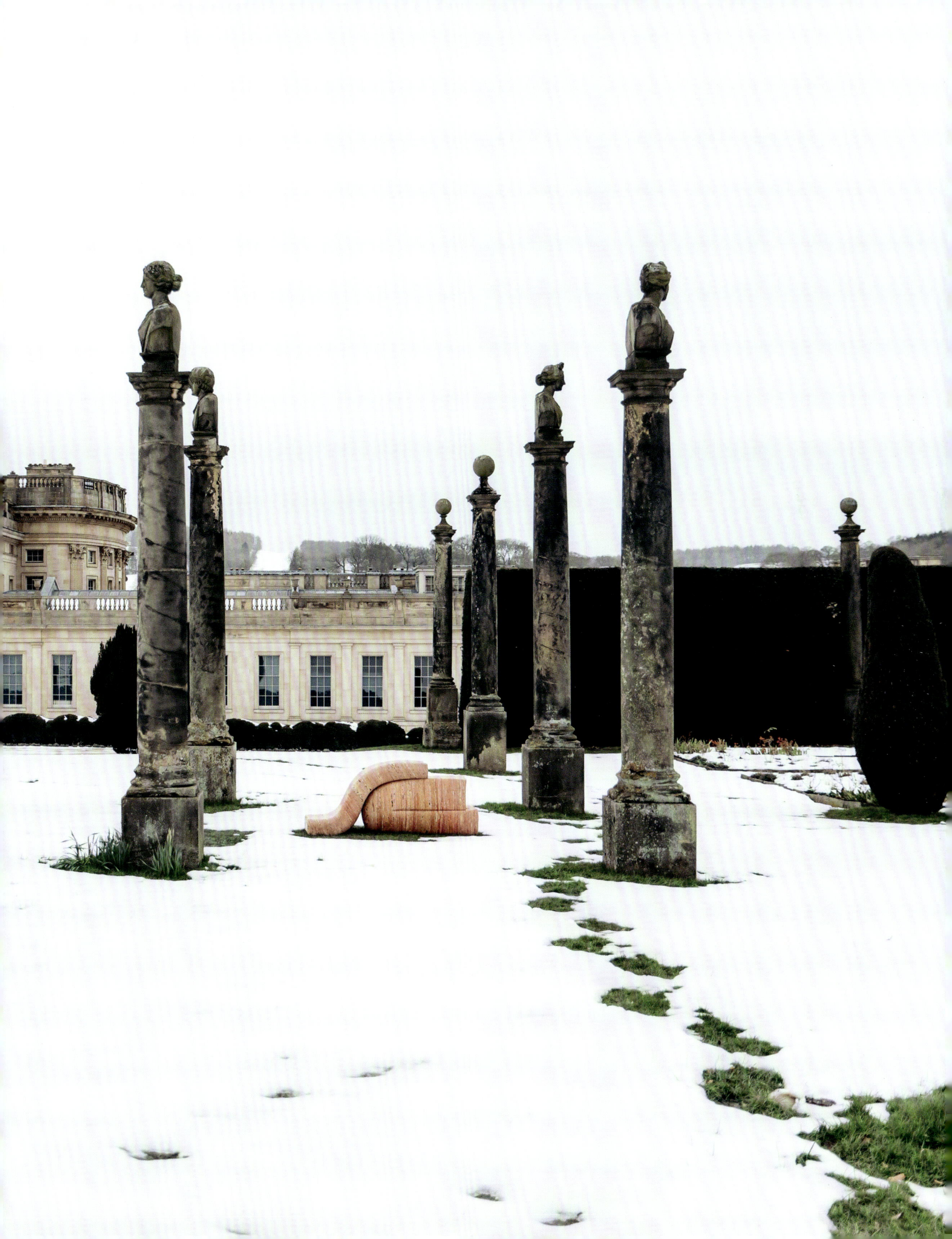

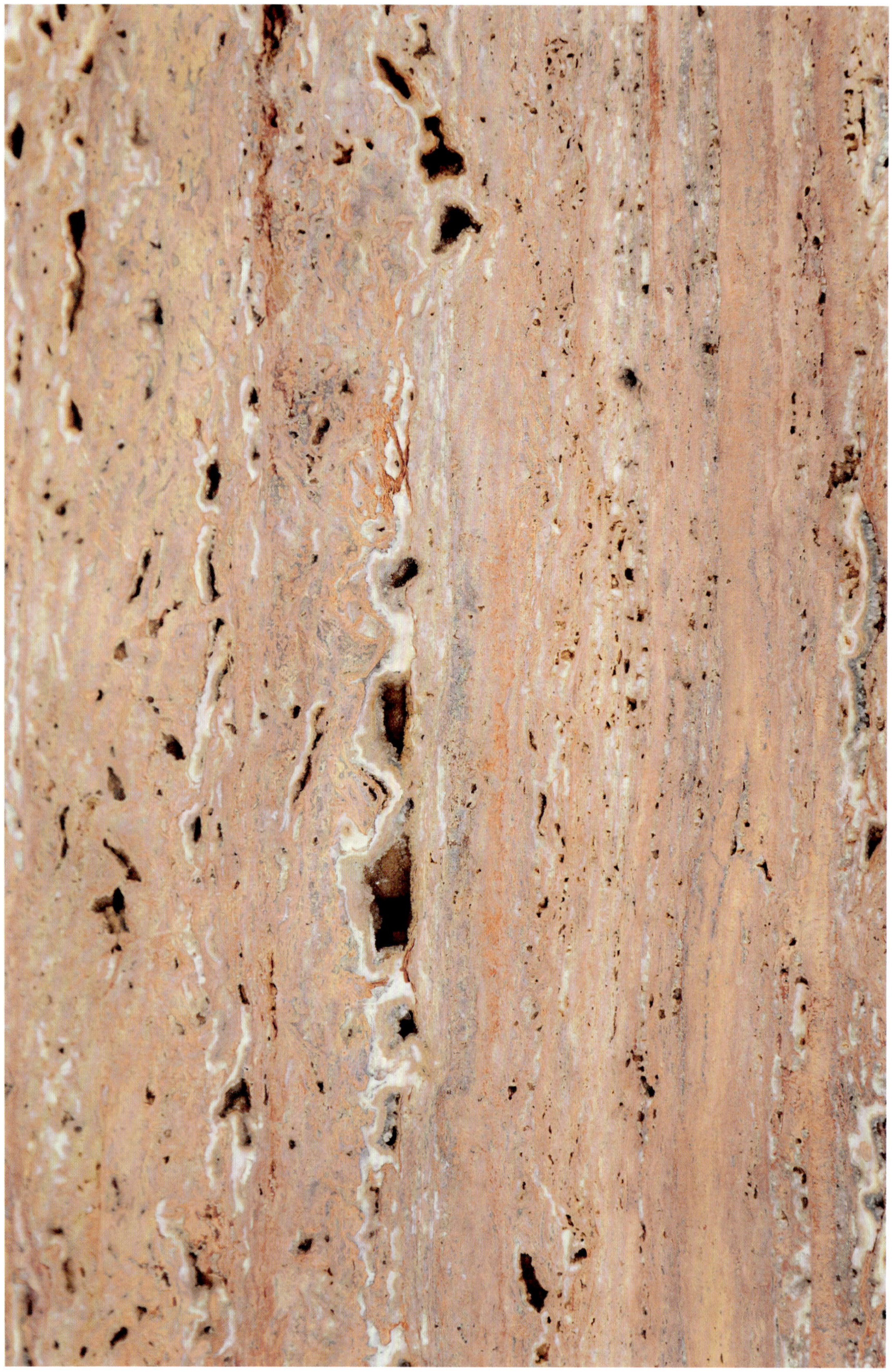

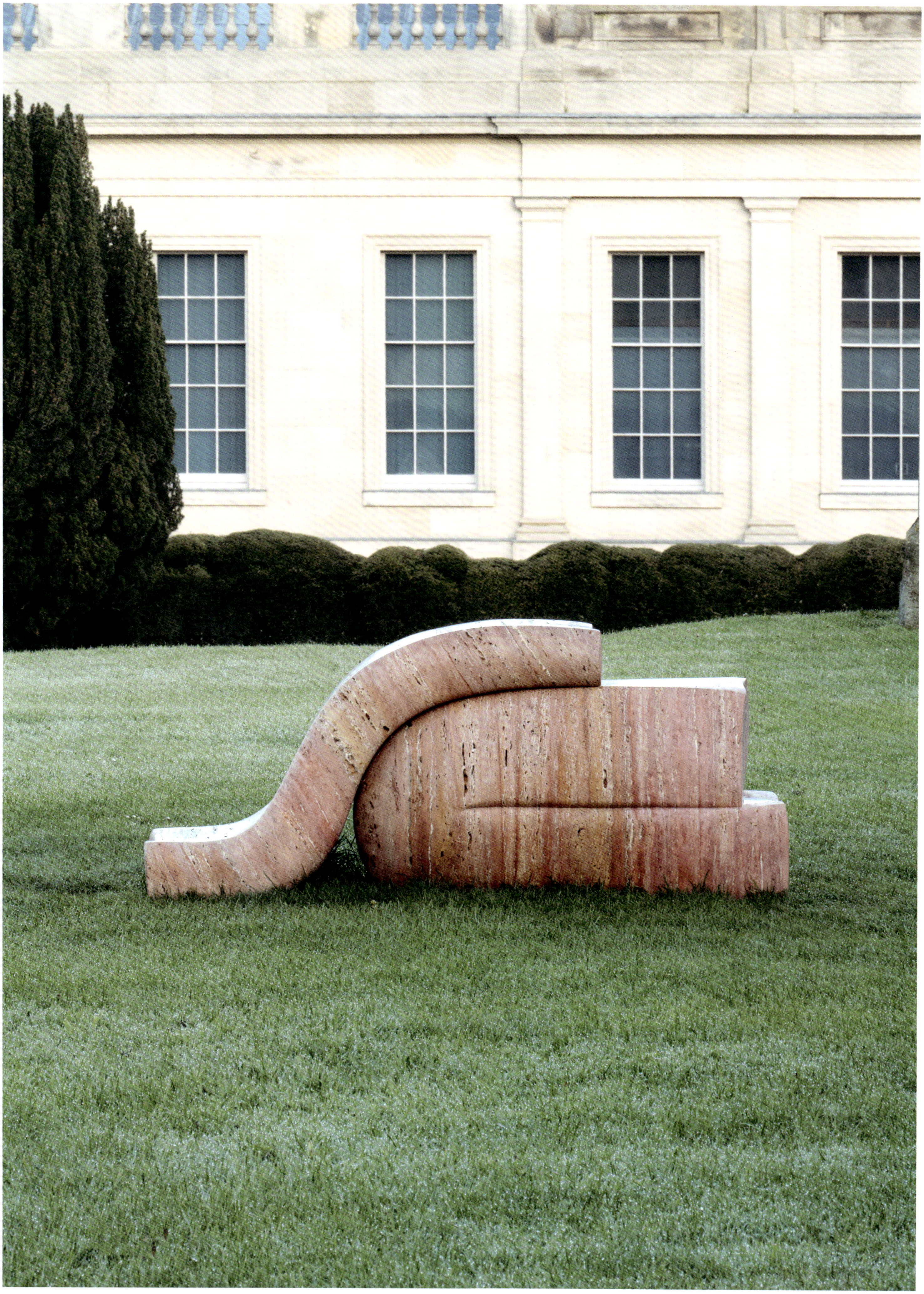

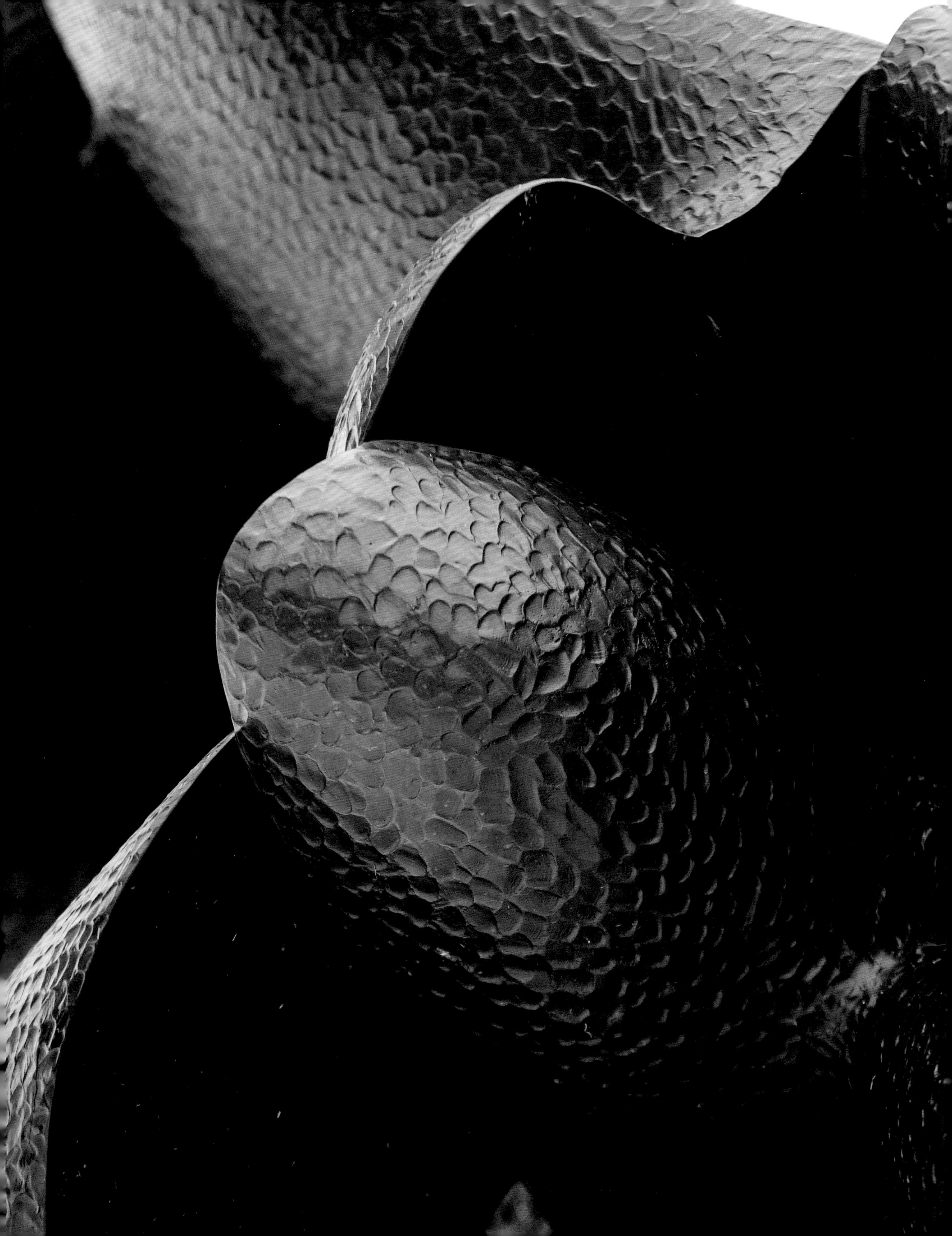

WENDELL

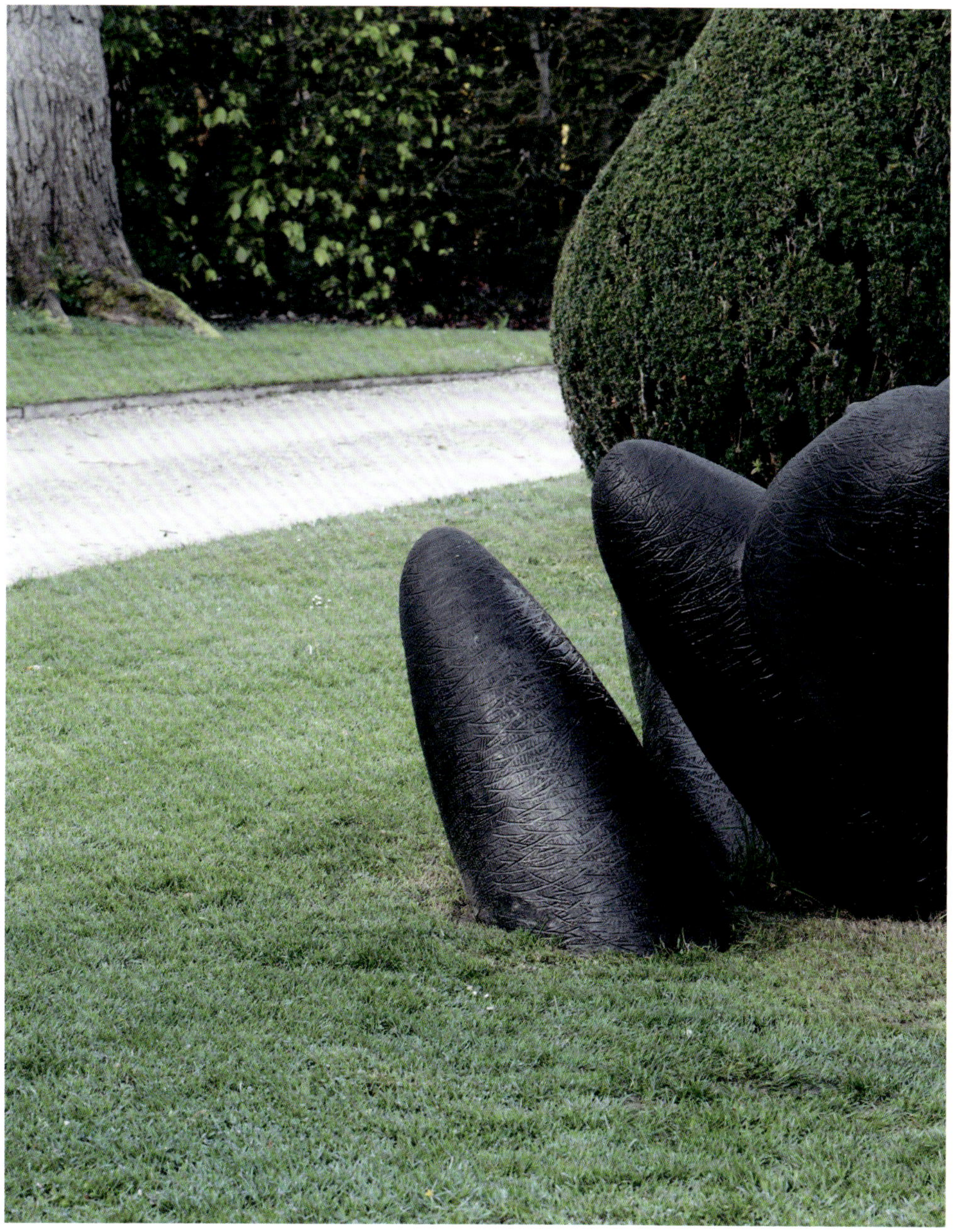

CASTLE

A CLOSELY RELATED RHYTHM

Although the late Wendell Castle (1932–2018) was the leading American furniture designer of his generation, he started his career studying sculpture, and never really left it. As far as he was concerned, the conventional methods of joinery and construction were less intriguing than the prospect of inventing his own way.

And this is just what he did. His breakthrough body of work, developed in the early 1960s, was made using an innovative technique called 'stack lamination', in which Castle glued shaped wood planks together, then contoured them using a chainsaw and other tools. The result was a curvaceous volume, wholly freed from the logic of conventional furniture. He could explore any shape he pleased, at massive scale.

Towards the end of his career Castle revisited these early works, making new stack laminated forms in timber, as well as related forms in bronze. These were based on hand-carved models, which were digitally enlarged, roughed out using a robotic carving tool, then extensively hand-finished; in the case of the bronzes, the pieces were then cast, and finally patinated. For *Mirror Mirror* we have gathered three bronze settees from this late body of work, placing them along the edge of a reflecting pool in Chatsworth's gardens. The trio shows the myriad possibilities of Castle's process. Each is a variation on a typology that he had introduced back in the 1960s, the three-person settee, but they vary in surface texture, patina, and overall composition.

In the first piece, *A New Seeing*, the concave seats are cut through at various angles, creating a strong contrast between gentle curvature and abrupt smash-joints. *Illusion-Reality-Truth* has a closely-related rhythm, but the seats are modulated into one another horizontally, and cantilevered from a cluster of vertical finger-like forms. *Temptation*, finally, is dominated by a single long seat that rides along an understructure of toppling forms, like a boat over waves. Together, the pieces testify to Castle's prolific imagination, a perfect match for the organic luxuriance of the surrounding gardens.

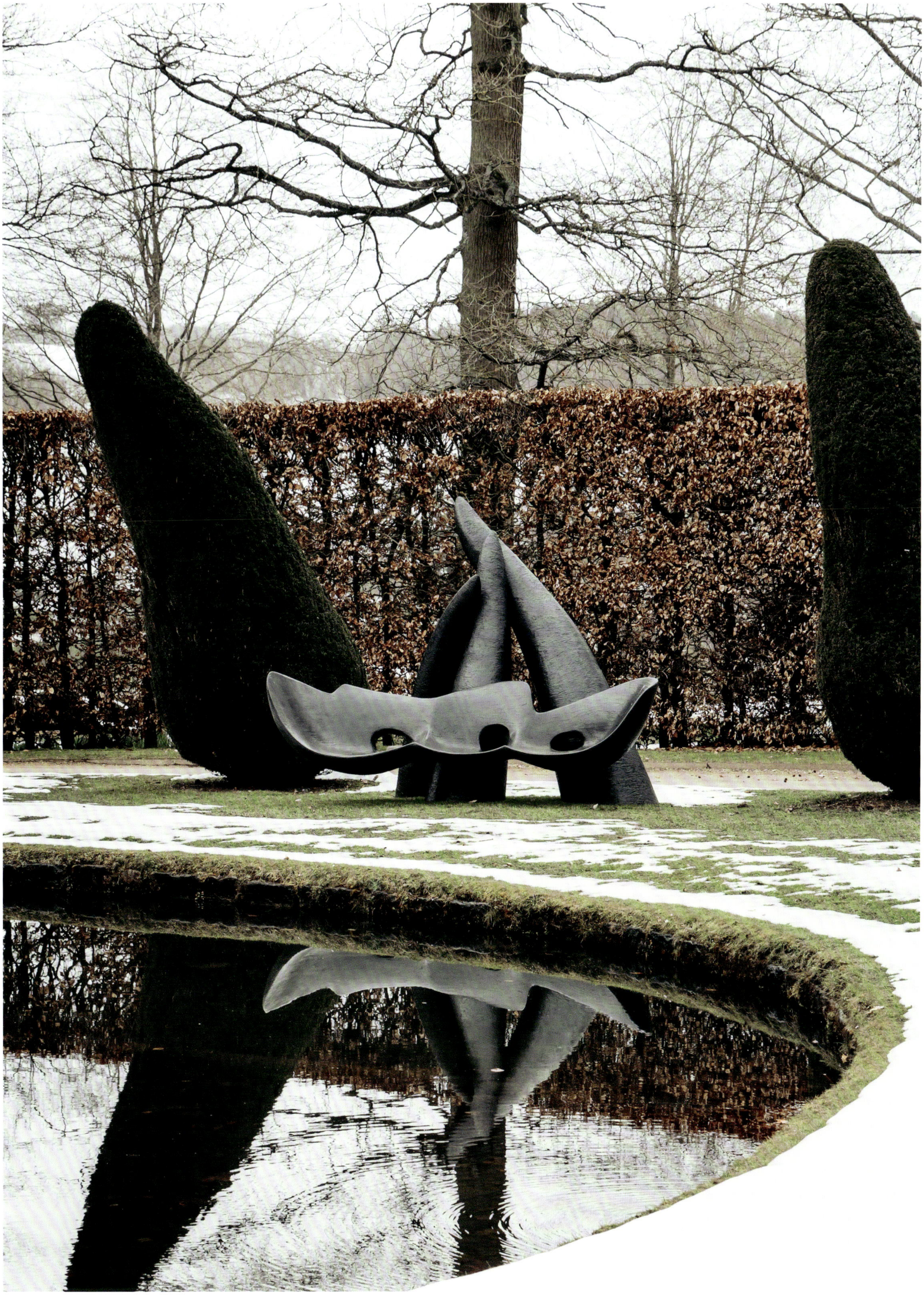

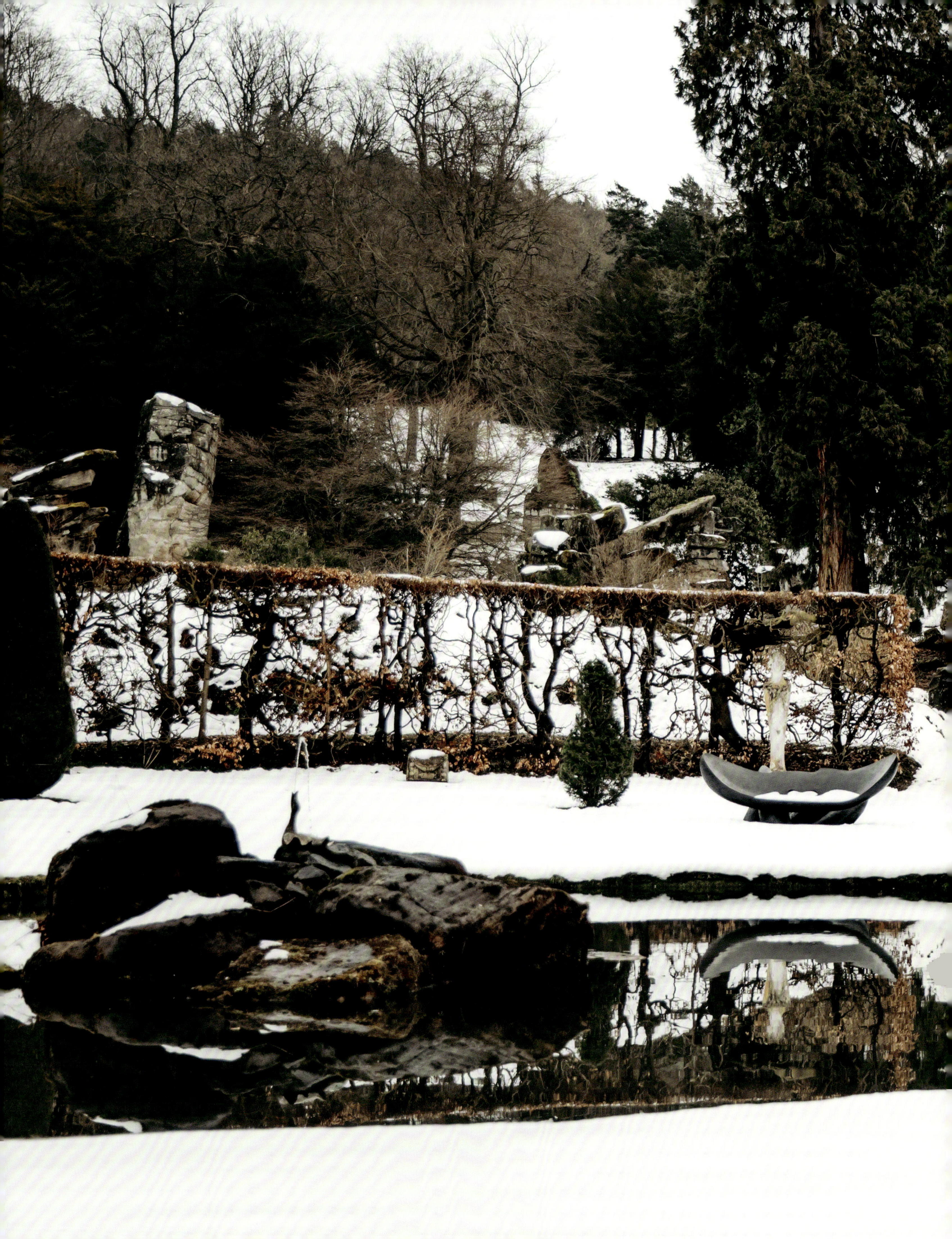

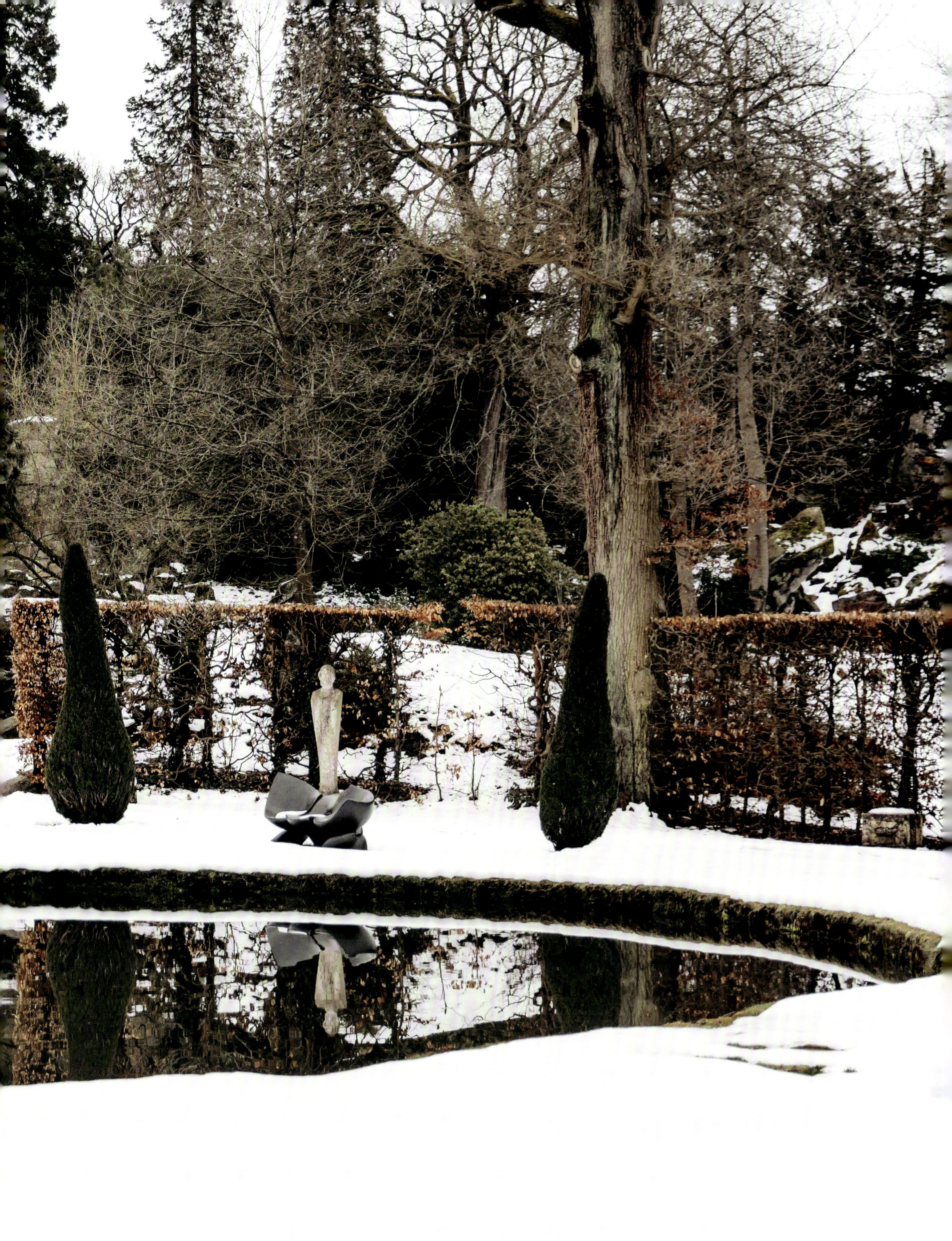

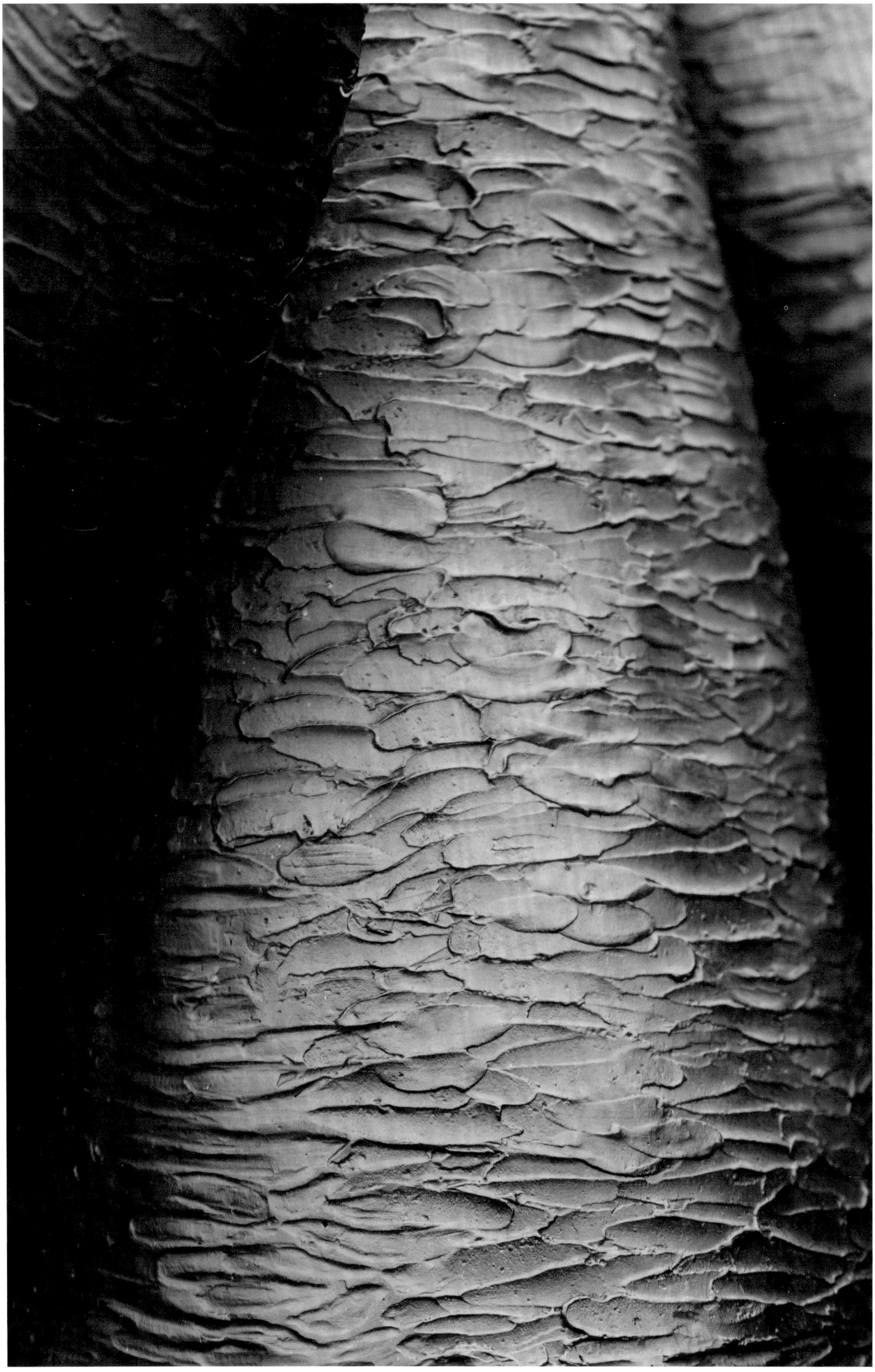

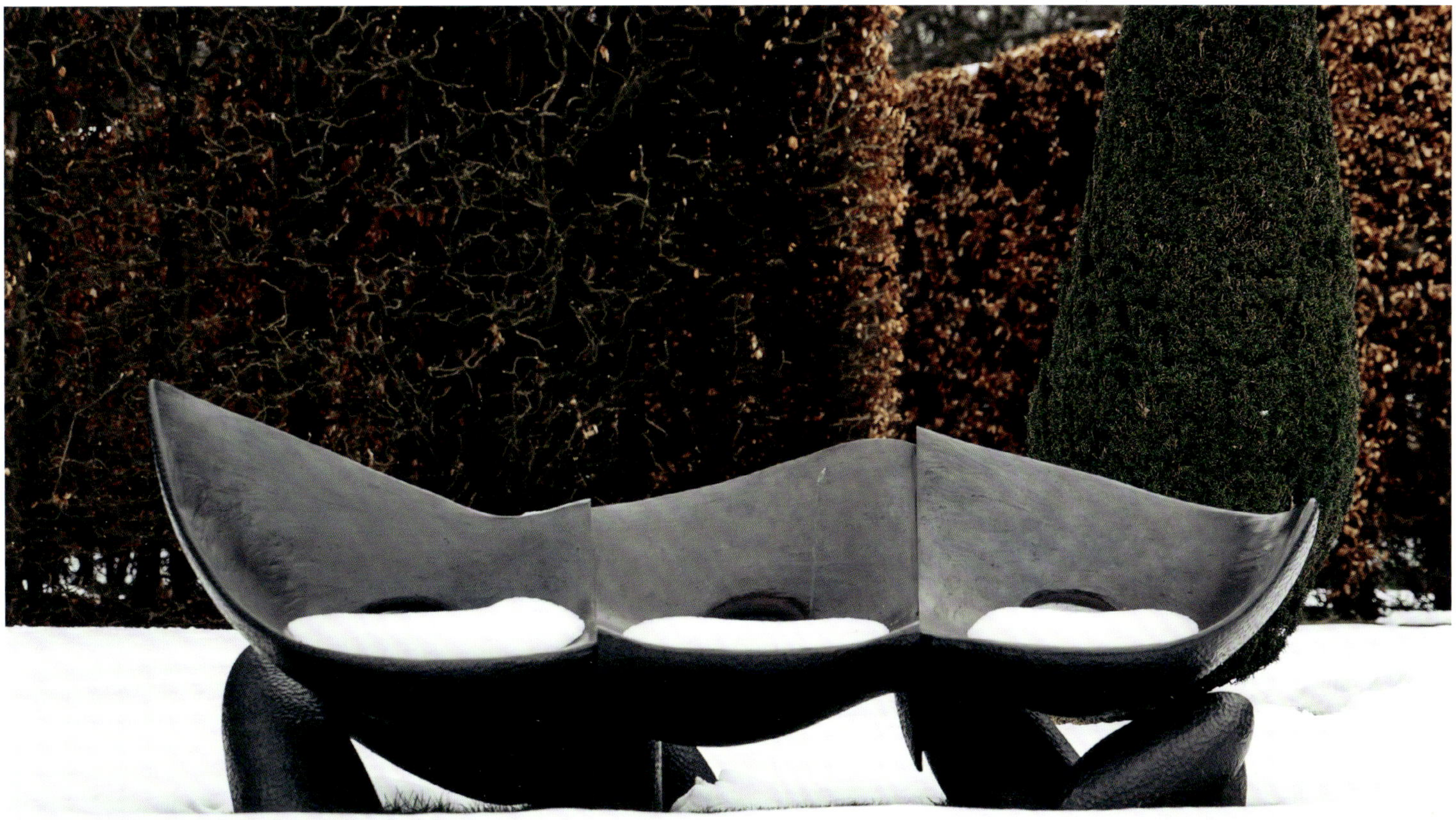

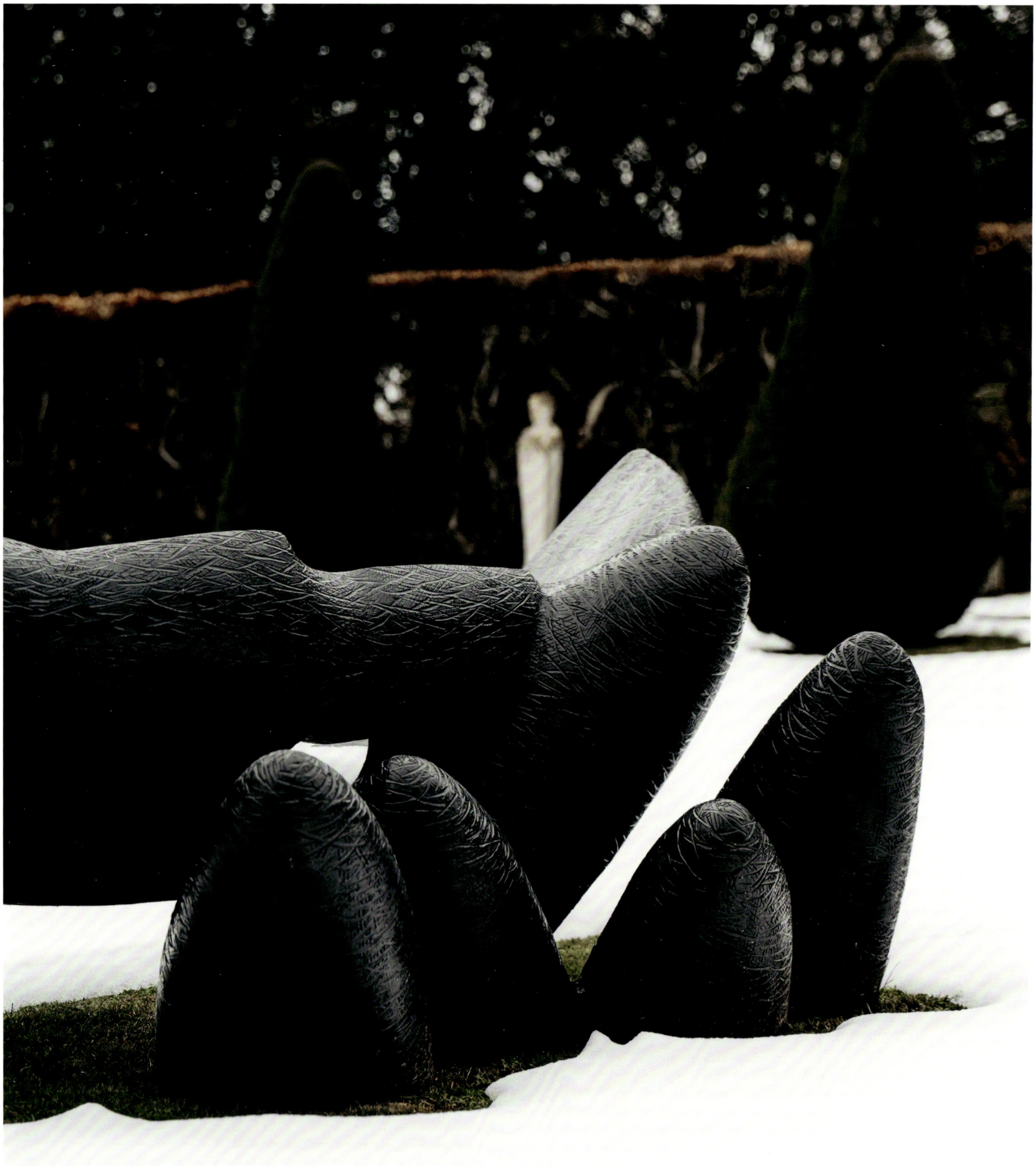

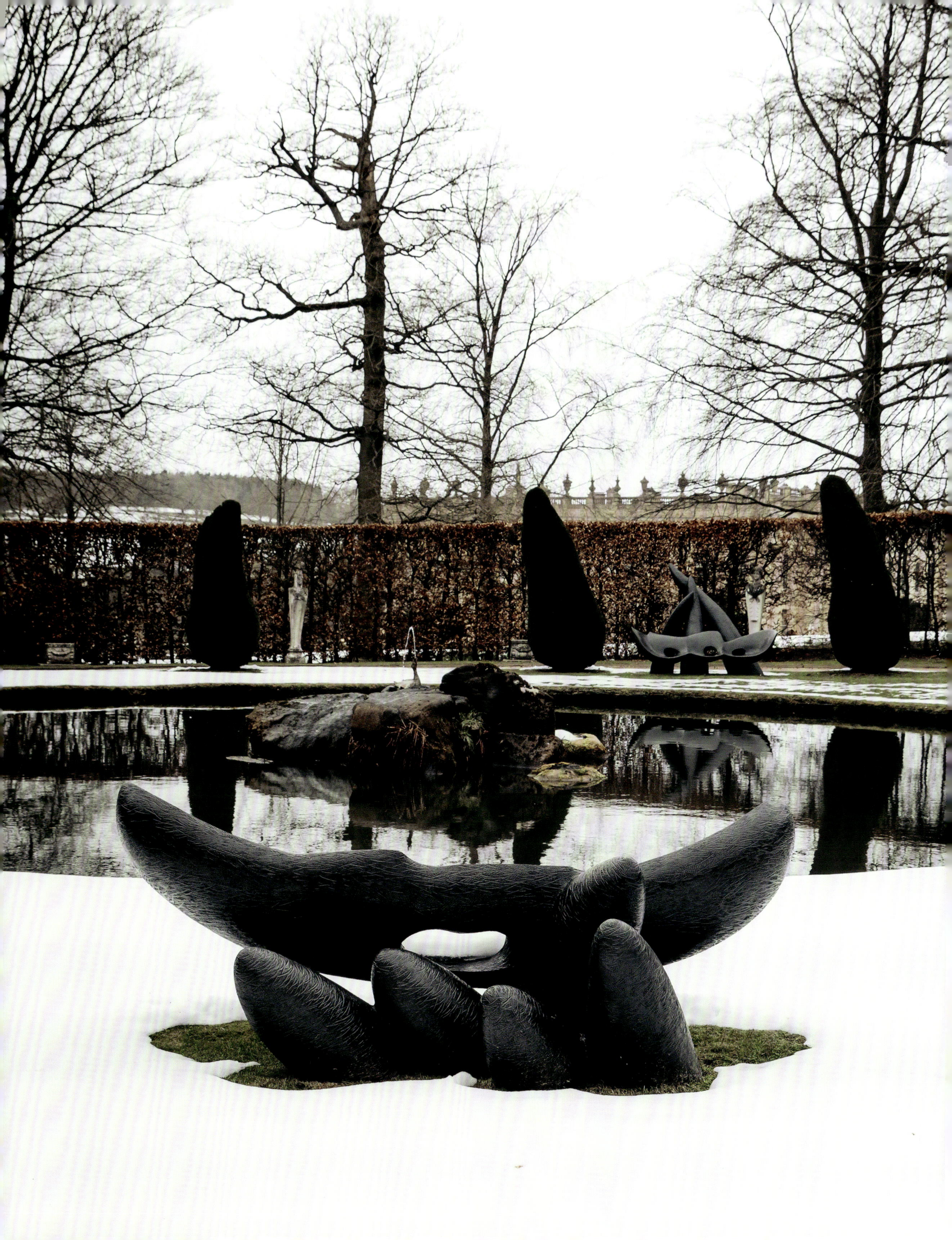

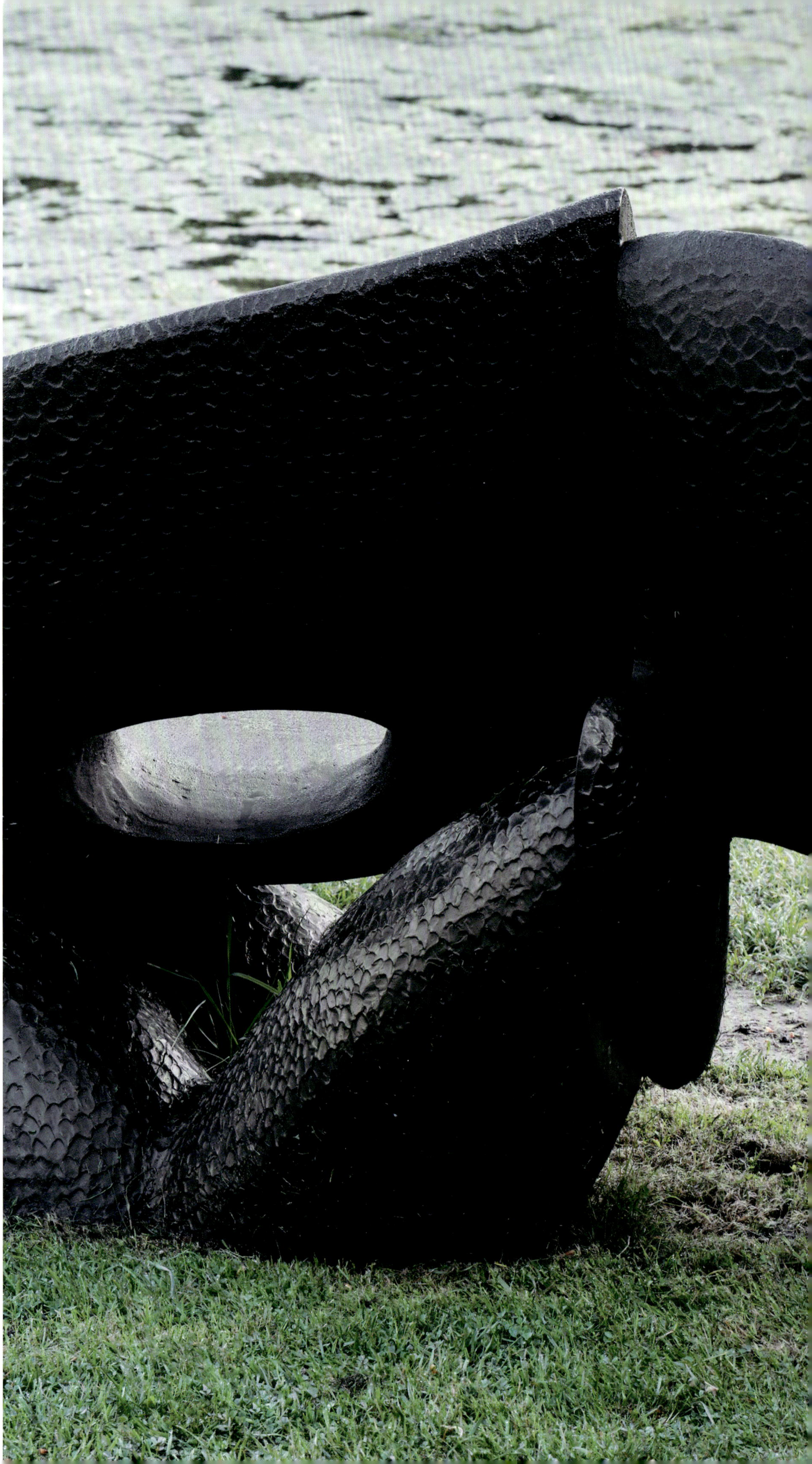

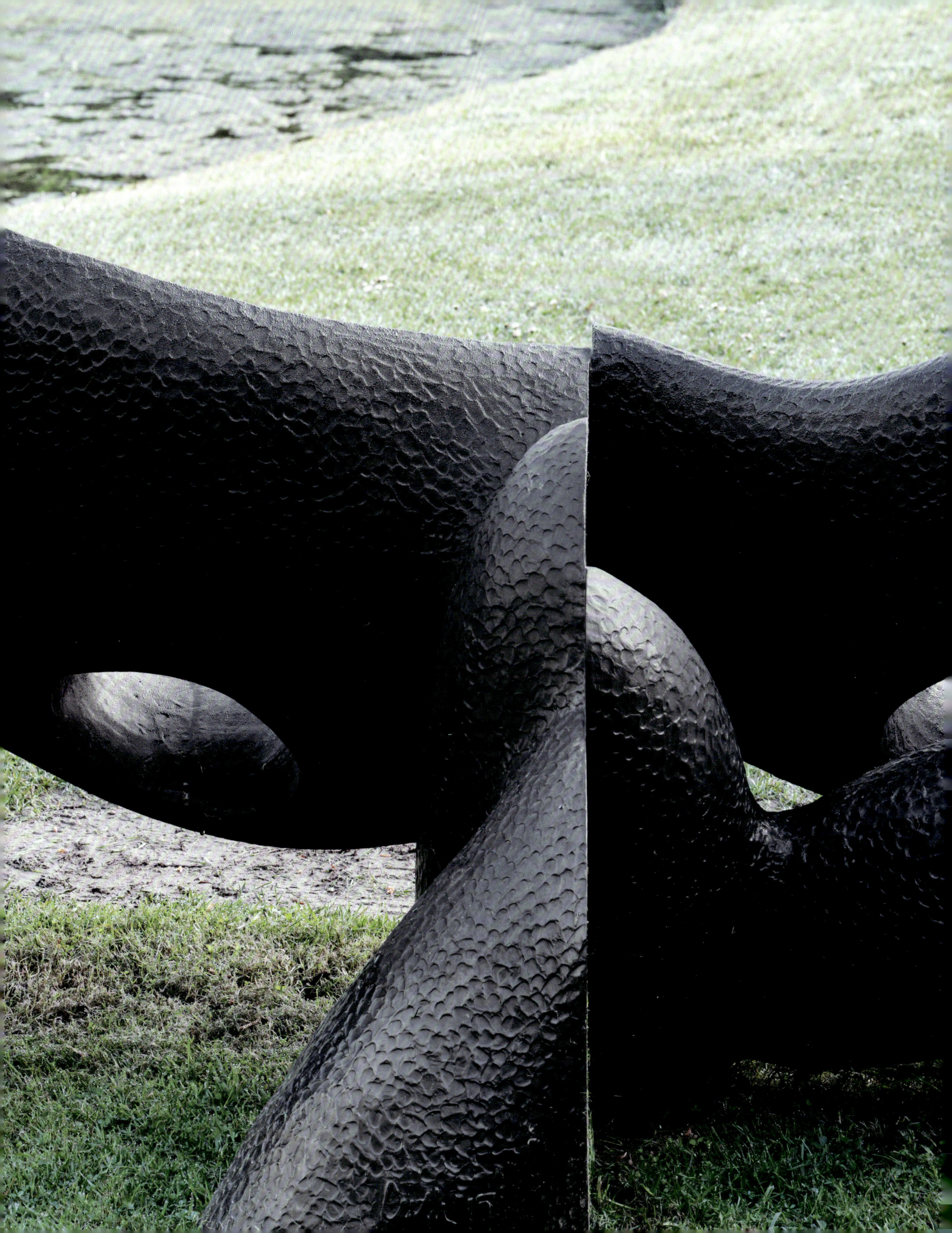

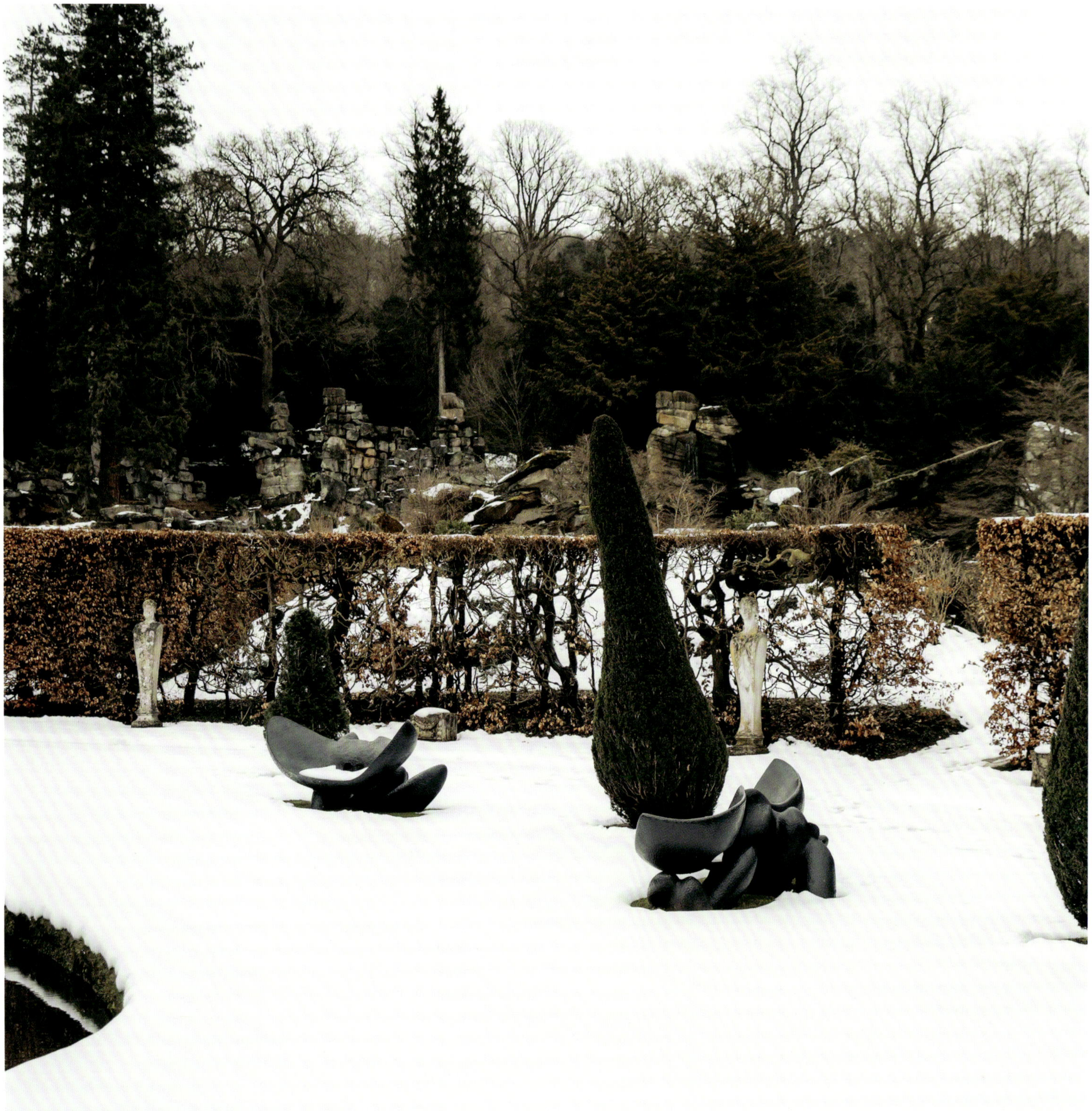

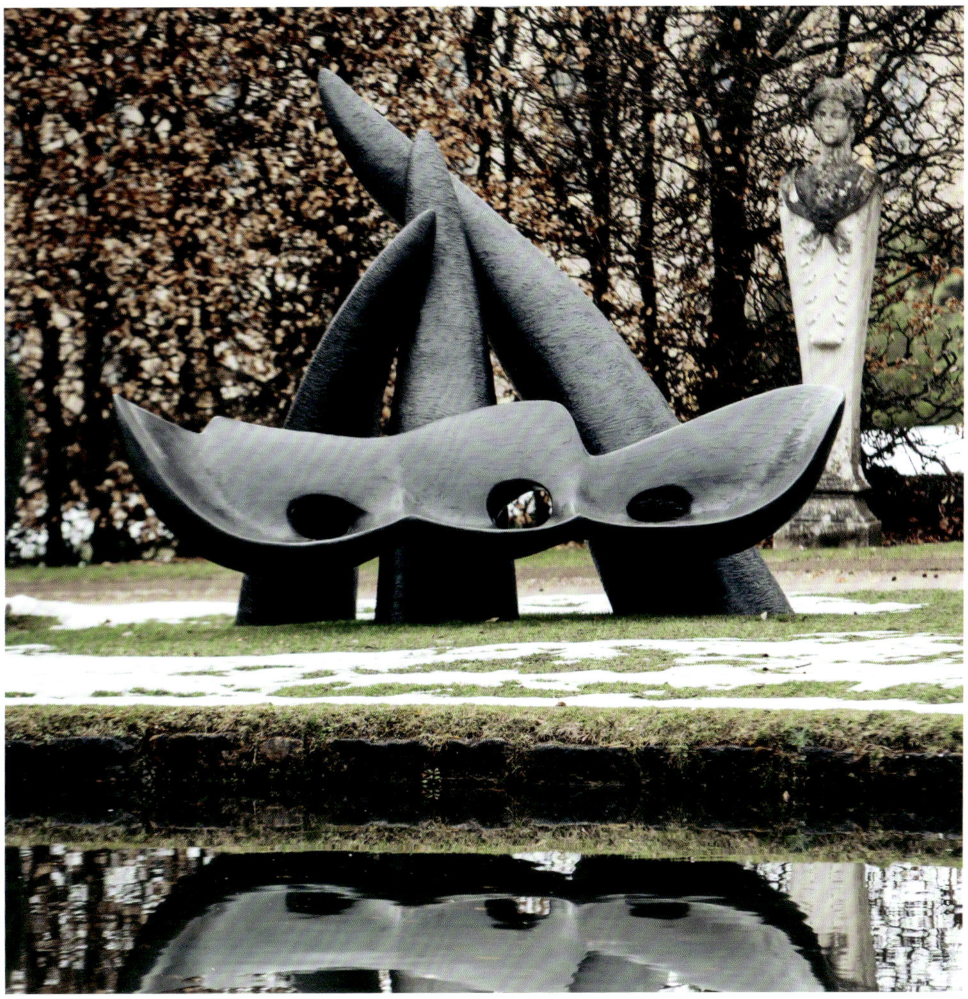

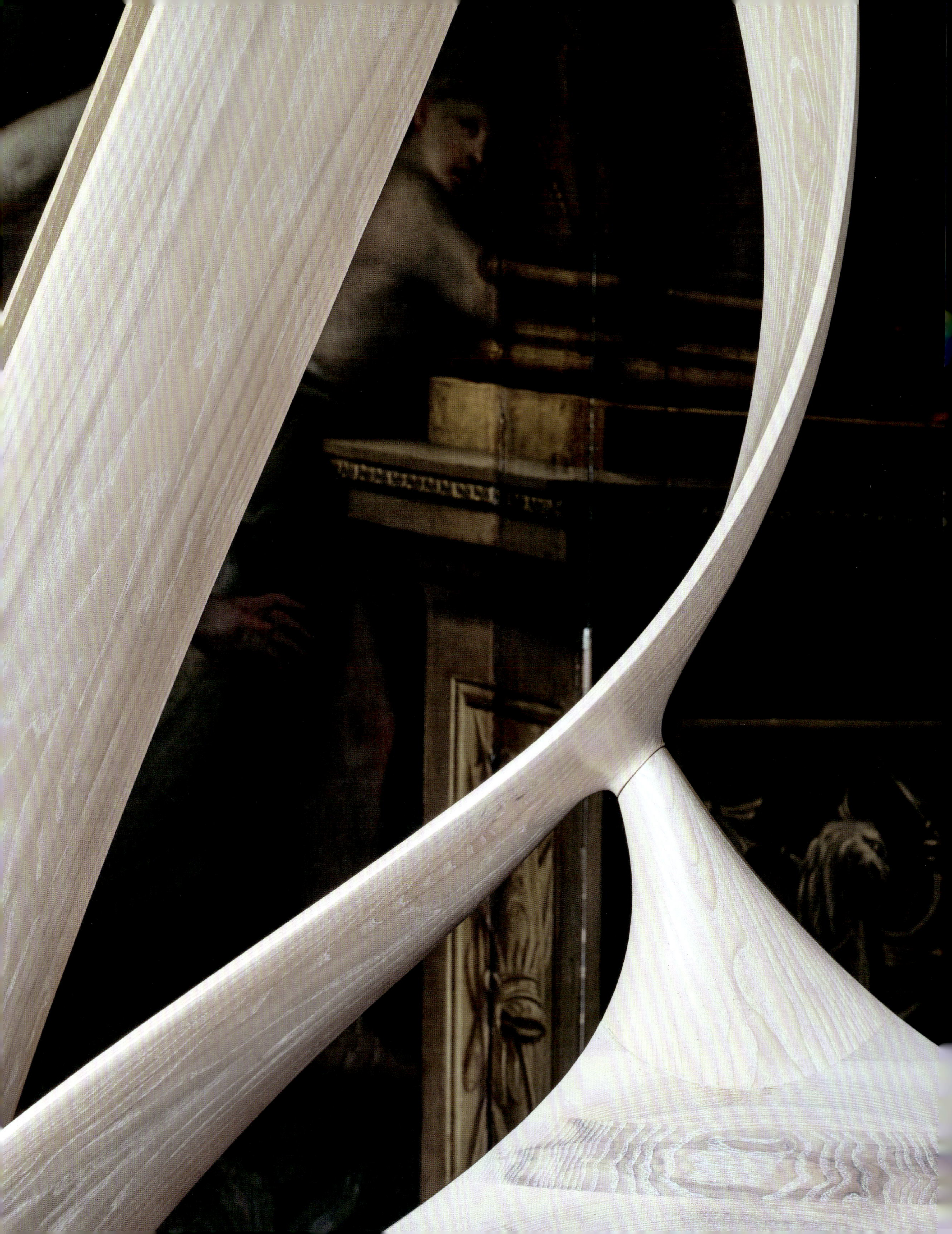

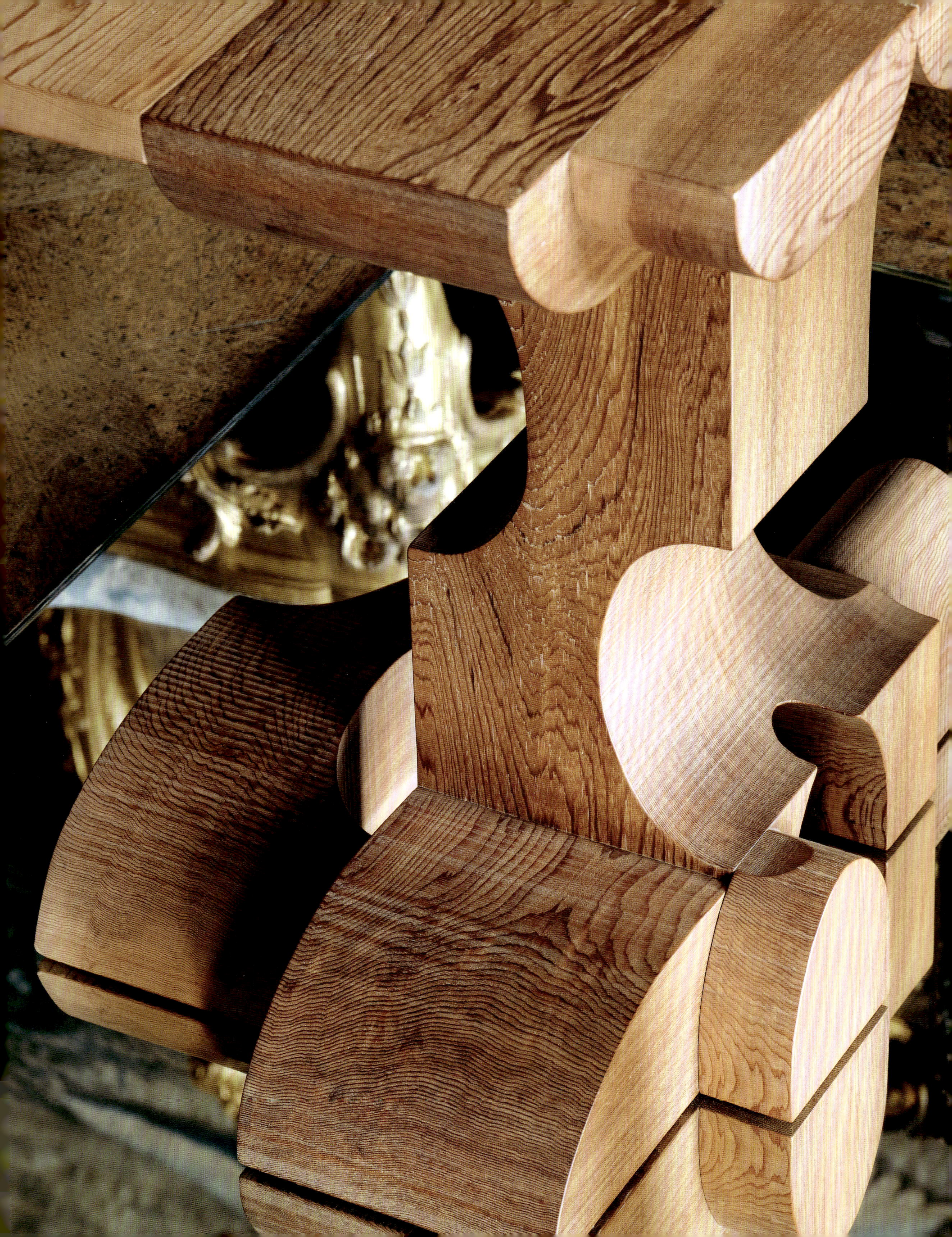

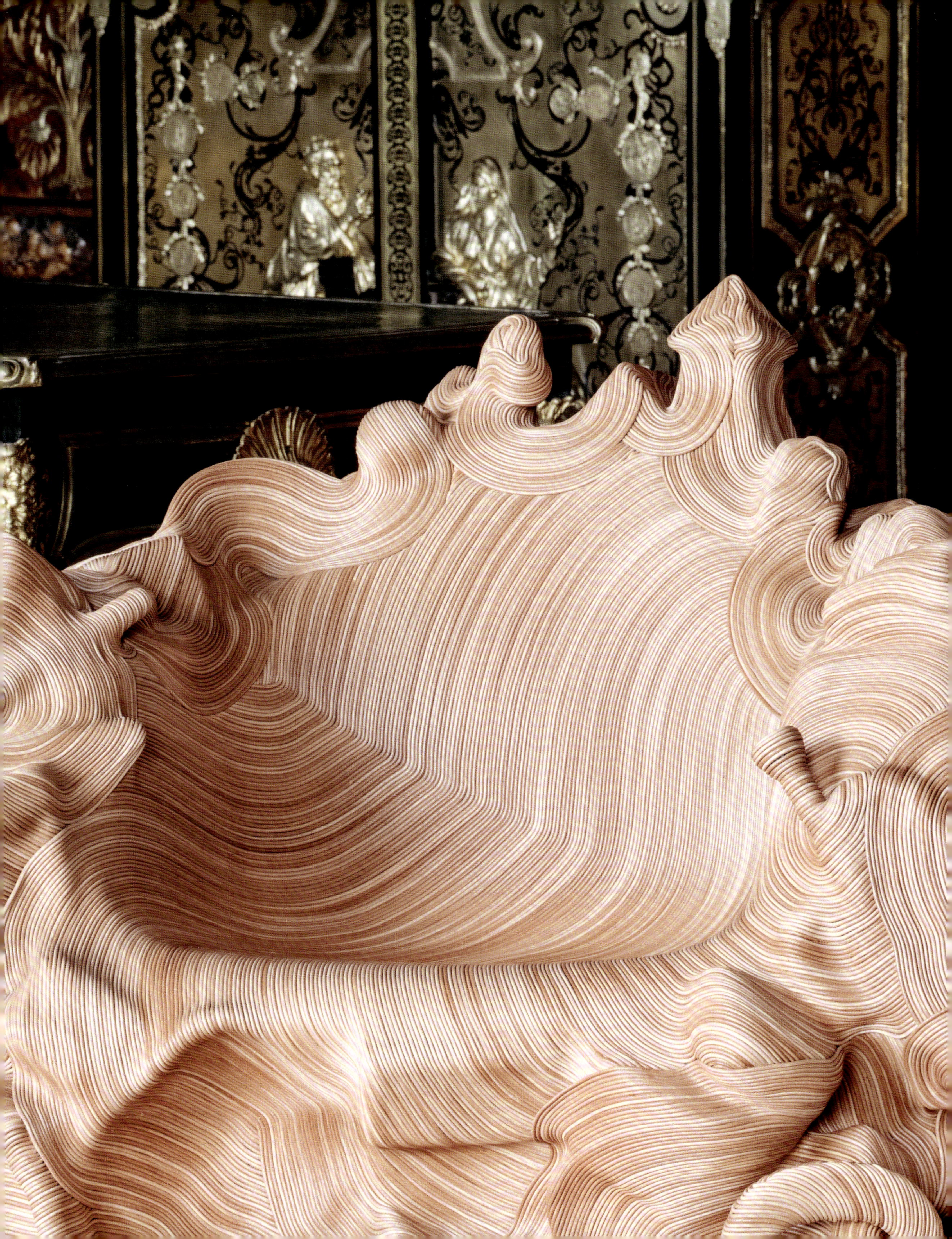

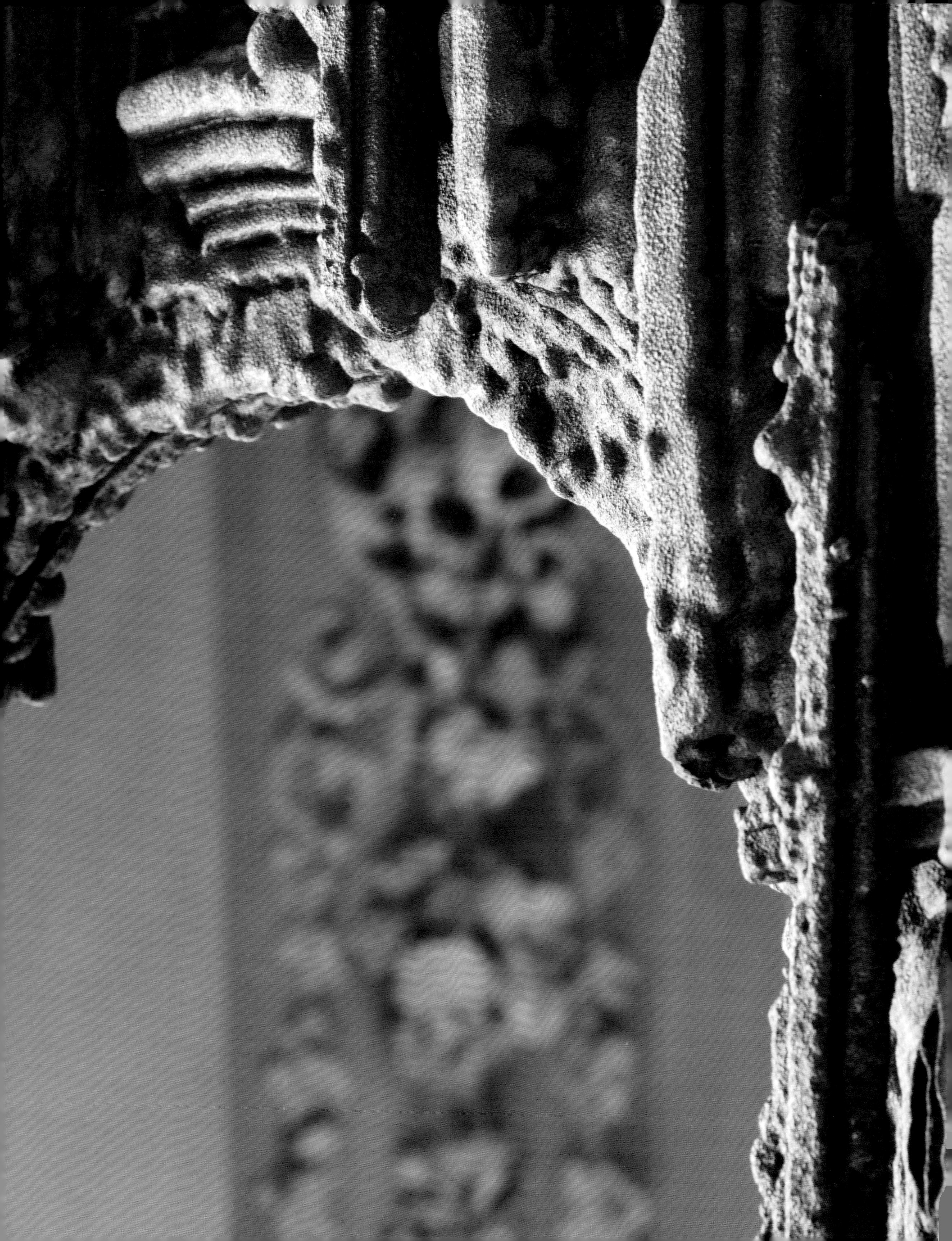

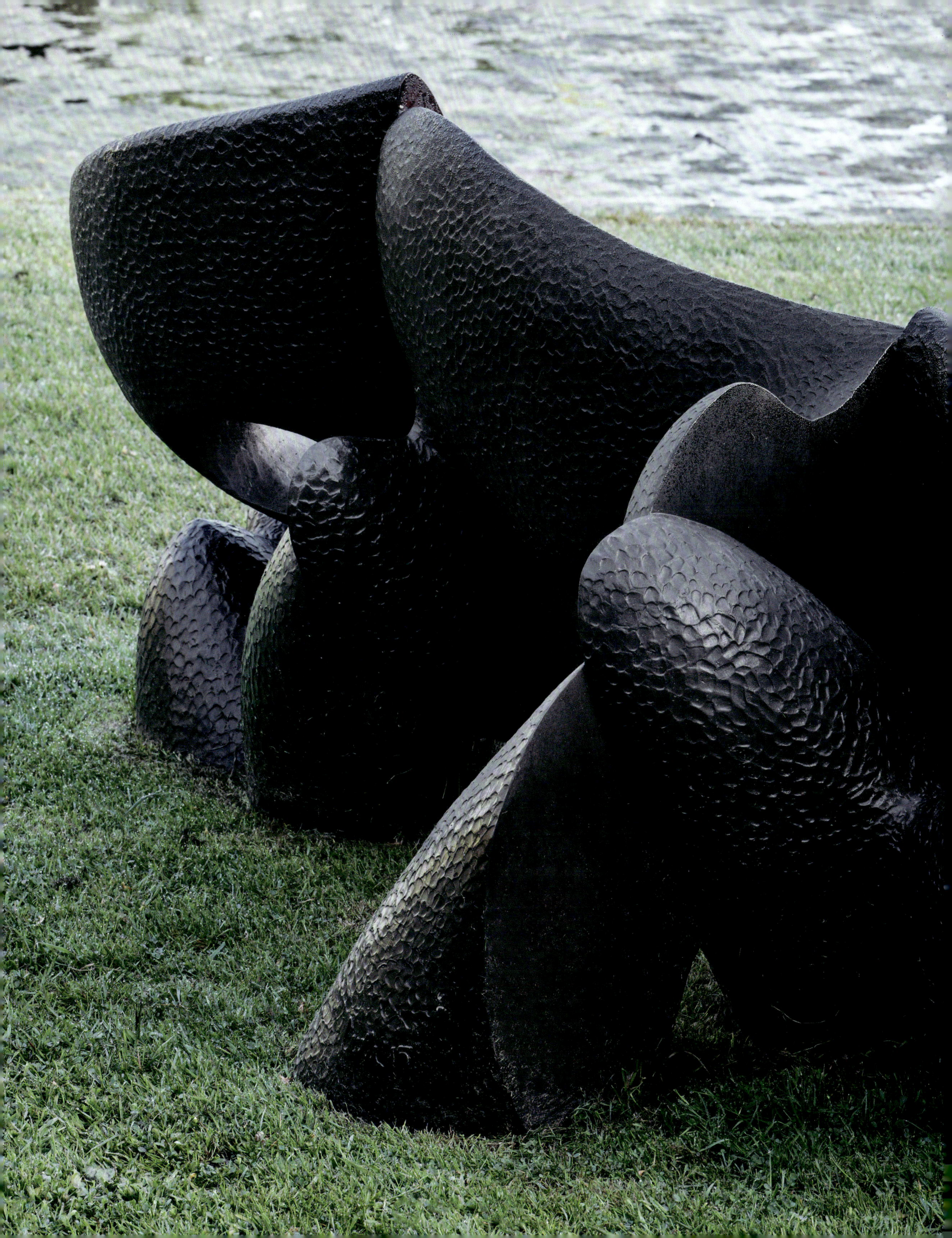

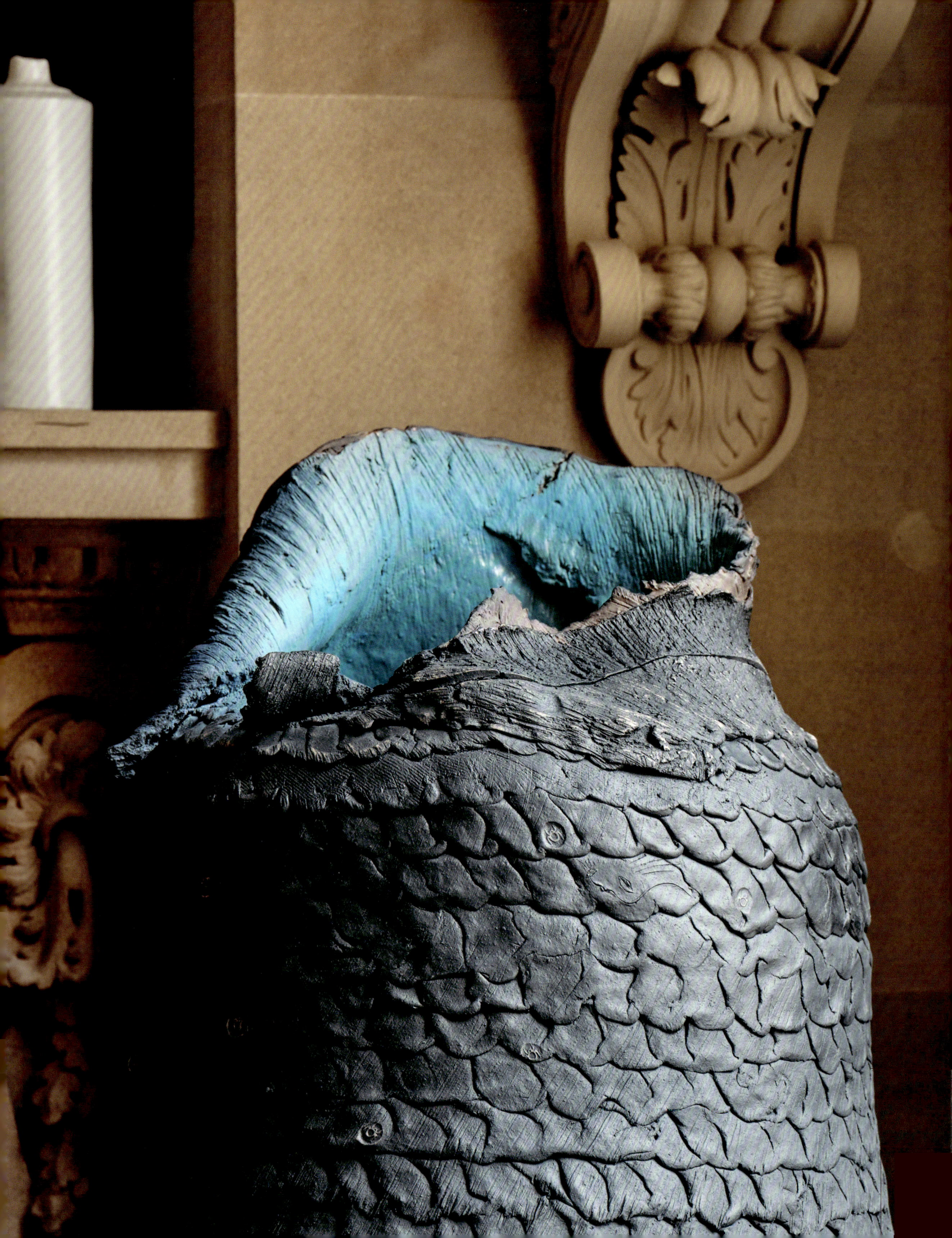

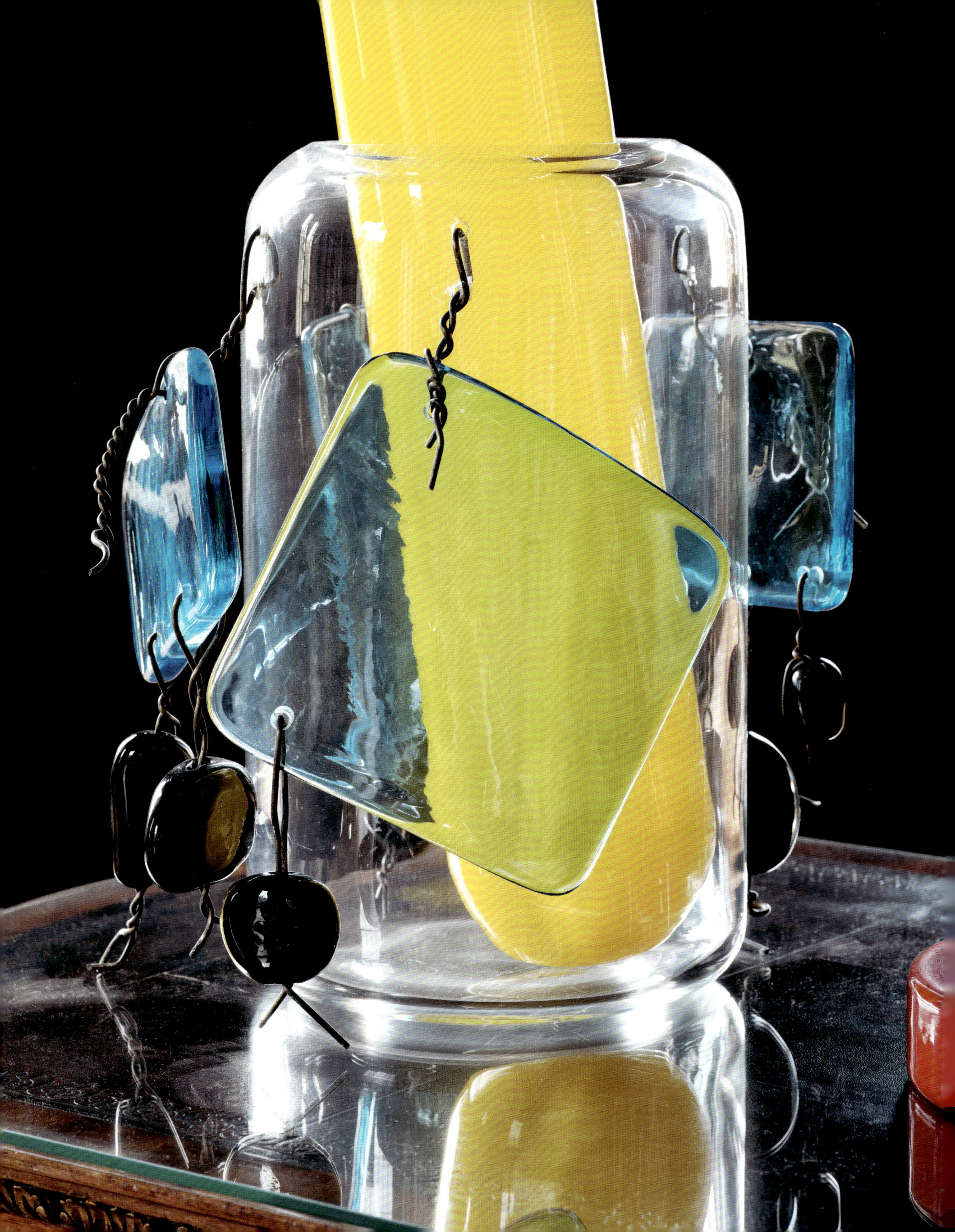

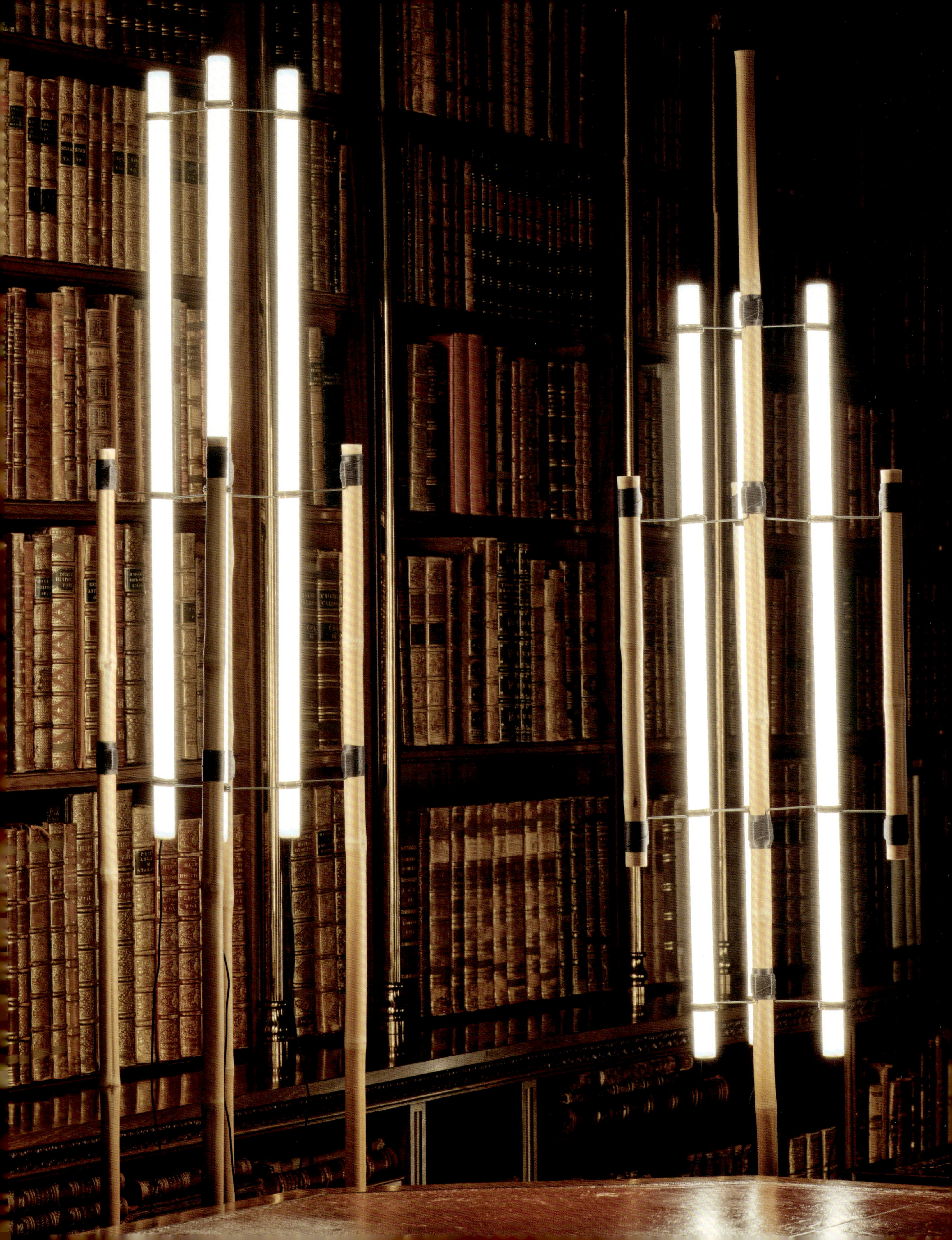

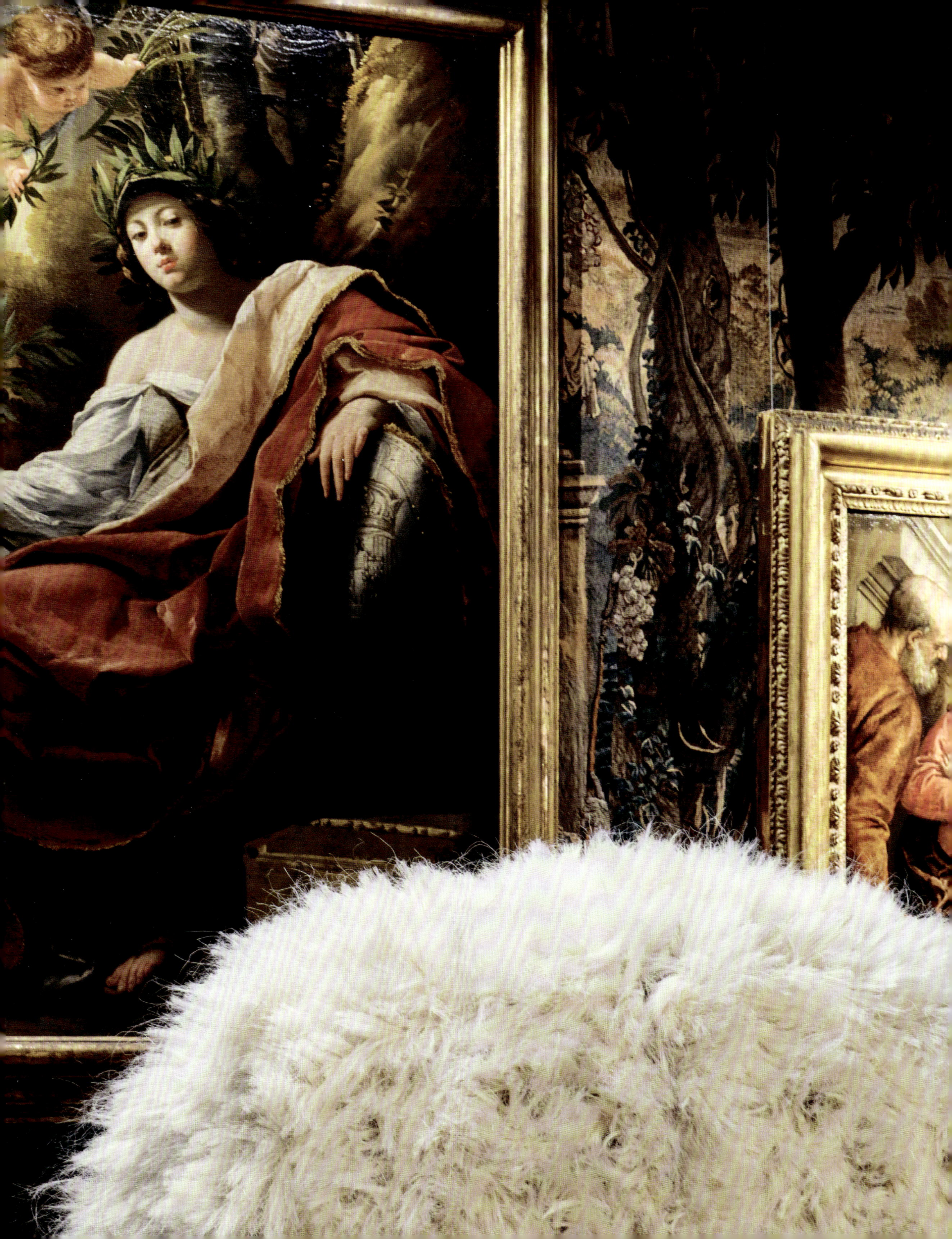

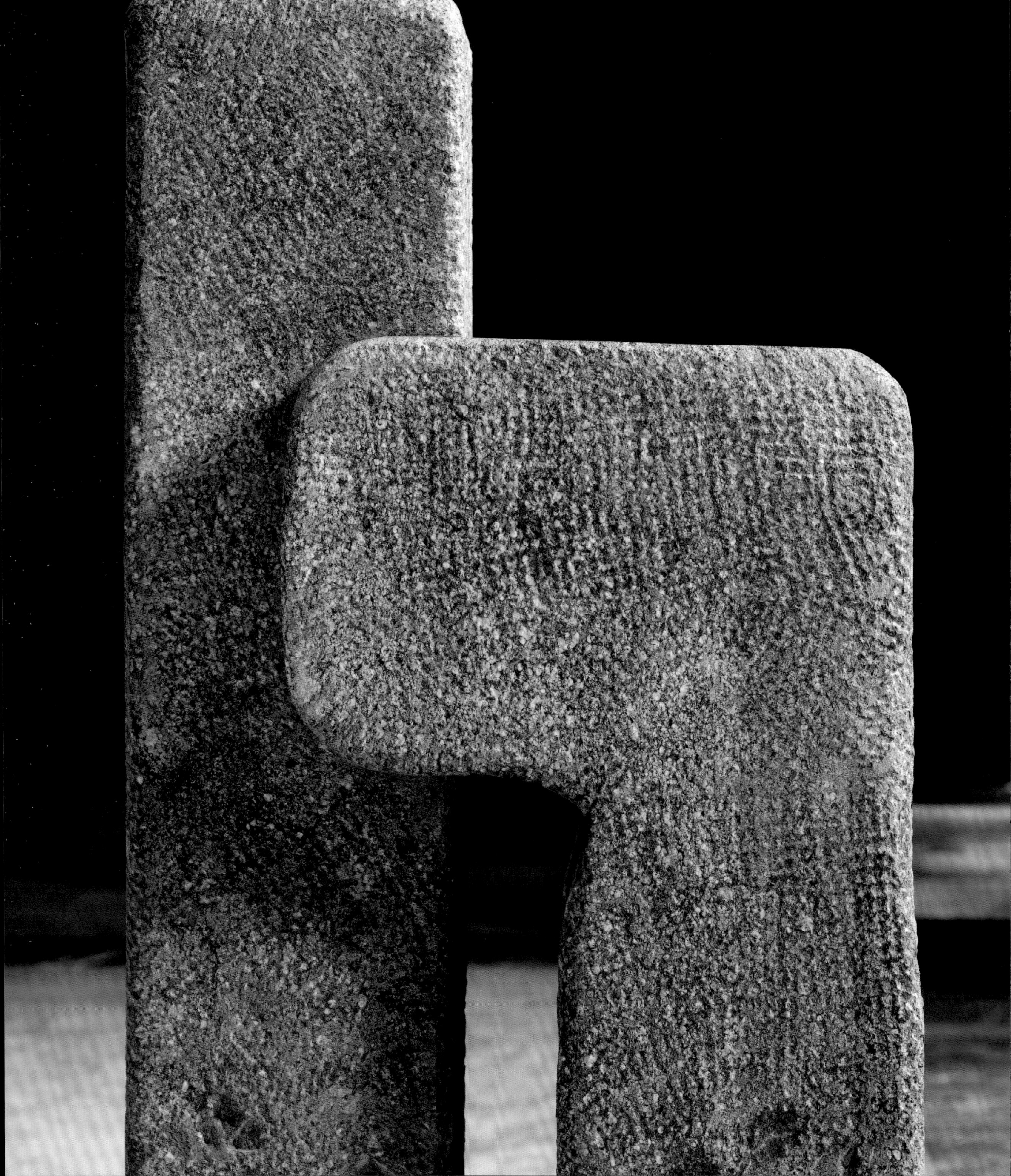

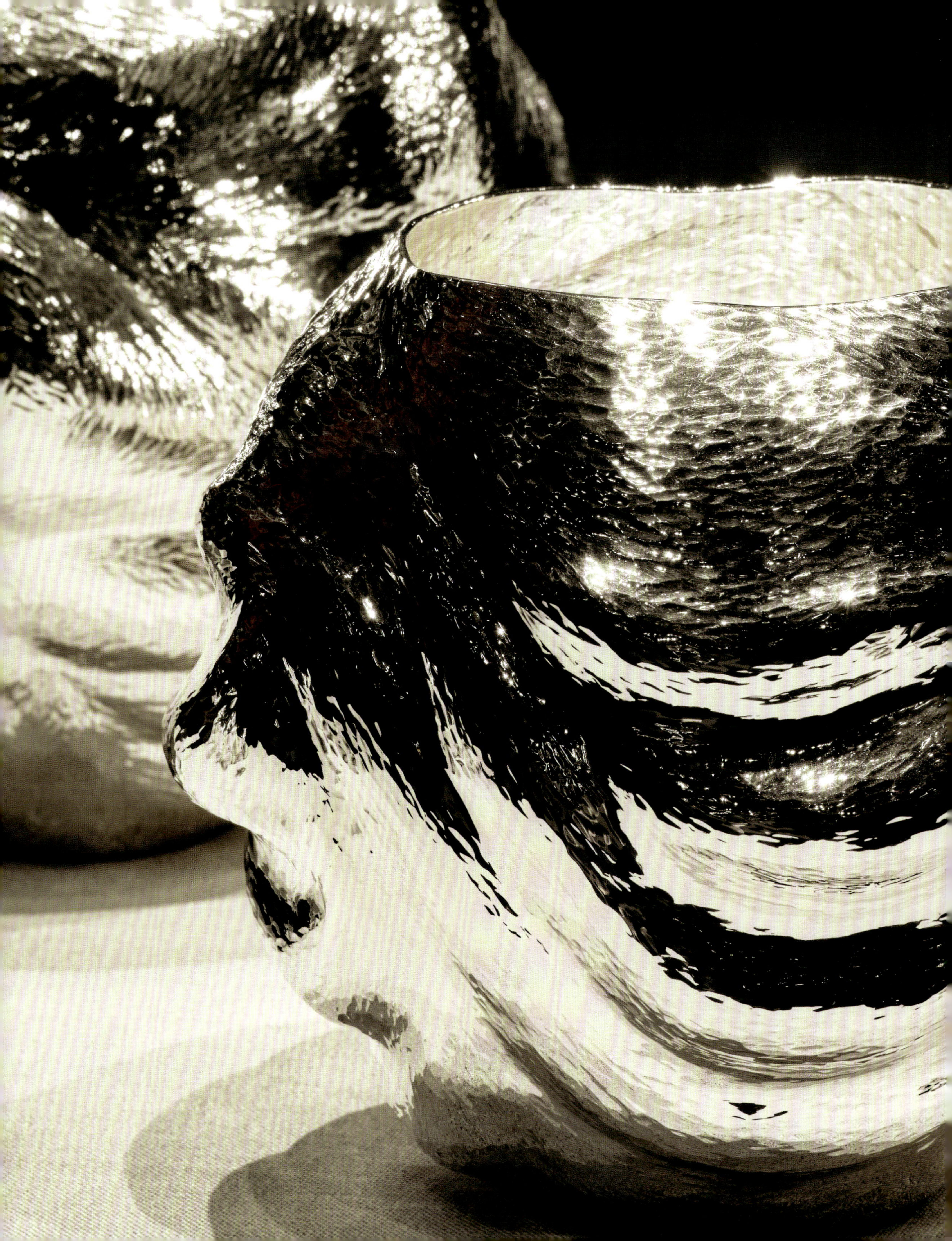

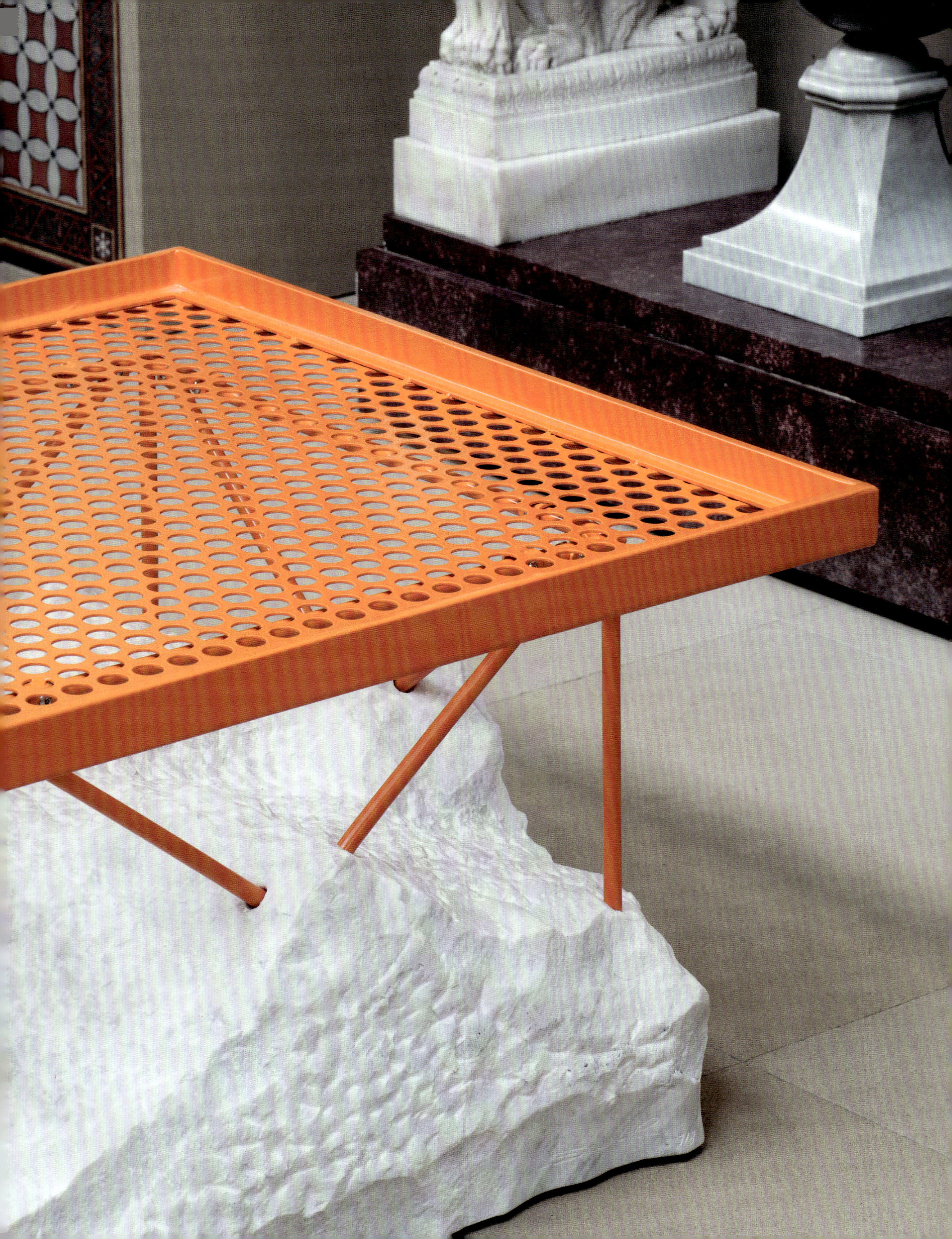

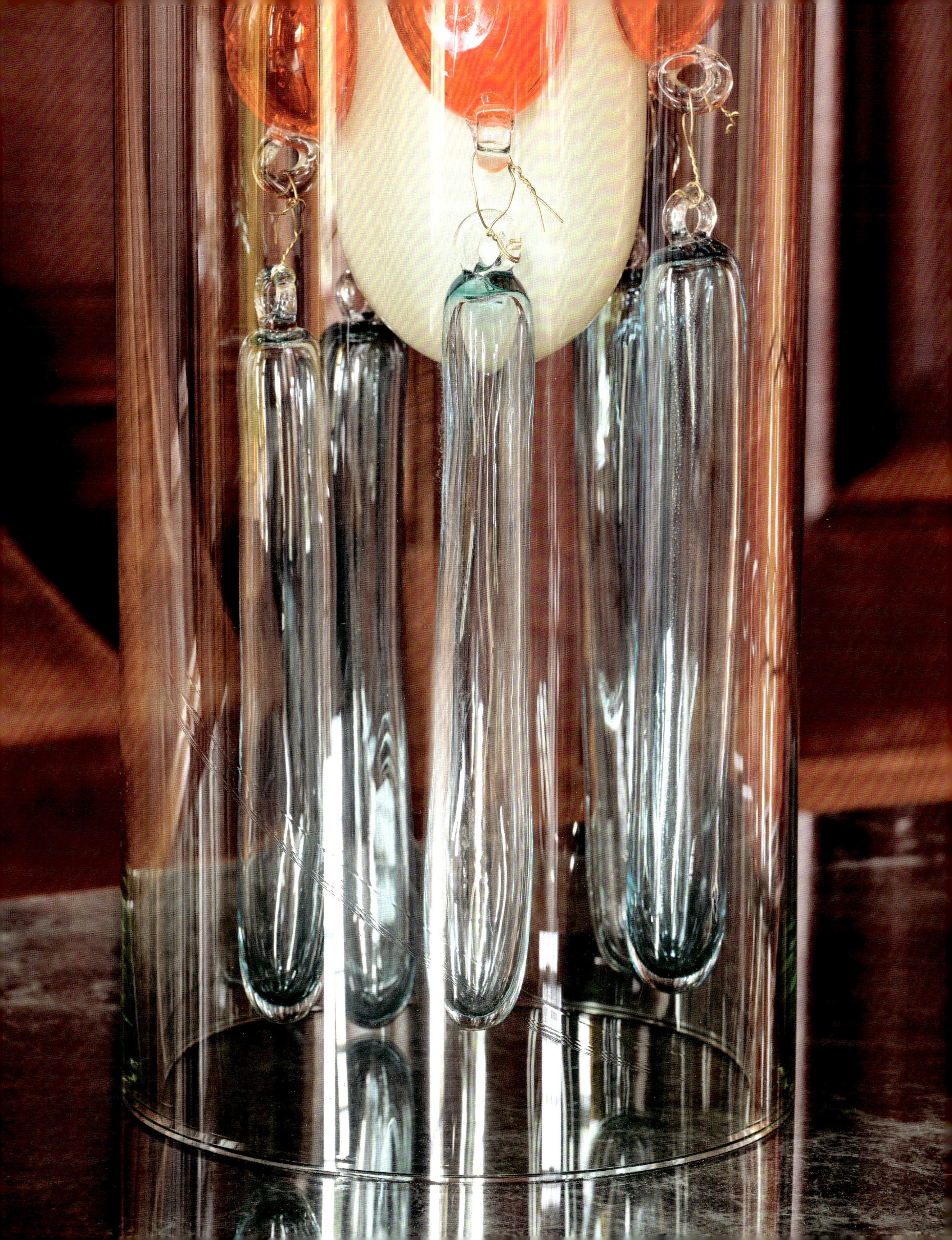

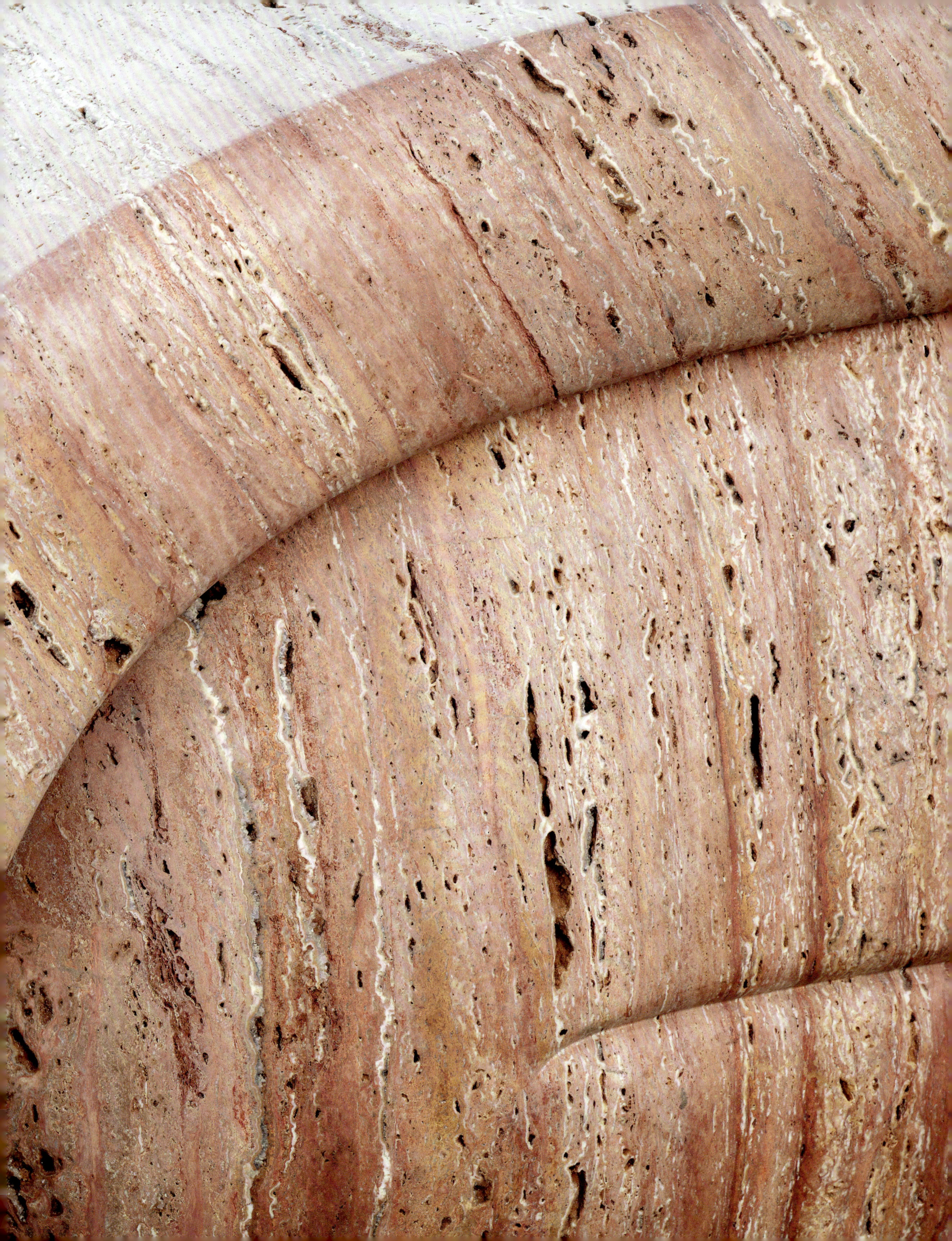

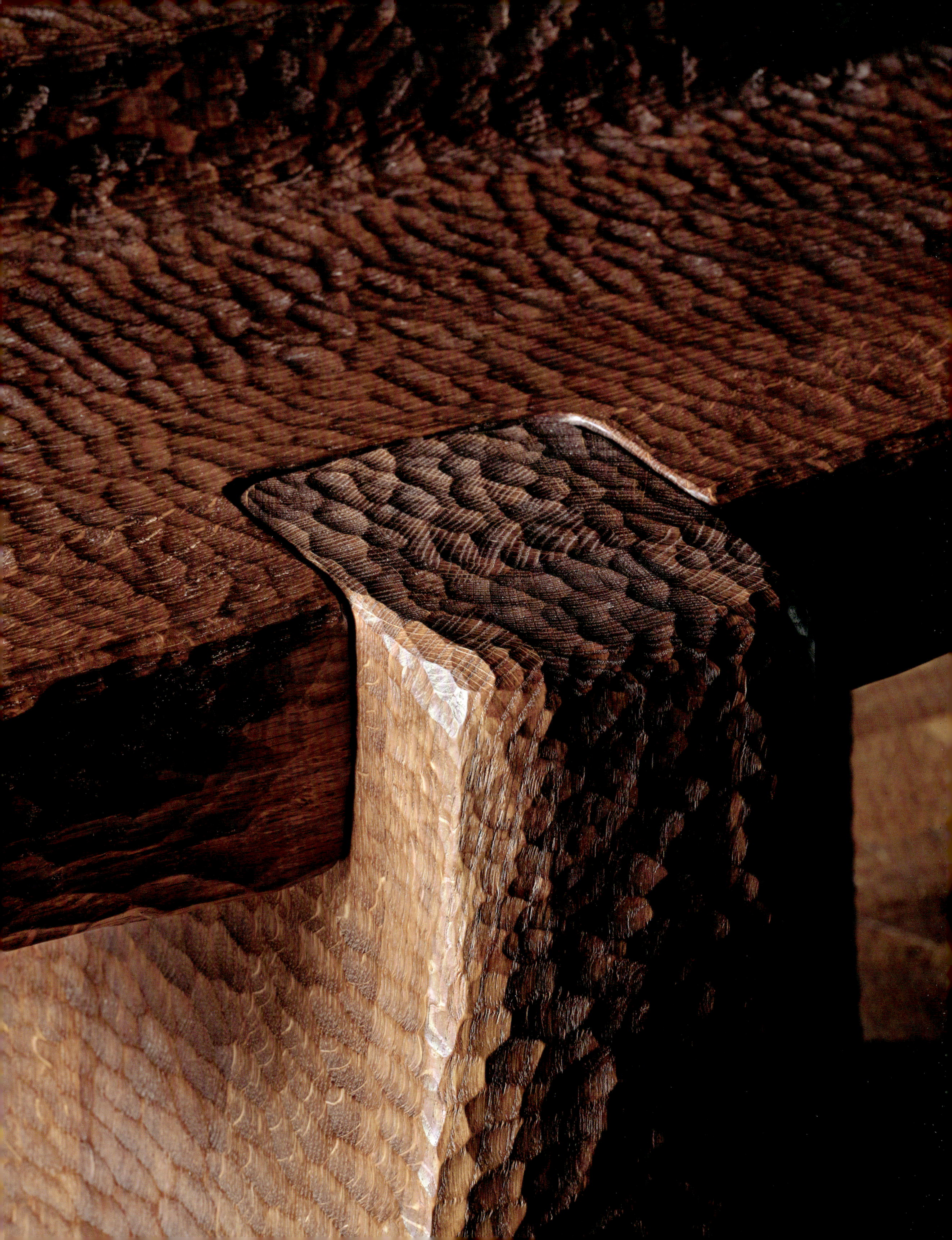

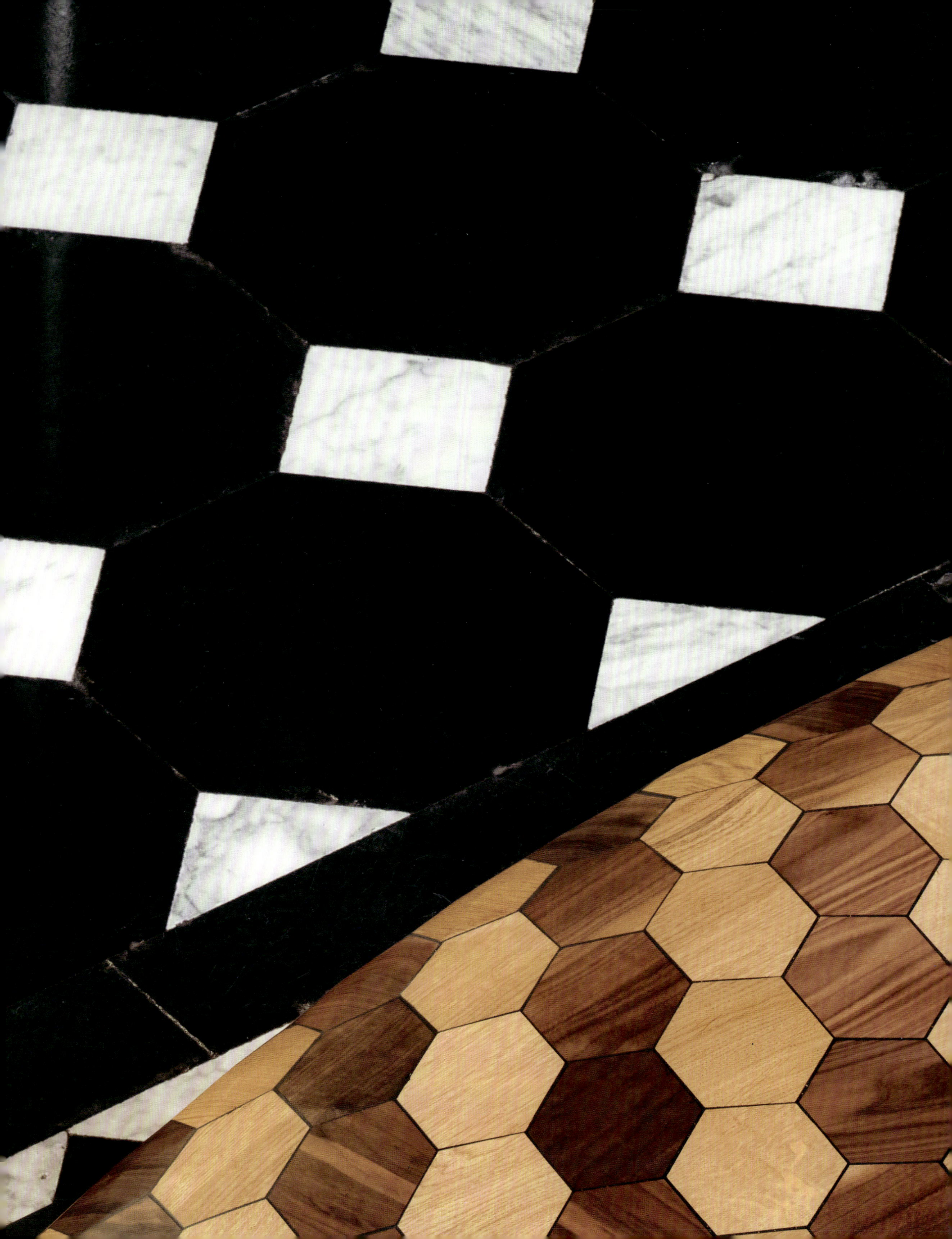

LOOKING FORWARD

SASH GILES
AND
ALEXANDRA HODBY

To enter the house at Chatsworth is to travel in time. The rooms and gardens have become palimpsests; original schemes are overlaid with new designs commissioned by its inhabitants over three hundred years. Changes in fashion and taste have shaped the spaces, as well as the desire for different form and function. The North Entrance Hall, so welcoming with its warm fire and leather porter's chairs, was once a kitchen. The staircase that rises from the Painted Hall was once divided in two, with an elegant sweep to the first floor. Corridors have been added to provide privacy and communication, as well as additional space for display. The Sketch Galleries were once places where 'sketches' (now called the collection of Old Master drawings) were hung floor to ceiling; but these galleries didn't even exist until the 6th Duke of Devonshire (1790–1858) commissioned Sir Jeffry Wyatville (1766–1840) to design and build them in the 1820s and '30s. In times of drought are revealed the curving archaeological remains of a parterre garden design from the 1600s: its ghostly pattern suddenly emerging in the dry grass.

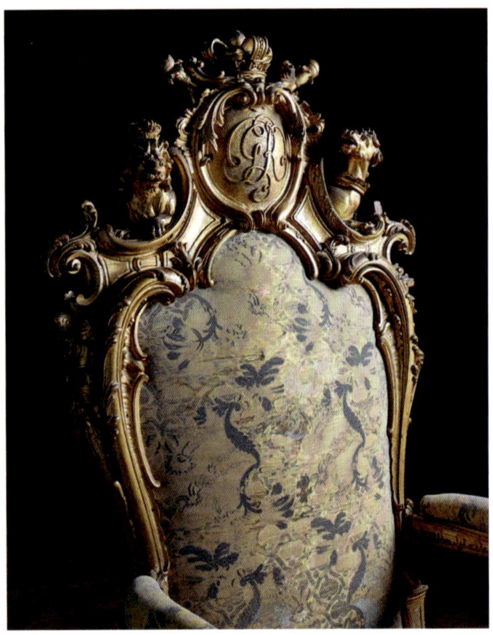

DETAIL OF CORONATION CHAIR
OF KING GEORGE III

In addition to these visible hints of its own complex history, Chatsworth today is also the product of exchange with other grand houses. The paintings hanging in the North Sub Corridor would have once been displayed at Chiswick or Devonshire House in London. A suite of chairs by William Kent was designed for Devonshire House, the family's principal London residence, which was demolished in 1924. The objects are now at Chatsworth, and have brought with them the echo of design schemes, tastes, and ways of life that have disappeared or been reconfigured beyond recognition.

Chatsworth, then, is an elegant repository of furniture and design from other ages and other places; the building continually shapeshifts to accommodate its contents, and *Mirror Mirror* is no exception. The project builds on a recent history of introducing contemporary artwork into the historic spaces, a sharpening of focus that extends the house's significance into the present. You might see one of Kent's chairs near a Michael Craig-Martin print from the *Art and Design* series (2012)—the Kent chair can arguably be seen as the ancestor of the chair in the artwork. A 2018 commission by ceramicist Natasha Daintry called *Sowing Colour* echoes the historic bookshelves installed by the 6th Duke of Devonshire, but instead is populated with vessels that celebrate the abundance of life and colour that can be glimpsed through the window and into the garden. When we encounter these interventions at Chatsworth, they remind us that the historic artefacts throughout the house were all, in their own time, new arrivals, often made and commissioned for the space. Chatsworth is an ever-evolving site-specific encounter that sends our thinking backwards and forward in time.

The garden too has been shaped by designers over the centuries. Our collection of maps and engravings can show us the original plans; the actual results, the traces of their work persist in the shape and sweep of the ground itself. The Cascade is a remake of an original design by Monsieur Grillet, a French hydraulics engineer with experience in decorative waterworks for Louis XIV of France. It's a remarkable survivor of a kind of design that was made popular by the 'naturalisation' of landscapes in the later 1700s. The huge gestures of those designs were epitomised in the sweeping statements of Lancelot 'Capability' Brown, who here instigated the movement of the river, creation of hills, and the planting of trees—a design on another scale entirely. Brown's designs, while appearing seamless with nature, are anything but. There is a complex balance between imposed and naturalistic forms, a balance that we are still trying to find today, as we endeavour to craft environments that are at one with the natural world.

The designer and engineer Joseph Paxton (1803–65) fashioned the Chatsworth landscape to his ambitions for water and heat. He used lakes to power gravity-fed fountains, and constructed hidden networks of tunnels to provide coal for the boilers of a great glasshouse, a precursor to his great Crystal Palace. Almost two hundred years later, in the first decades of the 2000s, landscape designers Dan Pearson and Tom Stuart-Smith added another layer to the plantings and infrastructure of the garden—now, seasonal changes shift its appearance, reinforcing Chatsworth as a place of creative inspiration across the year, and across centuries. This is a functioning ecosystem of horticulture and design, a microcosm of the world in the age of the Anthropocene, which models how functioning ecosystems can flourish in such disrupted places.

From the grand setting of the parkland and garden, the house itself comes into view. And it is in the

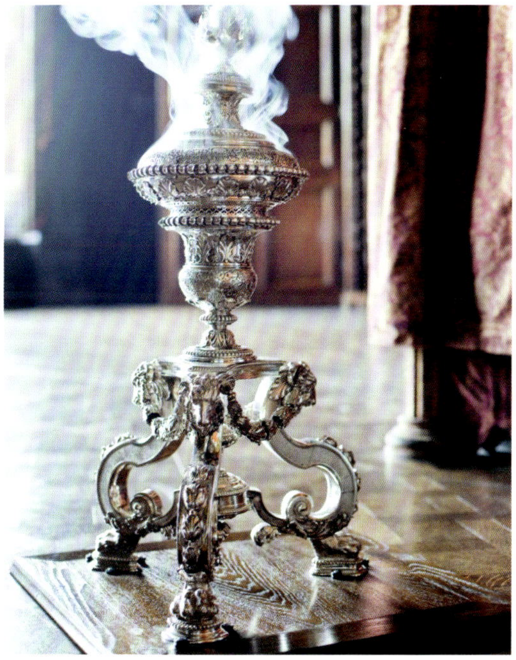

A WILLIAM AND MARY
SILVER PERFUME BURNER

details of the house that its complexity as a work of design comes to the fore. Almost every object at Chatsworth tells its own story, about its origins, persistence, and its continued presence in the world. Our archive can sometimes tell us about the individuals who were engaged to make or mend. Indeed, the house preserves much evidence of the emergence of what we might call 'design' in the modern sense of the word. Take, for example, the richly decorated interiors of the 1st Duke of Devonshire's house, carved by Samuel Watson (1633–1715). A local talent—he was born in Heanor, Derbyshire—Watson first appears in the records at Chatsworth in 1690 to 'carve the ornaments of lime tree worke for the great chamber according to the designe aprooved by his lord'. The carving was to be 'as good or better than any such like worke is hethertoo don'. That recognition of fine craft skill is also a distinguishing aspect of contemporary design. Designers working today, in contrast to mass-production, make individual works with attention to material and finish—not perhaps in the same way that Watson mimicked nature (though 'biomimicry' of a more process-led sort has a prominent place in the discipline), but with a similar sensitivity to the individual qualities of material and form.

Watson is credited with carving a pen 'indistinguishable from a feather' which once ornamented a door case originally placed in what is now the State Closet, but moved to the State Music Room by the 6th Duke of Devonshire.[1] His skill in carving was matched by his draughtsmanship; a volume of his drawings preserved at Chatsworth reveals Watson had a sensitive hand. This is a perfect example of Chatsworth's significance as a site of design history: with the building, its in situ archive, and collections of drawings, we can gather the evidence for the trajectory of Watson's presence and work as a designer—and, crucially, as a maker.

The labour of Watson's work is evident in the sheer abundance of his carvings; their tactile immediacy connects us to him and his skill, the trace of an idea from mind to hand, from pen to wood and stone. Watson, then, springs to life—though his presence was long missed, as, ironically, the very finesse of his work led earlier generations to assume it was by his more well-known contemporary, Grinling Gibbons, eclipsing Watson's authorship. Research in the archive at Chatsworth has reclaimed Watson, a character that could have easily eluded us.[2]

Also almost slipping from our grasp is the joiner Katherine (sometimes Catherine) Naish (fl. 1759–1772). We know little about her—but she is notable, because she was a woman working in a trade that at the time was led by men. In 1759 Naish (presumably her married name) succeeded her father, Henry Williams, as head of the family business and also took over the position of 'Royal Joyner and Chair maker', a position formerly held by her father, which she went on to hold for thirteen years. For the coronation of King George III and Queen Charlotte in Westminster Abbey on 22 September 1761, Naish supplied two thrones with footstools, at a cost of £36 per pair. These thrones now find their home at Chatsworth via William, 4th Duke of Devonshire (1720–1764), who was Lord Chamberlain to King George III and Queen Charlotte at the time of their coronation. The thrones were a perquisite—a 'perk'—of his role.

As royal joiner, Naish was tasked with supplying pieces for state purposes where monarchs asserted their authority. Her designs, then, were symbolic, loaded with political and cultural meaning—thrones are not just seats, but laden with the weight of many histories. We engage with her objects, and through them, we imagine her life and the weight of her responsibilities to satisfy the powerful and political machinations of the court. And, of course, today, at a time that design is at last becoming a more diverse field with respect to gender (and ethnicity, too), we remark on her achievement as a woman working in a world dominated by men. At Chatsworth, the material and documentary archive does privilege men's stories. But her four royal objects sing of their history—who can mistake the resonance of a throne and the footstools to support the royal feet?

From the generation preceding Naish, we have a contrasting abundance of evidence for the life and work of William Kent (1685–1748). Like many of his contemporaries, Kent was hugely interested in Italy and studied in Rome—through him we trace an influence from Andrea Palladio through Inigo Jones

1 At some point between 1907 and 1949 the carving was damaged. Its very existence had been doubted, until newly digitised photographs of the State Music Room door case gave confirmation of its inclusion in the trophy still in situ.

2 Joseph Tilley vociferously argued for Watson in 1892 as has, more recently, Trevor Brighton. Horace Walpole greatly influenced the attribution to Grinling Gibbons.

to a distinctive British style. We might today describe Kent as a 'cross disciplinary' creative: an artist, an architect and designer of gardens, furniture, theatre, and costumes. That pursuit of a wide range of creative application is a generative and creative force. It continues to be perpetuated in the interests of designers working today—including many of those featured in *Mirror Mirror*. We can see today's designers ranging across built architecture, furniture, environments, clothing, and performance, just as Kent did.

Kent was extensively patronised by both Richard Boyle, 3rd Earl of Burlington and his wife, Lady Dorothy (née Savile), at Chiswick House in London, over a period of about thirty years. This connection remains tangible at Chatsworth because the 3rd Earl's youngest daughter, Charlotte, married the future 4th Duke of Devonshire, bringing with her a significant inheritance of property and collections. Kent even lived as part of the family at Chiswick, sketching intimate moments from everyday life, which suggests an atmosphere of collaboration and discussion. The owl, the heraldic beast of the Savile family, appears on a suite of mirrors and desks he designed there; the furniture was almost exclusively used by Lady Dorothy, a direct commission by her from Kent. That tradition of design for a particular space has continued in design practice and is evident at Chatsworth in commissions for its spaces. It is further highlighted in *Mirror Mirror*, in the reactions of the designers to the spaces in which their work is positioned—some making direct connections to the function or appearance of a room.

In Kent's owl suite, we can read something of his aesthetic, a sort of proto-rococo: taking the voluptuousness of the baroque and funnelling those motifs into Palladian forms palatable, for those unsure of which direction the prevailing style would take. We may also be able to read a lot about Lady Dorothy's artistic interests, more than is generally realised. She and Kent spent time together, sketching and drawing, and Kent wrote when congratulating the Earl on his marriage his hope that 'architecture will flourish more': perhaps in Lady Dorothy, the 3rd Earl and Kent each found a kindred spirit.

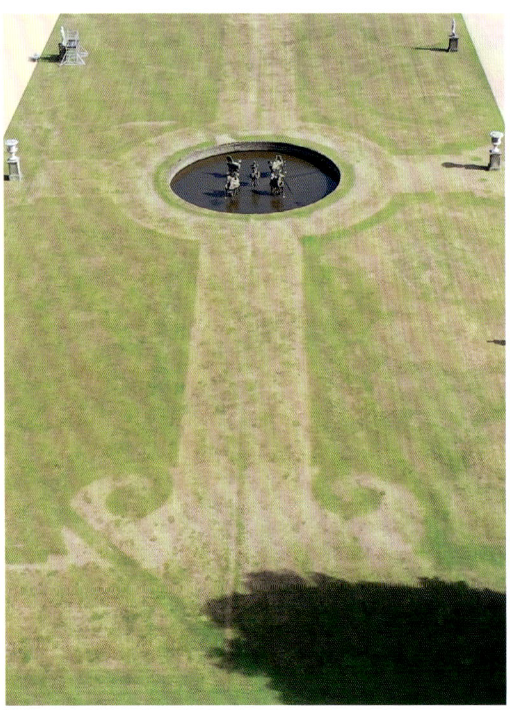

THE PARTERRE OUTLINE REVEALED IN THE SOUTH LAWN DURING A TIME OF DROUGHT IN 2022

Such linking of creative minds has long driven new directions at Chatsworth. Another example is the creation of the Sculpture Gallery, part of a new north wing at Chatsworth (1818–1838) designed by Sir Jeffry Wyatville. The space was purpose-built for the 6th Duke of Devonshire's collection of contemporary sculpture by artists such as John Gibson, Ludwig Michael von Schwanthaler, and, most notably, Antonio Canova, who became a close friend of the Duke. The Sculpture Gallery was lined with gritstone from local quarries; the matte quality of that backdrop was thought to show the sculptures to their best advantage.[3] In designing the space, the position of each of the new sculptures was decided by using skeleton models of the works—presumably to easily move them around, and a task that is far easier today in the virtual worlds enabled in computer-aided design environments. But the positioning of models was really a final touch to a process begun by the Duke years before, when he purchased and commissioned sculpture in Rome with the installation of his Sculpture Gallery in mind.[4]

We can, today, appreciate the Duke's vision for this space because of meticulous research undertaken to display the space according to his original design. This reassessment included not only sculpture, but also the columns, pedestals, tables, vases, and other objects. Also, secreted away in the wall of the gallery are some of Canova's tools—a tangible reminder that all this neoclassical grace had to be made by hand. What is found in the Sculpture Gallery, therefore, is representative of a collective approach to design in the assemblage of fine and decorative art found throughout the house.

While the original design for the Sculpture Gallery was recreated based on visual and written accounts, other pieces shine as individual examples—rare survivors of earlier design schemes. One such piece is the perfume burner that usually resides in the State Bedchamber at Chatsworth. It is a lone piece of silver furniture, never a common design type, but fashionable for a moment in the late 1600s, under the influence of the French court of Louis XIV, the Sun King. Silver is easily melted down to make new objects, in a manner that today we might think of

3 [The 6th Duke of Devonshire], *Handbook of Chatsworth and Hardwick*, London, 1845, pp.87–88.

4 Noble, C. and Yarrington, A. (2009) Like a poet's dreams: the redisplay of the 6th Duke of Devonshire's sculpture gallery at Chatsworth. Apollo, 170 (570), pp.46–53.

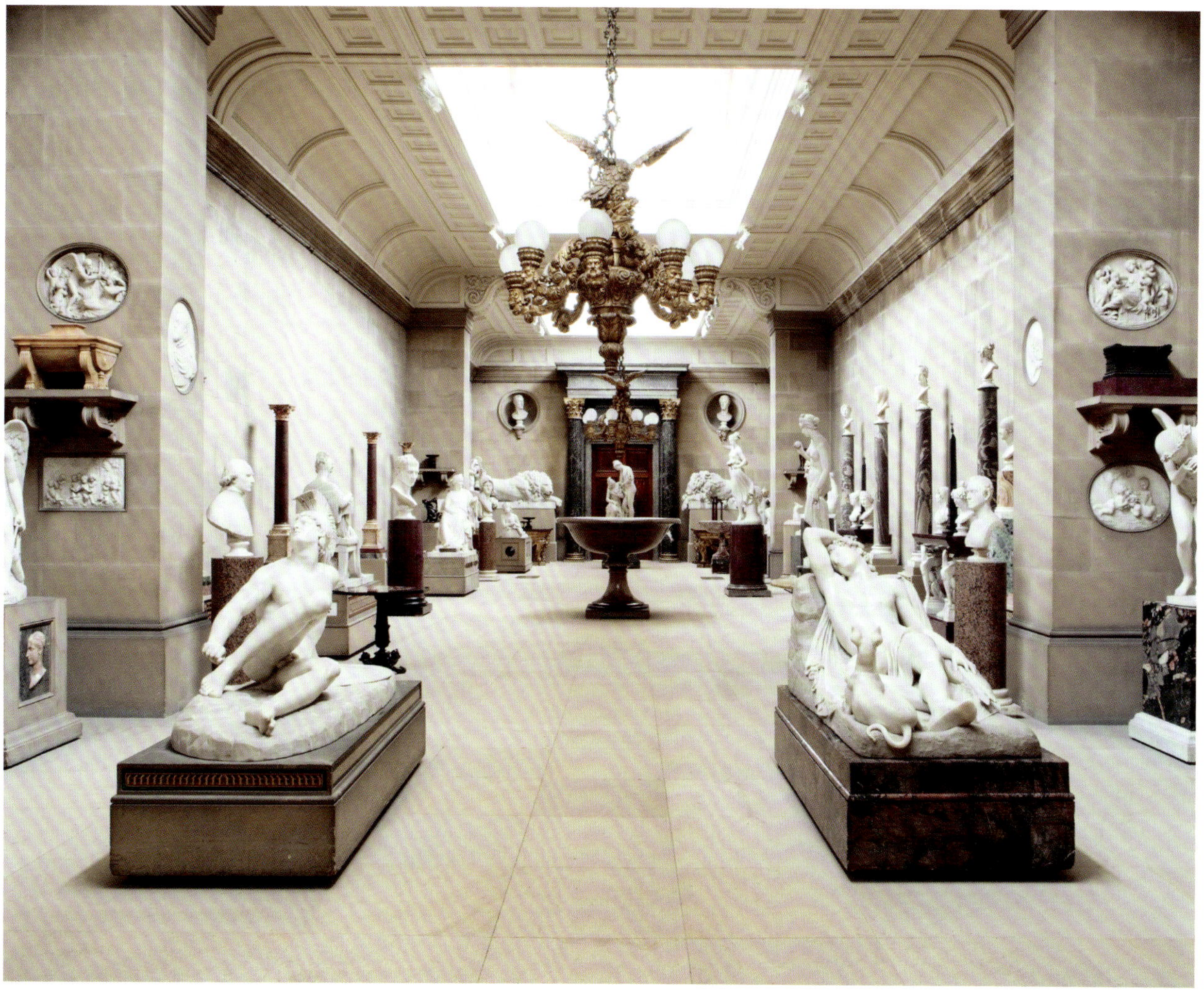

THE SCULPTURE GALLERY, CHATSWORTH

as recycling, or at least repurposing. When silver furniture fell from favour and fashion (probably due to the fact that silver tarnishes to black, and the way that the thin metal sheets, nailed on to light wood substrate, would sometimes loosen and look unsightly), most silver furniture was simply reworked for a more suitable purpose. The burner survived, perhaps because of its more solid construction and function. The ornament of the perfume burner—scrolls, acanthus leaves, paw feet, and various tiered sections—provides a rich setting for that function, the burning of scented oils or dried herbs on hot coals. Here at Chatsworth it remains, and is sometimes used. A trace of scent emanates from its pierced lid, an evocative conveyor of memory.

In some of Chatsworth's furniture we find surprising mechanics, of a type that even in a contemporary piece of design might seem outlandish. An unassuming oval writing table surprisingly flings open its contents at the press of a (delicately concealed) button. Two drawers fly out at both sides as a writing surface more sedately shifts towards you. Less dramatically, but more elaborately, a dressing table slowly reveals itself—a drawer slides out, a mirror emerges, and at the turn of a key, drawers and surfaces glide into view. These are two examples of pieces by father and son Abraham and David Roentgen—makers of furniture in the 1700s and patronised by the 5th Duke of Devonshire and Duchess Georgiana, as well as contemporaries Catherine the Great, Marie-Antoinette, and Louis XVI of France. The furniture is surprisingly heavy, packed as it is with internal mechanisms and a lot of metal inlay, locks, handles and catches. They are dense with potential and possibility.

Abraham Roentgen was a pioneer of manufacture, who split up tasks across his workshop to speed up production: a modern maker. His son David was financially shrewd and managed the business. They foresaw the rise of the fashionable neoclassical style, and in various business moves started to build their name into something akin to today's brands. In their workshop, they were able to attract skilled artisans, including such figures as Peter Kinzing, to design mechanical devices. From this workshop, the Duke and Duchess selected pieces; they are not unified designs, which suggests they were bought from stock, rather than commissions.

Most stately of the Roentgen pieces is a mahogany cylinder bureau mounted with gilt bronze and brass, recorded as being in the 5th Duke's bedroom in Devonshire House. At Chatsworth it usually resides in the South Sketch Gallery. As the name implies, the Sketch Galleries were built as part of major building works commissioned by the 6th Duke to accommodate what we now usually refer to as Old Master drawings.

The collection was initiated by the 2nd Duke of Devonshire, who is responsible for the acquisition of the majority of the works. However, significant additions also came via the Burlington connection.

Amongst the drawings, which often relate to great paintings, are also designs—drawings that map the thinking required to imagine another object. The word *design* has an etymology that relates to Latin, via Italian and French, and carries the meaning 'to mark out, to point out, or to devise'. Crucially, a drawing (in Italian, *disegno*) conveys not just draughtsmanship, but the capacity to imagine. While designers working today may use digital drawings, the dual role of that preliminary task is the same—both to imagine a form and to fix it, in order to communicate with fabricators. Some of the Old Master drawings are clearly instructional, intended for artisans to read. Take, for example, the drawings of Giulio Romano (1499?–1546). He was trained in the workshop of Raphael, eventually leading his own workshop in Mantua. While his workshop produced paintings and frescoes, from it also emerged designs for objects, particularly for gold and silver. In Chatsworth's collection are precise yet whimsical designs for smiths to work with, with imaginative motifs including tortoises and interlacing vine leaves. Romano's designs are functional but also inspired by the natural world—he was also an architect, which is evident in his rendering of structure and form. The drawings, like so much at Chatsworth, bear the sensibility of those who made them. Each piece is a crucial point in a network of objects, whose interrelationships tell of much larger schemes for design in houses made for their display.

In selecting only a few of the objects found at Chatsworth, we have tried to show how these innovative pieces confirm or prefigure later trends in design and making, which in turn have deep connections to this place as a centre for design and future thinking. Chatsworth has always been a place that embraces the innovations of its time—from architecture to furniture, from garden design to the technologies that underpin the functions of the house. Like the instruction to Samuel Watson to make work 'as good or better than any such like worke is hethertoo don', the continuing task of the designer is to make work that is deeply considered, and which resolves itself with its environment in a way that is satisfying: both appropriate and sustaining. As a collection and a designed space, Chatsworth remains an incomparably generative setting for the new.

MICHAEL ANASTASSIADES

BL001, 2021
Moso bamboo, waxed linen thread, pewter, spring steel, brass, borosilicate glass, components
91 × 16.75 × 14.75 in
231 × 42.5 × 37.5 cm
Edition of 3
p. 112

BL002, 2021
Moso bamboo, waxed linen thread, pewter, spring steel, brass, borosilicate glass, components
91 × 16.75 × 14.75 in
231 × 42.5 × 37.5 cm
Edition of 3

BL005, 2021
Moso bamboo, waxed linen thread, pewter, spring steel, brass, borosilicate glass, components
91 × 16.75 × 14.75 in
231 × 42.5 × 37.5 cm
Edition of 3

BL006, 2021
Moso bamboo, waxed linen thread, pewter, spring steel, brass, borosilicate glass, components
91 × 16.75 × 14.75 in
231 × 42.5 × 37.5 cm
Edition of 3

BL008, 2021
Moso bamboo, waxed linen thread, pewter, spring steel, brass, borosilicate glass, components
91 × 14.75 × 14.75 in
231 × 37.5 × 37.5 cm
Edition of 3

BL009, 2021
Moso bamboo, waxed linen thread, pewter, spring steel, brass, borosilicate glass, components
91 × 16.75 × 14.75 in
231 × 42.5 × 37.5 cm
Edition of 3

BL010, 2021
Moso bamboo, waxed linen thread, pewter, spring steel, brass, borosilicate glass, components
91 × 16.75 × 14.75 in
231 × 42.5 × 37.5 cm
Edition of 3
pp. 106, 110, 168

BL015, 2021
Moso bamboo, waxed linen thread, pewter, spring steel, brass, borosilicate glass, components
91 × 14.75 × 12.75 in
231 × 37.5 × 32.5 cm
Edition of 3
p. 113

BL018, 2021
Moso bamboo, waxed linen thread, pewter, spring steel, brass, borosilicate glass, components
91 × 14.75 × 12.75 in
231 × 37.5 × 32.5 cm
Edition of 3
pp. 110, 168

BL021, 2021
Moso bamboo, waxed linen thread, pewter, spring steel, brass, borosilicate glass, components
51.5 × 21.75 × 19 in
131 × 55 × 48 cm
Edition of 3
p. 109

BL023, 2021
Moso bamboo, waxed linen thread, pewter, spring steel, brass, borosilicate glass, components
51.5 × 21.75 × 19 in
131 × 55 × 48 cm
Edition of 3

BL025, 2021
Moso bamboo, waxed linen thread, pewter, spring steel, brass, borosilicate glass, components
91 × 16.75 × 14.5 in
231 × 42.5 × 37 cm
Edition of 3
p. 113

INI ARCHIBONG

Dark Vernus 1, 2021
Blued steel, glass
114 × 52 × 44.5 in
290 × 133 × 113 cm
pp. 114, 115, 117–119

WENDELL CASTLE

A New Seeing, 2015
Bronze
37 × 91.75 × 45.25 in
94 × 233 × 115 cm
Edition of 8
pp. 147, 151, 153, 156–158, 165

Illusion-Reality-Truth, 2015
Bronze
86.75 × 113 × 74.75 in
220 × 287 × 190 cm
Edition of 8
pp. 146, 149, 152, 155, 159

Temptation, 2014
Bronze
41.25 × 101 × 50.5 in
105 × 256 × 128 cm
Edition of 8
pp. 150, 154, 155, 158

ANDILE DYALVANE

Amaza (Waves), 2022
Glazed, hand coiled stoneware
36 × 22 × 22 in
92 × 55 × 55 cm
pp. 53, 54, 166

Cornish Waterfall, 2019
Stoneware
23.75 × 13 × 13 in
60 × 33 × 33 cm
pp. 54, 55

Ingxondorha (Volatile Rocky Terrain), 2022
Glazed, hand coiled stoneware
29 × 21 × 21 in
73 × 54 × 54 cm
p. 56

Isiziba (A Pool), 2022
Glazed, hand coiled stoneware
26 × 21 × 21 in
66 × 54 × 54 cm
p. 56

Rhythms Vase, 2014
White stoneware clay with stained highlights
40.5 × 18.5 × 18 in
103 × 47 × 46 cm
pp. 50, 51, 54

Umgodi (A Mine), 2022
Glazed, hand coiled stoneware
30 × 19 × 19 in
75 × 48 × 48 cm
p. 55

Umthombo (Spring), 2022
Glazed, hand coiled stoneware
30 × 20 × 19 in
76 × 50 × 48 cm
p. 57

NAJLA EL ZEIN

Seduction, Pair 06, 2019
Iranian red travertine
27.5 × 62.5 × 18.75 in
70 × 159 × 47.5 cm
Edition of 8
pp. 11, 14, 138, 139, 141, 143–145, 174

NDIDI EKUBIA

Turbine II Wine Cooler, 2013
Hammer-raised Britannia silver 958
8.5 × 10.5 in
22 × 27 cm
p. 97

Silver Palm Vase, 2020
Hammer-raised Britannia silver 958
6.5 × 7.5 in
16.5 × 19.5 cm
p. 96

Midrib Harmony Vase, 2020
Hammer-raised Britannia silver 958
6.25 × 5 in
16 × 12.5 cm
pp. 95, 97

Bowl, 2022
Hammer-raised Britannia silver 958
2 × 3.5 in
5 × 8.5 cm
pp. 95, 97

Cup, 2018
Hammer-raised Britannia silver 958
2 × 2.5 in
5.5 × 6.5 cm
pp. 95, 97

Cup, 2020
Hammer-raised Sterling silver 925
2.75 × 3 in
7 × 7.5 cm
p. 96

Journey Vase, 2001
Hammer-raised Britannia silver 958
6 × 7 in
15 × 18 cm
pp. 92, 93, 96, 171

FORMAFANTASMA
ANDREA TRIMARCHI
AND SIMONE FARRESIN

Glass Bottle, 2012
Carbonised oak log, mouth-blown glass
Carafe:
11.75 × 4 × 4 in
30 × 10 × 10 cm
Charcoal:
6 × 4.75 × 3.25 in
15 × 12 × 8 cm
pp. 69, 71, 73

Water Filter, Funnel, 2012
Carbonised oak wood, mouth-blown glass
13 × 8.75 × 8.75 in
33 × 22 × 22 cm
pp. 69, 70

Water Filter, Spoon, 2012
Carbonised oak wood, mouth-blown glass
11.75 × 10 × 10 in
30 × 25 × 25 cm
pp. 69, 70, 73

Water Filter, Stalactite, 2012
Carbonised oak wood, mouth-blown glass
11.75 × 8.75 × 8.75 in
30 × 22 × 22 cm
pp. 69, 71

Water Filter, Stalagmite, 2012
Carbonised oak wood, mouth-blown glass, copper
11.75 × 17.75 × 17.75 in
30 × 45 × 45 cm
pp. 66, 67, 69, 71, 72

Water Filter, Tongue, 2012
Carbonised oak wood, mouth-blown glass
10.75 × 10 × 5.25 in
27 × 25 × 13 cm
p. 70

JORIS LAARMAN

Chatsworth Symbio Bench, 2022
Gritstone, local bryophytes
18.5 × 67 × 34.75 in
47 × 170 × 88 cm
pp. 8, 130, 131, 133, 135, 136

Chatsworth Symbio Bench, 2022
Gritstone, local bryophytes
19 × 99 × 44.75 in
48 × 251 × 114 cm
pp. 8, 133, 135–137

Chatsworth Symbio Bench, 2022
Gritstone, local bryophytes
16 × 46.75 × 43.25 in
40.5 × 118.5 × 110 cm
pp. 134, 136

Maker Bench (Hexagon), 2018
Oak, walnut
17 × 75 × 43.25 in
43 × 190 × 110 cm
Edition of 3
pp. 24, 25, 27–30, 176

MAX LAMB

6 × 8 Chair, 2021
Western red cedar
29.5 × 15 × 19.75 in
75 × 38 × 50.5 cm
pp. 74, 75, 77, 78

6 × 8 Chair, 2021
Western red cedar
31.5 × 9.5 × 19 in
80 × 24.25 × 48.25 cm
pp. 77–79, 162

FERNANDO LAPOSSE

Black Furry Armchair, 2022
Dyed agave fibres, upholstered linen polyester blend, plywood
27.25 × 47 × 39.5 in
69 × 119 × 100 cm
Edition of 8
pp. 89, 91

White Agave Cabinet, 2021
Birch plywood, sisal, steel mesh, kiln dried Canadian maple
76.75 × 45.25 × 34.25 in
195 × 115 × 87 cm
Edition of 3
pp. 86, 87, 169

JAY SAE JUNG OH

Salvage Series Chatsworth Chair, 2021
Various plastics, leather, cord, plywood
39 × 44 × 37 in
99 × 112 × 94 cm
pp. 80, 81, 83, 85, 163

SAMUEL ROSS

Amnesia or platelet apparition?, 2021
Marble, powder-coated steel
32.25 × 47.25 × 13.75 in
82 × 120 × 35 cm
Edition of 8
pp. 120, 121, 123, 124, cover

Anxiety birthed corrosion, 2021
Marble, painted steel
19.75 × 32 × 32 in
50 × 81 × 81 cm
Edition of 8
pp. 126, 127, 172

Jut, impale, emerge, 2021
Marble, powder-coated steel
15.75 × 32 × 13.5 in
40 × 81.5 × 34.5 cm
Edition of 8
pp. 123, 125, back cover

Optimistic uncertainties solicit integration (Material Articulation), 2021
Fior di Pesca marble
23 × 77 × 22.5 in
58.5 × 195.5 × 57 cm
Unique
pp. 128, 129

CHRIS SCHANCK

Concretion, 2021
Aluminum
48.75 × 42 × 6 in
124 × 107 × 15 cm
Edition of 8
pp. 35, 36, 164

Cryo III, 2022
Steel, wood, polystyrene, polyurea, aluminum foil, resin, suede, onyx
83.5 × 30 × 30 in
212 × 76 × 76 cm
pp. 32, 33, 35, 36

ETTORE SOTTSASS

Vase no. 16, 2006
Glass and patinated aluminum wire
24 × 17 × 17 in
61 × 43 × 43 cm
Edition of 9
pp. 62, 65, 167

Vase no. 4, 2006
Glass and rope
26 × 13.5 × 13.5 in
66 × 34 × 34 cm
pp. 61, 63

Vase no. 7, 2006
Glass and rope
32.25 × 11.75 × 11.75 in
82 × 30 × 30 cm
Edition of 9
p. 61

Xiangzheng, 1999
Glass
31.5 × 12.75 × 12.75 in
80 × 32.5 × 32.5 cm
Edition of 6

Xiangzheng, 1999
Glass, polished and oxidised aluminum wire
28.5 × 13 × 13 in
72.5 × 33 × 33 cm
Edition of 6
pp. 59, 62, 64

Lingam, 1999
Produced by Cirva
Glass
37 × 10 × 10 in
94 × 25 × 25 cm
Edition of 6
pp. 62, 65

Lingam, 1999
Produced by Cirva
Glass
32 × 21 × 21 in
81 × 53.5 × 53.5 cm
Edition of 6
pp. 58, 62

Lingam, 1999
Produced by Cirva
Glass
36 × 8.25 × 8.25 in
91 × 21 × 21 cm
Edition of 6
pp. 61, 173

FAYE TOOGOOD

Hill, 2022
Hand-carved oak
30 × 86.75 × 47.25 in
76 × 220 × 120 cm
Edition of 8
pp. 46–49, 175

Hoard I, 2022
Hand-carved bog oak
17.75 × 13.75 × 13.75 in
45 × 35 × 35 cm
Edition of 3
p. 47

Hoard II, 2022
Hand-carved bog oak
16.5 × 12.5 × 12.5 in
42 × 32 × 32 cm
Edition of 3
p. 46

Lode II, 2021
Hand-carved Purbeck marble
34.75 × 47.25 × 13 in
88 × 120 × 33 cm
Edition of 8
pp. 38, 41

Pew Bench / Moon, 2016
Sand-cast bronze, silver nitrate
17 × 49.25 × 17.75 in
43 × 125 × 45 cm
Edition of 8

Plot II, 2022
Hand-carved Purbeck marble
14.5 × 62 × 41 in
37 × 157 × 104 cm
Edition of 8
pp. 41, 44, 45

Spoon Chair / Moon, 2016
Sand-cast bronze, silver nitrate
39.5 × 34.25 × 22 in
100 × 87 × 56 cm
Edition of 8
pp. 41–43

Trove I, 2022
Hand-carved Purbeck marble
59 × 17.75 × 20.5 in
150 × 45 × 52 cm
p. 41

Trove II, 2022
Hand-carved Purbeck marble
40.5 × 17.75 × 19.75 in
103 × 45 × 50 cm
pp. 39, 41, 170

JOSEPH WALSH

Enignum Brackets, 2022
Ash
Various Dimensions
pp. 104, 105

Enignum VIII Bed, 2015
Ash
240.5 × 90.5 × 111.75 in
611 × 230 × 284 cm
pp. 98, 99, 101, 103, 161

MICHAEL ANASTASSIADES

Michael Anastassiades's design philosophy is to produce exceptionally-designed objects of permanent value. He founded his studio in London in 1994 and established his lighting company in 2007. Anastassiades trained as a civil engineer at London's Imperial College of Science, Technology and Medicine before taking a Master's degree in Industrial Design at the Royal College of Art. His work is featured in permanent collections at the Museum of Modern Art in New York; the Art Institute of Chicago; the Victoria and Albert Museum, London; the MAK in Vienna; the Crafts Council in London; and the FRAC Centre in Orleans, France. Recent solo exhibitions include Norfolk House music room at the Victoria and Albert Museum in London (2010); Cyprus Presidency at the European Parliament in Brussels, Belgium (2011); *Time and Again at the Geymüllerschlössel*, MAK, Vienna (2012); *To Be Perfectly Frank*, Svenskt Tenn, Stockholm (2013); *Reload the Current Page*, Point Centre for Contemporary Art, Nicosia (2014); *Doings on Time and Light*, Rodeo Gallery, Istanbul (2015); *13 Mobiles*, Atelier Jesper, Belgium (2017); *Things That Go Together*, NiMAC, Nicosia (2019); and *Silver Tongued*, SHOP Taka Ishii, Hong Kong (2019).

Anastassiades's studio has designed products with various manufacturers including Flos, B&B Italia, Herman Miller, Cassina, Bang & Olufsen, Puiforcat, Fratelli Fantini SpA, Lobmeyr, Salvatori, Svenskt Tenn, Carl Auböck/Sigmar, Coedition, and SCP. He has designed signature limited edition collections for Nilufar Gallery, Milan; Dansk Mobelkunst, Copenhagen; and Taka Ishii Gallery, Japan.

Michael Anastassiades, who was born in Cyprus in 1967, lives and works in London.

INI ARCHIBONG

Ini Archibong's practice is characterised by a dedication to craftsmanship and to the integrity of materials, as well as a passion for world cultures and his own Nigerian heritage. 'Being a creator has always been a process of distilling my perception of the world around me into creations that can be understood by as many people as possible regardless of their background, point of view, or position in life', says Archibong.

Born in 1983 in Pasadena, California, Archibong originally trained in industrial design, and graduated with a Bachelor of Science in Environmental Design from the ArtCenter College of Design. Upon graduation, he moved to Singapore to work alongside Tim Kobe, who developed the Apple Store concept. He then relocated to Switzerland, where he received a Master of Arts in Luxury Design and Craftsmanship from L'École Cantonale d'Art de Lausanne (ECAL). Since establishing his own studio in 2010, Archibong has gone on to collaborate on numerous high-profile projects, including with Hermès and Knoll.

His works have been exhibited at museums and public institutions worldwide and most recently in the exhibitions *Speechless* (2019), co-organised by the Dallas Museum of Art and the High Museum of Art, Atlanta and *Connected* (2020) at the Design Museum in London. In 2021, Archibong's sail-like Pavilion of the African Diaspora was installed as part of the London Design Biennale, a symbolic gateway to the past, present, and future.

Ini Archibong lives and works in Switzerland.

WENDELL CASTLE

Throughout a career-spanning six decades, Wendell Castle introduced groundbreaking ways of looking at, thinking about, and making furniture. In doing so, he created a new sculptural vocabulary that became the cornerstone of his practice and established him as the father of the American studio furniture movement. Up until his death, Castle continued to defy categorisation through his sheer creative drive.

Born in Emporia, Kansas, in 1932, Castle received a Bachelor of Fine Arts in Industrial Design from the University of Kansas in 1958 and a Master of Fine Arts in Sculpture in 1961. He moved to Rochester, New York, to teach at the School for American Crafts, Rochester Institute of Technology, and established a permanent studio in the area which would remain active for almost sixty years.

In 1963, Castle pioneered the use of stack lamination, enabling him to compose volumes without being constrained by the inherent limitations of his signature material, wood. He soon gained international recognition and was included in key exhibitions, including the 1964 Triennale di Milano and the seminal touring show *Objects USA* (1969), which began at the Smithsonian American Art Museum in Washington, DC. During the last decade of his life, Castle realised some of the most ambitious work of his career by combining the laminating process with twenty-first-century digital technology and producing works in cast bronze, which had been a lifelong aspiration.

Castle was the recipient of numerous honors and awards, including four grants from the National Endowment for the Arts, three honorary degrees, a Visionaries of the American Craft Movement Award from the American Craft Museum (1994), the American

Craft Council Gold Medal (1997), Master of the Medium Award from the James Renwick Alliance of the National Museum of American Art (1999), and a Lifetime Achievement Award from the Brooklyn Museum of Art (2007).

His works can be found in the permanent collections of more than forty museums and cultural institutions worldwide, including Art Institute of Chicago; Los Angeles County Museum of Art; the Metropolitan Museum of Art, New York; Minneapolis Institute of Arts; Musée des beaux-arts de Montréal, Quebec; Museum of Arts and Design, New York; Museum of Fine Arts, Boston; Museum of Fine Arts, Houston; Museum of Modern Art, New York; Nelson Atkins Museum of Art, Kansas City, Missouri; Philadelphia Museum of Art; Renwick Gallery, Smithsonian Institution, Washington, DC; and the Victoria and Albert Museum, London.

Castle died in 2018 in Rochester, New York.

ANDILE DYALVANE

A leading voice in the field of contemporary ceramic art, Andile Dyalvane seeks to honor his Xhosa heritage through his practice. With ceramics, Dyalvane connects to his ancestors and shares his personal story of healing. 'Clay breathes. It's alive with becoming and moves with my energy, listens, and holds only what I've impressed upon it. It remembers and let's go in the fire, and then becomes stronger', says Dyalvane.

Dyalvane was born in 1978 on a cattle farm in Ngobozana, a small village in the Eastern Cape province of South Africa. His work with clay, or 'umhlaba' (mother earth), reinforces an innate human connection to soil, a foundational connection that Dyalvane made while learning to farm as a child. He received a National Degree in Art and Design from Sivuyile Technical College in 1999 and a National Degree in Ceramic Design from Nelson Mandela Metropolitan University in 2003. After graduation, Dyalvane founded Imiso Ceramics in South Africa's Western Cape in 2006.

He has exhibited extensively in South Africa and has been awarded residencies in Denmark, England, France, the United States, and Taiwan. Dyalvane's work is in the permanent collections of the Iziko National Museum, Cape Town, South Africa; Nelson Mandela Metropolitan Art Museum, Port Elizabeth, South Africa; and Yingge Ceramic Museum, Taipei, Taiwan.

Dyalvane lives and works in Cape Town, South Africa.

NDIDI EKUBIA

Born in 1973 in Manchester, England, Ndidi Ekubia is one of the world's leading silversmiths. She studied 3D Design at the University of Wolverhampton, then pursued a Master's in metalwork at the Royal College of Art in London, completing her degree in 1998. Ever since, Ekubia has been creating visually spectacular yet functional silverware.

Her method of making is founded on the idea of pushing sheet metal to its limits. The hand-finished, planished surfaces emphasise the fluid vitality of each form. This allows the viewer to become involved with a truly three-dimensional object, each side showing a completely different aspect. 'I am excited by the sensual and rich forms that can be created by the rhythmic process of making, and believe my nature is reflected through my work', she says. 'It is delightful to be absorbed in every stage, from design to the finished piece.'

Ekubia has been featured in many gallery and museum exhibitions, including *Colloquy*, Mary E. Black Gallery, Nova Scotia (2022); *Mastery: Women in Silver*, Ruthin Craft Centre (2021); *The Global Africa Project*, Museum of Arts and Design (2010); and *Silver Lives*, The Gilbert Collection (2001). Her work is in the collection of the Aberdeen Art Gallery & Museum, Aberdeen; Bristol City Museum and Art Gallery, Bristol; Crafts Council, London; Amgueddfa Cymru – National Museum Wales, courtesy of the P&O Makower Trust; Shipley Art Gallery, Gateshead; The Ashmolean Museum, Oxford; The Worshipful Company of Goldsmiths, London; and Winchester Cathedral, Hampshire.

Ndidi Ekubia lives and works in Manchester, England.

FORMAFANTASMA

Formafantasma is a research-based design studio investigating the ecological, historical, political, and social forces shaping the discipline of design today. Since founding the studio in 2009, Italians Andrea Trimarchi, born in 1980, and Simone Farresin, born in 1983, have championed the need for value-laden advocacy merged with holistic design thinking. Their aim is to facilitate a deeper understanding of both our natural and built environments and to propose transformative interventions through design and its material, technical, social, and discursive possibilities.

The practice embraces a broad spectrum of typologies and methods, from product design through spatial design, strategic planning, and design consultancy. Whether designing to a client's brief or developing self-initiated projects, the studio applies the same rigorous attention to context, process, and detail. Their portfolio is characterised by a coherent visual language and meticulously-researched outcomes.

For Formafantasma, this crossflow of knowledge and experience taken from both their commercial contracts and their more autonomous projects has benefitted and informed the other. It has also given them a unique perspective of the design industry, allowing them to acknowledge the legacy of industrial production as the fundamental source for the designer's expertise and agency in contemporary society while also addressing its historic contribution to environmental instability.

Formafantasma is based in Milan and Rotterdam.

JORIS LAARMAN

After graduating from the Design Academy in Eindhoven in 2003, Joris Laarman quickly became one of the leading creative voices of his generation. In 2004, together with his partner Anita Star, he founded Joris Laarman Lab, and now works in Amsterdam with a multidisciplinary team of coders, engineers, and craftspeople. The lab operates at the intersection of the digital and the physical world, connecting the magical possibilities of the future to indispensable elements of the past. Their work is at the intersection where nature, technology, and aesthetics meet: 'A future where truth is no longer stranger than fiction', he says, 'but where reality has also become faster than fiction. As unlikely as it may seem, we strive to unite both realities.'

Their work, involving experiments with artificial intelligence, digital and robotic fabrication, parametric modeling, and augmented and virtual reality is in the permanent collections and exhibitions of many renowned institutions including the Museum of Modern Art, New York; Victoria and Albert Museum, London; Centre Pompidou, Paris; and the Rijksmuseum, Amsterdam.

The lab's critically-acclaimed major travelling solo exhibition was shown at the Groninger Museum, the Netherlands; Cooper Hewitt, Smithsonian Design Museum, New York; The High Museum, Atlanta; and the Museum of Fine Arts, Houston.

Laarman is the winner of awards such as the *Wall Street Journal* Innovator of the Year, the European Union's Starts Prize, and multiple Dutch design awards. He has contributed to articles and seminars for *Domus Magazine* and has lectured at the Architectural Association School of Architecture, London; the Gerrit Rietveld Academy, Amsterdam; and the Design Academy Eindhoven.

Joris Laarman, who was born in Borculo, Netherlands in 1979, lives and works in Amsterdam.

MAX LAMB

Max Lamb is a designer well known for a deeply personal approach to creating works that resonate with materiality, location, and tradition. His creative exploration spans diverse media, which includes stone carving, bronze casting, and lost polystyrene casting. Lamb's approach, and his outlook on materials precious and inexpensive, natural and synthetic, has changed little since graduating from London's Royal College of Art in 2006.

Born in St. Austell, Cornwall, England in 1980, Lamb previously held a residency as the Wornick Distinguished Visiting Professor of Wood Arts at California College of the Arts in San Francisco. In 2016, Lamb's work was included in the Design Triennial *Beauty* at the Cooper Hewitt, Smithsonian Design Museum. In 2018, the Art Institute of Chicago presented his solo exhibition, *Exercises in Seating*, showcasing the variety and depth of Lamb's practice over the last two decades.

Max Lamb lives and works in London.

FERNANDO LAPOSSE

Born in 1988 in Paris, Fernando Laposse was trained at Central Saint Martins in London as a product designer. He specialises in transforming humble natural materials into refined design pieces.

Laposse has worked extensively with overlooked plant fibres such as sisal, loofah, and corn husks. His works are the result of extensive research that culminates into objects of 'endemic design' where materials and their historical and cultural ties to a particular location and its people take centre stage. He often works with indigenous communities in his native Mexico to create local employment opportunities and raise awareness about the challenges they face in a globalised world.

His projects have been exhibited in the Triennale di Milano, Cooper Hewitt Design Museum, The Design Museum in London, the Victoria and Albert Museum, and the World Economic Forum, to name a few. His work is held in the permanent collections of the Design Museum Gent, Le centre national des arts plastiques, Musée des Arts Décoratifs, San Francisco Museum of Modern Art, and the Victoria and Albert Museum.

Fernando Laposse lives and works in Mexico City.

JAY SAE JUNG OH

Jay Sae Jung Oh, born in Seoul in 1982, transforms everyday objects into something new and extraordinary —assemblages that are at once art and craft. Oh's ongoing *Salvage* series is composed of seemingly jerry-rigged structures made of household objects, which are intricately hand wrapped in leather. The manufactured plastic objects that lie beneath are transformed and unified into a sculptural design object, making a strong statement about the cultural condition of abundance and obsolescence.

Oh earned her Bachelor and Master of Fine Arts in sculpture at Kookmin University, Seoul, South Korea, and completed her Master of Fine Arts in 3D Design at Cranbrook Academy of Art, Michigan. She has served as a visiting professor of Industrial Design at the University of Illinois at Chicago, and has worked alongside maestro Gaetano Pesce. Her work is widely exhibited and featured in publications worldwide and can be seen in the permanent collections at the Carnegie Museum of Art, Cranbrook Art Museum, San Francisco Museum of Modern Art, and The Cooper Hewitt, Smithsonian Design Museum.

Jay Sae Jung Oh lives and works in Seattle.

DR. SAMUEL ROSS

British designer, creative director, and artist Dr Samuel Ross deftly mines the cross-sections of socio-geographic relationships, enlisting rhizomatic micro and macro references in the formulation of his works. Navigating themes located in anthropology, sociographic tendencies, and twentieth- and twenty-first-century industrialised societies, his output offers a commentary on equality, engagement, and collective experience.

Born in Brixton in 1991, Ross graduated with a Bachelor of Arts in Graphic Design and Illustration at De Montfort University, Leicester. After graduation, he embarked on a career as a product designer, working for several high-profile brands, advertising agencies, and industrial design practices, while concurrently focusing on his own creative endeavours spanning experimental film, street art, and garment design. He soon transitioned into fashion, working for Virgil Abloh, first as Abloh's first assistant for design, encompassing Off-White and various installations, then subsequently with Kanye West's creative content agency, Donda.

In 2015, at just twenty-five years old, Ross self-funded A-COLD-WALL*—renowned for its material investigation and innovation, married with incisive explorations of brutalist and abstract forms and precise execution. The label has since taken a leading role in redefining the parameters of streetwear and high fashion.

During the Hublot Prize exhibition at London's Serpentine Gallery in 2019, Ross launched SR_A (Samuel Ross & Associates), an industrial design studio operating within the fields of interior installation, architecture, furniture design, sound design, and sculptural/visual communication. Ross describes it as a vehicle for '...the progressive study of design and practical experience creation.'

Ross's accolades include being named the British Fashion Awards' Emerging Menswear Designer (2018) and receiving the Hublot Design Prize (2019). In 2020, he was named as one of *Forbes'* 30 under 30 [Europe] and won both the *GQ* USA Fashion Award and People of the Year British Fashion Award, the latter specifically for his philanthropic endeavours. He has also been a finalist for both the LVMH Prize and ANDAM Award. He has collaborated with brands, including Converse, Dr. Martens, Mercedes-Benz, Nike, and Oakley, as well as noteworthy artists Virgil Abloh, Daniel Arsham, Futura, and Takashi Murakami. Specific SR_A partnerships include those with Apple, Beats, Nike, Medicom, Hublot LVMH, Kohler, and Acqua Di Parma.

Samuel Ross lives and works in London.

CHRIS SCHANCK

Designer Chris Schanck's work embraces the tension between dilapidation and opulence, asking us to find unconventional beauty in the imperfect.

Schanck was born in Pittsburgh in 1975 and grew up in Dallas. He received a Bachelor of Fine Arts in sculpture from the School of Visual Arts and a Master of Fine Arts in design from Cranbrook Academy of Art. Upon graduating in 2011, Schanck founded a studio employing over a dozen artists, students, and craftspeople based in a former factory in a Detroit neighbourhood with a dense immigrant population. The local community plays a key role in Schanck's egalitarian practice, which brings 'outsiders' into design culture.

Schanck's efforts deviate from the mass-produced, instead reviving mundane materials by transforming them into unique objects of uncommon luxury. Schanck is best known for his ongoing *Alufoil* series, in which industrial and discarded materials are sculpted, covered in aluminum foil, and then sealed with resin. Despite overt references to fantasy and science fiction, Schanck's assemblages are grounded in the reality of humanity's neglect, necessity, and inventiveness with a vernacular inspired by his Detroit neighbourhood.

The Dallas Museum of Art commissioned Schanck to create a work in dialogue with a late nineteenth-century Martelé dressing table in their collection, which debuted in his first solo museum exhibition in January 2021. The Museum of Arts and Design, New York, presented his first retrospective exhibition in February 2022. Schanck's work is held in the collections of the Cranbrook Art Museum, Bloomfield Hills, Michigan; Dallas Museum of Art, Museum of Fine Arts, Houston; and the Montreal Museum of Fine Arts.

Chris Schanck lives and works in Detroit.

ETTORE SOTTSASS

One of the most significant and sustained challengers of modernism in design history, Ettore Sottsass, Jr. (1917–2007) brought his powerful artistic vision to a wide range of disciplines: architecture, ceramics, furniture, glass, industrial design, painting, and photography. Always, he was animated by sensual, spiritual, and humanist concerns.

Born in Innsbruck, Austria, and raised in Turin, Italy, Sottsass graduated from Turin University in 1939 with a degree in architecture. In the early part of his career, which ultimately spanned six decades, he moved skilfully between industrial design and independent experimentation. His bright red Valentine portable typewriter (1968) is just one well-known example from a broad range of products he realised for his most important corporate client, the office goods manufacturer Olivetti, for whom he also realised prescient designs for computing workstations.

During this time, he also created ceramics and furniture of great spiritual intensity, synthesising modernist abstraction with forms from ancient cultures. His ceramic *Totems* and laminated *Superboxes* of the 1960s alluded to functional typologies, while also asserting themselves as symbolic monuments. This syncretic approach, at once progressive and primordial, impossible to position within existing disciplinary structures, informed his contributions to numerous groups and projects, including Global Tools, Studio Alchimia, and the Milanese avant-garde group Memphis, which he founded in 1981.

Amongst his most exciting works are those he made in the successive decades, in tandem with his expanding architectural practice. His later works in glass, ceramics, and furniture show his formidable creative powers fully unleashed. Motifs from earlier in his career (totemic forms, plastic laminates) are brought back into play, as part of his ongoing experiment with the fundamentals of design—shape, material, and imagery—while also transcending any particular idiom. As he put it at the time, 'I don't design things in any style, even less so in any fashionable style. I design things for life states.'

Sottsass's work can be found in the permanent collections of numerous international museums, including the Centre Pompidou, Paris; Corning Museum of Glass, New York; Los Angeles County Museum of Art; M+ Museum, Hong Kong, Metropolitan Museum of Art, New York; Museum of Fine Arts, Houston; Philadelphia Museum of Art; Stedelijk Museum, Amsterdam; and Victoria and Albert Museum, London.

Ettore Sottsass died in 2007 in Milan.

FAYE TOOGOOD

Faye Toogood is amongst the most prominent figures in contemporary British design. 'Whether you are a fashion designer, a furniture designer, or an interior designer, the materials you can get your hands on are essential', she says.

Toogood was born in the UK in 1977 and graduated with a Bachelor of Arts in the History of Art in 1998 from Bristol University. Upon graduation, she worked as a prop stylist at *The World of Interiors* before establishing Studio Toogood in 2008. Working in a diverse range of disciplines, from sculpture to furniture and fashion, Toogood often reinterprets and reinvents classical tropes and references from art history by introducing a new aesthetic. Since the conception of her immediately recognisable voluminous *Roly-Poly Chair* (2014), she has been considered amongst the great form-givers of the twenty-first century.

Her career is marked out by the discrete *Assemblages*, each of which conjures a compact world of interrelated ideas, forms, and materials. *Assemblage 5*, for example, was inspired by a visit to Henri Matisse's Chapelle du Rosaire in Vence, France, and explored ancient animist notions of water, earth, and the moon through a personal lens. In *Assemblage 6*, Toogood set out to 'unlearn' the process of design and build a new vocabulary for furniture by recasting sculptural maquettes made from everyday materials found in the studio. Thirteen works from this expansive body of work were commissioned by Qatar Museum for a public setting at the Qatar National Theatre, titled *Clay Court*.

Her works have been acquired for the permanent collections of institutions worldwide, including the

Corning Museum of Glass, New York; the Dallas Museum of Art; the Denver Museum of Art; the High Museum of Art, Atlanta; National Gallery of Victoria, Melbourne; and the Philadelphia Museum of Art.

Faye Toogood lives and works in London.

JOSEPH WALSH

Joseph Walsh is an Irish designer and maker whose work reflects his passion for expression through material and form. From monumental scale sculptures to one-of-a-kind site-specific commissions, every piece within his body of work reveals an intuitive relationship with making, a sympathetic use of materials and an expressive engagement with form.

Walsh was born in 1979 in County Cork on the south coast of Ireland, where he established his own studio and workshop in 1999. With no formal training, he began to explore his passion for making, visiting master makers around Europe, and developing his own mastery of woodworking and deep knowledge of the material. From the outset, he pursued innovation in making based on traditional techniques, often from other craft forms, which enabled new making methods and forms. This led to significant commissions for various ecclesiastical clients, the Embassy of Japan, and the National Museum of Ireland.

From these early years of experimentation and development, Walsh began to break some of the traditional rules of making, and even his own rules, in order to create the truly bold and expressive forms for which he is known today, realised in an ever-widening range of materials, including wood, marble, and bronze. His achievements in design have been recognised by an honorary doctorate from University College, Cork; a major commission for the National Gallery of Ireland; and the acquisition of his works for many major international collections, including most recently the Metropolitan Museum of Art in New York.

Joseph Walsh lives and works in County Cork, Ireland.

NAJLA EL ZEIN

Najla El Zein's artworks explore the relationship between form, use, space, and emotion. El Zein's approach is rooted in her personal observations and experiences as she stresses the importance of expression through creation.

Born in Beirut in 1983, El Zein moved to Paris at the age of two, and later studied at the École Camondo there, receiving a Bachelor of Arts in Product Design and a Master of Arts in Interior Architecture and Spatial Design. Upon graduation, she worked in the Netherlands before moving back to Beirut in 2011.

Her first solo exhibition, *Transition* (2019), marked the debut of three bodies of work that acted as varied embodiments of El Zein's personal journey: *Distortion*, *Fragmented Pillar*, and *Seduction*. The communicative power of these series conveys not just the complexity, but also the fundamental importance of human connection by exploring themes such as the unconscious, sensuality, femininity, and desire.

To coincide with the World Cup 2022, El Zein was invited by Qatar Museum to intervene in two public spaces in Doha; one is *Us, Her, Him* at Flag Plaza, a monumental setting of sculptural benches, over one thousand feet long in total.

Her work has been exhibited at numerous public institutions, including at the Dallas Museum of Art's exhibition *Women + Design: New Works* (2018–2019). El Zein's pieces have been acquired for the permanent collections of museums such as the Dallas Museum of Art, and the Victoria and Albert Museum, London.

Najla El Zein lives and works in Amsterdam.

Published on the occasion of the exhibition
Mirror Mirror: Reflections on Design at Chatsworth,
organised by Chatsworth and Friedman Benda
March 18 – October 1, 2023

First published in the United States of America
in 2024 by

Rizzoli Electa
A division of Rizzoli International Publications, Inc.
300 Park Avenue South
New York, NY 10010
www.rizzoliusa.com

in association with

Chatsworth House Trust
Bakewell, Derbyshire
DE45 1PP, United Kingdom
Registered Charity No. 511149

Chatsworth House Trust is a Registered Charity, established in 1981, to look after the house, collections, garden, woodlands, and park for the benefit of everyone. Every penny of visitor admission income, fundraising, and membership goes directly to the Trust.

Located within the Peak District National Park, Chatsworth is home to the Devonshire family. It comprises a Grade I listed house and stables, a 105-acre garden, a 1,822-acre park, a farmyard, an adventure playground, and one of Europe's most significant private art collections.

Chatsworth plays an important role in the local community as a thriving cultural and educational destination, a nationally important historic landscape, and a working estate that operates with a mindful approach to the environment and sustainability. Chatsworth contains works of art that span four thousand years, from ancient Roman and Egyptian sculpture, to masterpieces by Rembrandt, Reynolds, and Veronese, to work by outstanding modern artists, including Felicity Aylieff, Lucian Freud, David Nash, and Edmund de Waal.

CHATSWORTH
www.chatsworth.org

For Rizzoli Electa
Charles Miers, Publisher
Margaret Rennolds Chace, Associate Publisher
Gisela Aguilar, Editor

Design: A Practice for Everyday Life

Special thank you to the Duke and Duchess of Devonshire and Lord and Lady Burlington.

Michael Anastassiades, Ini Archibong, Andile Dyalvane, Ndidi Ekubia, Najla El Zein, Formafantasma, Joris Laarman and Anita Star, Max Lamb, Fernando Laposse, Jay Sae Jung Oh, Samuel Ross, Chris Schanck, Faye Toogood, Joseph Walsh, and to every studio's exceptional team.

The Estate of Wendell Castle and Nancy Jurs.

The Estate of Ettore Sottsass, Barbara Radice, and Ernest Mourmans.

Alexandra Hodby, Sash Giles, and the entire Chatsworth team.

Glenn Adamson and Deyan Sudjic.

Mirror Mirror: Reflections on Design at Chatsworth was made possible by Chatsworth and Friedman Benda with support from Adrian Sassoon, Salon 94 Design, and The Gallery Mourmans.

Major support for this exhibition was provided by Sotheby's.

This catalogue is supported by Friedman Benda.

Library of Congress Control Number: 2023919471
ISBN: 978-0-8478-7395-1
2024 2025 2026 2027 / 10 9 8 7 6 5 4 3 2 1
Printed in Italy

FSC MIX Paper | Supporting responsible forestry FSC® C013123 www.fsc.org